# TRIBES AND RACES

## (IN TWO VOLUMES)

# TRIBES AND RACES

## A DESCRIPTIVE ETHNOLOGY OF ASIA, AFRICA & EUROPE

## (IN TWO VOLUMES)

By

**R. G. LATHAM**

**M .A. M .D., F .R.S.**

**LATE FELLOW OF KINGS COLLEGE. CAMBRIDGE. ETC.**

**VOL. I**

GYAN

ISBN : 978-81-212-0507-8(Set)

ISBN : 978-81-212-1394-3

Published, 2018

*Published by*

Gyan Publishing House
5, Ansari Road
Daryaganj, New Delhi-110002
Phone: 011-47034999, 9811692060
www.gyanbooks.com
E-mail: books@gyanbooks.com

*Printed at:* G. Print Process, Delhi.

# CONTENTS.

CHAPTER XVII.



CHAPTER XVIII.



CHAPTER XIX.



CHAPTER XX.



CHAPTER XXI.



CHAPTER XXII.



CHAPTER XXIII.



CHAPTER XXIV.



CHAPTER XXV.

# DESCRIPTIVE ETHNOLOGY.

---

## CHAPTER I.

Preliminary Remarks.—The Bhot Group.—The Mahometan Bhot of Bultistan, or Little Tibet.—Rongdo.—Skardo.—Parkuta and Khartakshi.—Shigar.—Chorbad, &c.—The Buddhist Bhot of Ladak.—Hungrung—Kunawer.

I FOLLOW the Horatian rule, and plunge, at once, *in medias res*. I am on the Indus; but not on the Indian portion of it. I am on the Himalayas, but not on their southern side. I am on the north-western ranges; with Tartary on the north, Bokhara on the west, and Hindostan on the south. I am in a neighbourhood where three great religions meet; Mahometanism, Buddhism, Brahminism. I *must* begin somewhere; and here is my beginning.

That these parts are my starting point means little; perhaps nothing. At any rate it does not mean that I hold them to be the centre of our civilization. Still less does it imply that they are the cradle of the human race. No hypothesis attaches to them. I must simply begin somewhere.

But why begin here? If I had begun elsewhere the same question might have been asked; and the same answer would be given. My object is to describe. If a certain amount of classification accompany the description, well and good. If speculations arise, they may or may not be pursued. At any rate they will form no notable portion of the work. As I have already stated, it is simply descriptive.

The group with which I begin contains the Tibetans, the Nepaul tribes, several populations of the Subhimalayan range, the Burmese, the Siamese, the natives of Pegu, the Cambojians, the Cochin-Chinese, and the Chinese; populations which cover, perhaps, one-fifth of Asia. They touch the ocean; they bound the Bay of Bengal on the east; they form the coasts of the China Sea. Upon the whole, however, their area lies inland; sometimes rising into the loftiest mountains of the world, sometimes broken by the watersheds of mighty rivers, sometimes spread out as alluvial plains, sometimes as hot and humid deltas. The Indus rises within the limits of this area. The Brahmaputra waters a long line of it. The great rivers of China fertilize its widest plains. The lengthy streams of Ava and Cambojia, the Irawadi and the Mekhong, from their unexplored sources, traverse it from north to south. They cut it vertically; as the Chinese rivers cut it horizontally.

As far as the physical appearance of its occupants is concerned, the phenomena presented by this large area are strongly and decidedly marked. Whatever may be meant by the term Mongolian, as applied to the complexion, the features, or the skeleton, has its application here. Though not actually occupants of the cheerless steppes of Mongolia Proper, the Chinese, the Tibetans, and the populations akin to them, have decidedly Mongol features; so Mongol, and so decidedly so, that few authors, however great has been their habit of drawing distinctions, have separated them from the typical members of the class. Indeed, some of them may be more Mongol than the Mongolians themselves.

In respect to their creed, though the majority are Buddhists, and (as such) representatives of anything but a primitive condition of society, several of the tribes of this part of the world are as pagan as the negroes of Africa; whilst, in language, they are, without any exception, the speakers of one of the least developed forms of human speech. I do not say that the Chinese and the other members of the great philological division to which it belongs, are either absolutely and wholly monosyllabic, or absolutely and wholly destitute of grammatical inflexions. I only say that they have been called monosyllabic; that they have been called uninflected; and that the terms are sufficiently free from any notable amount of error to pass current. They are not, of course, unexceptionable. Few are. They give us, however, a rough view of the real facts, and suggest an approximately correct notion, viz. that, notwithstanding a certain amount of civilization on the part of the speakers, the speech itself of the nations of south-eastern Asia in general is in a very primitive and rudimentary state. It must not, however, be inferred from this that the nations themselves are, what the Scythians of old were considered, the youngest of men. Nor yet that they are the oldest. The real fact is that of their languages having changed but slowly. Perhaps there has been an arrest of their development. Perhaps others have advanced with inordinate rapidity.

Be this as it may, a Mongol physiognomy, combined with a rudimentary form of speech, characterizes the populations under notice.

Their creeds vary. There come within the limits of the class thus described religions like that of the Koran on the one side, and the wildest forms of Paganism on the other. Both, however, are, to a great degree, exceptional. The belief of the majority is Buddhist.

The Mahometanism is a growth of yesterday. We shall find it where Tibet touches Persia.

For the Pagan tribes, the expositors of the primeval superstitions that preceded the spread of Buddhism we know, *à priori*, where to look. In the parts where the influences of India and China are at the minimum they will be found; chiefly, but not exclusively, in the forests and mountains of the Burmese, Siamese, and Chinese frontiers. In like manner the large towns of the alluvial valleys of the great rivers will give us the centres of the civilization.

Three great Empires represent the political power and importance of this stock—three great empires; the Chinese, the Siamese, and the Burmese. They profess to be conterminous. They profess to say that all that is not Siamese, is either Chinese or Burmese, and, *vice versâ*, that all which is not either Chinese or Burmese, is Siamese. They profess to divide the area amongst them. They scarcely do so in reality. Of the English and Hindu possessions we say nothing. They are of recent growth; and confirm, rather than invalidate, the rule. The exceptions lie in the land of a long list of semi-dependent and independent aborigines; Siamese, Burmese, Tibetan, or Chinese in respect to their ethnological relations, but not Chinese, Tibetan, Siamese, or Burmese in respect to their political position. Their political position is of no prominence whatever. Their ethnology is of the highest importance; and we easily see why it is so. In the great empires the original differences in the way of religion, art, and polity have, to a great extent, been obliterated by the diffusion of a common civilization; and the Buddhist populations of Asia, like the Christian populations of Europe, resemble each other in the more characteristic parts of their creeds. Yet, at one time, they differed;

and that on these very points. They differed as the Pagan of Gaul may have differed from the Pagan of Germany—*i. e.* with a difference, but with a certain amount of likeness as well. The interest then, with which we should contemplate (if there were such a thing) a remnant of the Druidism or Odinism of early Europe, attaches itself to such creeds as the Bodo, the Karien and the like, creeds of which the sequel will take notice; more notice than it will of the religions of China and Siam; inasmuch as it is supposed that the general character of these last is understood.

Our first group bears the name of *Bhot*. I spell it in this way because, according to theory, the *h* should be pronounced; even as the *h* in such words as *ab-hor* is pronounced. The generality, however, omit it in speech; and if learned men from the East would do the same in their spelling, the unlearned world might follow the example. The word, though unfamiliar in its naked form, is common enough under a slight disguise. It is the *Bult-*, in *Bult*istan, the *Bút-*, in *Bút*an, the *-bet*, in Ti*bet*. Sometimes, too, we hear of the *Bhoo*teeas; sometimes of the *Bho*tiyas. It is all the same word, a word that, in ethnology, has a wide meaning. In ethnology, it comprises the Little Tibetans, the natives of Ladak, the Tibetans of Tibet Proper, and the closely-allied tribes of Bútan.

The Tibet of the ordinary maps is too much of a table-land, plateau, or steppe. This is because it is imperfectly known; being a land under the dominion of the Chinese, and jealously protected against European exploration. Where enterprising travellers have actually penetrated, it has (to compare great things with small) been found to resemble the dales of Yorkshire, and the Lake district, rather than the sandy levels of Hampshire and Norfolk It has presented long and narrow valleys, or even gorges on the branches of great rivers. It has presented the level alluvia of drained lakes, pre-eminently numerous in Ladak and elsewhere. It has determined the industry of the inhabitants to a true and characteristic form of agriculture; for where water is scarce, and irrigation necessary, canal after canal, watercourse after watercourse, has to be constructed; and these, as we shall soon see, are to be found up to the very limits of the inhabited part of the Himalayas. Even when we follow the course of the Brahmaputra, (where we *can* follow it), the difference is only one of degree. There is still the river between its rocky and elevated banks. There is still the tract of alluvial and cultivated soil. The only difference is that the belts of cultivation are wider as the stream of the river grows stronger. If these be omitted in the maps it is because they have not been described; not because they are non-existent. Nevertheless, some portion of the Bhot area is what the ordinary representations make it—actual steppe or table-land, with the manners and customs of Tartary or Mongolia to match.

Of this vast tract of country we strike the western extremity, where we follow up the Indus towards its source. Move from India or Cashmír northwards, from Chinese Tartary southwards, from Bokhara eastwards, and you strike it. So that its frontiers are with Hindostan and Cashmír; with Little Bokhara, and with those strange and unknown countries to the north of the Cohistan of Cabul, the infidel districts of Kafer-istan.

It is not, however, *Kaferistan* or the *country* of the Kafirs, Guebres, or Giaours, with which we begin, but with *Bultistan*, or the country of the *Bulti*; for *stan* is the Persian for *country*, and *Bulti* is the Persian form of Bhot; and it is from the Persian frontier that the name has been propagated.

Far inland as Bultistan lies, it is not so far distant from Mecca as to lie wholly beyond the pale of the Koran; though it lies on the very verge and edge thereof.

It was Cashmír whence the Mahometanism of Bultistan was propagated; the districts in which it now predominates being petty chieftaincies, or captaincies, situated either on the main stream of the Indus, or its eastern feeders—the Shigar and the Shayok. They are, more or less, subordinate to Bultistan Proper, or Little Tibet in the limited sense of the term.

*Rongdo.*—Of these subordinate districts the most western is that of Rongdo, on the bend of the Indus, and on the frontier of the Gilgít and Hasora countries.

It is in Rongdo that the Indus makes its great bend from east to south, along with which a change in climate sets-in. The vegetation of Tibet graduates into that of the Eastern Punjab. The manners, however, of the Rongdo people are truly Tibetan. At the beginning of March, Dr. Thompson found them preparing for their crops, even before the snow was melted. They sprinkled thin layers of earth over it to promote its liquefaction. Below the level of 8000 feet it had, in favourable aspects, disappeared altogether. The artificial water-courses were filling, or full. Of the manure that had accumulated during the winter every particle was now forthcoming. It was carried to the fields in baskets, deposited in small heaps, carefully spread, carefully ploughed in. A pair of bullocks drew the plough, which was entirely of wood—share and all. The harrow was also of wood; a framework with no teeth, but weighted with stones, or a heavy board; sometimes made into a bush-harrow by means of thorns. The soil was freely hoed; its pulverization being an object of special care. The plough first, then the harrow, then the action of the air. This made a fine tilth, easily laid out in small square beds. Between these ran the last divisions of the watercourses; the irrigation being complete.

*Skardo.*—Little Tibet, in the limited sense of the word, comes next. It is better, however, to name it Skardo, or as those who, like the people of Cashmír, cannot pronounce the combination *sk*, call it *Is*kardo. Skardo, with its dependencies, was conquered for Gulab Singh, by his general Zoráwar Singh, in 1840. The contest was neither severe nor long. The invading army, which consisted of 15,000 men, was diminished by 200, no more. The defence cost about 500. The reigning chief, Ahmed Shah, was deposed, and his son Mahomed Shah, placed on the throne in his stead. The capital was surrendered after a slight resistance; and a garrison of Dogra troops left in a fort in its neighbourhood to ensure its fidelity; to ensure also the regular payment of a tribute of 7000 rupees.

Such is the recent political history and present condition of Skardo, and not only of Skardo but of Bulti, Bultiyul, Balor, Palolo, or Nang-koa; for by all these terms is the little district under notice designated. Nang-koa is the Tibetan, Balor the Dard, Skardo the native, name.

Like the men of Rongdo, the Skardo people are growers of corn, and cutters of watercourses. They plough, sow, irrigate, and reap. They are strong and hardy, simple in their habits; fond of out-of-door exercise, and manly games. One of these is noticed by Mr. Vigne. He calls it hockey on horseback. To those who have played the ordinary English game the name is a description.

Another of their sports is the hunting of the chakor. Throughout the valley of the Indus, and Tibet, the chakors, or painted partridges, are very common, and when the winter is sharp and the snow lies thick they come close up to houses. When they are hunted, the ground where they lie is surrounded by a ring of men who approach each other from all directions, so as gradually to make the circle narrower and narrower. When its diameter is no more than about 100 yards across, a horseman gallops about within the inclosure and disturbs the birds. Frightened and confused, they run from side to side till they sink exhausted, and allow themselves to be taken up by the hand.

The table-land of Deotsu, a thinly-inhabited steppe between Skardo and Cashmír belongs to Bultistan.

To the west of Deotsu lies a district marked as the Hasora country. It has already been mentioned as lying to the south of Rongdo. Whether this be Bulti, or other than Bulti, I am not prepared to say. Moorcroft specially states that the Tibetan language is spoken within its boundaries; if not over its whole surface. He also calls the district Dsungari. It will be noticed hereafter. At present I merely express the opinion that Hasora is partially Bhot.

Indeed, the exact limits of the frontier, along with the details of the mutual indentations into each other's areas effected by the Bhot districts of Dras, Suru, and Zanskar on the one side, and the Hindu regions of Cashmír and Kistewar on the other, are obscure; becoming clearer when we reach the British province of Lahúl. Yet, what do we know of the hill-ranges that form the northern margins of Cashmír? Some of the valleys may be Cashmiran, others Bhot. Where do Dras and Suru end? Where begins Cashmír? Again, what is the population of the valley marked Maru, and Wardwan in Strachey's map, the valley of the river which joins the Chenab at Kistewar? Some portion of this is, doubtless, Bhot, and some portion half Bhot and half Hindu.

Turning from these points to the Skardo frontier, we

find the three small districts of Shigar, on the river so called, of Parkuta, and of Khartakshi, on the main stream of the Indus. Then, on the Shayok, lie Keris, Khapalor, and Chorbad. They are all in the same relation to Skardo as Rongdo. They are all on high levels, Parkuta and Khartakshi at from 7000 to 8000, Chorbad at from 8000 to 9000 feet.

So many valleys, and so many Lords of the Valley—this is what we have seen in the list of the petty principalities that have been enumerated. I call the petty potentates chieftains or princes as the case may be. I also give their native titles; which are of some use as instruments in ethnological criticism. The native titles are Gyalpo, and Makpon; the latter word meaning General, and suggesting the notion of a military conquest. In the Shigar list of Gyalpos, the title of Tham is given to the men of the second, third, fourth, fifth, and sixth dynasties; a title which will appear elsewhere. The genealogy of them all is essentially the same. There is a Bikam in the list of the Kapolor Gyalpos, the tenth in descent from an ancestor named Biwân-cho; who is, in his turn, the 45th from Sultan Sikander (*i. e.* Alexander), who is succeeded by Abra-ham, who is succeeded by Isaac, who has amongst his posterity a Sultan Mahomed, a Malik Shah, a Balum Malik and other heterogeneous impossibilities. Of course, true history begins *somewhere* in these pedigrees; though I cannot say where. Bikam, whom Cunningham fixes A.D. 1650, has a name suspiciously like that of more than one other Bulti worthy. There is, for instance, Bokha, an adventurer who established himself about 1500, in these parts. Then there is a Fakir from whom the present Gyalpo of Skardo derives his origin. This was an ascetic of extreme sanctity, who lived during the days of a Gyalpo who had no son at all, and only one daughter.

Twelve chiefs sought her hand; but the sanctity of the fakir prevailed. The heiress was given to him; in proof of which there is the holy stone called Burdonas, on which the pious man was wont to sit, and on which the heir-apparent, on attaining manhood, undergoes certain ceremonies of inauguration.

Again—we shall find a Bikam in the so-called history of Nepaul.

Perhaps, Ali Sher, a cotemporary of Jehanguirs, is a truly historical character. He built the citadel of Skardo. He conquered Ladak; which his son Ahmed Shah lost. Shah Murad, the next in succession, conquered Gilgít, Hunz, Nagor, and Chitral; conquering and reigning from about 1720 to 1750.

Chorbad is divided from the Ladak district of Nubra by a ravine called Bogdan, narrow, tortuous, and steep. The descent upon it from the north-east is as much as 3000 feet, in less than a mile; Bogdan itself being some 13,000 feet above the level of the sea. It is the name, however, of a village as well as a pass; though only of a summer village. When winter sets-in the inhabitants move further down the stream. The Shayuk here is rapid, and the mountains that inclose it steep and barren. Their opposite faces are rarely more than a quarter of a mile apart; whilst spurs, projected at short intervals, intercept the outline of the narrow and impracticable valley, and throw its stream into zigzag channels. The road, in many places, quitting the bed of the river runs abruptly, and almost perpendicularly up the face of the rocky hills, and requires ladders and scaffoldings to make it accessible.

The Shayok, too, is rapid and deep, being in no place fordable. Meanwhile, the villages lie on its two sides alternately; so that whenever the traveller passes from one to another he must either miss every second one, or be continually crossing the river. The bridges, however, are numerous; chiefly made of the trunks of poplar-trees laid across, with a light rail to ensure safety. Sometimes a kind of pier is carried forward into the bed of the stream, and the ends of the bridge laid upon it.

The Shayok, here, as may be inferred from the notice, gives a *minimum* of alluvial soil; and this is not always to be depended on. In 1842 the village of Chulungka, in Chorbad, stood on the low level of the river side. But a flood washed it away. It now stands on a platform about 50 feet higher. It is a village. It consists, however, of but three or four houses. Lower down the fertility of the soil must be inexhaustible. Near Pranu there are isolated accumulations of alluvium to the depth of 600 feet. All the villages are surrounded by orchards of apricots and walnuts, mulberries and vines. The timber is from either the willow or the poplar—the timber and also the fuel; both being scarce.

It is not, however, either the districts of Chorbad, or the districts of Nubra, that we are noticing, so much as the impracticable block of land between them. This it is that makes a political division by separating Bultistan from Ladak. More than this, it separates the Mahometan, from the Buddhist, Bhot. The Mahometan religion, universal throughout the little principalities that have been enumerated, ceases at the ravine of Bogdan.

If this ravine of Bogdan have, as it seems to have, anything to do with the diffusion or arrest of Mahometanism, it may also have affected the spread of the earlier Buddhist creed. It may have acted as a barrier in one direction, even as it has acted as a barrier in another; due allowance being made for the difference between going up-hill and down-hill, between following a river and stemming its stream. *Valeat quantum.* The history of Buddhism is one thing, that of Mahometanism another; and the question which now suggests itself is this —what were the Bultistan States before they were Mahometan? What were they a few generations back? for Mahometanism, in some portions of them, is of recent introduction. To say that analogy is in favour of their being in the same category with Buddhist Ladak and Buddhist Tibet is inaccurate, and one-sided. It is like saying that men must be Welshmen in Shropshire because they are Welshmen in the neighbouring county of Montgomery. This is a blunder, and we know it is. We know, too, why it is one. We know that the analogy is all one way; that the western side of Shropshire has alone been taken into account. *Mutatis mutandis*, this applies to Bultistan. We have yet to take into consideration the countries that bound it on the west; countries which are not Buddhist, and which never appear to have been so. What are they? Some of them, as we may suppose, are Mahometan, the Mahometanism being new and imperfect. But some hold a creed *per se*. What it is I cannot say. It is not any of the great religions of the world in a clear and definite form. It is neither Christianity nor Judaism, neither Brahminism nor the doctrines of Zoroaster. As little is it a pure and peculiar form of primitive Paganism. It would be a creed of inordinate interest if it were so. But it is not this, though something of the sort. Its details, so far as they are known, will be given elsewhere. It is more Brahminic and Zoroastrian than either Buddhist or Jewish. It is as little Jewish as Christian. It is a creed *per se*.

Now the religion of the Bultis before their conversion may as easily have been this as Buddhism. It may *more* easily have been so. It may more easily have been so, because new religions, be they Mahometan or be they

Christian, are far more readily superinduced upon simple Paganism than upon any of the nobler, or less ignoble, superstitions; Buddhism, Brahminism, Parseeism. In a soil saturated with Fetichism or Shamanism, Christianity may take root; at any rate it should always be planted. Upon any of the above-named systems, and, still more, upon Mahometanism, it is scarcely worth engrafting. If missionary institutions reduced this to an absolute and invariable rule of action, they would save an enormous waste of power. The organization that will make one proselyte from the Koran, will make dozens and scores from the unlettered laxity of Paganism.

Whence came the present Bulti religion? From Cashmír as aforesaid. Whence came it into Cashmír? From Persia. Hence it is the Shiite, as opposed to the Sunnite, form of Mahometanism; the Turk tribes of the frontier being Sunnites, and, as such, hating their neighbours as heretics and, when convenient, robbing them as infidels. The Koran forbids its professors to sell one another into slavery. With infidels they are free to steal and sell. When infidels, however, are not to be procured, a heretic does instead. All along the northern frontier of Khorasan the Sunnite Turcomans of the southern part of Tartary kidnap the Shiite Persians. Some they keep for their own use, others they sell to the Uzbeks of Khiva. In either case they treat them as infidels.

*Ladak.*—Nubra, into which we pass from Chorbad, is Buddhist. The valley of Le, or Ladak Proper, is Buddhist. Zanskar, on the south, is Buddhist. In Dras, Suru, and Purik, in the direction of Cashmír, there is no Mahometanism. In general, however, Ladak is Buddhist.

In Ladak Proper, the valley of the main stream of the Indus, we have large villages, and even towns like Leh, the capital. In Nubra, on the Shayok, and in

Zanskar, on the river of that name, the levels are higher, the country more broken, and the population thinner. The villages are of the character of those in Chorbad, *i. e.* they consist of only three or four houses. Some of them are, probably, summer residences only. On the 2nd of July there were crops of barley and buckwheat growing at Nira, 12,000 feet above the level of the sea. At Yulchung (13,000 feet), vegetation was somewhat backwarder. Still there was vegetation, and occupation—in the month of July at least. Even Phutaksha, at 14,300, bears the name of village. Its cultivation ran along the side of the river to an elevation of 15,000 feet; but the crops were scanty. This is in Zanskar, on the Indian side of the Indus. The same vegetation, however, and the same occupation repeats itself in Nubra, on the north; between the Indus and the famous pass of Karakorum. The valley of the Nubra is fertile. Before, however, you reach the head-waters of the river itself, vegetation becomes scanty, and occupancy ceases. But, though no occupancy, there is trade. The road from Yarkend to Leh runs over the pass under notice; which one Englishman (Dr. Thompson) has visited. It lies at a height of 18,200 feet below the line of perpetual snow; above the line of any notable vegetation. At the same time, by the sides of stones, in protected crevices, and in spots where water collects, a few stunted plants are to be found—artemisiæ and tanacetums three or four inches in height, tufts of moss-like alsineæ, saussureæ, sibbaldiæ, prostrate astragali, prostrate myricareæ, a pyrethrum, a eurotia, biebersteinea odora, oxytropis chyliophylla, a species of primula, a white pedicularis, two or three cruciferæ, triglochins, carices, and grasses. Shingle along the main road, glaciers on the side, this is what the merchants find in the way between Leh and Yarkend. Their goods are carried by ponies; but the ponies must carry with them, besides the goods of their masters, their own provender. They faint by the way. In a small level plain, about 200 feet long and 50 broad (an evident halting-place), with a small pool of water, Dr. Thompson met a party on their way. The road was covered with skeletons of horses; and the miserable animals that he met alive were weak, emaciated, and, to all appearance, unfit for even the short remainder of their journey. At the top of the pass itself vegetation was entirely wanting; but the shingly ground was unfavourable to it. Otherwise, lichens, at least, might have been found. The only living animals observed were a bird about the size of a sparrow, a bright metallic carrion-fly, a small dusky butterfly, and several ravens. The ravens flew freshly and fastly, wending their way in arches overhead, not at all affected by the rarity of the atmosphere, and as much at their ease as they would have been at the level of the sea.

Not so, however, the traveller. His head ached and felt light during the whole time he was either on the pass or in its immediate neighbourhood.

Lieutenant Wood's account, of a similar feeling, I subjoin in his own words. He was at the head-waters of the Oxus, on the high plateau of Pamir, on the 20th of February, and at a level of 15,600 feet, or 62 feet lower than the summit of Mont Blanc, 2400 feet lower than the Karakorum pass. He is standing on the edge of the lake. "The water emitted a slightly fetid smell and was of a reddish tinge. The bottom was oozy and tangled with grassy weeds. I tried to measure the breadth of the lake by sound, but was baffled by the rarity of the air. A musket, loaded with blank cartridge, sounded as if the charge had been poured into the barrel, and neither wads nor ramrod used. When ball was introduced the report was louder, but possessed none of the sharpness that marks a similar charge in denser atmospheres. The ball, however, could be distinctly heard whizzing through the air. The human voice was sensibly affected, and conversation, especially if in a loud tone, could not be kept up without exhaustion: the slightest muscular exertion was attended with a similar result. Half a dozen strokes with an axe brought the workman to the ground; and though a few minutes' respite sufficed to restore the breath, anything like continued exertion was impossible. A run of fifty yards at full speed made the runner gasp for breath. Indeed, this exercise produced a pain in the lungs and a general prostration of strength which was not got rid of for many hours. Some of the party complained of dizziness and headaches; but, except the effects above described, I neither felt myself, nor perceived in others, any of those painful results of great elevation which travellers have suffered in ascending Mont Blanc. This might have been anticipated, for where the transition from a dense to a highly-rarified atmosphere is so sudden, as in the case of ascending that mountain, the circulation cannot be expected to accommodate itself at once to the difference of pressure, and violence must accrue to some of the more sensitive organs of the body. The ascent of Pamir was, on the contrary, so gradual that some extrinsic circumstances were necessary to remind us of the altitude we had attained. The effect of great elevation upon the general system had indeed been proved to me some time before in a manner for which I was not prepared. One evening in Badakhshan, while sitting in a brown study over the fire, I chanced to touch my pulse, and the galloping rate at which it was throbbing roused my attention. I at once took it for granted that I was in a raging fever, and after perusing some hints on the preservation of health which

Dr. Lord, at parting, had kindly drawn out for me, I forthwith prescribed for myself most liberally. Next morning my pulse was as brisk as ever, but still my feelings denoted health. I now thought of examining the wrists of all our party, and to my surprise found that the pulses of my companions beat yet faster than my own. The cause of this increased circulation immediately occurred to me; and when we afterwards commenced marching towards Wakhan I felt the pulses of the party whenever I registered the boiling point of water. The motion of the blood is in fact a sort of living barometer by which a man acquainted with his own habit of body can, in great altitudes, roughly calculate his height above the sea. Upon Pamir the pulsations in one minute were as follow :—

| | Throbs. | Country. | Habit of body. |
|---|---|---|---|
| My own . . . . . . | 110 | Scotland | spare |
| Gholam Hussein, Munshi . . | 124 | Jasulmer | fat |
| Omerallah, mule-driver . . | 112 | Afghan | spare |
| Gaffer, groom . . . . . | 114 | Peshawur | spare |
| Dowd, do. . . . . . | 124 | Kabul | stout." |

From the Sikkim Himalayas Major Sherwill writes thus :—The "rarefaction of the air is beginning to tell upon us; bleeding at the nose, a tightness across the back of the head, is what I most suffer from. The exertion of writing, making a false step amongst the rocks, of addressing any one, stooping to tie the shoe, or performing any act requiring but moderate exertion, is productive of the most distressing symptoms of suffocation, sharp, sudden pains in the chest, extreme beating of the heart, and violent action of the lungs, which, being fed with a thin and rarefied air, have to work hard to keep the blood purified. I have been so prostrated this day as to be fit for nothing; which is the more strange as our elevation is not a very great one; but, from all I can gather from travellers in the Himalayah, I suspect that their sufferings, commencing as they do from this elevation, are more acute, and more noticed, as being something new and, at first, very alarming. One of our Nepal coolies is in great agony, moaning in a most piteous manner."

When we come to the ethnology of the Cordilleras, and the populations of Ecuador, Bolivia, and Peru, the effect of the rarefaction of the air upon the lungs will again be brought under notice. It evidently varies with the constitution of the individual. It also stands in a decided ratio to his exertions. Rest awhile, and the distress ceases. At elevations of 17,000 feet and upwards (the highest passes range between this and 19,000), the traveller ascends with pain; and has to rest himself at short intervals. He suffers however, whether in motion or at his ease, from a dull headache. This, however, can be borne for two or three days—even more. Permanent occupancy is possible at altitudes of 13,800 feet at least; and, perhaps, somewhat beyond. Kibar, for instance, is at that high level. Cultivation reaches somewhat higher. It transcends 14,000.

It is fortunate for the ethnographer that our knowledge of the imperfectly-explored countries of the Himalaya is dependent upon the value rather than the number of observers who have visited and described them. Few Englishmen have written about them; but those who have done so have written fully. The earliest notices are Chinese, of high, but (in my mind) of not undoubted antiquity. Some one, however, either visited them early, or procured information concerning them; for it is surprising how closely the names of the classical geographers reappear in our most recent descriptions. The *Byltæ*, the *Cesi*, the *Akhassa regio*, the *Dabasæ* of Pliny and others, all come out with wonderful closeness in the still-existing names of *Bulti, Kie-chha,* and *d-Bus.* Neither does the marvellous story of Herodotus respecting the gold of the Iessdones, which was dug out of the ground by ants as large as foxes, fail in finding a plausible explanation in the two languages of Tibet and India combined with certain facts in their zoology. That in more than one district on the drainage of the Indus, an animal of the marmot family does the work of the gold-seeker, though he does it unconsciously, is attested by several independent authorities. He burrows in the auriferous clefts and sands, and gold is found in the earth at the entrance of his holes. This is collected by the natives of the district and traded in. Now the Bhot name for this marmot is *phyipa;* whilst the Indian name for the *ant* is *pipilaki.* Megasthenes relates that he never saw the animals themselves—that he never did this, but that he had seen some skins of them. But who talks of the skins of ants? The skin of the marmot is one of the commonest articles in the petty trade of India and Tibet. But the skin of an ant? The *names* seem to have been confused; not, however, by the Greeks, but by the Indians. "The people who dwell under the pleasant shade of the Kichakavenus, and along the Sailodá River, between the Moru and Mandara Mountains, the Khasas, Prádaras, Páradas, Ekásanas, Arkas, Kulindas, Tanganas, and Paratanganas brought to Yudhisthira lumps of gold a drona in weight, of the sort called *paippilika,* or ant-gold, which was so called because it was exfodiated, by the *pipilaka,* or common large ant." So runs an extract from the Mahabharata, by means of which Professor Wilson has illustrated this obscure but not uninteresting question. Subtract from *paippilika* the last two syllables, and the Bhot name remains, with scarcely the alteration of a single letter.

There was gold, then, in Ladak, and the trade that

grew out of gold. And this trade originated centuries ago. We know that it was directed towards India. We believe that it may also have been directed northwards. Before Herodotus wrote, Karakorum may have been a pass, laboriously traversed by weak ponies and panting drivers. And the names of certain Himalayan districts were known to the geographers of Greece and Rome. And those names still exist, some of them with a meaning in the present Tibetan. The present Tibetan, too, explains certain old Indian glosses.

The industry of Ladak is more or less commercial, and the energy of the natives has industriously contended against the obstacles of nature in making the country practicable. It is the country of a transit trade. No little labour has been expended on making roads in the direction of the neighbouring countries, *e. g.* the western road to the Punjab and Kabul through Kashmir, the south-western road through Jummú, the southern through Kullú and Lahúl to Lahore and Umritser, the south-eastern to Lhasa, the eastern to Chinese Tartary, the northern to Khoten and Yarkend, and the north-western to Little Tibet, Bulti, or Skardo. All these follow the lines of the rivers as far as they can, and are then carried over lofty and formidable passes, some more than 18,000 feet in height. The rivers are crossed by ferries or bridges; inflated skins for the former, suspensions for the latter. In Ladak the use of the skin is very general; that of the boat being rare and exceptional. The poorer travellers mount themselves on the hide of a single buffalo, carefully sewn up so as to be air-tight, which floats with the legs uppermost. The ferryman, who sits with his legs in the water, pushes it on by striking them out as in swimming, helping the propulsion by means of a small wooden paddle which he holds in his right hand. With his left he steadies the passenger, who holds on as he best can by one of the legs. Wealthy men indulge in the luxury of a raft (if so it may be called) made of a bed stretched across a pair of skins. The bridges are chiefly of wood, peculiar in construction,—especially the suspension bridges. The ropes are made of the twisted twigs of the birch-tree. They are suspended, side by side, about five feet apart from each other. The side ropes are also of birchen twigs; thinner, however, than the main suspenders. On these lies the roadway, which is again made of long ropes, joined by wickerwork or wattles.

In these bridges we have a fair measure of the Ladaki's power of construction. He shares it with the other populations of the group to which he belongs. The Bhot is a builder of suspension-bridges all Bhotland over. Other tribes akin to him are the same.

The industry of the Ladaki is agricultural; but not exclusively. He is a breeder of cattle; for the Ladak Fauna is eminently a Fauna of the domestic animals. Amongst horses, the Kyang, as the Bhot call it, and as it is named, even zoologically, by Moorcroft, has much that allies it to the quagga and zebra, much too, that allies it with the ass; standing about 14 hands in height, reddish-brown on the back, and white on the stomach, with the tail of a zebra, and the neigh of a horse.

The yak, like the native ox of Britain, is rare in its wild state. As a domesticated beast, both of burden and food, it is universal.

Of sheep no less than three species are Ladaki, and of goats more than three. To these add the Tibetan stag, the musk deer, and other animals, ruminant, though not domesticated.

With the exception of the yak, the exact relations of the actual domestic animals of Ladak to their wild congeners is (as elsewhere) a problem rather than an ascertained fact. The yak is used for carrying loads, being too unmanageable for the plough. The cow is kept for her milk and hair; for once a year, both the yak and the mixed offspring of the yak and cow are clipped. This hybrid is called the Dso, useful as a beast of burden, useful as a beast of draught (in the plough), useful in supplying milk of the richest quality. There are other half-breeds of less value.

Industrial habits in the way of commerce and agriculture on one side, a niggard soil and extreme climate on the other—such are the conditions of civilization in Ladak. They are much the same over the whole Bhot area; but we know the Ladaki portion of it best. Air rare; water either scarce or local; alluvial soil scarce and more local still. The cold of winter, but not all its characteristics. Little rain; as little snow. Everything to dry the atmosphere. Moorcroft was at Leh two years. Ten times, during that period, did it rain—ten times and no oftener. In the district of Dras the snow lies deep; and hence its Tibetan name of Hem-babs or the Snow Country. Elsewhere, however, there is rarely more than a few inches of depth even in the middle of winter. The cold, however, is intense. And so is the heat. Burning hot by day, parching cold by night—this is the Ladak climate, of which the extremes of temperature are determined by the hours of day rather than the months of the year. The mean temperature of the winter months is by no means excessive. It is the nights of the summer that bring the cold.

Such a country must be but thinly peopled. Hence, the calculations of Cunningham, which nearly coincide with those of that excellent observer Moorcroft, make the numbers, as distributed over the British, as well as the Sikh, district, to amount to no more than 433 persons to the square mile. But this scantiness of human life is due to other causes than severity of climate, impracticability of soil, or the domestic institution of polyandria. An epidemic, an emigration of the Lamas who were persecuted or insulted during the conquest by the troops of Gulab Singh, and losses during the war, give the following table:—

| | |
|---|---|
| Carried off by small-pox in 1834 . . . . | 14,000 |
| Lamas emigrated . . . . . . . . | 9,000 |
| Perished during the war . . . . . | 15,000 |
| Emigrants (chiefly Mahometans) . . . | 1,000 |
| Total decrease . . . | 39,000 |
| Moorcroft's census . . . | 165,000 |
| Present census | 126,000 |

The Sikh conquest seems, in Ladak, to have wholly broken up the system of petty chieftaincies; which, in Bultistan, it merely modified. Of the native Gyalpos, or Makpons of Zanskar, Rukshu, and Ladak Proper, we hear little. Nevertheless, we hear enough to indicate their existence; enough to show that the general rule of mountainous districts prevails in the mountains here. Dr. Thompson tells us how it fared with the native prince of Giah. He had a title, a very limited income, and no political power whatever. This was in 1847. When Moorcroft was there, he was kept by the same Gyalpos in a state of suspense as to how he was to be received, and whether he was to be allowed to go. Meanwhile, Giah itself is the valley of one of the smallest of the Ladak streams; 13,000 feet above the level of the sea.

In Ladak and in the Buddhist districts, in general, the females outnumber the males, whilst, in the Mahometan, the males outnumber the females. Moorcroft thought that the female population was as much as two to one against the male. The nuns and monks bear a large proportion to the rest of the population; a smaller one, however, than we are likely to find in Tibet.

The true Ladak physiognomy is found in its most typical form in the central parts of the Bhot area. On the confines of the Turk, Cashmirian, Dard, and Hindu frontier it changes; partaking of the character of the populations upon which the Bhot abut. In Shigar it is believed that the basis of the stock is Kirghís. In Kanàwer there is a notable amount of Hindu influences. So there is in Spiti and Lahúl; to say nothing of part of those districts being more or less Hindu. Then there is a great number of families known under the name of Arghon. These are half-bloods, Ladaki on one side, Cashmirian on the other. In the true Ladak districts, however, the type is definite, and the blood pure.

The Bhot of Ladak is strong, hardy, short, and square, with a decidedly Mongol physiognomy; by which is meant a flat face, broad cheek, depressed nose, oblique and narrow eye, curtained at the corners, hair black, stature low. In the following table a superiority of size in the Hindu and Mahometan districts is apparent; the district of Shigar alone being excepted. A third series of measurement, not given here, but to be found in Cunningham, gives more than four inches difference in favour of the class of landed proprietors, who are better fed, more warmly clothed, and more conveniently housed than the lower orders. They fare better, and labour less, ride when they travel, and indulge more liberally in the luxries of tea and animal food. Their average height for the Buddhist districts and Kunawer (the Mahometan landlords were not submitted to measurement) is 5 ft. 6·1 in. The ears of the Ladakis are inordinately large; one-half larger than those of Europeans.

STATURE.

| | MEN. | | | | | | WOMEN. | | | | | |
|---|---|---|---|---|---|---|---|---|---|---|---|---|
| | Tallest. | | Shortest. | | Average. | | Tallest. | | Shortest. | | Average. | |
| | ft. | in. | ft. | in. | ft. | in. | ft. | in. | ft. | in. | ft. | in. |
| BUDDHISTS: | | | | | | | | | | | | |
| Rukshu . . . | 5 | 1·5 | 5 | 0·0 | 5 | 0·9 | 5 | 0·0 | 4 | 1·0 | 4 | 8·2 |
| Spiti . . . . | 5 | 6.5 | 5 | 0·0 | 5 | 2·4 | 5 | 2·5 | 4 | 1·0 | 4 | 8·9 |
| Nubra . . . . | 5 | 7·0 | 5 | 4·0 | 5 | 2·7 | 4 | 7·0 | 4 | 0·0 | 5 | 9·8 |
| Ladak . . . . | 7 | 5·0 | 4 | 10.0 | 5 | 1·4 | 5 | 4·0 | 4 | 1·0 | 4. | 10·1 |
| *Average* | . . . | | . . . | | 5 | 1·8 | . . . | | . . . | | 4 | 9·2 |
| MAHOMETANS: | | | | | | | | | | | | |
| Chorbad . . . | 5 | 8·0 | 4 | 8·0 | 5 | 0·9 | 5 | 0·0 | 4 | 4·0 | 4 | 9·3 |
| Khapolor . . . | 5 | 7·0 | 4 | 6·0 | 5 | 0·7 | 5 | 2·0 | 4 | 2·0 | 4 | 9·1 |
| Keris . . . . | 5 | 5·0 | 5 | 0·0 | 5 | 2·9 | 4 | 11·0 | 4 | 8·0 | 4 | 10·6* |
| Parguta . . . | 5 | 9·0 | 4 | 10·0 | 5 | 3·5 | 5 | 4·0. | 4 | 4·0 | 4 | 8·5 |
| Skardo . . . | 5 | 11·0 | 4 | 9·0 | 5 | 2·3 | 5 | 0·0 | 4 | 6·0 | 4 | 9·7 |
| Shigar . . . | 5 | 5·0 | 4 | 4·0 | 5 | 0·4 | 4 | 11·0 | 4 | 8·0 | 4 | 9·4 |
| Rongdo . . . | 5 | 7·0 | 4 | 9·0 | 5 | 2·1 | 5 | 0·0 | 4 | 7·0 | 4 | 9·7 |
| *Average* | . . . | | . . . | | 5 | 0·8 | . . . | | . . . | | 4 | 9·5 |
| KANETS: | | | | | | | | | | | | |
| Upper Kanawer | 5 | 6·0 | 4 | 11·0 | 5 | 1·9 | 5 | 1·5 | 4 | 4·5 | 4 | 9·0 |
| Middle do. . | 5 | 6·0 | 4 | 9·0 | 5 | 2 0 | 5 | 5·0 | 4 | 9·0 | 4 | 11·1 |
| Lower do. . | 5 | 9·2 | 4 | 11·0 | 5 | 4·1 | 5 | 5·0 | 4 | 10·0 | 5 | 1·2 |
| *Average* | . . . | | . . . | | 5 | 2·0 | . . . | | . . . | | 4 | 9·7 |

The skulls, as far as I can judge by drawings, and the few I have seen or found described, are less referable to the extreme Mongolian type than is expected. Eighty is a fair facial angle for a European. A capacity of seventy-two cubic inches is that of many of the skulls found in English tumuli, and described as ancient British and Anglo-Saxon. The weight is important, because many of the Hindu skulls are very light and delicate, thin-boned, and of a fine texture. The truncation of the occiput is by no means remarkable.

| Skulls. | Facial Angle. | Cranial Capacity | Weight. | |
|---|---|---|---|---|
| | Degrees. | Cubic In. | lb. | oz. |
| No. 1 from Hanlé . . | 80 | 74·5 | 1 | 4·44 |
| No. 2 from Lé . . . . | 68 | 72·7 | 1 | 6·44 |
| No. 3 from Lé . . . . | 73 | 70·0 | 1 | 7·46 |
| No. 4 from Bultistan . | 75 | 72·0 | 1 | 2·40 |
| | 74 | 72·3 | 1 | 5·18 |

Ladak, like Bultistan, belongs to Gulab Singh, with the exception of two districts—Spiti and Lahúl, which constitute a part of British India. Spiti is wholly, Lahúl but partially, Bhot. It is Bhot along the banks of the Chandra, and Bhot along those of the Bhaga; but below the junction, and along the Chandra-Bhaga, or the result of the two combined streams, it is Hindu.

In Spiti the population is scantily spread along the banks of the river so called. In 316 houses, distributed in sixty villages, we find

| | |
|---|---|
| Adult males . . | 392 |
| Boys under 12 . . | 191 |
| Adult females . . | 593 |
| Girls under 12 . . | 238 |
| Priests . . . | 193 |
| | 1607 |

Their chief enemy is the small-pox; weakness of the eyes being common — goitre rare. The men marry between twenty and twenty-one, the women from fifteen to twenty. Polyandry prevails; and, side by side with it, polygamy. A man in good circumstances may have two or three wives; but, then, the priest has none. Of food they have but little variety, being without poultry, without vegetables.

The whole area of Ladak is as follows:—

UNDER GULAB SINGH.

| Districts. | Sq. Miles. | Mean Heights. |
|---|---|---|
| Nubra . . . | 9216 | 12,763 |
| Ladak . . . | 3960 | 11,500 |
| Zanskar . . . | 3030 | 13,154 |
| Rukshu . . . | 5580 | 15,634 |
| Purik, Suru, Dras . . . | 4200 | 11,196 |

BRITISH.

| | | |
|---|---|---|
| Spiti . . . . | 2312 | 12,986 |
| Lahúl . . . | 1872 | 11,063 |

*Hungrung.*—I know of no true ethnological difference between the Bhot of Hungrung and those of Ladak and Tibet. The district, however, belongs to the Rajah of Bisahur. The villages lie at different levels; ranging from 9,500 to 12,000 feet, the alluvia being numerous, and the climate, considering the altitude, favourable to cultivation.

On the very crest of the Hungrung pass, at a height of 14,800 feet, the dama grows in patches; the dama being the Tibetan name for the Caragana versicolor, a small shrub, that thrives at elevations where no other tree is to be found. This makes it valuable for fuel; the scarcest of the Bhot necessaries. The barleys are of two kinds, the common, and the Hordeum Ægiceros. Both are cultivated; and that after the ordinary Bhot fashion; *i. e.* by means of irrigation. On the lower levels are grown wheat, buckwheat, millet, a kind of rape, and apricots. On the higher, there are no fruit trees at all.

It is at Nako, in Hungrung, that Dr. Thompson finds occasion to remark upon the gradual character of the transition from India to Tibet, both morally and physically. It is by gradual transitions that Brahminism passes into Buddhism. It is by gradual transitions that the Hindu physiognomy becomes Bhot. The "gradual transition, in descending the Sutlej, from Hinduism to Buddhism is very remarkable, and not less so because it is accompanied by an equally gradual change in the physical aspect of the inhabitants; the Hindus of the Lower Sutlej appearing to pass by insensible gradations as we advance from village to village, till at last we arrive at a pure Tartar population. The people of Upper Piti have quite the Tartar physiognomy, the small stature and stout build of the inhabitants of Ladak, to whom they closely approximate in dress."

*Kunawer.*—In Lower Kunawer the language is Hindu

rather than Bhot; in Upper Kunawer it is Bhot rather than Hindu. Nor is this all. There are dialects and sub-dialects. The Milchan is the language of Lower Kunawer; Milchan being the Rampúr term for the language in general. In Súngnúm the forms are truly provincial, and, as the word Theburskud, or Tibberskud, is used as a name for all deviations from the ordinary speech, the Súngnúm dialect has been given as Theburskud. The Lubrung (or Kanam) and the Lidung (or Lippa) forms are varieties of the Milchan. The Súmchú is, perhaps, a fresh dialect.

| English | Milchan. | Theburskud. | Súmchú. |
|---|---|---|---|
| *Man* | mi | mi | mé |
| *Women* | chismi | shrí | esplung |
| *Head* | bul | pisha | pisha |
| *Tongue* | le | le | le |
| *Eye* | mík | mé | mí |
| *Ear* | kanung | rupung | repung |
| *Foot* | bung | bunk | bunkun |
| *Sun* | yúne | né | nímok |
| *Moon* | gulsung | gulsung | gulsung |
| *Star* | skara | karma | karma |
| *One* | ít | té | ít |
| *Two* | nísh | níshí | nísh |
| *Three* | súm | súm | húm |
| *Four* | pu | pí | pu |
| *Five* | gna | gnai | gna |
| *Ten* | saí | chúí | sa |

The differences here are slight. The infinitives, however, have peculiar endings:—

| | | | |
|---|---|---|---|
| Milchan . . . . | lonhmih' | or | lonhmig |
| Lippa . . . . . | lodenh' | or | lodent |
| Kanam . . . . | logma | | |
| Súngnúm . . . . | lopang | | |
| Súmchú (?) . . . | lomma | or | loma. |

Neither the Bhot nor the Hindu populations of Kunawer are truly pure. On the contrary, there are Bhot characters amongst the Hindus, Hindu characters amongst the Bhot. Buddhism, indeed, decreases in the central districts, and disappears in the southern. It is not, however, replaced by any pure form of Brahminism. Local gods and irregular priests appear here. Every hill has its deota or genius. Polyandry is general. To one family one wife; the elder brother being the more special husband. Minute and trenchant divisions of caste are wanting. There is, however, an approach to it. The Chumangs are regarded as outcasts, and no true Kane will eat with them, intermarry with them, or allow them to cross their threshold. Their skins are dark, and some are said to be woolly-haired. The same is said concerning the Rawi and Dom of Kumaon. They are not found in the Bhot districts. The people of the lower hills call them Koli; those of Rampúr, Chumars. Chumang is what they call themselves. They till the soil and weave. Polyandry is one of their habits, as well as one of their superiors'. They are liable to be pressed as porters.

So are the Domang, whose name is, word for word, that of the Dom of Kumaon.

So is the class of carpenters.

Hence, even in Kunawer, with its Buddhist frontier and its Bhot characters, there are no less than three castes; each of which keeps its members to itself in the way of intermarriage. A Dom will not intermarry with a Chumang.

To those who care about a general name for the two divisions of the Bhot family, which have been the subject of the present chapter, the valuable paper of Strachey on the Physical Geography of Western Tibet suggests one. All the members of the group under notice agree with each other in respect to their political relations. They are each and all other than Chinese. That this distinction is negative is clear; but it is not, for that reason, unimportant. The peculiar exclusiveness of the Chinese system makes the difference between what it applies to and what it does not, the difference between the known and the unknown. Now the non-Chinese portions of Bhotland are called by the Tibetans themselves Maryul, or Lowland; for *yul* means *land*, and *mar* means *low*.

Maryul, or the Lowlands, in respect to its politics, falls into two divisions; (1) British Maryul consisting of Spiti and North Lahúl, and (2) Sikh Maryul consisting of all the rest. This division is by no means natural. More natural is that which gives (1) Bultistan, which is Mahometan, and (2) Ladak, which is Buddhist.

Strachey's Maryul is as follows:—

I. *Bulti*—Hasora; Rongdo, or Rongyul; Shigar; Bulti Proper, or Skardo; Parkuta; Tolti; Khartaksho; Kiris; Khaypalu; Chorbat.

II. *Ladak*—Spiti; Zangskar; Purik; Suru; Hembabs (Dras); Ladak Proper, or Le; Nubra; Tanktse; Rong; Rupshu; Hanle.

In this list, Lahúl, Hungrung, and Kunawer are omitted as Indian; whilst Hasora is treated as Bhot.

## CHAPTER II.

**The Bhot of the Chinese Empire.—The Tibetans of Rudok, Garo, Guge, &c.—Of Lhasa and Tishú Lúmbú.—The Sifan.—The Lhopa of Bútan.—The Tak.—The Bhot of Gurhwhal, Kumaon, and Nepaul.—The Chepang.—Doubtful Bhot.—The Rhondur.—The Chak and Drok.—The Hor.—The Kolo.**

The difference between Ladak and Tibet Proper is chiefly political. It is the express statement of Strachey that the present diplomatic boundary coincides with the transverse range of mountains, which forms the watershed between the Sutlej and Indus, *for a small distance only*. As a general rule the line of demarcation is artificial. Neither can I make much in the way of a national division out of the word Maryul, notwithstanding its meaning. That portion of Chinese Tibet which gives us the actual sources of the Sutlej and Indus, not to mention the watershed between those great rivers and the Brahmaputra, must needs lie high. Yet so do Ladak and Bultistan. In any other part of the world they would form a highland, an alpine region, a Kohistan. However, they lie on the Lower Indus, just as Lower Germany lies on the Lower Elbe. Though we may use the word Maryul, if necessary, we may conveniently forget its meaning.

Tibet is Chinese, and, as such, inaccessible. Not that it is likely to be so until the end of time. The English frontier touches it. The Sikh frontier touches it. To the south lies Nepaul, the king whereof has lately manifested a spirit of either aggression or something like it. To the south-east Bútan is open to influences from

India, and likely to be still more so. At present, however, our knowledge is limited. Thus, whilst we know that, in the great essentials of language, religion, and physical conformation a Tibetan is a Ladaki, and a Ladaki a Tibetan (so little is the difference between them), we lack the knowledge of the differences between the Tibetans themselves. Some occupy the banks of the Brahmaputra in its upper and middle course. But others lie beyond its drainage; on steppes and plateaus, on the frontier of the Turks of Chinese Tartary, and the Mongols of Mongolia. Others lie eastward, on and within the frontier of China.

In the parts just to the east of the Ladak frontier, and the districts to the north of Gurwhal and Kumaon, lie the sources of both the Indus and the Sutlej, the parts about the Lake Manasarowar; visited by Lloyd and Gerard, and further explored by the Stracheys. East of these lie the heights that separate them from the drainage of the Tsanpú; the Tsanpú that flows eastwards to the north of the northern frontier of Nepaul and Bhútan until it turns to the south and west, and becomes the Brahmaputra of the great valley of Asam; partly Bhot, partly Indian. Where this great river rises we have the physical conditions of Tibet in their most extreme form. Before it becomes the Brahmaputra rice grows on its banks. Between the land of snow and ice on its head-waters and the hot alluvia of its lower course what intervenes? What, too, do we find on the Sutlej and Indus before we reach the drainage of the Tsanpú?

On the head-waters of the Sutlej and Indus, we find, in the provinces of Rudok, Garo, and Guge, much what we found in Ladak, except that the elevations are higher, and the alluvial soil of Guge is remarkable for its depth and extent.

Of the Upper Tsanpú we know less. The district that lies along the main channel is named Mangyul, or the land of *mang* whatever *mang* may mean. It lies parallel with Nepaul — there or thereabouts. It may be a little less inhospitable in soil and climate than the worst parts of Rudok and Nubra. It must, however, perforce, be cold and dry, containing a few villages, of which the names only, along with their relative positions, are known; so that the Land of Mang is pre-eminently the Terra Incognita of Tibet.

When we come, however, to the longitude of Sikkim, and reach the parts that lie to the north of Bhutan rather than Nepaul, the names, at least, of some of the localities, become familiar. There is Lhasa, the capital of the province U (spelt *DbUs*), and Tassisudon of Tsang.

And then there are the parts between Lhasa and Asam, like the parts along the Nepaul frontier, unexplored. They are, however, in patches at least, warm and alluvial.

What is the breadth of Tibet? There are three zones. The middlemost is traversed by the main axis of the drainage, whether it be that of the Indus or the Tsanpú. It has its mountain boundary to the south. It has also its mountain boundary to the north. The former gives us a district in geographical contact with India and Nepaul; a district of mountains and glaciers, of streams and valleys. The latter bounds Yarkend, Khoten, and parts of Mongolia. Where these begin is a doubtful point. But this is not all. Some part of these doubtful frontiers is steppe and desert, just like the great bare table-lands of Central Asia; so that the difference between the water system of the Indus and Tsanpú and the parts to the north of it is double — physical as well as ethnological, ethnological as well as physical. And the question that arises out of it is double. Where lie the most northern

Bhot? Are they tribes of the mountain valley, or tribes of the sandy steppe? Or where lie the most southern of the Turks and Mongols? Do any of them indent the area of the Bhot? Are any of them dalesmen?

Again—does the Bhot character change as the face of the country changes, becoming wilder as the area becomes more impracticable?

The average breadth of Maryul, from the Indian to the Turkish watershed, is laid by Mr. Strachey at about 150 miles; the Turkish watershed being formed by the prolongation of the Karakorum range, whatever that may be. Khoten, he thinks, extends further to the south than Yarkend, and, so doing, limits the breadth of Tibet as far as its eastern boundary in (about) 83 E.L. How broad is Mangyul, the district that overlies Nepaul? How broad are the provinces of which Lahsa and Tassisudon are the capitals? No one can say. Thus much, however, can be said viz.—that the industrial and monastic character of Tibet is confined within narrow limits.

The occupants of the middle zone are inconveniently near the Kyampo districts. Now Kyampo is the name of a lawless set of tribes which call themselves Rundur. They are independent robbers, barbarous in dialect, but still specially said to be Tibetan in language and features. They live on a steppe, and in tents. Make these Tibetan, and the Bhot area east of Khoten is widened, extending itself northwards. But what if they are Turks or Mongols? Of their language, *eo nomine*, I have seen no specimen.

The population, however, of the southern and middle zones appears to be homogeneous, the differences of dialect being slight, and the differences of creed next to none. And this is what we expect. The great bulk of the population is collected on the banks of the rivers; the tilth of the country being limited to these districts. As long as this is the case the habits of the occupants are agricultural, with much that reminds us of the careful industry of the Chinese. In a country almost destitute of wood, the dung of the sheep, yaks, and ponies goes for fuel just as it does in some parts of England, where it is beaten into caissons, dried, and burned. On the other hand, the highest value is put upon the refuse of towns, night soil, and human ordure. The business of the nightman is sufficient to employ a great proportion of the population. Every house has its privy, the contents of which are let or sold, with the same regard to their richness that a farmer has when he buys the manure of a crew-yard, and asks whether the beasts have been fed on straw or hay, or hay or oil-cake. Then there is the labour of irrigation: for where this is neglected there is no hope of a crop. It is carefully attended to. The fields are laid out in terraces, and the water that has enriched one of the higher, is then turned-off to fertilize the lower, levels. The barley—for this is the chief grain—is sown in April or May, and reaped in September or October. There is some rain in Tibet, far more than in Ladak; indeed, there is an approach to a rainy season. In the first, or early spring, which coincides with February, March, and April, there are showers and southerly winds. In the next three months there is also rain, with occasional thunder. In September there is heavy rain, and after that sharp frost; sharp frost, but not much snow, except on the mountains.

It is not, however, on the mountains that agriculture flourishes. The sheep and the yak belong to the broken surfaces of the higher levels. Of the domesticated yak there is the cross between the cow and the yak, and the cross between the yak and the bull; the latter being excellent milkers. Of the sheep—of which the numbers are numberless—there are four principal varieties, all well-savoured in flesh, all productive of useful wool, though of different qualities. There is also the goat, with its undercoat of shawl wool. This, however, in Tibet Proper is neglected. The pig, too, which the Tibetans and Chinese equally eat, and ducks and geese, which the latter delight in, but which the former abstain from, are abundant.

There is a little indulgence in the chase, or, at least, in shooting. No animal in Tibet is fiercer than the wild yak; the contrast, in many respects, of the domesticated animal. It is sometimes hunted on horseback, when the skill of the sportsman is shown in detaching it from the herd. At other times its favourite grazing-ground is discovered, and a loose enclosure of stones is thrown up. Then, near this, another; and then another not far off. In the first of these the shooter conceals himself, and fires. The yak, whether wounded or not, rushes furiously at the spot where he sees the smoke and vents his rage on the stones of the enclosure by knocking the wall to pieces. Meanwhile the shooter escapes to the next, and fires afresh from it; and so on, and so on, till the animal is brought down.

With woollen clothing, with barley bread, and with animal food in abundance the Tibetan is well protected against the extremities of his climate. In summer he eats, however, but little animal food. When winter sets in he has a great slaughtering-day. The animal is killed, skinned, gutted, and set upright in a free current of air. This dries and preserves him; the flesh becoming so dry as to rub to powder betwen the hands. The trade of butcher is often hereditary. Again, it is a public trade. Each village has its professional slaughterer.

Where the soil becomes unfit for agriculture, it often effloresces in salts, carbonate of soda, muriate of soda, borax. Saltpetre is made artificially at the large sheepfolds, where the compost of dung and earth determine its production.

The chief diseases are ophthalmic and cutaneous. Smallpox is guarded against by inoculation; though imperfectly. Sometimes its ravages are inordinately terrible. The laughing disease is one of which many die. It is said to consist of violent fits of laughter, with excruciating pain in the fauces: it is unaccompanied by fever. Dr. Campbell's notice of this is secondhand.

The Chinese dominion seems anything but oppressive. The whole number of the troops, all of whom are Mantshú, is only 4000; 2000 at Lahsa, 1000 at Digarchi, 500 at Giangtchi, and 500 at Tingri. The militia is native. The civil service is somewhat more celestial. The chief officers here are Chinese, but not all of them. The grand Lama is a Bhot.

There is, then, a fair amount of activity, and a fair amount of independence. Neither is the Buddhist creed, though it has studded the country with innumerable monasteries and nunneries, a notable cause of either idleness or mendicancy. The monks employ themselves on secular, as well as ecclesiastic, employments; employ themselves and find employments for others. The monastery is always an important part of the town. Tíshú Lúmbú, described by Mr. Turner, the second town in Tibet, is essentially either a monastery, or a collection of monasteries; as the old universities are collections of colleges. The ordinary monk, or priest, is the Gylong above whom are the Lamas, or presidents, and below whom are the Tohba and Tuppa. The Tuppa is a probationer, who is admitted into the establishment to which he would attach himself at the age of 8 or 10, and receives instr tion accordingly. At 15, he becomes a Tohba; and 24 a Gylong; provided his acquirements be satisfacto The Gylongs may become Lamas by being appointed perintendents, wardens, provosts, principals, masters, presidents of an endowed monastery; of which, it is ne less to say that the name is Legion. The nunneri too, are numerous; no man being allowed to pass a ni in a monastery, no monk being allowed to pass a night a nunnery. When the monastery of Tíshú Lúmbú established the number of its Gylongs was no less t 3700.

The class falls into two divisions; one containing th whose caps are yellow, the other those whose caps red. This is the distinction—the red and the yell the yellow and the red. The wearers of the yellow called Gyllúpka. The wearers of the red are cal Shammar. There are, of course, differences of doctri or rather discipline, as well; the Shammar allowing t Gylongs to marry. Originally, they were more pow ful than at present. Originally, the site of Tí Lúmbú was the occupancy of the Shammar. But normal state of quarrel between rival sectaries beg continued, and ended with the expulsion of the R caps, and the foundation of a monastery in the valley t had once cultivated.

On one side of Tíshú Lúmbú Turner saw the G gotha of the monastery, the place whither the dead v conveyed for exposúre; not for cremation, nor yet for terment (which is quite foreign to Tibet) but for posure. It was a spacious area, inclosed on one side natural rock, on the other by walls, open at top, wi narrow opening below. On the rock above was a form, from which the corpses were shot down into inclosure below. The hole in the wall was for the purpose of letting in dogs or other carnivora; the birds being free to descend from above. With these facilities, between beast and bird, the destruction of the fleshy parts of the dead bodies went on rapidly. Such is the ordinary mode of the disposal of the dead in Tibet; burial by deglutition, burial by invisceration, burial by means of the beasts of the field and the birds of the air, burial by exposure and absorption. Sometimes, however, the funeral ceremonies were, if such a term can be allowed, more private, and the deceased were carried to the top of some hill to be exposed. Sometimes, they were committed to the nearest stream of water. The chief exceptions to these exposures took place with the bodies of the Lamas. Those of the highest rank had shrines built over their remains, which were deposited entire; the shrines themselves being objects of religious awe and distant pilgrimages. Of the inferior saints the bodies were burnt, and the ashes preserved in little metallic idols which served as cases, and which were carefully kept in special cabinets sacred to the purpose of keeping them.

The resemblance between Buddhism and Roman Catholic Christianity has struck more than one investigator; most especially the Lazarist missionaries, whose opinions, as expounded in the works of Mr. Huc, are well known. They are extreme. The remarkable extent of it, according to the above-named writer, is neither explained by the convenient doctrine of accidental resemblance, nor yet by the more scientific hypothesis of the uniformity of the human mind, and the similarity of its modes of operation under similar circumstances. Direct influence from Europe is supposed to explain it. The reasoning runs thus. In the fourteenth century the relations between the populations of Central Asia and the Europeans were close.

The Mongols sent embassies to Rome, to France, and to England. England, France, and Rome sent missions in return. The visitors of the West were struck by the pomp and ceremony of the western rites, and carried back to their residences the profound impressions which such rites, magnificently solemnized, had made on their memories. The desire to reproduce them at home grew up. A reformer arose in a district to the south of Koko Nor. A shepherd born in these parts was visited by a stranger with a large nose and brilliant eyes. Messrs. Huc and Gabet were likened to the traditional likeness of this stranger. He implanted the desire of recasting the institution of Buddhism in the breast of Tsong Kaba; for so the reformer was named. He founded the monastery of Kounboum, or the 10,000 images; but not until a miracle had occurred. It was his mother's miracle rather than his. According to the custom, she cut off his hair when she devoted him to a religious life, and when she threw it away, a tree sprung up from the spot on which it was thrown. This tree is now alive. It is not more than 8 feet high, but so thick that three men cannot grasp it. It may be seen at Kounboum; Huc indeed saw it. He smelt it. It was of the scent of cinnamon. In summer it puts forth a beautiful red flower. But what is strangest of all each of its leaves bears the figure of a letter of the Tibetan alphabet; we are not told which. No fraud on the part of the Lamas was suspected by the missionaries; but they scarcely seem to have thought of the mark being natural, just like the Greek Gamma, and the English C on the wings of certain moths and butterflies. Doubtless "people will smile at our credulity." It is too honest and straightforward to be smiled at; besides which it is consistent, being shown in other things as well. Thus, a *bokti*, or holy man, ripped up his stomach with a knife, disembowelled himself, and walked away as if nothing had happened. It was his business to act a miracle. Yet the worthy missionaries believed in it. It was Satan's doing. We should know thus much of their way at looking at matters before we pin our faith on all they tell us. However, Tsong Kaba's monastery still exists. The Lamas are distributed into four classes, that of the mystics, that of the directors of the religious ceremonies, that of the physicians, that of the prayers. Call these the faculties of Philosophy, Arts, Medicine and Divinity and you have a university. The victor in one of the periodical disputations is mounted on the shoulders of the Lama he has vanquished. Call this keeping an act and opponency. The subjects are not very different from those that were discussed in mediæval Europe. "Why are birds without the functions of other animals?" This was the subject of the one part of Huc's master in the Thibetan language. The moderators keep order with a crow-bar. It is not impossible, then, that European discipline may have been imitated in the monastery of Kounboum.

A short distance from Kounboum is Tshogortan; famous for its contemplative Lamas; men who again remind us if not of Europe, of Egypt and Syria. They occupy cells on the steepest sides of the most inaccessible mountains, like swallows' nests. They cut themselves off from all intercourse with their fellow-creatures, and (in some cases) a sack and a long cord serves to supply them with food. So much for the eremites. Tshogortan is on the Sifan frontier, and the more secular districts in its neighbourhood get robbed accordingly.

In a little islet on the Koko Nor is another monastery. No one visits it from the shore. No boats were seen on the lake. Solitude, except so far as it is broken by the intercourse of the recluses with each other, is the lot of the isolated beings who live here.

The mendicants have also their analogies. The vagabond Lamas, a definite class, travel from place to place, taking no care of the morrow. They stop at the tent; they seat themselves on the hearth; they tell their story; they receive hospitality. They visit all accessible, or possible, countries; China, Mantshuria, Mongolia, Turkestan.

The rivers and lakes, with their strongly-marked physical characteristics, stimulate the Bhot fancy into the usual rude etymologies and ætiologies of simple-minded speculators. The five great rivers flow from the mouths of five animals; the Ganges from a cow's, the Indus from a lion's, the Sutlej from an elephant's, the Gogra from a peacock's, and the Brahmaputra from the holy horse of Sakya, named Ta-chok.

The Tshomoriri Lake took its name from the cry of a woman who rode into it. She was mounted on a yak, and the yak run away with her, till he reached the water. He plunged into it. At first the woman (*tshomo*) was pleased with the excitement and novelty. At last she got frightened, and, when the animal began to sink, cried *ri-ri*; whence the name of the lake.

As travellers are often in trouble for want of horses, the Lamas have the following way of helping them. They cut out a number of horses in paper, ascend a high mountain, pray, and fling up the lot into the air. The wind carries them in all directions: Buddha changes them into flesh and blood. Weary travellers get the use of them.

If Tíshú Lúmbú be a town of monks, Lahsa is both monastic and mercantile. The palace of the Dalai Lama, the Chinese garrisons, and traders from the east, west, north, and south, help to secularize it. As far as the inhabitants themselves are concerned, it is (unlike the towns of China) free to all who wish to either buy or sell. It is not the Tibetans who keep the English out of Tibet. It is the Chinese who garrison the land. They are not numerous. They are enough, however, to close the country.

Few writers touch upon Tibet without noticing what they call its Polyandria. It is a word that speaks for itself; in ethnology as well as in botany. It is the reverse of polygamy, or polygynia, and, as such, it is usually considered. In the East, in general, one man has many wives. In Tibet, and certain other countries where Tibetan habits are practised, one woman has many husbands. The contrast is sufficiently strong to command attention. So is the apparently exceptional character of the instances. The bearings, too, of the fact upon questions of social statics are as evident as they are important. What is the effect of Polyandria upon morals? What its effect upon population? In addition to this, the ethnologists ask whether it is found elsewhere? whether the Tibetan practices are nearly so exceptional as they seem? Have they anything to do with the physical condition of the country, especially with its enormous altitude? Have they anything to do with the religious habitudes of the people, especially with the system of monasteries? The monastic system can have little or nothing to do with it. On the contrary, it should make men scarce instead of overabundant; for, though there are nunneries as well as monasteries in Tibet, the latter are the more numerous and the better filled.

I am slow to believe that polyandria can be an institution of any kind in its normal state. I was once slow to believe that the evidence in favour of a number of brothers having but one wife amongst them at the same time was unexceptionable. I must take it, however, as I find it. Turner especially states that women in Tibet, with their three or four husbands, were just as jealous as a Turk polygamist could have been of the virtue of his harem. One woman he saw who had five brothers all alive, and all her husbands. At the same time he shows that the chief, perhaps the real, husband was the elder brother. He it was who chose. He it was who went through the marriage ceremonies. He it was who represented the union.

Along with this I take the Jewish practice of one brother, on the death of another, taking to himself the relict of the deceased. The question upon this point, by which the Sadducees tempted our Lord, need only be alluded to. Seven brothers married one and the same woman, but they married her in succession; one dying before the other succeeded. Now this is a practice which is not only less improbable *à priori*, but one which is known to be of no very uncommon occurrence. Can the Tibetan polyandry be an abnormal case of this? The wife *in esse* of one brother is the wife *in posse* of another. She is family property; much after the manner of an entailed estate. Given certain events, she knows who will, and she knows who will not, be her husband. This keeps her to the brotherhood. Let one, or more, of the reversionist brothers anticipate his nuptial rights, and polyandry is the result—not a normal, but not an unlikely, one. Just as, in entails, the protector of the settlement may find it convenient to come to an agreement with the remainder-man, and allow him to realize, by anticipation, his contingent rights, so may the elder brother allow his possible successors in the wifedom to act as husbands before their turn. I only suggest this. Polyandria, pure and simple, with the licence which the rest of Asia allows to the men transferred to women I do not believe in. Neither do I believe that the latitude which Europe allows to men is a womanly privilege in Tibet. It argues too great a reversal of the ordinary sentiments of human nature. Still, however, if a certain amount of evidence establish the fact, we must take it as it comes before us. The *descensus per umbilicum* of the Malabar coast is akin to polyandry. Again, amongst the Mongols, in the time of Kublai Khan, and according to the express evidence of Marco Polo, brothers not only took to themselves deceased brothers' wives, but children succeeded to the wives of their fathers. When a man died his son took all the wives he left behind him, with the single exception of his own mother.

*The Sifan—Amdoans—Gyarung—Manyak—Thochu.*—I give the notices of the Sifan as I find them, being satisfied that they are, not only incomplete, but partially inaccurate, and committing myself to nothing in the way of etymology, however currently received. The class itself, then, is provisional. It may or may not turn out natural. The word itself is said to be Chinese; *si* meaning *western*, and *fan* meaning *barbarians;* so that the compound = *the barbarians or strangers of the* West. In China this expression would point toward Tibet. On the other hand, the Sifan, in the eyes of a Tibetan, would be in the direction of China, and, if they were deemed *barbarians* at all, would be the *barbarians of the East.* At any rate they would not be Sifan *eo nomine.* They need not, indeed, have a Tibetan name at all. It seems, however, that one of their constituent tribes is called Gyárung; word for word, the same (I think) as Gurung, the name of a population in Nepaul. The Gyárung are a powerful nation, consisting of as many as eighteen banners; and, although they are at the present time satisfied with the recognized supremacy of the Celestial Empire, they have once, and more than once, been independent. Yet Gyárung is no native name. Each tribe has its special denomination, the whole collection none. It is the Tibetans who use the word. They apply it to the eighteen banners of the Gyárung Proper, and they also apply it to the tribes of the Chinese frontier in general. If so, the Gyárung, or Gyárungbo, are the Sifan under a Tibetan, the Sifan being Gyárung, or Gyárung-bo, under a Chinese appellation. Whether, however, the two names (supposing both to be accurate) apply to precisely the same tribes depends upon the breadth and length of the area. If the belt of barbarism between China and Tibet be narrow, the Gyárung may be Sifan—tribe for tribe. But what if the belt be broad? In that case it may extend far into China, and the most eastern of the Sifan may be neither more nor less than ruder members of the Chinese stock, separated from the rest on account of their wildness, just as certain hill tribes of India, from the fact of their being pagan rather than Brahminic, are separated from the other Hindus. And what if the belt be long? In that case it may embrace Mongols, and even Turks, at its northern, Siamese and Burmese at its southern, extremity.

One fact alone is certain, viz.—that the only known samples of the Sifan forms of speech are Tibetan.

The chiefs of the different Gyárung tribes are called Gyapo, word for word the Gyalpo of the Bultistanis.

The question now arises as to the habits on which the name Sifan—supposing it to mean barbarian—is founded. I can scarcely think that it rests on any difference of creed. I have looked in vain for any traces of Paganism in the few notices we possess. At the same time it should be added that these apply to the northern part of the area only. The most irreligious act in the eyes of a Buddhist, of which I can find any of the tribes guilty, is that of having made an inroad upon some holy ground, broken some images, and turned-off the waters that worked the prayer mills. But Buddhists of lax principles might do this, just as lax Christians may rob churches. I imagine that it is founded chiefly on their nomad habits, and on the associated habits of plunder and robbery.

With a thoughtful Sifan, whom he met in the Amdoa country, Mr. Huc had the following conversation:—

"Aha! brother," said we, "it is the first time that we have come to seat ourselves in your tent."

"I am old," he replied; "my legs cannot support me, otherwise I should have been to Tchogortan, to offer you my khata. From what I have heard the shepherds of the black tents say, you are from the sky of the west."

"Yes; our country is far from here."

"Are you from the kingdom of Samba, or that of Poba?"

"Neither one nor the other; we are from the kingdom of the French."

"Ah! you are of the Framba; I have never heard of that. It is so large that West; the kingdoms there are so numerous. But at bottom it makes no difference; we are all of the same family, are we not?"

"Yes, certainly; all men are brothers, whatever their kingdom is."

"What you say is founded on reason; but nevertheless there are on the earth three great families, and we are all of the great Thibetan family."

"Aha!—do you know whence come these three families?"

"This is what I have heard the Lamas say, who have

studied the things of antiquity. At the beginning, there was on the earth only a single man; he had neither house nor tent, for at that time the winter was not cold, and the summer not hot; the wind did not blow so violently, and there fell neither snow nor rain; the tea grew of itself on the mountains, and the flocks had nothing to fear from beasts of prey. This man had three children, who lived a long time with him, nourishing themselves on milk and fruits. After having attained to a great age this man died. The three children deliberated what they should do with the body of their father, and they could not agree about it; one wished to put him in a coffin, the other wanted to burn him, the third thought it would be best to expose the body on the summit of a mountain. They resolved then to divide it into three parts; the eldest had the body and arms—he was the ancestor of the great Chinese family, and that is why his descendants have become celebrated in arts and industry, and are remarkable for their tricks and stratagems. The second son had the breast—he was the father of the Tibetan family, and they are full of heart and courage, and do not fear death. From the third, who had the inferior parts of the body, are descended the Tartars, who are simple and timid, without head or heart, and who know nothing but how to keep themselves firm in their saddles."

The Amdoan tents are not, like those of the Mongols, made of felt, though black is the common colour with both. They are of linen, hexagonal, and without any framework of wood. The side angles are nailed to the ground, the top being supported by cords fastened to poles on the outside, and placed horizontally. These are fixed to the ground by cords and rings. They look like "monstrous black spiders."

The evidence that the difference between the nomad and the tiller of the ground is due to a difference of soil rather than to anything called race, is manifest in the case of the Tibetan populations. Where there is a dry plateau, there there are flocks and herds. Where there is a water-course, there there is irrigation and agriculture. We may, if we choose, disparage this kind of industry, and call those who practise it gardeners rather than farmers. It is, however, as true and good agriculture as that of the greater part of the French farmers and vine-growers.

The following samples of the Sifan languages are from Hodgson :—

| English. | Gyarung. | Manyak. | Thochu. |
|---|---|---|---|
| *Man* | tirmi | chhoh | nah |
| *Head* | tako | wulli | kapat |
| *Hair* | tarni | mui | hompa |
| *Eye* | taimek | mne | kan |
| *Ear* | tirne | napi | nukh |
| *Tooth* | tiswe | phwih | sweh |
| *Blood* | tashi | shah | sah |
| *Bone* | syarhu | rukhu | ripat |
| *Hand* | tayak | lapcheh | jipah |
| *Foot* | tami | lipchheh | jako |
| *Sky* | tumon | mah | mahto |
| *Sun* | kini | nyima | mun |
| *Moon* | tsile | leh | chhap |
| *Star* | tsine | krah | ghada |
| *Fire* | timi | sameh | meh |
| *Water* | tichi | dyah | chah |
| *Stone* | rugu | wobi | gholopi |
| *One* | kate | tabi | ari |
| *Two* | kanes | nabi | gnari |
| *Three* | kasam | sibi | ksiri |
| *Four* | kadi | rebi | gzari |
| *Five* | kunggno | gnabi | wari |
| *Six* | kutok | trubi | khatari |
| *Seven* | kushnes | skwibi | stari |
| *Eight* | oryet | zibi | khrari |
| *Nine* | kunggu | gubi | rguni |
| *Ten* | sih | chechibi | paduri |

| Measurements. | Amdóan. ft. | in. | Hór. ft. | in. | Gyárúng. ft. | in. | Manyak. ft. | in. |
|---|---|---|---|---|---|---|---|---|
| Height without shoes | 5 | 8½ | 5 | 7½ | 5 | 8 | 5 | 4 |
| Length of head, from crown to chin, with calipers | 0 | 8½ | 0 | 8½ | 0 | 9 | 0 | 9½ |
| Girth of head | 1 | 10 | 1 | 9¼ | 1 | 10¾ | 1 | 10¾ |
| Length of head, fore and aft, or forehead to occiput | 0 | 7¾ | 0 | 7¾ | 0 | 8 | 0 | 8 |
| Width of head between parietes | 0 | 6½ | 6 | 0 | 0 | 6⅞ | 0 | 6⅞ |
| Crown of head to hip | 2 | 4¾ | 2 | 4 | 2 | 8½ | 2 | 8 |
| Hip to heel | 3 | 3¾ | 3 | 3½ | 2 | 11½ | 3 | 1 |
| Width between the shoulders | 1 | 4 | 1 | 1 | 1 | 1½ | 1 | 4 |
| Girth of chest | 3 | 1 | 2 | 9 | 2 | 11¼ | 2 | 11¾ |
| Length of arm and hand | 2 | 6¾ | 2 | 6 | 2 | 4⅝ | 2 | 4 |
| Length of arm | 1 | 0 | 1 | 0 | 0 | 11⅜ | 0 | 11¼ |
| Ditto of fore-arm | 0 | 11 | 0 | 10 | 0 | 9½ | 0 | 9¾ |
| Ditto of hand | 0 | 8 | 0 | 7¾ | 0 | 7¾ | 0 | 7¼ |
| Length of thigh | 1 | 8 | 1 | 7 | 1 | 6½ | 1 | 7 |
| Length of leg to ankle | 1 | 4½ | 1 | 5 | 1 | 3 | 1 | 5 |
| Ditto of foot | 0 | 11 | 0 | 10 | 0 | 9½ | 0 | 9¼ |
| Width of hand | 0 | 4¾ | 0 | 4⅛ | 0 | 4 | 0 | 4 |
| Ditto of foot | 0 | 4¾ | 0 | 4¼ | 0 | 4⅛ | 0 | 4 |
| Girth of thigh | 1 | 9 | 1 | 4¾ | 1 | 6¾ | 1 | 7½ |
| Ditto of calf | 1 | 3½ | 1 | 1¾ | 1 | 2 | 1 | 1½ |
| Ditto of fore-arm | 0 | 11 | 0 | 9¾ | 0 | 10 | 0 | 9½ |

*Bútan.*—Bútan is best known from Captain Turner's account of his embassy, published in the first year of the present century. The attempt was made to reach Lhassa, but the legation got no further than Tíshú Lúmbú. This, however, was in Tibet; so that the whole breadth of Bútan was traversed, and its capital, Tassisudon, visited, a palace and monastery constituting a town, a town in a valley, much after the manner of the small towns or large villages of Ladak and Bultistan. For, like Ladak and Bultistan, the whole of Bútan is broken up in valleys and glens, with mountains, covered with June and July snow, looking down upon them, feeding their streams, and fertilizing their small patches of alluvial soil; fertilizing them, but not without the supplementary aid of human labour.

The system of artificial irrigation is adopted by the industrious and agricultural Lhopa of Bútan, even as it is by the agricultural and industrial Ladaki. In the valley of Tassisudon, a narrow slip of fertile soil, about four miles long and one mile broad, through which the Tshentshein winds its way to the Ganges, the melted snows of the surrounding mountains are carefully conducted from farm to farm and from bed to bed. Productive crops of rice are the chief result.

The castle, or palace, a solid building of stone, has its windows small, and inconspicuous, and placed in the upper part of the building, the walls being about thirty feet high, and slightly sloping from the foundation to the top. Like the Bhot buildings in general, it is built as much against the violence of the wind as any other agent—solidly and strongly. Its galleries, verandahs, terraces, are all, more or less, Indian. It stands by itself, or nearly so. The town consists of scattered clusters of houses belonging to the farmers of the well-cultivated soil of the valley.

More characteristic than the Raja and his Court are the 15,000 gylongs, or monks, of the monastery. Bound to celibacy, they assemble in their chapels three times a day, for the performance of a morning, noontide, and evening service. Their duty, or rather the regularity with which it is done, agrees with them. They are cleaner than the rest of their countrymen; larger-limbed; fairer-skinned. The goitre is general; but, with this exception, they are free from ailments. As to the Lhopa in general, their physical description runs thus: they have "invariably black hair, which it is their fashion to cut close to the head. The eye is a very remarkable feature of the face; small, black, with long pointed corners, as though stretched and extended by artificial means. Their eyelashes are so thin as to be scarcely perceptible; and the eyebrow is but slightly shaded. Below the eyes is the broadest part of the face, which is rather flat, and narrow from the cheek-bones to the chin; a character of countenance appearing first to take its rise among the Tartar tribes, but is by far more strongly marked in the Chinese. Their skins are remarkably smooth, and most of them arrive at a very advanced age before they can boast even the earliest rudiments of a beard; they cultivate whiskers, but the best they produce are of a scanty straggling growth. In this heroic acquisition I quickly surpassed them; and one of my Mogul attendants, for the luxuriancy of his, was the admiration of them all. Many of these mountaineers are more than six feet high; and, taken altogether, they have a complexion not so dark by several shades as that of the European Portuguese."

One of the industrial arts of the Lhopa of the parts about Tassisudon, is paper-making. The bark of a tree called Deah is shredded, steeped in a ley of wood-ashes, drained, beaten to a pulp, cleansed, and formed into sheets. This is done by spreading it over a frame of reeds. These the manufacturer dips into the water which contains the pulp, until he has covered their surfaces. Then he raises them perpendicularly, and has nothing further to do beyond the drying and pressing.

Another of the arts is that of making alcoholic drinks by means of distillation. Fermentation is a common practice, half the world over. Distillation is rarer. The populations of the class under notice seem to have a general knowledge of the process, the Lhopa being by no means the only artists in this department.

They first make the chong by fermentation. Chong is an ordinary preparation from wheat, barley, or rice. To a "given quantity of grain is added more water than will completely cover it, and the mixture is placed over a slow fire till it begins to boil; it is then taken up, and the water drained from the grain, which is spread abroad upon mats, or coarse cloths, to cool. When it is cold, a ball of the composition, here termed Bakka (which is the blossom of the Cucalia Saracenica collected and rolled together in small balls) is crumbled, and strewed over the grains, and both are well mixed together. The usual proportion is a ball, the size of a nutmeg, to two pounds of grain. The grain thus prepared is put into baskets lined with leaves, and pressed down with the hand slightly, to draw off the superfluous moisture. It is then covered with leaves and cloths, to defend it from the external air; and put in a place of moderate warmth, where it is suffered to stand three days. It is afterwards deposited in dry earthen jars; a little cold water is sprinkled upon the top, in the proportion of about a tea-cup full to a gallon of grain; the vessel is then covered close, and the cap fortified with some strong compost, or stiff clay. It remains thus, at least, ten days before it is fit for use; and, if it be suffered to continue longer, it always improves from age. To make the chong, when required, they put a quantity of the fermented mass into some capacious vessel, pouring boiling water upon it, sufficient to completely cover it, and stirring the whole well together. A short time is sufficient for it to digest; a small wicker-basket is then thrust down in the centre, and the infusion called chong immediately drains through and occupies the vacant space. This liquor is with equal expedition distributed to the expecting guests, the segment of a gourd, fastened upon a staff, serving the purpose of a ladle. Each person holds a shallow wooden cup upon the points of his fingers, for its reception, and is seldom satisfied with one supply.

"A short experience proved to me that this was a most grateful beverage, being slightly acid, and possessing no powerful spirit. It was the custom, in these regions, to drink this liquor warm; a practice at the same time safe and agreeable, and which might be recommended to universal imitation, wherever fatigue and heat induced intemperate thirst."

They first make chong, which is fermented; then *arra* (word for word the same as *arrack*), which is distilled; the details of the apparatus being as follows:—

There are three vessels of earthenware; one small, one without a bottom, one in which the chong is put. This last stands over the fire-place. In it stands a tripod; over it the jar without the bottom. On the tripod, above the vessel that holds the chong, and within the one which has no bottom, stands the smallest of the three. Over the top of this, and resting on the rim of the other, is an iron saucer; with its convex side downwards. It just stands over the opening of the little jar in the middle. Now light the fire. The vapour of the chong compartment ascends. It passes into the second vessel, because that vessel, though it has sides, has no bottom. Up these sides it passes. It settles on the lower and convex surface of the iron saucer. This is kept cool by water, poured in and renewed as it loses its coldness. This acts as a condenser. The drops from the lowest part of its under surface fall into the smaller vessel, which stands within the one without a bottom, which rests upon the tripod, which stands upon the vessel which contains the chong, which stands above the fire. The fire may be of any sort. The engraving, however, in Turner suggests the notion of some done on the scale of a manufacture. It is almost a furnace. It is made of clay, has an opening for fuel and air, and five chong-stands on its upper surface.

The Lhopa of Bútan differ from the true Tibetans in dialect, in being somewhat more exposed to Hindu influences, and in their greater independence of the central government in China. The Deb Raja of Bútan is nearly an independent prince. His country falls into small districts, each with its chief, captain, makpon, gyalpo, or raja, who stands in the same relation to the Deb Raja as the little potentates of Bultistan do to the chief of Skardo. Notwithstanding this, the real ethnological differences between the Lhopa and the true Tibetans are small. From the frontier of Kafaristan to that of Asam the language is the same. The religion is the same from Asam to Bultistan. As we move westward the dialect changes. For the parts between 90 and 91 E. L., we have a vocabulary termed Changlo.

| English. | Written Tibetan. | Spoken Tibetan. | Lhopa. | Changlo. |
|---|---|---|---|---|
| *Man* | mi | mi | mi | songo |
| *Head* | *m* go | go | gutch | sharang |
| *Hair* | *s* kra | kra | kya | cham |
| *Eye* | mig | mik | migo | ming |
| *Ear* | sa | amch | navo | na |
| *Tooth* | so | so | soh | shia |
| *Blood* | khrag | thak | thyak | yi |
| *Bone* | ruspa | ruko | rutok | khang |
| *Hand* | lagpa | lango | lappa | gadang |
| *Foot* | *r* kangpa | kango | kanglep | bi |
| *Sun* | nyima | nyima | nyim | ngam |
| *Moon* | *z* lava | dawa | dau | lani |
| *Star* | *s* karma | karma | kam | murgeng |
| *Fire* | me | me | mi | mi |
| *Water* | chhu | chhu | chhu | ri |
| *Stone* | *r* do | do | doh | lung |
| *Tree* | *l* jonshing | shingdong | shing | shing |
| *One* | *g* chig | chik | chi | thur |
| *Two* | *g* nyis | nyi | nyi | nyik-ching |
| *Three* | *g* sum | sum | sum | sam |
| *Four* | *b* zhi | zhyi | żhi | hhi |
| *Five* | hna | gna | gna | nga |
| *Six* | druk | thu | dhu | khung |
| *Seven* | *b* dun | dun | dun | zum |
| *Eight* | *b* rgyud | gye | gye | yen |
| *Nine* | *d* gu | guk | gu | gu |
| *Ten* | *b* chu | chu | — | se |
| — | thamba | — | chatham | shong |

The word *Changlo*, in the language so called, means *black*. That the Changlo are smaller, less muscular, and darker-skinned than the ordinary Lhopa is especially stated—"their skin possesses a deeper isabelline tint." Their alphabet is that of Bútan; their levels are comparatively low; their habits agricultural. They probably belong to the *turai*.

*The Tak.*—A line drawn in a south-eastern direction from Lhassa to Jorhat in Asam cuts through a district marked Tacpony. It overlies the north-eastern half of Bútan, and is inclosed within the great bend of the Brahmaputra. I know of no one who has described it from personal knowledge. It is a compound word; as we see a Kenpony, and a Conepony on its frontier. It is the name of the country of the Tak. It is the country (even though not exactly defined) of the Tak of the forthcoming vocabulary. Dakpo, certainly, Gagpo and Gangpo, probably, are the same word.

It is also the country marked Towang, or Raj Towang in the ordinary maps. In like manner Kenpony is the province of Kongbo, to the east of Takpo; its occupants being, as Strachey surmises, the barbarians who, in conjunction with a noxious climate, oppose the ascent of the English explorers from Asam. They may be Aka, or Dofla, or Abor, or Mishmi, or a mixture of tribes rather than true Bhots.

| English. | Takpa. | Lhopa. |
|---|---|---|
| *Man* | men | me |
| *Head* | gokti | gutoh |
| *Hair* | pu | kya |
| *Eye* | melong | mido |
| *Ear* | neblap | navo |
| *Tooth* | wah | soh |
| *Blood* | khra | thyak |
| *Bone* | rospa | rutok |
| *Hand* | la | lappa |

| English. | Takpa. | Lhopa. |
|---|---|---|
| *Foot* | leme | kanglep |
| *Sky* | namdung | nam |
| *Sun* | plang | nyim |
| *Moon* | leh | dau |
| *Star* | karma | kam |
| *Fire* | meh | mi |
| *Water* | chhi | chhu |
| *Stone* | gorr | doh |
| *Tree* | shendong | shing |
| *One* | the | che |
| *Two* | nai | nye |
| *Three* | sum | sum |
| *Four* | pli | zhi |
| *Five* | liagni | gna |
| *Six* | kro | dhu |
| *Seven* | nis | dun |
| *Eight* | gyet | gye |
| *Nine* | dugu | gu |
| *Ten* | paki | chatham |

I think that the Tak, or Takpa, may be Shammar Tibetans, of nomad habits, and a well-marked dialect. I consider them to be this because Turner, in his notice of the quarrels between the Yellow Bonnets and the Red Bonnets, states that the Shammar being worsted retired to a barren and inhospitable part of the country, where some of them still continue to live in tents.

I also think that the Tak and Thochu may be the same people. They both seem to occupy a frontier. Now in Mongol a Thakar means a Borderer. If so, the populations so called may be what the Marchmen and Marcomanni are in the German, and the men of the Ukraine in the Slavonic, countries. Tshakar itself is a vast camp, wherein the cultivation of the soil is not only neglected but discouraged, perhaps forbidden. The men must be ready to march at any time. In order to be this they must live on their pay, and on the produce of their flocks and herds. This, however, is in Mongolia, so that the doctrine that the Tak, Thochu, and Tshakar may all be Borderers is only suggested.

As a general rule the Himalayas divide Hindostan from Bhotland. There are Bhot, however, in several parts south of the crest of those mighty mountains. That there were Bhot in Kistewar we surmised. We noted those of Lahúl. We now come to those of

*Gurwhal and Kumaon.*—The productive and habitable portion of the Bhot area in Kumaon and Gurwhal is confined to the passes and their neighbourhood, all the rest being either snow or rock. Their minimum height is about 6000 feet. The paths to them coincide with the head-waters of the following rivers.

| | | |
|---|---|---|
| The Mana Pass is on the | Saraswati | Feeders of the Ganges. |
| The Nítí Pass „ | Duli | |
| The Juwar Pass „ | Gaúri | Feeders of the Sarda or Gogra. |
| The Darma Pass „ | Dhouli | |
| The Byanse Pass „ | Kali | |

The evidence to the gradual extension of the zone of snow is strong. The passmen state that ridges, which, within the memory of man, were covered with forests, are now covered with snow; that pastures to which their fathers drove their flocks in summer are now non-existent; that avalanches from the higher regions are on melting found to contain trees in their centre. With such a neighbourhood it is easy to imagine that the passes themselves are of no ordinary difficulty. The watercourses that run up to them require bridges; the roads by the side of them require continual repairs. The snow blocks them up; masses of rock obstruct them; beasts of burden are often unable to proceed alone, and must be raised or lowered by means of slings passed round their bodies. The Niti pass is the best, the Juwar the worst. Respecting the latter the story runs thus—that when a Bhot army, under Raja Bag Bahader Khan, invaded Kumaon, the commander inspected the making of the road himself, and paid a rupee for every cupful of earth. This is not given as a fact. It is given as a measure of the belief of the natives in the engineering difficulties that presented themselves during its construction. The number of well-built stone houses (for well-built houses of stone are required to stand their ground) in the Bhot districts is as follows:—

| | Villages. | Houses. |
|---|---|---|
| In Mana | 3 | 125 |
| In Níti | 10 | 219 |
| In Juwar | 13 | 455 |
| In Darma | 24 | 342 |
| In Byanse | 9 | 184 |
| | 59 | 1326 |

A portion of the population consists of slaves, who, with their families, live under the same roof with their masters. They help in the cultivation of the soil; for here, as elsewhere, the Bhot is an agriculturist. Marse a species of amaranth, wheat, two kinds of barley, two kinds of buckwheat, are the chief products; to which add, as cultivated vegetables, turnips and leeks, and as wild ones, garlic, celery, rhubarb, a kind of frankincense. Few or no fruits receive any culture. The walnuts and hazel-nuts are small, the apricots and peaches ill-flavoured. Gooseberries, currants, strawberries, and pears, grow wild. The domestic animals are those of Ladak and Tibet.

In the Mana, Níti, Juwar, and Byanse passes the population is generally believed to have emigrated from Tibet within the historical period, inasmuch as many of the chief families trace their family to some Tibetan locality. They encroached upon an earlier body of Hindus, and drove them downwards. With the inhabitants of the

Darma pass the case is different. They are considered to be descendants of a body of Mongols left in Kumaon by Timúr. If so, the difference of origin is considerable; if so, the occupants of the Darma pass are no true Bhots, but Mongols, who have learned the Bhot language. They differ from the rest in dress (especially that of the females) and in certain customs. All the passmen burn their dead; but the Darma make a general ceremony of the cremation and reserve it for the month Kartik. Those who die at any other time of the year are interred, but only for a time. When the month Kartik approaches they are taken out of the ground, and transferred to the funeral pile. But what if a Darma die away from his native village? In such a case his relations take a clue of worsted and draw it from the dead body to the house of the deceased, keeping it unbroken if they can. The object of this is to enable the spirit to join those of its ancestors.

The details, then, of the Bhot area in Kumaon require further investigation. Again,—in the districts of Dewara and Bágeswar vestiges of some population other than Hindu, and, perhaps, other than Bhot, are to be found. They consist, chiefly, of tombs constructed of large flat tiles, different in their external character from those of the other inhabitants, who call them the Mogul sepulchres.

At the same time the people repel the doctrine that makes them Mongol; the term Mogul being too closely associated with the Mahometan religion. Of their language we have no specimens. In their creed there are probably peculiarities; at any rate the practice of divination is spoken of as if it were more Darma than aught else. The omens are taken from the warm and reeking livers of sheep, sacrificed for the purpose, whenever an undertaking of importance is in hand.

Another distinction—the Mána, Nítí, and Juwár Bhots pretend to consider the men of Darma as their inferiors;—but, as they have the same low opinion of those of Byanse, this either proves too little or too much. Are the Byanse Mongol also? The fact of their being classed with the Darma in the matter of caste is not their only Darma characteristic. The women of the two passes dress alike. A piece of cloth, folded round the body, descends from the waist to the ankles, like a petticoat, being fastened round the waist with a girdle. Above this is a shift without sleeves, reaching to the knee. Over the head is a hood, with a tail behind, which reaches nearly to the heels. The ornaments are remarkable for their mass; the pewter ear-rings being compared to large house-keys.

Again,—whilst the Mána, Nítí, and Juwár Bhots abstain from beef of all kinds, the Darma and Byansė indulge in the flesh of the yak, and would not abstain from that of the common cow if the law permitted them to eat it. But there is, in the province, a general prohibition against the slaughter of this holy animal.

The difference of rank, along with the other details akin to it, is worth our notice, if it be only for its suggesting the probability of the Darma and Byanse populations being other than Bhot. But there is another reason for giving prominence to it. The feeling of caste is, by no means, Buddhist; and Bhots as Buddhists ought to have nothing whatever to do with it. They have it nevertheless. This is because their creed is no longer pure; but Buddhist *plus* certain Brahminic influences. The Hindu doctrines on one side contend with the Tibetan on the other; and the contest has not been wholly unfavourable to them. A Bhot, in want of a priest, will accept the services of either a Brahmin or a Lama. The Juwar Bhots go further in the direction of Hinduism. They affect many of the Hindu prejudices in regard to food. They occasionally practise Suttí. The use of the Hindu language is most widely diffused amongst them. Their trade is the most considerable.

Trade is important to the whole Bhot population of the passes; but it is most considerable within the Juwár country. A periodical fair for Tibetan goods takes place every September, at Gartokh, the residence of the Lahsa viceroy. The Bhots of Hindostan are freer to visit this fair than the Hindus; and the Juwars freer than the other Bhots of Hindostan.

The Bhots of the passes are subjects of the East India Company; without being, wholly and absolutely, disconnected from Tibet. Many of their suits are decided in Tibetan courts; and if a Bhot commit a crime on Tibetan soil, he is judged as a Tibetan. He seems to be responsible for the peaceable condition of the passes to the Chinese Government as well as to the Company's.

It is just through the Bhot of Kumaon that British India comes in contact with China; the passes in question being the roads from that portion of Hindostan which abuts upon the Chinese empire to the Tlbetan province called Nari or Gnari. Westward of these passes lies Ladak, wherein the British provinces of Lahúl and Spiti are separated from the Chinese frontier by the Sikh possessions, whilst eastward are the independent rajahships of Nepaul and Sikkim. Beyond these, the northern frontier of Bengal touches the southern frontier of Bútan; but Bútan, though a Chinese dependency, is a dependency of a much looser kind than Tibet Proper.

For this reason I shall enlarge upon the government of the important province of Gnari—the province of China which the Bhot of Kumaon, about the five passes of Nítí, Mána, Juwar, Byanse, and Darma separate from British Hindostan. What is the machinery by which the Chinese keeps up its exclusiveness in these parts, an exclusiveness to which, as is reasonably believed, the Tibetans themselves are no parties?

The general government of the province is entrusted to the two Garphan; one of which is called the Urgú Ma, the other the Urgú Ya. They are Tibetans; and natives of Lahsa. They hold their office for three years, and are, then, replaced. They reside at Gartokh.

Under the Garphan or governors of the province are the district officers; also two in number; and named Deb and Vazir. Like the Garphan, the Deb holds his office for the limited period of three years; the Vazir *quamdiu bene se gesserit*. They are Tibetans.

The troops seem to be either Turk or Mongol; or, perhaps, Mantshu. This is an inference from the notion which the Bhots entertain concerning their habits of eating. They are believed to feed upon horseflesh; which no Tibetan and no Chinese would do. The force consists of about 200 men. All beyond is native. Each town and village has its number of militiamen, who may be called out whenever their services are required. A horse post keeps up a rapid communication between Gartokh and Lhasa. The stages are from 15 to 20 miles apart, and four horses, with their riders, are kept at each.

As each district has its Deb and Vazir, and each Deb and each Vazir has his residence, there are so many little capitals. Four of these are named as follows:—(1) Chaprang, (2) Dapa, (3) Kiunlang, (4) Taklakol; with these, four out of the five passes coincide; each having its special and peculiar market to which it is limited. Thus:—

| | | | | |
|---|---|---|---|---|
| Mana | is free of | the market | at | Chaprang. |
| Niti | „ | „ | „ | Dapa. |
| Dharma | „ | „ | „ | Kumlang. |
| Byanse | „ | „ | „ | Taklakot. |

The Juwári can trade with any and all of these.

*The Ráwat.*—What are the Ráwat? The Ráwat, or Raji, are certain occupants of the forest districts of Kumaon. They pertinaciously adhere to certain customs other than Hindu; though the exact details as to what these are and what they are not are unknown. They are reduced to (say) twenty or thirty families—so, at least, runs the statement in Mr. Traill's report. They represent themselves as the descendants of one of the ancient princes of Kumaon who fled to the jungle when his country was invaded; and, on the strength of this royal pedigree, they refuse the ordinary salutation to all men alike, high or low. Whatever be your rank a Ráwat will show you no respect. Their language, by its "total dissimilitude" from the Hindu of the Kumaon, marks them out as a different race. What is this language? We have no specimens of it. What is it likely to be? It is likely to belong to the same class with the Bhot dialects, without being actually Bhot in the limited sense of the word. Against its being this is the probable antiquity of the Ráwat population. It is considered to represent the aborigines of the district. If so, it must differ from the Bhot, as well as resemble it.

*The Doms.*—What are the Doms? The lowest class of the Kumaon population are thus called. Many of them have dark, and almost black, complexions, with crisp curly hair. They are supposed to be the descendants of the aborigines. That these may be represented by the Ráwat has just been stated. It has also been stated that the Ráwat may belong to the same class with the Bhot. Hence, the Dom and Ráwat may be in the same category.

*The Bhot of Nepaul and Sikkim.*—These fall into two divisions, the civilized and the rude. Indentations of the proper Bhot area may easily occur, along the whole of the frontier. In this case the population will be neither more nor less than the Bhot population of Lahúl, Kunawer, and the Kumaon passes. But there may also be the analogues of the Ráwats.

A Serpa vocabulary of Mr. Hodgson's represents one, at least, of the Bhot populations of Nepaul. It is all but actual Tibetan.

| English. | Serpa. | Tibetan. |
|---|---|---|
| *Man* | mi | mi |
| *Head* | go | go |
| *Hair* | ta | ta |
| *Eye* | mik | mik |
| *Ear* | amchuk | amcho |
| *Tooth* | so | so |
| *Blood* | thak | thak |
| *Bone* | ruba | ruko |
| *Hand* | lango | lango |
| *Foot* | kango | kango |
| *Sky* | nam | nam |
| *Sun* | nimo | nimo |
| *Moon* | oula | dawa |
| *Star* | karma | karma |
| *Water* | chhú | chhú |
| *Stone* | doh | do |
| *Tree* | dongo | shindong. |

Far more interesting are three rude tribes named *Chepang*, *Haiyu* and *Kusunda*; of which, as far as there are degrees in rudeness, the Kusunda are the rudest. I give the only account of them in Mr. Hodgson's words:—

"Amid the dense forests of the central region of Népál, to the westward of the great valley, dwell, in scanty numbers and nearly in a state of nature, two broken tribes having no apparent affinity with the civilized races of that country, and seeming like the fragments of an earlier population.

"They toil not, neither do they spin; they pay no taxes, acknowledge no allegiance, but living entirely upon wild fruits and the produce of the chase, are wont to say that the Rajah is Lord of the cultivated country as they are of the unredeemed waste. They have bows and arrows, of which the iron arrow-heads are procured from their neighbours, but almost no other implement of civilization, and it is in the very skilful snaring of the beasts of the field and the fowls of the air that all their little intelligence is manifested.

"Boughs torn from trees and laid dexterously together constitute their only houses, the sites of which they are perpetually shifting according to the exigencies or fancies of the hour. In short, they are altogether as near to what is usually called the state of nature as anything in human shape can well be, especially the Kusundas, for the Chépángs are a few degrees above their confrères, and are beginning to hold some slight intercourse with civilized beings and to adopt the most simple of their arts and habits. It is due, however, to these rude foresters to say that, though they stand wholly aloof from society, they are not actively offensive against it, and that neither the Government nor individuals tax them with any aggressions against the wealth they despise or the comforts and conveniences they have no conception of the value of.

"They are, in fact, not noxious but helpless, not vicious but aimless, both morally and intellectually, so that no one could without distress behold their careless unconscious inaptitude."

He continues—

"During a long residence in Népál, I never could gain the least access to the Kusundas, though aided by all the authority of the Durbar: but, so aided, I once in the course of an ostensible shooting excursion persuaded some Chépángs to let me see and converse with them for three or four days through the medium of some Gúrúngs of their acquaintance. On that occasion I obtained the accompanying ample specimen of their language; and, whilst they were doling forth the words to my interpreters I was enabled to study and to sketch the characteristic traits of their forms and faces. Compared with the mountaineers among whom they are found the Chépángs are a slight but not actually-deformed race, though their large bellies and thin legs indicate strongly the precarious amount and innutritious quality of their food. In height they are scarcely below the standard of the tribes around them—who, however, are notoriously short of stature—but in colour they are very decidedly darker or of a nigrescent brown. They have elongated (fore and aft) heads, protuberant large mouths, low narrow foreheads, large cheekbones, flat faces, and small eyes. But the protuberance of the mouth does not amount to prognathous deformity, nor has the small suspicious eye much, if anything, of the Mongolian obliqueness of direction or set in the head. Having frequently questioned the Durbar whilst resident at Káthmándú as to the relations and origin of the Chépángs and Kusundas, I was invariably answered that no one could give the least account of them, but that they were generally supposed to be autochthones, or primitive inhabitants of the country. For a long time such also was my own opinion, based chiefly upon their physical characteristics as above noted and upon the absence of all traceable lingual or other affinity with the tribes around them. So that I took them to be fragments of an original hill population prior to the present Tibetan inhabitants of these mountains; and to be of Tamulian extraction, from their great resemblance of form and colour to the Aborigines of the plains, particularly the Kóls. It did not for several years occur to me to look for lingual affinities beyond the proximate tribes, nor was I, save by dint of observation, made fully aware that the Mongolian type of mankind belongs not only to the races of known northern pedigree, such as the mass of the sub-Himálayan population, but equally so to all the Aborigines of the plains, at least to all those of Central India. Having of late, however, become domiciled much to the eastward of Káthmándú, and having had more leisure for systematic and extended researches, those attributes of the general subject which had previously perplexed me were no longer hindrances to me in the investigation of any particular race or people. I now saw in the Mongolian features of the Chépángs a mark equally reconcilable with Tamulian *or* Tibetan affinities; in their dark colour and slender frame, characteristics at first sight indeed rather Tamulian than Tibetan, but such as might, even in a Tibetan race, be accounted for by the extreme privations to which the Chépángs had for ages been subject; and in their physical attributes taken altogether I perceived that I had to deal with a test of affinity too nice and dubious to afford a solution of the question of origin. I therefore turned to the other or lingual test; and, pursuing this branch of the inquiry, I found that with the southern Aborigines there was not a vestige of connection, whilst, to my surprise I confess, I discovered in the lusty Lhópás of Bhútán the unquestionable origin and stock of the far removed, and physically very differently characterized Chépángs!"

That their language is akin to the Lhopa is clear from

the specimen ; clearer from the table which Mr. Hodgson has given of the affinities. Whether they are more especially Lhopa than Tibetan is doubtful. I give the table as it is given by its author :—

| English. | Chepang. | Lhopa. | Tibetan. |
|---|---|---|---|
| *Sun* | nyam | nyim | nyimá |
| *Sky* | nam | nam | namkháh |
| *Mountain* | rías | rong | rí |
| *Star* | kar | kam | karma |
| *Free* | sing-tak | shing | jon-shing |
| *Salt* | chhí | chhá | tsá |
| *Road* | liam | lam | lam |
| *House* | kyim | khim | khyim |
| *Fire* | mí | mí | mé |
| *Arrow* | láh | dáh | dáh |
| *Dog* | kúi | khi | khyi |
| *Buffalo* | mísha | méshi | mahi |
| *Fish* | gná | gná | nyá |
| *Hog* | piak | phag | phag |
| *Horn* | róng | róng | rá |
| *Two* | nhí-zho | nyi | nyis |
| *Three* | súm-zho | súm | súm |
| *Give* | búi | bin | búh |
| *Take* | lí | ling | lan |

Are the Chepang, Haiyu, and Kusunda remnants of the earlier occupants of the soil? or are they wanderers from Tibet degenerated? I only submit that they are in the same category with Ráwat, so that what the Chepang are, that are the Ráwat also.

I shall now notice a few populations, which may possibly be truly Bhot; but which, nevertheless, have a slight shade of doubt over their purity.

1. The *Rongdur* have already been mentioned. Neither in habits nor locality can the Rongdur be very distant from

2. *The Drok or Brog, and (? or) the Chak or Jag.* These are occupants of the central parts of northern Tibet. The language of the Chak is stated to be ordinary

Tibetan. That of the Drok has yet to be investigated. Mr. Hodgson believes them to be a mixed population—robber-bands recruited from all quarters. The ordinary Tibetans, peaceful-minded men, separate them from themselves. The difference of habits, however, is enough to account for this. They may be Tibetan, or Tibetan *plus* other elements, nevertheless. They may be Rongdu or Kyampo under another name. They may be actually Kyampo *eo nomine*—the change from *m* to *k* being a very likely one. This, I think, is the case.

3. *The Hor.*—The Hor call themselves Ighur, and are called by the Chinese Kao-tse; Hor (Hor-pa) being the Tibetan names. Their occupancy of the Hor, of Mr. Hodgson's researches, is the north-western frontier of Tibet, on the confines of the Turk districts of Little Bokhara and the Mongolian districts of Dzungaria. Even in Tibet some of the Horpa are Mahometans; so are some in Dzungaria. In Little Bokharā, a Mahometan district, there are more. This is a repetition of what we found in Bultistan.

Mr. Hodgson makes them Turk at once. I cannot, however, separate the following Hor Ighur, or any other, form of the vocabulary from the Bhot, still less connect it with the Turk.

| English. | Hor. | Tibetan.* | Ighur. |
|---|---|---|---|
| *Man* | vzih | mi | er, kishi |
| *Head* | gho | go | bash |
| *Hair* | spu | kra | satsh |
| *Eye* | mo | mik | kusi |
| *Ear* | nyo | amcho | kulak |
| *Tooth* | syo | so | tish |
| *Blood* | sye | thak | khan |
| *Bone* | rera | ruko | sungguki |
| *Hand* | lha | lango | ilik |
| *Foot* | ko | kango | adakhi |

* Spoken form.

| English. | Hor. | Tibetan.* | Ighur. |
|---|---|---|---|
| *Sky* | koh | namkhâh | tengri |
| *Sun* | gna | nyima | kun |
| *Moon* | slikno | dawa | ai |
| *Star* | sgre | karma | yuldus |
| *Fire* | umah | me | oot |
| *Water* | hrah | chhu | suw |
| *Stone* | rgame | do | tash |
| *Tree* | nah | shindong | yikhatsh |
| *One* | ra | chik | bir |
| *Two* | gre | nyi | iki |
| *Three* | su | sum | utsh |
| *Four* | pla | zhyi | tort |
| *Five* | gwe | gna | bish |
| *Six* | chha | thu | alty |
| *Seven* | zne | dun | yidi |
| *Eight* | rhiee | gye | sekis |
| *Nine* | go | guh | tochus |
| *Ten* | sga | chuh | on |

* Spoken form.

Still they call themselves Ighur, a Turk name. Are they Turks, who have adopted the Bhot language, or is there an error in the history of the vocabulary?

Again, in Strachey's map there is a district (a population) marked Horba on the eastern bank of the Lake Manasarowar, on the very frontier of Nepaul. Are these in the same category with the Horpa of the frontier? Are they Turk settlers? Not improbably.

4. *The Kolo.*—These I treat as Mongolian, and when the Mongolians Proper come under notice the Kolo will do the same. They *may*, however, be Bhot.

Upon the whole, the Tibetan stock is pure. The extent of its area favours its being so. So does the exclusive character of the Chinese government; so does polyandry. On the other hand, slavery is a Tibetan institution, and wherever there is slavery there is an intermixture of blood. It may not be prominently conspicuous—it may not be recognized at all—it may be studiously concealed. Still it exists. It exists along the frontier most; but it extends inland as well. The Turk tribes to the north-west, the Mongols to the north and north-east, easily assimilate. They are all but Tibetan as it is, differing chiefly in language; the Turks in creed also. Then there are the Chinese on the east. Wherever there is a Chinese frontier there is encroachment. In Mantshuria this goes on with the greatest rapidity. Look to the old maps—the geographical names are Mantshú. Look to the newer ones—they are Chinese. The evidence to intermixture here is express. Huc enlarges upon it. In the Sifan districts there is encroachment also. Then there are the military establishments of the Chinese. Wherever there are these there is intermarriage, or its equivalent. Upon this there is direct evidence. Along the Indian frontier there are numerous half-bloods; dark-skinned on one side, fair on the other. In Lhasa the population other than Tibetan is notable. The Pebúns (the name is from Huc) are Indians, whose business is trade, and whose residence is permanent. The Katshi (the name is also Huc's) are Cashmirians; Mahometan in creed, and with an inclination to remain so. The first settlers took Tibetan wives. Since then they have married and intermarried amongst themselves. When we know more of Tibet we learn the characters of these mixed races. On the side of Bultistan the frontier is Paropamisan and modified Persian. The Kafirs of Kafaristan are Paropamisan. So are the natives of Gilghit, Astor, Hunz, and Nagor. There is slavery here—consequently intermixture. Again, in Ladak we have seen that the half-bloods between the natives and the Cashmirians are numerous, and that Argon is their name.

Again, Ladak was once under the dominion of China, so that Chinese soldiers have been on Ladak ground, introducing Chinese blood. At present it is partly subject to the Sikhs, partly to England. The Indian element is likely to be greater than the British.

As he passed through the belt of hot and humid forest that lies along the southern frontier of Bútan, Mr. Turner noticed what he calls a half-blood between a Lhopa and a Bengal. He describes him in most unfavourable terms; under-sized, badly made, dark-skinned. I take his notice as it stands; thinking, however, that instead of a half-blood he saw a sickly Bodo, and that intermixture may have been an inference. Be this particular case, however, as it may, there is no difficulty in believing that between the Lhopa division of the Bhot and the Bengali Hindu there is a considerable number of intermediate varieties. The same applies to other parts of the frontier.

The amount of Paropamisan, Cashmirian, Sikh, Bengali, Chinese, Mongolian, and Turk blood within the actual limits of the Bhot family, as it stands at the present, is one thing. The amount of Bhot blood beyond the present frontier of Bhotland is another. It may exist from two causes; from simple migration, and from an earlier increase of area. Of the first we find but few traces—practically none. There may be a few Tibetan soldiers in China, a few Bhots in India, Cashmir, and on the Paropamisan, Turk, and Mongol frontiers, sometimes as traders, sometimes as captives. There may be this because we have noticed that, notwithstanding the apparent want of business in the numerous monastic and semi-monastic towns of Tibet, there was still a great deal of real mercantile industry in the metropolis. There may be this because we have noticed the system of robbery and kidnapping which is practised along the frontiers. There may be this; but there is little besides. Tibet is one of the most land-locked countries in the world; nowhere touching the sea, nowhere near it; so that there is no maritime enterprise to spread the Tibet sailors over islands and archipelagoes; neither is there any activity in their movements upon the land. They are anything but a population of colonists.

That their area was at one time larger than it is at present is probable. Say that it extended beyond its present limits in the direction of Cashmir, Nepaul, and Hindostan. In this case the Hindu, Nepalese, and Cashmirians, who first encroached on the soil of the Bhot, may have taken to themselves Bhot wives, and half-blood children may have been the result. Of this there is, doubtless, a good deal. If the Bhots Proper did not extend far—very far—into India, some of their nearest congeners did. And this, except for the purposes of the minutest ethnology, is enough. The question, however, as thus put, will appear when we treat of India; and a very prominent question it will be. It will bring something either Bhot or Bhot like, as far south as the Ganges, at least, and that in a part where the river and the Himalayas are widely distant. For the parts where the stream approaches the mountains (or the mountains approach the stream), as is done in the parts about Calcutta, there are Bhot congeners within sight of the Ganges at the present moment. That the banks of the Sutlej were, at one time, more Bhot than at present is stated by Major Cunningham. The Bhot population stretched further down the stream. This he inferred from certain geographical names. They were of Bhot origin, even where the present area was Hindu.

The great extent of ground over which the Bhot language is spoken is less remarkable than the paucity of strongly-marked provincial forms of speech, and the little difference that has, as yet, been found between its extreme dialects. The Bulti of Little Tibet, the Lhopa of Bútan, the Proper Tibetan of Lhasa are mutually intelligible, as well as intelligible to the Ladaki of Leh, and (I think) to even the Chepang and the Sifan. From this we infer that the diffusion of the tongue over a great portion of its present area is recent. I do not mean by this that it took place within the last few generations, or even centuries. *Recent*, in ethnographical philosophy, may mean something of great historical antiquity. It may mean something earlier than the time of which history takes cognizance; and I think from its uniformity that the spread of the Bhot tongue *is* recent. Upon the next point I speak less decidedly. As far, however, as I have investigated the matter I find that the uniformity increases as we go westward, and that it is least in the Sifan and Thochu neighbourhoods. If so, its direction has been from east to west, rather than from west to east. Such was, probably, the case. This, however, is a question which connects itself with others, and has yet to receive its final consideration.

Such is the ethnological sketch of a country concerning which our information is as imperfect as it is recent, a country of which the Southern frontier alone has been explored with any approach to accuracy; and even here the survey has been partial. Southern Tibet has yet to be penetrated from Nepaul, from Sikkim, and from the eastern parts of Bútan. The jealousy of the Chinese government, is the chief, though not the only, cause of the obscurity that involves it. To the north of the hills above Asam there are rude and independent tribes of mountaineers who impede explorations—Bor Abors, Dophlas, and the like. These, though more or less akin to the Bhot, will be described in the sequel.

A Tibetan calls—

| | |
|---|---|
| His own country | Bodul. |
| China | Gyanak. |
| Chinese | Gyami. |
| India | Gyagar. |
| Russia | Gyaser. |
| Europe | Filing. |
| British India | Gya Filing. |
| Turkistan | Hor-yul. |
| Mongolia | Sok-yul. |
| Asam | Ashong. |
| The Indian Himalaya | Mon-yul. |
| Butan | Lho-pato, Lho-mon, Lho-duk. |
| Sikkim | Demojongs. |
| Nepaul | Palbo. |
| Kumaon | Kyunam. |
| Gurwhal | Galdiya. |
| Kunawer | Kunu. |
| Kashmír | Kache-yul. |

Lho-duk is, doubtless, word for word the same as Ladak.

## CHAPTER III.

The Nepaul Tribes.—The Sunwar.—The Magar.—Gurung.—Jareya.—Newar.—Murmi.—Kirata or Kichak.—Limbu.—Lepcha.—The Denwar, Durré, and Bramho.

Of the tribes of Nepaul, other than Hindu, and, at the same time, not so decidedly Bhot, as the Serpa and their allied tribes, the most western are

*The Sunwar.*—Of these I only know that they lie in the north-west, and at a high level, conterminous (I believe) with the true Bhot. Then come

*The Magar.*—It is the *lower* levels, chiefly on the *east* of the Kali, which are occupied by the Magar. They are the occupants of the lower levels; a point worth notice, because when we approach the mountain-tops the population changes. The forces which have changed the character of the indigenæ of western Nepaul, Gurwhal, and Kumaon are in continuance, directing themselves eastwards. Hence, the Magar may, at some future time, be what their neighbours to the west are at present, thoroughly Indianized. Their present condition is, more or less, transitional. Their physical conformation is their own, being that of the Bhot in general. At the same time there has been much intermarriage, and amongst the Hindus we may find the flat faces of the aborigines; amongst the aborigines the oval outlines and prominent, regular, or delicate features of their conquerors.

The language of the Magar is their own; essentially what is called monosyllabic; essentially in the same great class with the Tibetan, Chinese, Burmese, and Siamese. If it were not so they would scarcely find their place in this part of the work. There are elements, however, here which betoken transition, inasmuch as numerous words of Hindu origin have become incorporate. Besides this, many Hindus speak the Magar; whilst many Magar have either unlearnt their own tongue or use the Hindu in preference. This is more especially the case with the soldiers, many of whom are separated for long periods of time from their fellow countrymen at home, doing service in garrisons in other parts of the kingdom.

Upon the whole, the approximation to the Hindu type has been sufficient to lead more than one author to designate the Magar as Kshatrias—Hindu Khsatrias neither more nor less. They are not this. On the contrary, they are members of the same great group with the Bhot, &c.

The Magar alphabet is of Indian origin; indeed, this may be said of the alphabets of all the languages now coming under notice in general. In one or two cases we may hear of a native alphabet. If such exist it will still be of Indian origin, having been introduced earlier, having been adapted differently, having been modified by the course of time. A truly native alphabet is to be found neither at the foot of the Himalayas nor at their sides, nor yet at their tops, nor yet anywhere round about them. There has been (in the very decided opinion, at least, of the present writer) but one native alphabet in the world.

But the real hybridity appears in the religion. Without being scrupulous in other meats the Magar abstains from beef. Utterly unscrupulous in the way of drinks, he indulges freely in the use of fermented liquors, and makes anything in the way of a feast or festival an occasion and excuse for intoxication. His excess in this matter is notable.

Then he has his own priesthood, or, at any rate, an Indian priesthood, with a Magar nomenclature. His Brahmins are all Achars. In the pagan times a priest was called a Dami; Dami being the name for a priest in more than one of the tribes akin to the Magar at the present moment. We shall meet with the word when we get to the Bodo and Dhimal. Have we not, indeed, met with it already? There is a change in form and a change in sense—both being slight—but, surely, the Dami of the Magar is, word for word, the Jam and Tham of the Bulti populations, and of others far away from Bultistan.

Imperfect as is our information for the early history and social constitution of the Magar, we know that a trace of a tribual division (why not say an actual division into tribes?) is to be found. There are twelve thums. All individuals belonging to the same thum are supposed to be descended from the same male ancestor; descent from the same great mother being by no means necessary. So husband and wife must belong to different thums. Within one and the same there is no marriage. Do you wish for a wife? If so, look to the thum of your neighbour; at any rate look beyond your own. This is the first time I have found occasion to mention this practice. It will not be the last; on the contrary, the principle it suggests is so common as to be almost universal. We shall find it in Australia; we shall find it in North and South America; we shall find it in Africa; we shall find it in Europe; we shall suspect and infer it in many places where the actual evidence of its existence is incomplete.

(2.) *The Gurung.*—The tribes that lie equally westward with the Magar, but differ from them in occupying a higher place on the mountain sides, are those of the Gurung. These are decidedly and eminently pastoral; the breeders of sheep. They use, too, the sheep as a beast of burden, and lay upon its patient back such light loads as their chapmanship requires them to move about with. The higher the level of his occupancy the more the Gurung is said to thrive. The heat of the plains is better borne by the Magar.

Their language is their own; different from that of the Hindus; different from that of the Magar; not very well known even to professed philologues; but known from a sufficiency of samples to enable us to place—or rather to isolate—it. It is the medium by which the Gurung priests propagate a Buddhist creed; for the Hindu religion, though not unknown to some of the Gurung, has yet to make its way to any notable extent. That it will encroach on the earlier creed is likely. On the other hand, it is not certain that even Buddhism has wholly replaced the original Paganism. A tribe, or collection of tribes, called Bhujal Gharti is accused of numerous impurities in the way of food; for they eat anything except, perhaps, milk. At any rate they eat beef. When the details of the Bhujal superstitions are known they will probably turn out to be those of the Bodo and Dhimal; neither Buddhist nor Brahminic, but yet tinctured with an early Brahminism, which, in its present state, is either a rudiment of something that has to be developed, or a fragment of something that has fallen into decay. Like the Magar the Gurung fall into tribes; some of which are the Nisi, the Ghali, and the Thagsi; the Thagsi being the occupants of the highest altitudes, and constituting the truly Alpine division of the family.

(3.) *The Jaryas.*—Of the Jaryas I can give but an indifferent account. They lie to the south of the Gurung, with whom they are intermixed, and with whom they intermarry. Hamilton says that they have a peculiar dialect; but of this he gives no specimen. Mr. Hodgson denies the existence of a Jareya form of speech altogether. They are eminently Hindu both in creed and manners, notwithstanding which they may easily be as separate from both Gurung and the Magar, as those two families form one another. But they may also be either Gurung, or Magar, or Newar.

(4.) *The Newar.*—For now comes the notice of a new section thus named. The main portion of the central valley of Nepaul Proper was originally Newar, and Newar it is now, save and except the Hindu populations of the conquest. Favoured in respect to both soil and climate, at a lower level than the sheep-feeding Gurung, the Newar occupy a strong clay soil, fitted for brick-making, tile-making, and tilth. And this determines their industry and their architecture. The Newar are agriculturists and masons. No better cultivation, no better domestic architecture, is to be found than that of the Newar. The houses, as a general rule, are well-built and three stories high. They form large villages or small towns. The morals their occupants exhibit in the way of the sexes is by no means exemplary; indeed, the freedom (to use no stronger term) of the women is notorious.

Of their primitive Paganism no traces have been noticed. Perhaps they have no definite and tangible existence. Analogues to the Bujal Gharti amongst the Gurung there are none; so, at least, runs the evidence as it stands. On the other hand, there is no small portion of Hinduism engrafted upon the original Buddhism. There is also a great deal of true, or slightly-modified,

Brahminism. Still it is Brahminism with a difference. A Newar priest is not a Hindu Brahmin, but a native Achar. Then there is the class of surgeons and physicians called Jausi. These are the sons of Brahmin fathers and Newar mothers.

A little before the Ghurkha conquest Hinduism took root in the Newar country, when some influential proselytes to the worship of Siva were made. These have developed themselves and their successors into a definite division of the population. Nowhere, however, is there absolute purity. Like the Magar the Newar eat beef; like the Magar the Newar drink alcoholic liquors. We have seen that, like the Magar, they have a priesthood, Brahminic in many respects, but not Brahminic in name and origin. A worshipper of Siva will both kill and eat his beef; one of Buddha will eat but not kill it. They burn their dead.

On the 11th of August a curious operation is effected in the matter of frogs. The Newar farmer on that day goes forth into the field, takes with him some mashed rice, looks out to find the frogs, and gives them the rice to eat.

| English. | Sunwar. | Magar. | Gurung. | Newar. |
|---|---|---|---|---|
| *Man* | muru | bharmi | mhi | mijang |
| *Head* | piya | mitalu | kra | chhong |
| *Hair* | chang | chham | moi | song |
| *Hand* | table | hutpiak | lapta | palaha |
| *Foot* | kweli | mihil | bhale | pali |
| *Eye* | michi | mik | mi | mikha |
| *Ear* | nopha | nakyeh | nabe | nhaipong |
| *Bone* | nishe | miryaros | nugri | kwe |
| *Blood* | usi | hyu | koh | hi |
| *Tooth* | kryu | siak | sak | wa |
| *Day* | nathi | namsin | dini | nhi |
| *Sun* | na | namkhar | dhini | suja |
| *Star* | soru | bhuga | pira | nagu |
| *Fire* | mi | mhe | mi | mi |
| *Water* | pankhu | di | kyu | lau |

| English. | Sunwar. | Magar. | Gurung. | Newar. |
|---|---|---|---|---|
| *Tree* | rawa | sing | sindu | sinia |
| *Stone* | phunglu | thung | yuma | lohong |
| *One* | ka | kat | kri | chhi |
| *Two* | nishi | nis | ni | ni |
| *Three* | sang | song | song | son |
| *Four* | le | buli | pli | pi |
| *Five* | gno | banga | gna | gna |
| *Six* | ruk | — | tu | khu |
| *Seven* | chani | — | nis | nhe |
| *Eight* | yoh | — | pre | chya |
| *Nine* | guh | — | kuh | gunh |
| *Ten* | sashi | — | chuk | sanho |

(5.) *The Murmi.* (6.) *The Kirata* or *Kichak.* The Sikkim frontier is now near, so that the remaining populations, in all probability, belong to the two kingdoms. Of the four that stand over for notice, the first two are the Murmi and the Kirata.

Of the former I only know that they are Buddhists, with a less amount of Hinduism amongst them than any of the aforesaid.

Of the Kirata, or Kichak, half may be Buddhist, half Brahminic. Brahminic, however, as that half is, it either eats beef or unwillingly abstains from it.

(7.) *The Limbu.*—The Limbu are called Chung by the Lepcha.

The Limbu intermarry with the Kirata, and are somewhat less Buddhist, and somewhat more Brahminic than their situation leads us to expect. It has been the policy of the Nepaul rulers to conciliate them.

The few known notices concerning the Limbu make them hardy and hardworking. They cultivate grain, feed cows, pigs, and poultry. Their huts are neat and well made; the walls being of split bamboo, the roofs of the leaves of the wild ginger and cardamon. They are guyed down to the ground by long rattans, to steady them against the winds—violent, frequent, unexpected.

A glimpse at the nature of a Limbu festival is got from another part of Captain Sherwill's narrative. All the men, women, and children, amounting to about twenty, were drunk. And they were hospitable. The best of what they had was laid out before his party of sixteen—*chee* (the *chong* of Bútan) to drink, fowls and rice as food; and not only fowls and rice but milk, against which so many of the populations akin to the Limbu have a prejudice. At the house of the principal man of the neighbourhood some thirty men and women were sitting on the ground, drinking hot chee. Some beat drums. In the middle a young girl, highly excited, in a fantastic dress fringed with the teeth of beasts, the beaks and spurs of birds, the claws of bears, and cocks' tail feathers, was dancing. Her action was slow and monotonous at first, then livelier and more rapid, then most lively and most rapid, then hurried and irregular, then frenzied and uncontrollable. The noise, too, increased; the humming or singing became a shout; the drums beat louder and more discordantly. There was a fire in the middle of the circle; the poor girl dashed into it, and with her naked feet sent the burning ashes over the floor. Then a propensity to mischief set in. She would pull down the frames upon which the domestic utensils were hung; she would burn down the house. The next morning she was as quiet and demure as any decent little Limbu could be.

(8.) *The Lepcha.*—The Lepcha is hemmed in between the Newar and the other tribes of Nepaul, and the Lhopa of Bútan; the Lepcha area being barely sixty miles in breadth. Darjeling is the town wherein the Lepcha is most found; Sikkim the district which he more peculiarly calls his own. His decidedly Mongolian physiognomy has been admitted and insisted on by all who have noticed him—by Hodgson, Hooker, &c. The latter expressly states that of his Mongolian kindred he is more specially Tibetan than either Newar or Lhopa—"he differs from his Tibetan prototype, though not so decidedly as from the Nepalese and Bhotanese." The stature is short, varying from four feet eight inches (which is *very* short) to five feet; the face broad and flat, nose depressed, eye oblique, chin beardless, skin sallow or olive; the lip shows a little moustachè. Broad-chested and strong-armed the Lepcha is still fine-boned; at least, his hands are small, and his wrists thin. In like manner the legs of the Lepchas are stout, the feet small. The expression of their features is more mild and frank than cunning and quarrelsome, and this seems to agree with their real character. The Ghorkas are brave and fierce, the Lhopa quarrelsome and cruel, but not brave; the Lepcha timid and peaceful; such, at least, is Hooker's statement. He adds, that in their dealing with each other they are an honest people.

The chief article in a Lepcha dress, scantier and cooler than the altitude of their occupancy would suggest, is a cotton cloak, which is loosely thrown round the body, so as to leave the arms free, striped with blue, and worked with white and red. In cold weather an upper garment, with loose sleeves, is added. The hat, when worn, which is only on occasions, is made of the leaves of one of the *Scitamineæ* spread out between two thin plates of bamboo, extravagantly broad, wide-brimmed, and with a hemispherical crown. This is when the weather is rainy. When dry it is changed for a conical one, ornamented with peacock's feathers, and flakes of talc. The umbrella is a hood rather than a true umbrella, reaching from the head to the thighs. A Lepcha in a shower is like a snail with its shell on.

The ornaments—amulets as well as ornaments—are

chiefly of Tibetan make, some of great beauty, others of great value, having in them little idols, charms, copies of prayers, bones, hairs, and nail-parings of Lamas. The hair, an object of pride and care, in the dressing of which a female will assist a male, is collected into a large tail—simple or plaited, flat or round. The women wear two tails, and when in full dress are much less ungainly in their costume than the men. Besides the skirt and petticoat they wear a small sleeveless woollen cloak, covered with crosses, and fastened by a girdle of silver chains. A coronet of scarlet cloth adorns the head. The common dress (as with the Bodo) is of silk, coarse in kind, and spun by a worm peculiar to the country which feeds on the leaves of the castor-oil plant.

The Lepcha knife is long, heavy, and straight, serving for all purposes to which a knife can by any human ingenuity be applied; it is always worn, but rarely drawn in anger. They drink out of little cups turned in the knots of maple and other woods. A common one costs but *4d.* or *6d.*; but, besides these, there are several fancy articles (so to say) polished or mounted in silver. These are dearer. If made of a peculiar wood, paler than the common material, they are supposed to serve as antidotes, and of these the price is extravagant—say forty times as much as that of the common ones. Mr. Hooker gave a guinea for one hardly different from the ordinary kind in its outward appearance. The knots, from which they are shaped, are the modified roots of the oak, &c., as attacked by the balanophora, a parasite.

Their stimulus is the fermented juice of the Eleusine Coracana (Murwa grain). It is acidulous, refreshing, slightly intoxicating, and not unlike hock or sauterne in its flavour; is not common, above 6000 feet elevation; is presented in a joint of a bamboo, and sucked through a hollow reed. Word for word it is Murmi *chee*, the Bútani *chong*.

The only musical instrument, described as Lepcha, is a kind of flute, made of the cane of the bamboo, with four or six holes burnt in it considerably below the mouth-piece. The tone is low and sweet, and its sound monotonous, but not unpleasant, like that of the Æolian harp. The Lepcha songs are monotonous also.

Marriages are contracted in nonage, and even in childhood. Brides are purchased either by money or service. The violation of the marriage tie is sharply punished. The children of mixed marriages belong to the country of the father.

Though the Lepcha is no Buddhist, the Buddhist religion has considerably modified some of his customs and ceremonies. The priests, for instance, called Bijua, profess mendicancy, like the begging friars of Tibet; carry the Mani or prayer-machine, and wear Buddhist rosaries and amulets. The natives, who treat them with no little respect, liberally answer to their applications for charity, and so freely admit their sanctity, that a little energy in the business of conversion would, doubtless, be followed by a large amount of Lepcha proselytism. As it is, however, the original creed is but little interfered with. In this the priest is the medicine-man, the exorcist, and the director of feasts, ceremonies, and sacrifices. These are to the evil rather than the good spirits. "Why should we sacrifice to *them?* They do us no harm. The evil spirits, who dwell in every rock, grove, and mountain, are constantly at mischief, and to them we must pray, for it is they who hurt us."

Omens are sought for in the entrails of fowls, and superstitions of all kinds are rife and common. A list of Lepcha charms is long and heterogeneous. The dog-tooth of a leopard, the dog-tooth of the barking deer, an ornamented brass bead, a piece of ginger, a clove of garlic, the hard seeds of some tree—all these at once strung on a thread did Major Sherwill see on the neck of a Lepcha child.

A list of Lepcha vegetables is peculiar. Mountain spinach, fern tops, fungi, are what a Lepcha will contrive to exist on amongst the hills; but he adds to his mess of spinach a sauce of stinging-nettles, crushed, but raw.

The Lepchas are one of the many rude tribes who are skilful in kindling a light by means of two pieces of wood. One lies horizontally, and has a hole in it; another is worked vertically, and is sharpened to a point. Both are prepared beforehand, highly-dried, and smoked. The point of the vertical, is fixed in the hole of the horizontal, piece, and rapidly revolved; the friction at the points of contact soon produces fire. This is just how it is done amongst the Dyaks of Borneo, also amongst some of the American tribes. It is effective. When "lucifers, matches, flint-and-steel, and several other modes of procuring fire were utterly unavailing in these damp mountains, the Lepchas were never at a loss." They rubbed the sticks and got a light. After about a minute's working the wood catches fire. It is the wood of a particular tree, and resembles willow. Two men do the revolutionary part of the operation. One begins at the top of the upright stick. As his hand gradually slides downwards another succeeds. So that before the light is kindled four hands are in action.

The Lepchas believe that dysentery is infectious, and, accordingly, take certain sanitary precautions to prevent its spread. It was at Hee when Major Sherwill was on his survey. The people begged him not to go there, refusing to follow him if he did. Ere long he came upon two upright posts, one on each side of the path. They were connected at top by a horizontal pole—gallows-fashion. From this pole hung two bundles of sticks, near them two cudgels; a few feet further stood two more posts, but without any pole or bar to join. The meaning whereof is this. Any one coming from the side of the two unconnected posts may pass on; any one coming from the side of the two connected ones must not pass on. If he do he will be beaten by the cudgels, and fined thirty rupees; thirty being the number of the sticks in the two bundles—fifteen in each.

The chief Lepcha diseases are small-pox (the most dreaded of all), goitre, remittent fevers, and rheumatism.

The dead are burnt or buried, sometimes burnt first and buried afterwards.

| English. | Murmi. | Kiranti. | Limbu. | Lepcha. |
|---|---|---|---|---|
| *Man* | mi | mana | yapme | maro |
| — | — | — | yembocha | tagri |
| *Head* | thobo | tang | thagek | athiak |
| *Hair* | kra | moa | thagi | achom |
| *Hand* | ya | chukuphema | huktaphe | kaliok |
| *Foot* | bale | ukhuro | langdapphe | dianghok |
| *Eye* | mi | mak | mik | amik |
| *Ear* | nape | naba | nekho | anyor |
| *Bone* | nakhu | saiba | sayet | arhet |
| *Blood* | ka | hau | makhi | vi |
| *Tooth* | swa | kang | hebo | apho |
| *Day* | dini | len | lendik | sakne |
| *Sun* | dini | nam | nam | sakhak |
| *Moon* | ladima | lava | lavo | dau |
| *Star* | karchin | sangyen | kesva | sahor |
| *Fire* | me | mi | me | mi |
| *Water* | kwi | chawa | chua | ong |
| *Tree* | dhong | sangtang | sing | kung |
| *Stone* | yumba | lungta | lung | long |
| *One* | grik | ektai | thit | kat |
| *Two* | gni | hasat | nyetsh | nyet |
| *Three* | som | sumya | syumsh | sam |
| *Four* | bli | laya | lish | phali |

| English. | Murmi. | Kiranti. | Limbu. | Lepcha. |
|---|---|---|---|---|
| *Five* | gna | gnaya | gnash | phagnon |
| *Six* | dhu | tukya | tuksh | tarok |
| *Seven* | nis | bhagya | nuksh | kakyok |
| *Eight* | pre | reya | yetsh | kaken |
| *Nine* | kuh | phangya | phangsh | kakyot |
| *Ten* | chiwai | kip | thibong | kati |

Three other populations seem to belong to the same group with the Ráwat, Kúsúnda, Haiyu, and Chepang. They occupy the districts where the soil is moist, the air hot, the effluvia miasmatic. They are named, but not described in full, by Mr. Hodgson as Durre, Denwar, and Bramho. Word for word, I believe these names to be Tharu, Dunghur, and (possibly) Rawi. No specimen of their language is published. It may be akin to the Chepang; it may be more akin to the Dhimal and Bodo of the next chapter.

## CHAPTER IV.

The Kocch.—Dhimal and Bodo.—Western Bodo of Sikkim and the Bútan frontier.—Eastern Bodo, or Borro, of Asam and Cachar.—The Garo.—The Kasia.—The Mikir.

FAREWELL, for awhile, Buddhism and welcome Paganism. We may say this and mean it; for Paganism is both more instructive than Buddhism and more practicable. It is more instructive, because it exhibits the thoughts and feelings of an earlier period in the history of humanity. That it is more practicable is known to every commercial man and every missionary. It presents fewer obstacles to those who look for work; fewer obstacles to those who would make proselytes to Christianity. This is because its hold on the mind is weaker, and its prejudices fewer. Asia tells us this, speaking through the mouth of Parsís, Brahmins, and Buddhists. Africa tells us as much. A Pagan country is a promising, a Mahometan a hopeless, field for the missionary.

Farewell, too, for awhile, white, yellow, and brown skins. You are about to grow black. It is no longer the high and rare atmospheres of the snow-line and the parts in its neighbourhood that will now be respired. It is no longer even the healthy breezes of the hill-side; no longer even the fresh air of the level and cultivated plain. We are moving on a lower level, and in a medium tainted with malaria. We are in India, and not in the best parts of it. We are in a belt of forest fatal to Europeans, fatal, in many cases, to even the Hindu of the healthier localities.

Upon the extent that these unfavourable conditions affect the human frame, the evidence is conflicting. The Saul forest, full of malaria everywhere, but fullest in the range to the east of the Kosi, is endured by no human being, save and except the remarkable individuals that have, for ages, made it their dwelling-place. Yet the Dhimal, the Bodo, and others thrive in it, love it, leave it with regret. When others show in their fever-stricken aspects the inroads of the poison of the atmosphere, these breathe it as common air. Nay, they prefer it to the open and untainted air of the plains; where the heat gives them fever. So writes Mr. Hodgson; and so his communicants informed him. Yet they may easily have been exceptions to their countrymen, stronger in body, more patriotic in spirit. They may, also, have exaggerated. It is certain that all our testimony is not to this effect. It is certain that other writers have noticed the unhealthy complexion, and undersized limbs of the foresters of the Saul belt, the so-called aborigines of the district.

What we have seen in the tribes of Nepaul we shall see in the tribes coming under notice, or, at least, with the greater part of them. There will be a certain amount of Hindu influence; sometimes sufficient to disguise the original ethnological characteristics. So that there will be varieties and sub-varieties, as we expect *à priori*. Never mind, for the present, how these are named. They exist. They will come under notice when India becomes our subject. They will all be explained on the same principle; the principle that gave us the varieties and subvarieties of the Magars and Newars. They will all represent an intermixture of Hindu and Himalayan elements; sometimes of language, sometimes of creed, sometimes of blood.

Of the populations about to be noticed we meet with

branches within the confines of the Indian Peninsula. They extend, however, beyond it, into Assam as well as Bengāl, into Assam and the parts beyond. They extend also, I think, into Bútan. If so we are on a class which connects India, Tibet, and the Transgangetic Peninsula.

*The Kocch* (*Koktsh, Koksh*, or *Kúksh*).—The Kocch are the Kavach of the Yogini Tantra, where they are noticed as Mlekhs, or barbarians; as, without doubt, they *then* were, one and all. They are not all barbarians now; but, on the contrary, fall into three divisions; two of which are sufficiently modified to disguise their real affinities. Two are disguised after the manner of the modified Magars and Newars; or rather they are in the condition of the Jareyas where the concealment of the original character is greater. What this arises from we can anticipate; though not altogether. Brahminism has something to do with it. Has Buddhism also? No. We are anticipating too much here. We are no longer in Tibet and Nepaul, but in India, where Buddhism is said to be banished. It is not, then, a case of Brahminism and Buddhism, but one of Mahometanism, and Brahminism. When the Mahometan power was established in Bengal the kingdom of the Kocch bounded it on the north, extending from 88 to 93° E. L., and from 26 to 27° N. L. It may have touched the south-eastern extremity of Nepaul. At any rate it lay along the southern frontier of Sikkim, and Bútan, extending itself into Assam, with Kocch Bahar for its metropolis. Such a kingdom as this was powerful; and, although the Hindu and Mahometans called it the Kingdom of Kavach, or Kocch, its ethnological constituents were heterogeneous. In fact, they consisted of all the tribes under notice; one being as much Kocch as the other, the name being, when first given, general, though now exceedingly limited. At present a Kocch is one thing, a Dhimal another, a Bodo another. Some centuries ago they were all Kocch. Suppose the sub-alpine regions of Lombardy and Piedmont to have been called Barbary, by the Romans, without distinction of the tribes which composed their population. Suppose this population to have been heterogeneous. Suppose some portion of one division of it to have become Romanized; and, so changed, to have abandoned the name of Barbari; the remainder retaining it. The name would, in all probability, be anything but a complimentary one. Meanwhile, the kingdom breaks up, and the other divisions are no longer blended with the general mass of Barbars, but known in details; or, supposing them to be taken *en masse*, the name by which they are known to the Romans is changed. What could now befall the primitive Barbari, *i. e.* those who were not Romanized? They would be the only section of the population that retained the original name, which would now have become special and particular—general and collective—as it had been originally. They might or might not be proud of it. They might be proud of it if left alone; yet easily made to abandon it by being acted upon from without. Its discreditable nature might be enlarged on: and, in the course of time, its application might become equivocal. *Mutatis mutandis*, this seems to have been the case with the word under notice. The Bodo of the immediate neighbourhood call the population we are considering Kocch. The more distant Bodo of Asam call them Hásá. The Dhimal call them Kamul (? Dhimal). But what do they call themselves? The Mahometan and Hindu members of the class have, as aforesaid, abandoned the name. But the unconverted portion; what of it? They called themselves Koocch when "not perplexed with Brahminical devices;" by which I understand that, when they are persuaded that the same is a badge of rudeness, they are easily put out of love with it.

The unconverted Kocch, the only ones at present under consideration, live in the woods, and cultivate the soil with the hoe. They move from spot to spot as the soil gets exhausted. They are well fed and fairly clothed; of average strength and vigour. They abstain from beef; but respect and admire the Garo who do not, and *because* they do not; for they hold that the less a tribe is restricted the more exalted it is. They eat no tame animal without sacrificing some part of it to the gods, two of whom are Pushi and his wife Jago. They sacrifice, too, to the sun, moon, and stars, to the deities of the rivers, hills and woods, to their deceased parents. The chief feast is at the harvest. The end, too, of the rainy season is a time for solemn sacrifices. The sacrificant priest is called a Deoshi. He is chosen by his employer, marries, and works like the rest, and has no hereditary authority. Of the victims, the blood goes to the deities, the flesh to their worshippers. The dead are kept two days, during which time the family mourn, the friends feast. They are then burnt, by a river's side, where the mourners bathe and have done with their mourning. There is also a sacrifice of pigs. Whoever marries out of his tribe incurs a fine, and whoever incurs a fine without paying it must become a bondsman until his wife can redeem him. And here we come in contact with a strange piece of social economy. The property of the husband is made over to the wife; when she dies it goes to her daughters, and when he marries he lives with his wife's mother. Marriages are arranged in the nonage of the parties concerned; though not without consulting the inclination of the contemplated bride. Ante-nuptial frailties are overlooked, and a girl can always marry her lover. After marriage however, the morality becomes strict, and polygamy or polyandria, concubinage and adultery, are punished with fines. The general character of the social organization of the Pani Kocch is patriarchal. The elder of the settlement decides between contesting parties.

The northern parts of Rungpúr, Púrnea, Dinajpúr, and Mymansing, are the chief Kocch localities.

At the risk of being accused of improperly rationalizing on historical statements I cannot forbear taking an exception to the account of the Kocch kingdom during the days of its supremacy, as given in Buchanan, and endorsed by Hodgson. It is to the effect that its founder's name was Hájo, that he lived more than three hundred years ago, at the end of the fifteenth, or the beginning of the sixteenth, century, that he had no son, that his daughter was his heiress, that he gave her to a Bodo chief in marriage, that he thus founded the kingdom, and successfully defended it against its three most formidable enemies, the Sauman, the Plov, and the Javan. In all this there is nothing intrinsically improbable, and if it were not for two out of the five names in the narrative no objection would arise. But Hájo is a suspicious denomination. It has all the appearance of being such a word as Romulus in the history of Rome and Hellen in that of the Hellenes. We shall see the name Hojai as that of a population before we get three degrees eastward, if we have not seen it already in the word Hásá. I suggest, then, that Hájo is a fabulous individual, no real founder of the Kocch or any empire; but an eponymus hero. Then comes Javan. In the ordinary translation of ordinary statements it is rendered Greek, being neither more nor less than Ion and Javan. Here, however, it is said to mean Mahometan; Saumar meaning the Ahoms of Upper

Asam, and Plava the men of Bútan; Phih or Pruh being the name by which the Lepchas designate the Bútani.

*The Dhimál.*—The Dhimál live to the north and east of the Kocch, between the open plains and the higher levels of the mountains (both of which they avoid); also between the rivers Konki and Dhorla, touching the Bodo districts as well as the Kocch; indeed, the Bodo and Dhimál are intermixed, though each population occupies separate villages.

Neither do the two divisions intermarry. Of these the Dhimál is the smaller, amounting to no more than some 15,000 souls, a number that decreases rather than increases. It was the opinion of Mr. Hodgson, founded upon four months' intercourse with the Dhimál as well as the Bodo, that their traditions were nothing worth; that their area, however, had once been larger than it is he inferred from the fact of there being a tract in North Bengal still called Dhimáli, lying considerably beyond the present limits of the reduced and receding Dhimáls. Again, although no chief of the Dhimál tribes now exists, a migration from Kamba to the Tengwa, and from the Tengwa to the Konki, in order to escape the oppressions of the Ghurkas of Nepaul, a migration from west to east, is still within the memory of man, having happened no more than sixty years ago.

I am probably wrong in departing from the plan so well illustrated by Mr. Hodgson in his valuable monograph on these tribes, wherein, on the strength of the little difference between them, and the great extent to which an account of the one serves as an account of the other, the two divisions of the Bodo and Dhimál are treated together, the *minutiæ* in which they differ being pointed out as they arise. Nevertheless, as it is my wish to give special details rather than to advance generalities, I adhere to the distinctions with which I have begun, and continue the notice of Dhimál as one separate from that of the Bodo, though not wholly, as will be seen in the sequel. Whatever may be their similarity in other respects—

1. The languages of the two populations are different.

2. The Pantheon of the two populations is different. This, however, is a difference of less importance than it appears to be at first sight, inasmuch as the chief objects of reverence with both the Bodo and the Dhimál are the rivers of their respective districts, which are sometimes invoked under the name of the deity that is supposed to preside over them, sometimes by the simple geographical designation. Thus, as examples of the former, we have the names Timai, Lakhim, and Chima, denoting the Teeshta, the Mahamada, and Kosi Rivers respectively, Timai, Lakhim, Chima, being three sisters. On the other hand, however, the names of the Konki, Mechi, Soran, Boas, and Dubelly Rivers are simply Kankai, Menchi, Sonusi, Bonasi, and Dhulpi. Some of these are of the masculine, others of the feminine gender; *i. e.* some are gods, others goddesses.

3. The details of the marriage ceremony are different. The Dhimál priest propitiates Dáta and Bidáta by invocations and offerings of betel-leaf and red-lead—Dáta and Bidáta being the deities who preside over wedlock. This is a cheaper operation with the Bodo than with the Dhimál; for with the Dhimál the marriage feast may be prolonged to the third day, and cost from thirty to forty rupees; whereas the Bodo ceremony may be gone through for four or six. When Dáta and Bidáta have been invoked, the bride and groom are placed side by side, each with five pauns, with which they feed each other; the parents of

the groom then cover the couple with a sheet, when the priest completes the nuptials by sprinkling them with water.

4. If the Dhimál weddings are dearer than those of the Bodo, their funerals are cheaper, for the Bodo practise more formality. A Bodo, when the funeral feast is ready, repairs with his assembled mourners to the grave of the deceased, and, if he be the nearest of kin, takes a little food, and presents it to the departed one with these words:—" 'Take and eat: heretofore you have eaten and drunk with us; you can do so no more: you were one of us; you can be so no longer: we come no more to you; come you not to us.' After this each member of the meeting breaks and casts on the grave a bracelet of thread; proceeds to the river and bathes, and having thus lustrated himself, repairs to the banquet, and eats, drinks. and makes merry."

5. That the names of the Dhimál festivals should differ is nothing more than what we expect from the difference of language. There are differences, however, in their number and details as well—not very important, nor yet calling for description. Still they are differences.

Word for word, I believe Dhimál, Kamul, and Tamul to be the same.

*The Bodo*.—The Bodo area extends much further than the Dhimál, the Bodo population being by far the more important of the two. Its western branch belongs to Bahar and Bengal, to the Sikkim and Bútan frontiers; and it is described in the valuable and well-known monograph of Mr. Hodgson, along with the Kocch and Dhimál. The eastern branch occupies Asam and Cachar.

The western Bodo build their houses and lay out their little villages in the same manner as the Dhimál; and building houses, and clearing grounds, are matters in which the two populations intermix and help each other. The chief material with which they work are the jungle grass and the bamboo. From ten to forty of the huts thus rudely made form a village. If the family be large each house forms a court or enclosure. First, the main dwelling-house; secondly, a cattle-shed, stable, or fold opposite it. Then, if needed, there are two wings on each side so as to form a quadrangle. The roof projects. The body of the houses falls into two compartments, one to sleep, the other to cook in. A bedstead, a few stools, a few mats and shelves, constitute the furniture—all home-made, as is, also, the earthenware. For the metal pans there must be a little barter at Kocch markets. They are all of brass—none of copper, none of iron. Neither is there any manufacture or use of leather. Ropes of grass, and baskets of cane do instead. In the way of clothing, they use silk and cotton, (but no wool); which they spin, weave, and dye. Their sandals are of wood: their ornaments, few in number, like their pots and pans, are purchased. Rice, maize, millet, fresh-water fish, and a fair allowance of meat, constitute the chief Bodo aliment, and Jo their chief drink. This is made of rice or millet, the grain of which is boiled, and flavoured by the root of a plant called Agai-chito. It then stands, nearly in a dry state, to ferment for two days. Water is then added, and the whole, after three or four days, is fit for drinking. The plant is grown for the purpose. Hodgson compares the Jo of the Bodo with the Aji-mana of the Newari of Nepaul. I think he might have done more. He might have suggested that the name of the Newari beverage was the name of the Bodo plant (Aji-mana, Agai-chito). Beside their Jo, the Bodo use tobacco—both freely; but not hemp, nor yet opium.

The Bodo are tillers of the soil; but their agriculture is imperfect, and quasi-nomadic; since they are not fixed but erratic or migratory cultivators. They have no name for a village, no sheep, no oxen, no *fixed* property in the soil. Like the ancient Germans, *arva in annos mutant, et superest ager.* They clear a jungle, crop it as long as it will yield an average produce, and then remove themselves elsewhere.

The Bodo villages are small communities of from ten to forty huts. The head of these communities is called the Grá. It is the Grá who is responsible to the foreign government (British, Tibetan, or Nepaulese), for the order of the community, and for the payment of its tribute. In cases of perplexity the Grás of three or four neighbouring communities meet in deliberation. Offenders against the customs of the community may be admonished, fined, or excommunicated.

The Bodo religious ordinances are simple. The birth, the weaning, and the naming of children are all unattended with ceremonies requiring the presence of a priest. At funerals and marriages, however, the priest presides. This he does, not so much as a minister to the essential ceremony, as for the sake of the feast that accompanies it. No Bodo or Dhimál will touch flesh which has not been offered to the gods: and this offering a priest must make.

Marriage is a contract rather than a rite. Polygamy or concubinage is rare: the adoption of children common. All the sons inherit equally; daughters not at all. A Bodo can only marry to one of his own people. Divorce, though practicable and easy, is rare; the wife and daughter have their due influence. Children are named as soon as the mother comes abroad, which is generally four or five days after her confinement. The idea that the delivery involves a temporal impurity is recognized; so that all births (and deaths also) necessitate a temporary segregation and certain purificatory forms.

A price—Jan—must be paid by the bridegroom elect for the intended bride. If the former have no means of discharging this sum, he must go to the house of his father-in-law elect, and there literally earn his wife by the sweat of his brow, and labour for a term of years.

When any person is afflicted by witchcraft "the elders assemble and summon three Ojhás or exorcists, with whose aid and that of a cane freely used, they endeavour to extort from the witch a confession of the fact and the motives. By dint of questioning and of beating, the witch is generally brought to confession, when he or she is asked to remove the spell, and to heal the sufferer; means of propitiating preternatural allies (if their agency be alleged) being at the same time tendered to the witch, who is, however, forthwith expelled the district, and put across the next river, with the concurrence of the local authorities."

"When sickness takes place, it is not the physician but the exorcist who is summoned to the sick man's aid. The exorcist is called, both by the Bodo and Dhimáls, Ojhá, and he operates as follows. Thirteen leaves, each with a few grains of rice upon it, are placed by the exorcist in a segment of a circle before him to represent the deities. The Ojhá, squatting on his hams before the leaves causes a pendulum attached to his thumb by a string to vibrate before them, repeating invocations the while. The god who has possessed the sick man, is indicated by the exclusive vibration of the pendulum towards his representative leaf, which is then taken apart, and the god in question is asked, what sacrifice he requires? a buffalo, a hog, a fowl, or a duck to spare the sufferer. He answers (the

Ojhá best knows how!) a *hog;* and it is forthwith vowed by the sick man and promised by the exorcist, but only paid when the former has recovered. On recovery the animal is sacrificed, and its blood offered to the offended deity. I witnessed the ceremony myself among the Dhimáls, on which occasion the thirteen deities invoked were Póchima or Waráng, Timai or Béráng, Lákhim, Konoksiri, Ménchi, Chímá, Danto, Chádúng, Aphói, Biphói, Andhéman (Aphún), Tátopátia (Báphún), and Shúti. A Bodo exorcist would proceed precisely in the same manner, the only difference in the ceremony being the invocation of the Bodo gods instead of the Dhimál ones."

The great Bodo festivals are four; the Shúrkar, held in December or January, when the cotton-crop is got in; the Wagaleno for February or March; the Phúlthépno for July or August, when the rice comes into ear; and the Aihúno in October, or bamboo festival.

The Wagaleno was witnessed by Dr. Campbell and Mr. Hodgson. A noise of voices by the wayside between Siligori and Pankhabari drew them from the direct road to the spot whence it came. This was the bed of the river, where they found thirteen Bodo men, in a circle, facing each other, and each carrying a long bamboo pole, with different articles of wearing apparel streaming forth as its ornaments and a yak's tail at the end. Of three men who stood within the circle, the first danced to the singing (for the thirteen around him were solemnly chanting a kind of chorus) and gesticulated. The second was a priest; the third a servitor or assistant. It was a priest, clothed in red cotton, who set the tune to the thirteen chanters. The servitor had a brush and a water-pot. More important, however, than either servitor or priest was another actor, the seer, prophet, or inspired one. He it was who, full of the God, answered such questions as were put to him about the prospects of the coming seasons. He was Déódá, or Possessed. "When we first discerned him, he was sitting on the ground panting, and rolling his eyes so significantly that I at once conjectured his function. Shortly afterwards, the rite still proceeding, the Déódá got up, entered the circle, and commenced dancing with the rest, but more wildly. He held a short staff in his hand, with which, from time to time, he struck the bedizened poles, one by one; lowering it as he struck. The chief dancer, with the odd-shaped instrument, waxed more and more vehement in his dance; the inspired grew more and more maniacal; the music more and more rapid; the incantation more and more solemn and earnest; till at last, amid a general lowering of the heads of the decked bamboo poles, so that they met and formed a canopy over him, the Déódá went off in an unaffected fit, and the ceremony closed without any revelation—a circumstance which must be ascribed to the presence of the sceptical strangers."

The Aihúno is a domestic ceremony. The "friends and family being assembled, including as many persons as the master of the house can afford to feast, the Déóshi or priest enters the enclosure or yard of the house, in the centre of which is invariably planted a Sij or Euphorbia, as the representative of Báthó who is the family as well as national god of the Bodo. The Báthó, thus represented, the Déóshi offers prayers, and sacrifices a cock. He then proceeds into the house, adores Mainou, and sacrifices to her a hog. Next, the priest, the family, and all the friends proceed to some convenient and pleasant spot in the vicinity, previously selected, and at which a little temporary shed has been erected as an altar, and there, with due ceremonies, another hog is sacrificed to

Agráng, a he-goat to Manásho and to Búli, and a fowl, duck, or pigeon (black, red, or white, according to the special and well-known taste of each god) to each of the remaining nine of the Noŏni madai. The blood of the sacrifice belongs to the gods—the flesh to his worshippers, and these now hold a high feast, at which beer and tobacco are freely used to animate the joyous conclave, but not spirits, nor opium, nor hemp."

Mannou is the wife of Báthó, an eminently domestic goddess. She is found in every house, under the guise of a bamboo pole, about 3 feet high, with one end in the earth, and with a small earthenware cup of rice on the other. Such the symbol; which has its annual and its monthly offerings. The annual one has been described; the sacrifice being that of a hog. The monthly offerings are eggs, and they are made by the females.

*The Borro of Cachar.*—The Eastern Bodo (Borro), or Cachar, are divided into the Cachars of the hill-country and the Cachars of the plains; and these again are subdivided according to their difference of creed. A hill Cachar may be either a Hindu or a Pagan, though he is oftener the latter; and a Cachar of the lower levels may be the same, though he is generally, perhaps always, the former.

A Cachar of the plains is called a Hazai, Hojai, or Hajong, and this is what is meant by the Hojangs of Assam, and the parts about are spoken of. They are Hindu in creed, more or less Hindu in language and manners, Cachar in blood.

The Hojai have had rajahs of their own. Again, the title Burmon, or Brahmin, is applied as a mark of distinction to some of their nobler families, families which, notwithstanding their title, are a tribual aristocracy rather than an aristocracy of caste. Of this they have little; so little as to make them but loose and imperfect Hindus. They eat freely of both fowls and pigs. They sacrifice them to their deities. They indulge freely in fermented liquors; in short, they depart widely from what a Brahmin of Benares would consider orthodox. Their education is Hindu, their alphabet of Hindu origin. Those that read and write are prone to leave their ordinary agricultural industry and become collectors, policemen, and the like; showing no want of intelligence or activity in their new employments, but by no means showing the simplicity of character they maintained as cultivators of the rice and cotton of their fertile soil. In office they become adepts in chicanery, corruption, and oppression, imitating the worst practices of the Bengali.

The hill Cachar is more simple and unsophisticated, stouter, hardier, and more turbulent; more formidable, too, in the eyes of the neighbouring marauders of the Naga family. However little an Anjami Naga may hesitate to attack a Mikir village, he generally abstains from the occupancies of the hill Cachar.

Of the hill Cachars each head of a family lives in a separate house, of which from 20 to 100 go to constitute the village; the batchelors living in the *dekha chung*, or *warriors' house*. This is a large building in the centre of the village more like a club than an ordinary dwelling. The young men who have attained a certain age and have not chosen for themselves a wife, support it, and in it they live, their parents having eliminated them from the houses of their nativity. The Nagas have the same practice.

The great locality of the Borro of Assam is a frontier district, named Chatgari, between Desh, During, and the

Bútan hills, where their numbers may amount to 30,000, half the whole Borro population.

| English. | Kocch. | Dhimál. | Bodo. |
|---|---|---|---|
| *Man* | beta-choá | waval | hiwa |
| ——— | ——— | diang | manshi |
| *Head* | mura | purung | khoro |
| *Ear* | kan | nhatong | khoma |
| *Eye* | chaku | mi | mogon |
| *Blood* | lohu | hiki | thoi |
| *Bone* | harwa | hara | begeng |
| *Tooth* | dant | sitong | hathai |
| *Hand* | hath | khur | akhai |
| *Foot* | bhori | khokoi | yapha |
| *Sun* | bela | bela | shan |
| *Moon* | chand | tali | nokhabir |
| *Star* | tara | phuro | hathotkhi |
| *Fire* | agni | men | wat |
| *Water* | jal | chi | doi |
| *Stone* | pathai | unthur | onthai |
| *One* | ek | elong | mancho |
| *Two* | du | nhelong | manne |
| *Three* | tin | sumlang | mantham |
| *Four* | char | dealong | mambre |
| *Five* | panch | nalong | manba |
| *Six* | choe | tulong | nando |
| *Seven* | sat | nhilong | manchini |
| *Eight* | ath | yelong | ——— |
| *Nine* | noze | kuhalong | ——— |
| *Ten* | das | telong | ——— |

*The Garo.*—The mountaineers of the Garo Hills, to the north-east of Bengal, have long commanded the attention of investigators, and a good account of them is to be found in the third volume of the Asiatic Researches, by Mr. Eliot. Their language, of which a specimen is there given, is left unplaced in the Asia Polyglotta of Klaproth. It is, however, a member of the class under notice, and was known to be so when the Bodo and Dhimál were considered Indian.

The Garo, like so many mountaineers, are hardy, stout, and

surly-looking, with a flattened nose, blue or brown eyes, large mouth, thick lips, round face, and brown complexion. They have a prejudice against milk; but in the matter of other sorts of food are omnivorous. Their houses, called *chaungs*, are built on piles, from three to four feet from the ground, from ten to forty in breadth, and from thirty to one hundred and fifty in length. They drink, feast, and dance freely; and, in their matrimonial forms, much resemble the Bodo. The youngest daughter inherits. The widow marries the brother of the deceased; if he die, the next; if all, the father.

The dead are kept for four days; then burnt. Then the ashes are buried in a hole on the place where the fire was. A small thatched building is next raised over them, which is afterwards railed in. For a month, or more, a lamp is lit every night in this building. The clothes of the deceased hang on poles—one at each corner of the railing. When the pile is set fire to, there is great feasting and drunkenness.

The Garo are no Hindús. Neither are they unmodified Pagans. Mahadeva they invoke; perhaps worship. Nevertheless, their creed is mixed. They worship the sun and the moon, or rather the sun *or* the moon; since they ascertain which is to be invoked by taking a cup of water and some wheat. The priest then calls on the name of the sun, and drops corn into the water. If it sink, the sun is worshipped. If not, a similar experiment is tried with the name of the moon. Misfortunes are attributed to supernatural agency; and averted by sacrifice.

Sometimes they swear on a stone; sometimes they take a tiger's bone between their teeth and then tell their tale.

Among them "a madness exists, which they call

transformation into a tiger, from the person who is afflicted with this malady walking about like that animal, shunning all society. It is said, that, on their being first seized with this complaint, they tear their hair and the rings from their ears, with such force as to break the lobe. It is supposed to be occasioned by a medicine applied to the forehead: but I endeavoured to procure some of the medicine thus used, without effect. I imagine it rather to be created by frequent intoxications, as the malady goes off in the course of a week or fortnight. During the time the person is in this state, it is with the utmost difficulty he is made to eat or drink. I questioned a man, who had thus been afflicted, as to the manner of his being seized, and he told me he only felt a giddiness without any pain, and that afterwards he did not know what happened to him."

In a paper by Captain C. S. Reynolds, we have the notice of a hitherto undescribed superstition; that of the *Korah*. A *Korah* is a dish of bell-metal, of uncertain manufacture. A small kind, called Deo Korah, is hung up as a household god and worshipped. Should the monthly sacrifice of a fowl be omitted, punishment is expected. If "a person perform his devotion to the spirit which inhabits the Korah with increasing fervour and devotion, he is generally rewarded by seeing the embossed figures gradually expand. The Garo believe that when the whole household is wrapped in sleep, the Deo Korahs make expeditions in search of food, and when they have satisfied their appetites return to their snug retreats unobserved."

The greater part of the Garo population is independent. A part, however, is British.

It is the northern members of the family that are in

this predicament; their area being on the boundary of the Calúmalúpara pergunnah. This pergunnah is divided into shares of six and of ten annas; a fact which has engendered the names Cheanni (6 anna) and Dusanni (10 anna). There is Cheanni portion of Calúmalúpara, and there is Dusanni portion also; and it is the Calúmalúpara people who are either Dusanni or Cheanni. The terms, however, have been extended to the Garo, who lie along the frontier, those opposite the Cheanni parts being Cheanni; those opposite the Dusanni parts being Dusanni. Though "we have hitherto considered the Dusanni and Cheanni Garows as separate tribes, I believe that they are both of one Abengyas, and that this distinction is without a difference. They consider themselves one and the same people." Word for word, *abengyas* is, doubtless, the same as *buniah*, a term used by Eliot, and applied to the Garo chiefs. In the passage before us it seems to mean chieftaincy.

In 1822–23 the pergunnah of Calúmalúpara was sold to the Company, and the Garo mehauls seem to have gone along with it. These were troublesome possessions, for the Garo of Currybari were in actual revolt, and the whole occupancy had been a source of annoyance rather than gain.

Soon after its transfer the chiefs made their submission, and agreed to pay a revenue of 196 rupees *per annum;* the chiefs of each village paying it. In 1832, however, there were arrears, a demonstration against them, and a settlement which lasted till 1848; when another demonstration was necessary. A murder had been committed; and, as the murderer was not given up, Captain Reynolds, from whose narrative this notice is taken, made an inroad into their territory, burnt a village, and exacted promises of better behaviour for the future. He found the road barricaded in several places, and planted with panjis, or bamboo stakes, short, sharp, and dangerous. One end is set in the ground. The other wounds the feet of those who tread on it. So effective are they, that the troops, in one place, were an hour and a half getting over 200 yards of ground. They had to shave them off close to the soil before they could proceed. I draw attention to this, because, in another notice of the mode of warfare of the tribes of south-eastern Asia, these panjis will appear again. Several Malay tribes use them, and find them more formidable than either spear or sword. They are not above four inches long—little better than strong thorns. The whole weight, however, of the body, comes down on them, so that they penetrate to the bone—and this through the sole of a shoe or boot.

The expedition ended in the following agreement, signed by fifteen Locmas of village chiefs. It gives us a better insight into what the people are, and what the Company wishes them to be, than a longer notice.

"*Art.* 1*st.*—We agree to abstain from committing murder, either in our own clan or in any other, nor will we permit any amongst us to do so, or to commit any other heinous offences that we may be able to prevent.

"*Art.* 2*nd.*—It was our former custom to hang human skulls in our houses, we hereby agree to abstain therefrom for the future.

"*Art.* 3*rd.*—All disputes which may occur in our jurisdiction requiring investigation, we will endeavour to settle with the assistance of a punchyat of four or five of the most influential chiefs amongst us, and in presence of the disputing parties, and should we be unable to settle it ourselves, we will report the same to the Hunt Mohurir, with a view to its being settled by your lordship.

"*Art. 4th.*—When any officer or government servant may have occasion to travel through our country, we agree to clear the roads in our several jurisdictions, and to furnish him with coolies, and render him every assistance in our power.

"*Art. 5th.*—When any officer or his deputy may arrive at Bengal Katta and summon us to attend him, we will instantly do so, and if it is necessary for us to attend him at any other place, we agree to do so on his summons.

"*Art. 6th.*—We agree to prevent any independent Garros from entering the government territories through our jurisdictions with intent to murder or commit any other disturbances.

"*Art. 7th.*—When any officer orgovernment servant arrives at our Doar, we agree, on being called on, to pay, without delay the revenue due by us.

"*Art. 8th.*—The road which has been cleared from Bhayamara to Kuntanangiri, and Bengal Katta to Ripoogiri, we agree to keep clear every year throughout our respective jurisdictions from twenty-four to thirty feet wide."

The Dusanni Garo occupy twenty villages, the smallest consisting of a single house paying one rupee, and the largest of 100, paying 100. The whole number of houses is 306, each holding (say) ten persons. Hence, the total population of the Dusannis is 3060. In the Cheanni country the number of villages is twenty-five. In each district the names of them end in either *-giri* or *-parrah*, as Repúgiri, Rungtupara. This, however, is Indian, so that the British Garo, at least, have been Indianized in respect to their language, always assuming that the names in question are native, *i. e.* names given by the Garo themselves, and not names given by the Hindus of the frontier.

| English. | Garo. | Borro. | Bodo. |
|---|---|---|---|
| *Man* | mande | manse | hiwa |
| *Head* | skho | khoro | khoro |
| *Eye* | mikran | nigan | mogon |
| *Ear* | nachil | khama | khoma |
| *Tooth* | wagom | hathai | hathai |
| *Blood* | anchi | thoi | thoi |
| *Bone* | greng | begeng | begeng |
| *Hand* | jak | nakhai | akhai |
| *Foot* | jatheng | atheng | yapha |
| *Sun* | sal | san | shan |
| *Star* | jashki | hatolthi | hathotki |
| *Fire* | wal | wat | wat |
| *Water* | chi | doi | doi |
| *Stone* | rong | lanthai | onthai |

Due east of the Garo country comes that of

*The Kasia*, which falls into petty rajahships, and, by so doing, exhibits a little more political organization than that of their western neighbours, where the constitution seems to be simply patriarchal. The difference between the Garo and Kasia tribes seems but slight. Both abstain from milk. Both chew pawn. A Kasia man expresses his contempt of a Bengali by saying that he "has white teeth."

In his accounts of rude tribes an ethnologist must take what he can get in the way of information without asking too minutely whether each particular fact tallies with the rest of his description. He is in the hands of his informants, and it rarely happens that they examine the phenomena which come under their notice from the same point of view. One describes the dress, another the customs, another the manners of a country, a fourth its religion. Others notice certain facts because they are common, others because they are rare. Two tribes may be so closely allied as to have, in all fundamental points, the same ethnological character. The details, with few exceptions, may be the same. Yet if the descriptions of them be imperfect (as most descriptions are and must be), it is possible that the similarity may be concealed. Let one writer note what the other omits, and this will be the case.

I have no doubt but that many isolated facts in the description of a Garo apply to a Kasia also, though in the notices of the Kasia they may be non-apparent, and *vice versâ*. I find, for instance, no notice of the Kasia believing in men becoming tigers; yet it is, probably, a Kasia superstition. The Kasia, on the other hand, have an especial fear of the snake. The Garo *may* have this also. No account, however, has been taken of it. From the Garo alone, or from the Kasia alone, we get but a slight notion of the mythology of the parts to which those families belong. Combine the two and our *data* increase. One account becomes the complement to the other. The fragmentary character of our material is at the bottom of this. If every section of every class had its full and complete description we might condense, generalize, connect; as it is we must take facts when we can get them, not caring overmuch whether they be isolated or systematically connected.

The construction of the Garo house is, at present, an isolated fact. When we get further southwards, and further eastwards, we shall find that the large house on a frame of piles is the ordinary structure.

The Garo panjis are in the same predicament. As has been stated, they will re-appear in Borneo.

Numerous rude nations catch fish by means of traps. I find, however, the Kasia fish-trap particularly noticed. Like the large houses, and the panji spikes, it will be noticed again, *i. e.* in Java, Borneo, and Sumatra.

Most of the tribes of the Bhot alliance are not only thirsty drinkers, but skilful distillers. No one, however, has told us this as a general fact; on the contrary, a certain number of observers have stated that such and such tribes practised such and such contrivances, and indulged in such and such potations.

So it is. There are some facts which we must note because they are peculiar, others because they are common. They may be trifling; still they should be noted. Of course when they appear and re-appear too frequently they may be pretermitted. Until, however, they have re-appeared once or twice they should be noted. Otherwise we may assume likenesses improperly.

The *living* bridges of the Kasia country may be commoner elsewhere than the existing descriptions make them. In the present state of our knowledge, however, they claim attention. On the bank of the river that runs between Ringhot and Cherra grows a large India-rubber tree. Whilst its fibres are young and pliable they are stretched across the stream, and fastened by their free ends on the soil at the other side. They take root, grow, and form a bridge of live wood. Sometimes two trees are planted on the two sides of the river opposite each other, in which case their fibres join in the middle. I subjoin Captain Yule's account. The tree throws out "a multitude of roots. Two or three of the long fibres, whilst still easily pliable, have been stretched across the stream, and their free ends fastened on the other bank. There they have stuck firmly into the earth, and now form a living bridge of great and yearly-increasing strength. Two great roots run directly one over the other, and the secondary shoots from the upper have been bound round and grown into the lower, so that the former affords at once a hand-rail and suspending chain, the latter a footway. Other roots have been laced and twisted into a sort of ladder as an ascent from the bank to the bridge. The greatest thickness of the upper root is a foot, from which it tapers to six or seven inches. The length of the bridge is about eighty feet, and its height about twenty above the water in the dry season.

"This bridge was constructed by the people of the village of Ringhot, and forms their communication with Cherra during the rains; the present generation say it was made by their grandfathers. This was the first and most remarkable bridge of the kind that I saw in the Kasia Hills, and I supposed it to be unique, perhaps half accidental. But I afterwards found it to be an instance of a regular practice, and saw such bridges in every stage, from that of two slender fibres hung across the stream, to such as I have described above, and there are not less than half a dozen within as many miles of Cherra. One I measured ninety feet in clear span. They were generally composed of the roots of two opposite trees (apparently planted for the purpose) bound together in the middle."

From living bridges to dead stone the transition is, perhaps, abrupt. The analogues, however, of the Cromlechs and Stonehenges, numerous in most countries, have been specially described in Kasia. Groups of erect oblong pillars, hewn or unhewn, are common; the number generally odd—from three to thirteen. The middle one is generally the highest, and is sometimes surmounted by a circular disk. A flat table stone near the village of Sailankot stood five feet above the ground, was two feet thick, and thirty-two by fifteen in circumference. Many of the villages take their name from these monuments. Mau means stone; and the villages Mau-smai, Mau-inlu, Mau-flong, and Mau-mlu, mean the Stone of the Oath, the Stone of Salt, the Grassy Stone, the Upturned Stone, &c. The upright stones are said to be cenotaphs, and if a Kasia be asked why his ancestors erected it, the answer will be that "he did it to preserve his name." Yet the name is rarely remembered. So much for the credit due to the traditions of rude nations. Others are believed to have been erected as memorials of a compact. "There was war between Cherra and Mausmai, and when they made peace and swore to it, they erected the stone as a witness." So said Umang, an intelligent native. Nevertheless, the stone may be older than the war, and the oath have been sworn on it because it was where it was, not because it was erected for the occasion. The name, however, favours Umang's view. Then there is the Mau-mlu, or the Salt Stone. To eat salt from the point of a sword is said to be a Kasia mode of oath-taking.

The names of persons are short, as Tess, Bepp, Mang, Sor, Mir, Bi; and fathers are sometimes addressed by a title taken from their children. "How is it with Pabobon, the father of Bobon? How is it with Pahaimon, the father of Haimon?" Not that the link between fathers and sons is of the strongest. On the contrary, when a child has grown up he leaves his father, and all but treats him as a stranger. The details of this account want criticism. The son of the sister inherits. The male child of a Raja may be a labourer, whilst his cousin may succeed to a large property once his (*i.e.* the labourer's) father's. As a rule, the matrimonial relations are lax. In other matters the habits of the people are such as encourage the missionary. The heads of a large village near Cherra invited one (Mr. Jones) to settle amongst them, offering, if he would do so, to build a house for him. This was in 1842.

The children spin peg-tops. In how many more countries do they do the same? No man knows. How to observe has yet to be applied to children's games. There is ethnology, however, in all things—even in peg-tops.

One of their ordeals is that of water. The man who can hold his head under water longest, wins.

They draw omens from broken eggs, noting the way in which they break.

The moon, once a month, falls in love with his wife's mother: she, to repel his addresses, throws ashes in his face. In days of old the stars were so many individuals, who climbed to the top of a tree. Others from below cut this tree. The company in its upper branches are the stars. The group of the Pleiads is called the Hen-man (man and chickens).

Every fourth day is a market-day in each village; the great and little markets being held alternately. The space between two of these is the Kasia week.

A Kasia before drinking a glass of brandy dipped his finger four times in the glass, first filliping a drop of the spirit over each shoulder, then dropping one along each side. "Why do you do this?" "For the name of the God." The name, however, of the deity is not given. It seems that Nat worship is the culture of the Kasia.

A superstition in respect to snakes has been alluded to. It is this. If a snake dwell in your house you may sell and consume what you like and your store will not diminish.

Kano Likai, or Lika's Leap, is a waterfall near Cherra. "Once on a time, a man of foreign race came to the hills, married a woman named Likai, and settled with his wife in a village north of Maumlu. They had two children, a boy and a girl. One day the woman betook herself to the forest as usual to cut firewood, and in her absence the father killed his two little children, and cooked them; on his wife's return, he invited her to feast on what he had prepared, and she did so; he then disclosed what she had eaten. Then said Likai, 'It is no longer good to remain in this world,' and, hurrying to the adjoining precipice, leapt over."

Another legend, concerning the wife of Ula. "Ula was a great warrior at the court of the Raja of Linkardyem, and the Raja married his sister.

"Now in those days there were but twelve households in Cherra, and the Raja of Linkardyem, making war on the Raja of Cherra, drove him with his people to the woods, where they ate leather, and the rind of certain fruits. But the Raja of Linkardyem was a savage, and abused his wife, the sister of the brave Ula. For he placed her on a frame of bamboos, and lighted a fire beneath; and so, being roasted, she died. So Ula was wroth, and he went to the Raja of Cherra, and said, 'Make me a great man and I will avenge thee on thine enemy.' So he of Cherra agreed; and Ula, having cut off the head of the Raja of Linkardyem, brought it to him of Cherra, and so became first counsellor of the Raja.

"One day, as Ula was going forth on his avocations, with others of the village, he said to his wife, 'Clothe thyself with my arms and garments.' Meantime the new Raja of Linkardyem came against Cherra with a mighty host of four thousand men. Now the village of Cherra was well girt with palisades and ditches, and the wife of Ula went forth to the barriers in her husband's arms and clothing, and the other women, doing likewise, went with her; and when the army of Linkardyem beheld the arms and the shield, they shouted in terror, 'Ula! Ula!' and turned their backs in flight, for great was their fear of Ula; and the wives of Cherra and the men who remained, went forth with the wife of Ula, and chased the Linkardyemians, and smote them sorely. From these twelve households come the twelve tribes which now exist in Cherra. My informant was of the house of Ula."

*The Jaintia Tribes*—East of the Kasia range, lies that of the Jaintia hills, the occupants of which may differ from the Kasia about as much as the Kasia differed from the Garo. Instead of being independent, these are under the Company. Instead of being nearly pagan, they are tinctured with Hinduism; the Saiva form of worship being partially and recently introduced.

Of the tribes *in situ*, or in their actual Jaintia occupancies amongst the hills, I have seen no full account. There is a population in Cachar and Asam which is considered to represent them. Whether it do so or not is another question. This is that of—

*The Mikir.*—In Cachar, and in the Asam district of Nowgong, the Mikir, whose name is, I believe, word for word, that of the Mekhs, occupy a considerable area; the lowest computation of their numbers amounts to 26,000. They cultivate rice and cotton, changing their localities every four or five years. *Arva in annos,* &c. We have seen this already. *Arva in annos,* &c. We may quote the sentence *ad libitum* in the notices of these parts.

The Mikir are, in the matter of name, Mekhs, Mlecchas or impure infidels; the word being of Hindu origin. So, at least, it seems; although I am not able to affirm that they call themselves differently. And they are what their designation is supposed to suggest, either unbelievers or imperfect converts. The latter are forbidden to drink spirits, but allowed to chew opium; and in this they indulge.

They hold, too, as many of their original superstitions as are compatible with the profession of Brahminism—and these are numerous. This is the story of the Converted and Unconverted Kocch over again. Like the Bodo, the Unconverted Mikir delight in festivals, and in the drunkenness which attends them. Like the Bodo, they have no prejudices in the way of eating. The cow is rarely killed; but this is because it is inconvenient rather than because there is any prejudice against beef. Pork is eaten freely. The sacrifices of fowls are common. These they offer to the sun, the moon, and the invisible deities attached to trees and rocks remarkable for either size or shape.

There are the Mikir of the plains, and the Mikir of the hills; the Cachar distribution over again. The Mikir of the plains belong to Nowgong in Asam rather than to Northern Cachar; the Mikir of the hills belong to Northern Cachar rather than Asam. The evidence of their connection with the Jaintia tribes is partly inference, partly what is called tradition. It is capable of improvement.

Stewart writes that they were *originally* settled in or near their present districts; that they lived under chiefs of their own; that the Cachar Rajas oppressed them; that they fled to the Jaintia Hills; that they were oppressed there; and that they returned. He merely, however, says that this is tradition. I take exception to it. The descent from the Jaintia Hills is, probably, true. The previous occupancy of Cachar is doubtful. The single movement is historical. There is no evidence of the double ones. On the contrary, the statement that in settling in Cachar they were only retaking their own, is one likely to develope itself from a *minimum* amount of fact.

Robinson says that they have a tradition that their ancestors came from the Jaintia Hills, and he adds that they have a few Jaintia words in their vocabularies. But he superadds that he has not compared the two forms of speech.

Again—the Mikir physiognomy is Kasia. So is the Mikir dress, which consists of two pieces of striped cotton cloth made bag fashion and with holes for the head and arms.

If the Jaintia tribes be Kasia, these affinities may be real.

But what are the Jaintia tribes? I wait for a full account of them. Meanwhile, I remark that whatever they may be, and whatever may be the relation between them and the Mikir, the latter have decided Naga affinities in the way of language. It is probable that in these parts the transition from the Garo to the Naga may be found. It is possible, too, that the Mikir may always have been where they are; that they may know as a matter of fact that they resemble the Jaintia tribes in language and customs, and that they may explain this likeness by the assumption of a descent. Extremes meet. Learned ethnologists theorize thus, and savages do the same; one consciously, the other unconsciously.

The Mikir of North Cachar are the mildest and least courageous of the numerous populations of that district. The Kutcha and Angami Nagas of their neighbourhood, attack the hill Mikir with impunity, burn their villages, enslave their women and children. And the Mikir resist slowly and inefficiently; the story running that, long ago they attempted to throw off the dominion of the Rajah of Asam, failed, and were disarmed; that habitual cowardice arose out of the disuse of their weapons; that it has become hereditary, and has been transmitted to the present generation. The present Mikir carry the dhao; carry the spear—but they do not use them for actual warfare.

Their arts are the arts of peace. They are manageable, industrious, regular. They keep clear of the courts of law, grow rice and cotton, sell them to the Kasia, and pay their taxes regularly. When not at work in the fields they fell timber, make canoes, float them down to Lower Asam, and realize profits on their labour, and humble enterprize. The ground that they work is forest-land rather than jungle, and (as such) requires more clearing.

They are obliged to work harder than their neighbours, and have established a more industrial character accordingly.

They build their houses on platforms. One of them may contain as many as forty individuals; men, women, and children, members of the same family, or of different ones, as the case may be. Of these large houses, jointly occupied, we have seen something, and shall see more.

| English. | Kasia. | Mikir. | Naga. |
|---|---|---|---|
| *Man* | uman | arleng | minyan |
| —— | —— | penso | —— |
| *Woman* | ka kantei | arloso | dehiek |
| *Head* | kakli | iphu | kho |
| *Eye* | ka kamat | mek | mit |
| *Ear* | ka skor | ino | na |
| *Nose* | ka kamut | inokan | kho |
| *Mouth* | ka shintur | ingho | tun |
| *Tooth* | ka baniat | isso | pa |
| *Tongue* | —— | ade | —— |
| *Hand* | ka thallid | ripa | thali |
| *Foot* | ka kajat | kengpak | da |
| *Sun* | ka sngi | arni | san |
| *Moon* | ubanai | cheklo | da |
| *Star* | uklur | *cheklo longsho | merik |
| *Fire* | kading | me | van |
| *Water* | kaum | lang | jo |
| *Stone* | man | arlong | long |
| *Wood* | kading | theng | pan |

* Little moons.

## CHAPTER V.

The Hill-tribes of Asam.—Northern Boundary.—Aka, Dofla, Abor, and Miri Tribes.—The Bor Abor.—Eastern extremity and South-eastern margin.—The Mishmi.—The Muttuk, Singpho, and Jili.

The main part of the valley of Asam is either Indian or Indianized. Not so the hills round it.

The mountain-range that forms the northern boundary is a continuation of the hills of Bútan, the occupancy of the tribes whose languages are represented by the Tak and Changlo vocabularies.

The details of the Bútan frontier are but imperfectly known; since the populations are rude, inaccessible, and independent. We know, however, that the four following belong to the same class; at any rate their languages are closely allied.

*The Aka.*—On the western extremity of the northern range lie the Aka tribes, of which, though there is a sample of the language, there is no good description. I can only say that they are succeeded by

*The Dofla.*—No less than 180 petty chiefs are said to hold authority in the numerous Dofla villages of the Char Dwar.

Char Dwar means the Four Marches; the Char Dwar being but one of the Dofla areas.

The Dofla are succeeded by—

*The Abor.*—The hills on the right bank of the Dihong belong to the Pasial and Mayong, those of the left to the Padú, Sibú, Nibú, and Goliwar, Abor; tribes which were visited in 1825 by Major Bedford, whose notice of them finds place in Major Wilcox's report upon Asam.

In the matter of food they were well-nigh omnivorous; but expressed a horror for those who eat beef. Whether or no they drank milk is not stated. The generality of the mountain tribes of the Himalaya eschew it. Each warrior had a bow and quiver; some of the arrows being poisoned. Their dress was from the bark of the Uddal tree. It was tied round the loins and hung down behind in loose strips. It served for a rug to sit down on by day, and for a pillow to sleep on at night. Some wore basket caps; some caps made of cane and skin; some caps made like helmets, and ornamented with stained hair. Every man had something woollen in his possession; sometimes a waistcoat, sometimes a blanket; sometimes coloured, sometimes figured. When first visited they were in the habit of making periodical descents from their highlands and taking tribute, or levying black mail, from the villagers of the level country. They also took slaves; for amongst the Abors of Pasial many Asamese captives were found. This has now been put a stop to.

The buffalo is the animal they most especially hunt. They wound him with a poisoned arrow, and follow his tract, until they find him either dead or dying. The favourite ornament for their caps is the beak of one of the toucans, or horn-bills, the Buceros (? Nepalensis). With this at the front, and a red chowry behind, the appearance of their head-gear is imposing.

If the derivation of the word *Abor* be accurate, the term *Bor Abor* is something like a contradiction. *Bor* means *tribute*; whilst *a* (like the Greek *α*) = *not*. Hence, *Abor* = *free from tribute*. It is no native word at all; but one used to the Asamese; consequently, it can be applied to more populations than one. They may, for instance, be Bor Naga who pay tribute, and Abor Naga who do not; the latter being called simply Nagas. But what if one tribe more pre-eminently independent than the rest get called Abor, κατ' ἐξοχὴν? Such a thing may easily be. And what if a portion of it lose its independence, as it may easily do? In such a case it becomes Bor Abor, or the Tributary Independent, and we get an oxymoron.

This really happens. The population which the Asamese call Abor call themselves Padam, of which they are two divisions, the Bor and the Abor, the payers of no tribute, and the payers of tribute.

This really happens if the current explanation of the words Abor and Bor be accurate. But I take exception to it. The Bor Abors are the stronger, the more distant, the more independent population. Besides which, there is a branch of the Khamti called the Bor Khamti. Does Bor mean great? I have seen a statement to this effect; indeed, it appears in the very paper wherein we find the other etymology. It should be remembered, however, that it may do this and not mean much in the way of superiority of magnitude. Magna Græcia was not so large as ordinary Greece. Can it mean the mother country? In some cases it seems to do so. What it means in the case of the Bor Abor and the Bor Khamti remains to be decided.

A Padam village on the river Shiku consisted of 100 houses, with granaries at a distance (for security against fire), and a morang in the centre. The morang is a large building for the reception of strangers, for the transaction of public business, and for the residence of the unmarried men, who live in it as in a common club or boarding-house. At the dawn of day the boys go round like watchmen, bawl out the time, and tell the half-awakened sleepers that it is time for them to be at work.

In their politics there is unlimited freedom, both of voting and of speaking. The people pass the resolutions, each individual having a vote. And this they cherish carefully, jealously; their constitution being essentially democratic. Age and oratory have some weight. Upon the whole, however, the legislation lies with the masses, small though they be.

Their creed is simple. They sacrifice to certain deities of the woods and hills. The conical mountain, Regam, is the abode of an ill-natured, not to say malignant demon, who would cause the death of any one who should pry into the secrets of his dwelling, which is at the very top of the peak.

*The Miri.*—The Miri are in closer relation to the Asam government than the Abor, for it is against the Abor that the Asam government protects them. The bow and arrow—the arrow poisoned—are the chief Miri weapons. Their occupancy is on the eastern frontier of the Abor area.

| English. | Dofla. | Abor. | Miri. |
|---|---|---|---|
| *Man* | bangni | amie | ami |
| *Hair* | dùmùk | dumid | dumid |
| *Head* | dompo | dumpong | tupko |
| *Ear* | niorung | narung | ierung |
| *Eye* | nyuk | aming | amida |
| *Blood* | ui | yi | yie |
| *Bone* | solo | along | along |
| *Foot* | laga | ale | leppa |
| *Hand* | lak | elag | elag |
| *Sun* | dani | arung | dainya |
| *Moon* | polo | polo | polo |
| *Star* | takar | tekar | takar |
| *Fire* | ami | emme | umma |
| *Water* | esi | asi | achyo |
| *One* | aken | ako | ako |
| *Two* | ani | ani | aniko |
| *Three* | aam | angom | aumko |
| *Four* | apli | api | apiko |
| *Five* | ango | pilango | angoko |
| *Six* | akple | akyo | akengko |
| *Seven* | kanag | konange | kinitko |
| *Eight* | plagnag | pini | piniko |
| *Nine* | kayo | kinide | konangk |
| *Ten* | rang | iinge | uyingko |

*The Bor Abor.*—The Bor Abor, probably, belong to the same division of the same class as the Abor. The evidence, however, of their speaking the same language is incomplete. They lie to the back of the Abor, on the higher hills, and in a more inaccessible country. They are rude, independent, powerful, and but little known.

As we approach the head of the valley, and prepare for turning round towards its south-eastern margin, we come to the country of

*The Mishmi.*—The Mishmi frontier touches that of the Padam, or Abor, being on the drainage of the Dihong and Dibong. The details of the area beyond it are unknown. Its villages are small. Jillee and Anundea contain from thirty to forty families, Mabúm ten, Alonga twenty, Chunda twelve; making, in all, eighty.

The Mishmi, differing from the Padam in language, and in the shrine at which they worship, acknowledge them as relations, and are acknowledged by them; a common origin being claimed by the two populations. They also eat together. On the other hand, they quarrel and fight, and when the Mishmi of the above-named villages were visited by Captain Wilcox, they were at variance with the Padam of the Dihong and certain members of their own stock as well. They were variously dressed. None, however, were observed to wear anything woollen. Some wore rings beneath the knee, some caps of cane. Their ears were pierced, and their ear-rings various; now of metal, now of wood. Their arrows were poisoned so effectively that they were said to kill elephants. The wounded part was cut out; the rest eaten.

They described the tribes with which they were at war, but which were as Mishmi as themselves, unfavourably. Those of Bubhajia were accused of cannibalism.

The hut of the chief of the Thethong Mishmi was

strangely and filthily ornamented. Long poles of bamboo were hung with the blackened, smoke-dried skulls of all the animals with which the owner had ever feasted his friends and retainers. The smokiness of the huts has told upon the physiognomy of the Mishmi. They habitually contract their eyebrows. What is the mortality of the children? In Iceland, and the island of St. Kilda, where the reek is as impure as it is profuse, the deaths of infants from *trismus neonatorum* are inordinately numerous.

Some of the tribes turn up the hair and tie it in a knot, whilst others are closely cropped. The lower classes dress scantily; the chiefs well; in Chinese and Tibetan cloths, and with Chinese and Tibetan ornaments. The cross-bow is a common weapon.

Polygamy is common; the limit to the number of wives being the means of the husband. For each wife so many heads of cattle. Ghalim, one of the more powerful chiefs, had ten or twelve in his house, and a large remainder in separate establishments, or quartered amongst their relations. The women mix with the men, and join them in every labour but that of the chase.

For even ten wives a man must have a large house. Ghalim's was about one hundred and thirty feet long, and eleven wide. It was raised on posts. He was proud of the skulls that adorned it. It showed the number of cattle he had killed in the exercise of a noble hospitality. When he dies they will all be cleared away, and buried near the burial-place of the chief himself. And then his son will take his pride and pleasure in filling the house afresh. A chief who was either shabby or ostentatious retained the skulls of his father's time, and bragged of them as his own. He was voted an impostor accordingly.

The calf of the leg of the daughter of the Gam of Dilling measured more round than both Captain Wilcox's put together. What was the size of the captain's? Was the enlargement natural? In more than one savage country artificial means of thickening the legs are resorted to. Men should remember this, and make inquiries accordingly, when the legs of young ladies are twice as thick as their own.

When trouble comes upon a Mishmi he sacrifices fowls or pigs to the rural deities, and places the branch of a tree over his door to inform strangers that his house is under a temporary ban, and that it must not be entered.

The Mishmi are traders. Every man amongst them will either buy or sell. They are also blacksmiths, and forge their own spear-heads, though they buy them as well. They are skilful, too, in making suspension bridges.

The Taying and Mijhu of the following table are Mishmi tribes; the Miri being Abors, Dofla, or Aka, rather than Mishmi.

| English. | Taying. | Mijhu. | Miri. |
|---|---|---|---|
| *Man* | nme | ktchong | ami |
| *Head* | mkau | kau | tupko |
| *Eye* | mollom | mik | amida |
| *Ear* | nkruna | ing | ierung |
| *Blood* | rhwei | vi | yie |
| *Bone* | lubunglubra | zak | along |
| *Hand* | ptoya | yop | elag |
| *Foot* | mgrung | mpla | leppa |
| *Sun* | ring-nging | lemik | dainya |
| *Moon* | hho | lai | polo |
| *Fire* | naming | mai | umma |
| *Water* | machi | ti | achye |
| *One* | eking | kmo | ako |
| *Two* | kaying | kaning | aniko |
| *Three* | kachong | kacham | aumko |
| *Four* | kaprei | kambum | apiko |
| *Five* | mangu | kalei | angoko |
| *Six* | tharo | katham | akengko |
| *Seven* | uwe | nun | kinitko |
| *Eight* | elyeni | ngun | piniko |
| *Nine* | konyong | nyet | konangk |
| *Ten* | halong | kyep | uyingko |

*The Singpho, &c.*—The group that now comes under notice seems to fall into three (or more) divisions; (1) the Mutkuk, (2) the Singpho Proper, (3) the Jili. There may be others. These, however, are all we know; and these we know imperfectly. Error, therefore, in the classification is excusable.

Up to the very bank of the river, on its southern rather than its northern side, and at no great distance from its entrance into the valley from the north-east, lies the country of—

(1.) *The Muttuk.*—Muttuk, Moran, and Moameria, or Mowameria, are all names of the same population, the subjects of the Barsenaputi, a vassal of the Raja of Asam.

The Muttuk are Hindu in creed, worshippers of Vishnu, but worshippers of a very equivocal orthodoxy.

I have no vocabulary of their language *eo nomine.* The statements, however, concerning it are these—that though spoken by a small population, and in districts not more than a day's journey apart, it falls into no less than seven dialects, sufficiently unlike each other to be understood with difficulty. That of the Khaphok tribe is just intelligible to a Singpho. In Khanung there is still a resemblance to the Singpho; but no mutual intelligibility. The Khalang and the Nogmún forms of speech are, again, like the

(2.) *The Singpho Proper.*—The Singpho Proper are a powerful intrusive population, of the physical appearance of the populations with which they come in contact, partly in Asam, partly in Manipur, partly in the unexplored tracts to the east. Their religion is Buddhism, tinctured with Paganism, or Paganism modified by Buddhism. They live in separate villages under chiefs, captains, or elders called Gams. The Bisa Gam's account of his nation is as follows:—

"In the beginning, the Great Gosein (the Supreme Being) created man, and regarded him with especial kindness and favour. He gave him the whole earth to dwell in and enjoy, but forbade him to bathe or wash in the river called *Rámsíta* under a threatened penalty of being devoured by the *Rákhas* (Demon), and totally destroyed; as the forfeit of his disobedience. If, on the contrary, he refrained, the Rákhas should have no power over him, and he should inherit the earth eternally. Mankind, however, soon disobeyed the injunction, and the whole race was devoured by the *Rákhas* with the exception of a man called *Sírí Jía* and his wife *Phaksat.* These were seated under a tree, when the Gosein caused a parrot, perched on a bough, to speak, and give them warning to avoid the north, and fly to the southward, by which they would escape the *Rákhas's* hands.

"The man *Sírí Jía* obeyed, but *Phaksat* took the other road, and fell into the clutches of the Rákhas. When *Sírí Jía* saw *Phaksat* in the power of the Demon, he was divided from them by the river *Rámsíta,* the forbidden stream, and forgetting, or disregarding, the prohibition, he immediately crossed it to her rescue, and was also taken by the Rákhas, who prepared to devour them. In the act, however, of lifting them to his mouth, a flame issued from all parts of his body, and consumed him on the spot, since which time no *Rákhas* have been seen on the earth, in a palpable shape. The great Gosein, having then fully instructed *Sírí Jía* and *Phaksat* in all useful knowledge, placed them on the *Mújaí Sangra-bhúm* hill, and from them the present race of men are descended."

The Satao Gam's narrative—"The race of man having killed and roasted buffaloes and pigs, which they devoured, without offering up the prescribed portions in sacrifice to the gods, the Supreme Being, in his anger, sent an universal deluge, which covered the earth, and destroyed the whole race of man, with the exception of two men, called *Kung-litang* and *Kulíyang*, and their wives, whom He warned to take refuge on the top of the *Singra Bhum* Hill, which remained above the waters; from them the present race are descended. A brother and sister, belonging to a race superior to man, were also saved. The Supreme Being directed them to conceal themselves under a conical mound of earth, taking with them two cocks, and nine spikes of bamboo; the latter they were to stick through the sides of the mound, and pull them out one by one daily. They did so for eight days, but the cocks took no notice. On drawing out the ninth, the light appeared through, and the cocks crew, by which they knew that the waters had subsided. They then went out, and, as they were in search of fire, they encountered the old woman belonging to the Demon *Rákhas*, who endeavoured to seize them; they, however, effected their escape to the ninth heaven, where they were deified, and are sacrificed to by the *Singphos*, with cocks and pigs.

"The name of the brother is *Kai-jan*, and the sister *Giung*."

The Singpho seem from these narratives, each of which suggests the idea of a migration, to have encroached upon a population akin to themselves from the east.

They held, and hold, their own. When necessity compels, one of the Gams takes an increase of influence and power, and becomes the head, not of a village, but of a small confederacy.

Of the Singpho tribes we know the names of four; the Thengái, the Mayang, the Lubrang, and the Mírip (Miri, Mru, &c.). A Singpho in a state of dependence (we may call it domestic slavery) is called a Gúm Lao. A Gúm Lao may be, in all other respects, a true Singpho. He may be a poor man, who has sold himself to some richer countryman into bondage; either for life, or for a term of years. Sometimes, too, men earn a wife for themselves, even as Jacob earned Leah and Rachel; in which case they are incorporated with the family, and treated as members of it.

The law of succession is remarkable. The whole property is divided between two brothers—the eldest and the youngest. The eldest takes the land, the house, and the title; the youngest, the personal chattels, arms, implements, flocks, and herds. The intermediate take nothing at all, but remain with the families, attached to the head of it, as clansmen to a chief.

Polygamy is practised without restriction, and without any loss of caste to the children of foreign mothers, of which there are many. Since the Singpho area has been brought up to the Asam frontier, the inroads into that country have been numerous, and Asam slaves are frequent in the Singpho houses.

More important, however, are their relations to the Kaku. The Kaku religion is more or less Buddhist, and the chief object of their worship is Gautama. But, besides this, there is the god of the elements, Megh Duta, to whom they sacrifice buffaloes, hogs, and poultry; and, besides Megh Duta, there are the Ningshi, who may, possibly, be the most indigenous of their deities; Lares and Penates when domestic, elemental spirits when worshipped out-of-doors. To the Ningshi they hang up, in their houses, the sculls of buffaloes previously sacrificed. They dedicate, also, to the Ningshi such of their enemies as they may kill in battle. Of true anthropothysia, or the sacrifice of living human victims, I find no notice. The account I follow runs thus:—"They are in the habit of deifying any Singphos whom they may kill in action, during a fray with some other tribe or village, and of sacrificing them to the Penates."

Word for word, I hold that Kaku is Kuki. It is also Kakui, and Kakhyen, names which will appear again, when their ethnological relations will be considered. At present it is enough to say that the Kaku are mixed with the Singpho, and intermarry with them; forming an inferior but scarcely a servile population.

*The Jili.*—Of the Jili I only know that they are conterminous with the Singpho Proper, and that 70 per cent. of their language is Singpho, and 22 per cent. Garo. Add to this that it has decided Burmese affinities, and its transitional character becomes apparent.

| English. | Singpho. | Jili. | Aká. |
|---|---|---|---|
| *Man* | singpho | nsang | bangne |
| *Hair* | kara | kará | demuk |
| *Head* | bong | nggum | dumpa |
| *Ear* | na | kaná | nyárung |
| *Eye* | mi | njú | nyek |
| *Blood* | sai | tashai | oyí |
| *Bone* | nrang | khamráng | sala |
| *Foot* | lagong | takkhyai | lágá |
| *Hand* | letta | taphán | lák |
| *Sun* | jan | katsán | dahani |
| *Moon* | sita | satá | polo |
| *Star* | sigan | sakan | takar |
| *Fire* | wan | tavan | ummah |
| *Water* | ncin | mchin | issí |
| *Stone* | nlung | talóng | elung |
| *Tree* | phun | phún | sangná |
| *One* | aima | —— | —— |
| *Two* | nkhong | —— | —— |
| *Three* | masum | —— | —— |
| *Four* | meli | —— | —— |
| *Five* | manga | —— | —— |
| *Six* | kru | —— | —— |
| *Seven* | sinit | —— | —— |
| *Eight* | macat | —— | —— |
| *Nine* | tsekhu | —— | —— |
| *Ten* | si | —— | —— |

# CHAPTER VI.

## The Hill Tribes of Asam.—The Nagas.

THE valley of Asam is Indian, or Indianized. Not so the hills around it.

On the eastern frontier of the Mikir and Cachar comes a population rude and pagan; or, if not wholly pagan, with a *minimum* amount of Buddhism or Brahminism. The numerous tribes which compose it are on the boundary of the British dominions—some of them within it. Expeditions have been made by British officers against them. Like all pagans, however, they are fitter objects for the missionary than the soldier; and missionaries are finding their way to them. The fullest notice of their dialects is to be found in the American Oriental Society (vol. ii.), where specimens of no less than ten of their dialects are to be found. They fall into four groups.

(1.)

| English. | Namsang, &c. | Joboka, &c. |
|---|---|---|
| *Man* | minyan | mi |
| *Woman* | dehiek | tunaunu |
| *Head* | kho | khangra |
| *Hair* | kacho | kho |
| *Eye* | mit | mik |
| *Ear* | na | na |
| *Tooth* | pa | va |
| *Hand* | dak | chak |
| *Foot* | da | taha |
| *Sky* | rangtung | rangphum |
| *Sun* | san | ranghan |
| *Moon* | da | letlu |
| *Star* | merik | letsi |
| *Fire* | van | van |
| *Water* | jo | ti |

| English. | Namsang, &c. | Joboka, &c. |
|---|---|---|
| *Stone* | long | long |
| *One* | vanthe | tuta |
| *Two* | vanyi | anyi |
| *Three* | vanram | azam |
| *Four* | beli | ali |
| *Five* | banga | aga |
| *Six* | irok | azok |
| *Seven* | ingit | annat |
| *Eight* | isat | achat |
| *Nine* | ikhu | aku |
| *Ten* | ichi | ban |

(2.)

| English. | Mulung, &c. | Tablung, &c. |
|---|---|---|
| *One* | cha | cha |
| *Two* | ih | ih |
| *Three* | lem | lem |
| *Four* | pell | peli |
| *Five* | nga | nga |
| *Six* | vok | vok |
| *Seven* | niath | neth |
| *Eight* | thuth | thuth |
| *Nine* | .her | thu |
| *Ten* | pan | pan |

(3.)

| English. | Tengsa, &c. | Khari. |
|---|---|---|
| *One* | khatu | akhet |
| *Two* | annat | anne |
| *Three* | asam | asam |
| *Four* | phale | phali |
| *Five* | phungu | phanga |
| *Six* | thelok | tarok |
| *Seven* | thanyet | tani |
| *Eight* | thesep | sachet |
| *Nine* | thaku | taken |
| *Ten* | thelu | tarah |

(4.)

| English. | Angami. | Mozome Angami. |
|---|---|---|
| *One* | po | po |
| *Two* | kena | kane |
| *Three* | she | sus |
| *Four* | da | deh |
| *Five* | pengu | pangu |
| *Six* | soru | soru |
| *Seven* | thena | thene |
| *Eight* | thetha | thetha |
| *Nine* | theku | thaku |
| *Ten* | kerr | kurr |

The Naga houses differ from the Mikir; so does the Naga dress—or rather un-dress. From this they are supposed to have taken their name, which is anything but native. Indeed, it is not likely to be so. Few tribes so rude as these mountaineers have any general or collective name at all amongst themselves. Amongst themselves everything is particular or specific. Each tribe has its name, but the whole stock none. It is the neighbours who know them in their collective capacity. Now, in the languages of the plains, *nunga* equals *naked.* I do not, however, find that the Nagas are actually this: they have some clothing, though not much. It is, moreover, home-made; manufactured by the Naga women, dyed by them.

The name Naga, as we may easily believe, is, in general, foreign to the Nagas. There is one tribe, however, in North Cachar that so denominates itself. The Aroong Nagas call themselves what the neighbours call them.

In one respect they differ from the Mikir, Kukis and Cachar, with whom (in some portions of their area at least) they come in contact; and that notably. All the above-named tribes, though not migratory, are easily moved to a change of residence. They crop the ground around their settlements, and when it is exhausted go elsewhere. The Nagas crop the ground also, and exhaust it; but when, having done this, they find it necessary to make a fresh choice of ground, they go to a distance, cultivate their allotments, and never mind the trouble and labour of bringing the produce home. This is the sacrifice they make for the love of their old localities. The field is changed; the house remains where it was. Of Naga houses, some twenty, thirty, or one hundred constitute a village, the situation of which is generally on the tops of the hills. Can this extraordinary affection for particular spots be accounted for in an otherwise not over-active community? I think the suggestion of Stewart is correct—viz. that the habit of burying the dead near the houses promotes it. The Nagas inter their deceased relations at the very threshold of their homes, rolling a stone over the grave to mark the spot. The village streets are full of these rude memorials, some falling into neglect, but others fenced-in and ornamented with flowers.

When no blood has to be avenged the Naga is simple, social, and peaceful. His government is so pre-eminently patriarchal as to be no government at all. A quarrel, however, between two villages, or even between two families of the same village, leads to miserable results—blood for blood, treacherous surprises, cruel punishments.

The first deity of the Naga Pantheon is Semeo, the god of riches.

The next (perhaps) is the god of the harvest, or Kuchimpai.

The chief malignant deity is Rupiaba, a Cyclops, not only with one eye, but with that in the middle of his forehead, even as the eye of Polyphemus. But—

*Inter cœcos regnat luscus.* His assistant Kangniba, bad-tempered and malicious, is blind altogether. He must, however, be propitiated. And this can be done cheaply. A fowl is the sacrifice; but the sickliest and smallest of the roost will do. He can only feel what room it takes. So the crafty Nagas put the little bird in a big basket, and so deceive Kangniba the sightless.

The custom of the Genna is this. When certain occasions call for the preliminary rite, the whole village is closed. Work is suspended. The fires are put out. Eating and drinking, however, are believed to go on with more than usual vigour. A buffalo, or some animal, is sacrificed. When a fresh piece of jungle is cleared the ceremony of the Genna precedes ; and the fire used for the purpose is made by rubbing two pieces of wood together. The ordinary light of a household hearth would be improper.

| English. | Cachar. | Kuki. | Angami. | Mikir. |
|---|---|---|---|---|
| *Man* | subung | mi | ma | arleng |
| *Woman* | masainjoo | wamei | thenuma | arloso |
| *Head* | khoro | loo | uchu | iphu |
| *Eye* | ma | met | umhi | mek |
| *Ear* | kumao | bill | uneu | ino |
| *Nose* | gung | na | unheu | inokan |
| *Mouth* | khu | kum | ume | ingho |
| *Tooth* | hatai | ha | uhu | isso |
| *Hand* | yao | khutpang | ubiju | ripa |
| *Foot* | yapha | kengpang | uphi-ju | kengpak |
| *Sky* | nakhasu | vanpi | keruke | shineng |
| *Day* | saing | ni | ja | arni |
| *Sun* | saing | ni | naki | arni |
| *Moon* | daing | lha | thírr | cheklo |
| *Star* | hatri | ashi | themu | cheklo longsho |
| *Fire* | wai | mei | mi | me |
| *Water* | di | tui | zu | lang |
| *Stone* | lonthai | shong | keche | arlong |
| *Wood* | bon | thing | si | theng |
| *One* | masi | khut | po | hisi |
| *Two* | maguni | ni | kana | hini |
| *Three* | magtham | thum | se | kithom |
| *Four* | mabri | le | da | phili |
| *Five* | mabonga | nga | pengu | phanga |
| *Six* | mado | gup | shuru | therok |
| *Seven* | masni | suggi | thena | theroksi |
| *Eight* | majai | get | thata | nerkep |
| *Nine* | masku | ko | theku | sirkep |
| *Ten* | maji | som | kerr | [illegible] |

## CHAPTER VII.

The Burmese Group.—The Khumia and Kuki of Sylhet, Tipperah, and Chittagong.—The Old and New Kuki of Cachar.—The Mugs of Arakan.—Tribes of the Koladyn River.—Mhru, Kami, and Kumi.—Sak.—Shendu, or Heuma. — The Khen of the Yoma Range. — The Karien.

THE Naga dialects lead so decidedly to those of Munipúr, and the northern portions of the area now coming under notice, that the present chapter is, in many respects, their proper place. It was chiefly for the sake of the reader that they were separated. It was convenient to carry him round the great Asam valley as continuously as possible.

We have seen how it is bounded on the south. First come the Garo, then the Kasia, then the Jaintia Hills; then the occupancies of the Nagas in North Cachar, and Nowgong; then those of the Singpho, which take us up to the great bend of the Brahmaputra. Now all the native populations of all these localities, so far as they have already been enumerated, are, more or less, akin to the populations of the Burmese Empire; the Naga being somewhat less so than the rest.

South of the Nagas lies Munipúr and its dependencies; leading to Ava.

South of the Jaintia, Kasia, and Garo ranges lie the districts of Tipperah, Sylhet, and Chittagong, leading to Aracan.

In all these the population is equally Burmese. But it is not equally unmixed. The nearer we are to Hindostan, the greater the amount of foreign influences; the greater, too, the amount of Hindu blood. Sylhet, Tipperah, and Chittagong are like Asam—Indian, or Indianized.

*Khumia and Kuki.*—Khum means village; Khumia, a villager. The Khumia occupy the skirts, the Kuki the tops, of the hills. Except so far as the difference of level may develop differences in their mode of life, a Kuki is a Khumia, a Khumia a Kuki.

The Kuki, however, are, as may be expected, the ruder, and more truly pagan tribe; the creed being, nevertheless, tinctured with Indian elements. They "have an idea of "a future state, where they are rewarded or punished, ac-"cording to their merits in this world. They conceive "that nothing is more pleasing to the Deity, or more "certainly ensures future happiness, than destroying a "number of their enemies. The Supreme Being they "conceive to be omnipotent, and the Creator of the "World, and all that it contains. The term in their "language for the Supreme Being is Khogein Pootteeang. "They also worship an inferior deity under the name of "Sheem Sauk, to whom they address their prayers, as a "mediator with the Supreme Being, and as more imme-"diately interesting himself with the concerns of indi-"viduals. To the Supreme Being they offer, in sacrifice, "a gyal as being their most valued animal; while to "Sheem Sauk they sacrifice a goat only. In every "parah they have a rudely-formed figure of wood, of the "human shape, representing Sheem Sauk; it is generally "placed under a tree, and to it they offer up their prayers "before they set out on any excursion or enterprize, as "the Deity that controls and directs their actions and "destiny. Whenever, therefore, they return successful, "whether from the chase, or the attack of an enemy, they "religiously place before Sheem Sauk all the heads of the "slain, or of their game killed, as expressive of their de-

"votion, and to record their exploits. Each warrior has "his own particular pile of heads; and according to the "number it consists of, his character as a hunter and "warrior is established in the tribe. These piles are "sacred; and no man dares attempt to filch away his "neighbour's fame by stealing from them to add to his "own. They likewise worship the moon, as conceiving "it to influence their fortunes in some degree. And in "every house there is a particular post, consecrated to the "Deity, before which they always place a certain portion "of whatever food they are about to eat. In the month "of January they have a solemn sacrifice and festival in "honour of the Deity; when the inhabitants of several "neighbouring parahs (if on friendly terms) often unite, "and kill gyals, and all kinds of animals, on which they "feast; and dance, and drink together for several days. "They have no professed ministers of religion, but each "adores the Deity in such manner as he thinks proper. "They have no emblem, as of Sheem Sauk, to represent "the Supreme Being." (*Account of the Kookies, or Lunctas, by J. Macrae, Esq. Asiatic Res.*, vol. vii. 1801, p. 195.)

Such is the belief of the Kuki of Sylhet, Tipperah, and Chittagong, of whom the Kuki of Cachar are an offset.

The Kuki, who about sixty years ago came from the jungles of Tipperah to settle in Cachar, were, at first, in the same category with the Nagas, *i. e.* naked. In the course of time they ceased to deserve the name. They not only wear clothes now, but are skilful in the cultivation and weaving of cotton. They are well clothed and well fed; on a level with the Angami Nagas for physical strength, as also with the Kasia—these being the ablest-bodied of the frontagers of Asam.

In Cachar they are called the Old Kuki. They fall

into three divisions—the Rhángkúl, the Khelma, and the Betch, the first being the largest. The whole, however, are under 4000.

The Old Kuki of Cachar have a New Kuki to match. Both came from the south—both from the ruder parts of Tipperah and Chittagong. They came, however, as the name implies, at different times, and, as their language suggests, from different districts. The New Kuki form of speech is not always intelligible to an Old Kuki. Mr. Stewart saw one of the Khelma tribe as much puzzled with what a New Kuki was saying to him as he would have been with a perfect stranger. On the other hand, the Manipur dialects and the New Kuki are mutually intelligible. I do not think that the vocabularies verify this doctrine; either in the way of likeness or of difference. It may, nevertheless, be accurate.

It was the Lushai (Looshais) who caused the flight of the New Kuki into Cachar; the Lushai who inhabited the same parts only further to the south, the Lushai who spoke (and speak) a Kuki dialect, the Lushai against whom we had to protect the fugitives. In 1848-49 four Kuki tribes—the Thadon, the Shingshon, the Chúngsen, and the Lumgúm—driven from their native districts, poured themselves into Cachar, and were pursued by the Lushai. Three hundred men of the Sylhet Light Infantry Battalion, under Colonel Lister, were not long in coercing them. They drove them beyond the frontier, and returned to settle and protect the Kuki.

Some had settled themselves. Some, however, hung on the skirts of the Lushai, and only waited for the opportunity of being revenged on them. To prevent the chronic state of warfare that would have originated from this, Colonel Lister enlisted them as soldiers, officered by their own clansmen, but trained and disciplined according to English tactics. The measure succeeded. The Kuki soldiers are found to constitute excellent posts on the frontiers of both the Lushai and the Angami countries.

Of the fugitives some fixed themselves in Manipur, some in South Kachar, some in North.

The Lushai I hold the same population, as that which in the paper of Macrae's, just quoted, is called Luncta; a population scarcely differing from the ordinary Kuki, or rather, a population of ordinary Kuki under another name.

The best observer of the New Kukis credits them with clearer and more definite notions in the way of religion than any of the tribes of their neighbourhood. This is, perhaps, the actual fact. It may, however, be otherwise. The Kuki creed may simply be the one best known. It recognizes one deity, more important than the rest, whose name is Puthen. His passions are human; though, on the whole, he is benevolent, and is interested in the welfare and virtue of the Kuki family; perhaps in that of the world at large. He visits sin with sickness in this world; punishes it in a world beyond the grave. He is sometimes invoked in order that he may abate his own anger; sometimes that he may intercede with other deities. Sometimes animals are sacrificed to him.

The family of Puthen is large; though it is not certain that every one charged upon it is a true member. Ghumoishe, for instance, is doubtful. He is the deity who exercises the worst influence on mankind. He does a great deal of mischief, and delights in doing it; for his disposition is naturally malevolent. If he show himself to a Kuki, death ensues. If he inflict disease, the symptoms are of the worst sort. What, however, is his relation to Puthen? Some say that he is his illegitimate son. Some deny the paternity altogether.

Ghumoishe has a wife—and a very bad one too—whose name is Khuchom, and whose special delight is to inflict colic and pains in the stomach. It is no good praying to either of them. You may avert their wrath by sacrifices, but you will never get any positive services. You may obtain, too, the intercession of Puthen; but direct prayer in reliance of any amiability on the part of either Ghumoishe or Kuchom is useless. Hila, the daughter, is the Goddess of Poisons, or, at least, of indigestion. She can make viands otherwise edible poisonous, disturbing healthy stomachs by means of wholesome food. To keep her from mischief you must apply to Puthen.

Thus far Puthen may or may not be the father of a family; Ghumoishe's best claim being but a bastard one. With Nongjai and Thila the case is different. The former is the wife, the latter the son. Thila, without being absolutely malignant or diabolical, is harsh, ill-conditioned, and vindictive. His anger, however, can be averted by prayers and sacrifices; either at first-hand (in which case they are made direct to him) or mediately, through the intercession of Puthen or Nongjai.

If Thila has *his* faults, his wife has *hers*. Ghumnu is her name; a name which, even when you pray to Thila, it is not well to omit. She is pre-eminently sensitive on this point. When you pray to her husband, pray to her also. If you don't you may take a headache, a toothache, or some similar ailment.

Khomungnu is the household, Thingbulgna the forest, god. Then there are the gods with the compound names; names wherein Puthen simply means deity. Such are Tui Puthen the Water God, Thi Puthen the Iron God.

From the Pantheon to its priests is but a short step. The Thempu are initiated priests, skilful (in the case of god-sent diseases) to divine the offended deity, to point out the propitiations he expects, to conduct the propitiatory ceremonies. In a large Pantheon, whereof more than one member is mischievous, the office of a Thempu is a medical necessity. As often as disease occurs, his services are wanted. Necessary, however, as they are, they are not always to be obtained. The Thempu are not a caste. Novices from the people at large who choose to undergo the initiatory ordeal, may become Thempu. But so formidable is the initiation that few covet the honour. Indeed, so great is the fear—physical or superstitious—of its pains or dangers, that, in order to prevent the order from dying out, the rajahs have, on occasions, been obliged to coerce their unwilling subjects into the privilege of holding communion with the deities. The details of the initiation are unknown. One, however, of its formulas is a prayer of indemnity on the part of the neophyte. Should anything go wrong during the ceremony, let the punishment fall on his head—not on the heads of his teachers. Another known fact is the use of a mysterious language, unintelligible to the people at large. Judging from what we know elsewhere, it is, probably, a mixture of slang and archaism.

The details of the initiation are unknown. Not so, however, the professional practice of the Thempu. When a villager feels ill, he gets the Thempu to feel his pulse, and ask him certain questions concerning the place and time of the first ailment, the nature of his recent occupations. On this he meditates. He then names the offended god, and enjoins the necessary propitiation. The sacrifice may be a fowl; in which case the remedy is cheap. Or it may be a pig, a dog, or a goat; in which case there is an entertainment as well as an oblation. Or it may be a cow, or methin; in which case there is an expensive feast, and the remedy is as bad as the disease.

The Kuki country lies to the south of the Garo, Kasia, and Mikir areas or the hill-ranges of Garo, Jaintia, and Cachar, in Sylhet. Tipperah, and Chittagong.

Manipur lies to the south of the Naga districts, eastward of the Kuki area, and on the drainage of the Irawadi.

Of the frontier between the southern members of the group represented by the Nagas and the northern tribes of Manipur, I can give no account. It seems, however, that over and above the civilized and Buddhist occupants of the capital and the parts around, the phenomena which we have seen in the Naga districts repeat themselves. From the southern slope of the Patkoe range the feeders of the western branch of the Irawadi cut channels and fertilize valleys; the occupancies of rude tribes, whose dialects differ notably from each other. Eleven of these are known, through vocabularies; the percentage of proper Manipur words in each being as follows:—

| | |
|---|---|
| In the Songpu | 21 |
| ,, Kapwi | 41 |
| ,, Koreng | 18 |
| ,, Maram | 25 |
| ,, Champhung | 28 |
| ,, Luhuppa | 31 |
| ,, North Tankhul | 28 |
| ,, Middle ,, | 35 |
| ,, South ,, | 33 |
| ,, Khoibu | 40 |
| ,, Maring | 50 |

When we have said this, we have said nearly all we can say. The three Tankhul forms of speech are said to be all but mutually unintelligible. The Kapwi is a very small tribe. The Champhung consists of but thirty or forty families. The resemblance between the words Songpú and Singpho should be noticed. So should the re-appearance of the root *mr* in Maram and Maring. It has already appeared as Miri, and will do so again as Mru and Mrung. Luhuppa is very like Lhopa and (?) Lepcha. At any rate the terminations *-pa, -po, -pu,* are old acquaintances. Then there are the names for Manipur, some of which appear in the maps as Moitay and Kathi, or Kassay; which is Kasia.

East of Chittagong lies the Jo country; the language of which is neither more nor less than a rude dialect of the ordinary Burmese; the population being Burmese also.

The same is the case with the Mugs; Mug being the name by which the native population of the towns and villages of Arakan is designated. The Mugs amount to about six-tenths of the whole population; one-tenth being Burmese, and the remainder Hindu. The only town of importance is the capital. Some of the Mug villages lie but just above the level of the sea; others are on the sides, others on the tops, of hills. The early history of Arakan, so far as it may be dignified by that name, makes it an independent state, sometimes with Chittagong and Tipperah in subjection to it, sometimes with Chittagong and Tipperah separate.

The island of Ramri, Cheduba and Sandoway are parts of Arakan; Mug in languages, British in politics.

In the hill-country the type is changed, and instead of the comparatively-civilized Mug we get tribes like the Kuki and Naga. The best known of these are—

*The Tribes of the Koladyn River.*—The tribes of the Koladyn River form a convenient if not a strictly-natural group. The Koladyn being the chief river of Arakan, and Arakan being a British possession, the opportunities for collecting information have been favourable; nor have they been neglected. Of the names of tribes, and of specimens of tribes, we have no want; rather an *embarras de richesse*. There Buddhism, as a general rule, is partial and imperfect; partial as being found in some tribes only, imperfect as being strongly tinctured with the orginal Paganism when it is found. And of unmodified Paganism there is, probably, not a little. The forms of speech fall into strongly-marked dialects; in some, into separate languages; by which I mean that, in some cases, they may be mutually unintelligible. The government seems to be patriarchal during a time of peace, ducal during a time of war; ducal meaning that a tribe, or a confederacy of tribes, may find themselves, for the time, under the command of some general chief. That such occasions are by no means unfrequent, we infer from the history of certain sections of the population rather than from any direct account of their wars. The story of almost every tribe is the same. It came upon its present locality a few generations back, having originally dwelt elsewhere; somewhere northwards, somewhere to the south, somewhere to the east. It dispossessed certain earlier occupants. But these earlier occupants may, in their turn, be found in fragments, consisting of a single village, or of a few families. The form that the history (if so it may be called) of these marchings and countermarchings, of these fusions and amalgamations, of these encroachments and displacements assumes, is deserving of notice. Ask a Khyen how he came to be where he is, and he will answer that his ancestors came there as soldiers and invaders in some Burmese army long ago, that they remained on the spot, settled, propagated their kind, and left issue. Is this true? No. Is it a tradition? No. What is it? It is an inference. It is the narrator's mode of accounting for a phenomenon which he knows as a fact, but has not ethnology enough to explain. It is his mode of accounting for the likeness in language between himself and more powerful neighbours. Lest any one should condemn this as so much rationalism out of place, I will add that it is not in one place, nor in two, but in many that these accounts are to be found. We shall find them amongst the Shans, *mutatis mutandis*. Now there cannot well have been a succession of armies with a succession of stragglers who became colonists. More than this, the story is sometimes absurd. In one case it runs that the part which was left behind consisted of lazy or tired men who fell asleep, and stayed where they were, whilst the others kept awake and left them behind. Child's play this. Child's play, but still dignified by the name of tradition. Traditions do not grow on every tree. The Mring state that their ancestors were brought as captives from the Tipperah hills. This is more probable, since removals of this kind are commoner than armies leaving stragglers. At the same time it is not safe, even here, to believe more than this, viz. that the tribes who tell the story believe that they have congeners in the quarters where they lay its venue; their belief being *primâ facie* evidence of the fact.

Does any one believe this, viz. that one of the forms of tribute to one of the conquerors of one of the branches of the Khyens was the payment of a certain number of beautiful women? To avoid this the beautiful women tattooed themselves, so as to become ugly. This is why they are tattooed at the present time. So runs the tale. In reality, they are tattooed because they are savages. The narrative about the conqueror is their way of explaining it. Should you doubt this, turn to Mr. Turner's account of Tibet, where the same story repeats itself, *mutatis mutandis.* The women of a certain town were too handsome to be looked at with impunity; for, as their virtue was proportionately easy, the morals of the people suffered. So a sort of sumptuary law against an excess of good looks was enacted; from the date of which to the present time the women, whenever they go abroad, smear their faces with a dingy dirty-coloured oil and varnish, and succeed in concealing such natural charms as they might otherwise exhibit.

There is another class of inferences; for which, however, learned men in Calcutta and London are chiefly answerable. Some of the tribes are darker-skinned than others. The inference is that they have Indian blood in their veins. They may have this. The fact, however, should rest upon its proper evidence. I venture to guess that, in most cases where this darkness of complexion occurs, the soil will have more to do with it than any intercourse with the Hindus. There will be least of it on the hill-tops, less on the hill-sides, most of it in the swampy bottoms and hot jungles. At the same time, *some* Indian influences are actually at work.

The tribe which, most probably, is in the closest geographical contact with the Kuki of Chittagong is the

*Mrú, or Túng Mrú.*—The name is native. It is also Rukheng. It means in Rukheng, or the language of Arakan, over and above the particular tribes under notice, all the hill-men of the surrounding district; this being the high country between Arakan and Chittagong. That the Mrú are the same as the Mrúng, who deduce their origin from Tipperah, I have no doubt; though I doubt the origin. They were all parts of one and the same division. At the present moment, the Mrú are in low condition; fallen from their ancient, high estate. For at one time, a Mrú chief was chosen king of Arakan; and when the Rukheng conqueror invaded the country, the country was Mrú. However, at present, the Mrú are despised. Their number in Arakan amounts to about 2800. Their present occupancy is somewhat west of their older one. This was on the Upper Koladyn; whence they were expelled by—

*The Kami, or Kumi.*—The Kami or Kumi are themselves suffering from encroachments; gradually being driven westwards and southwards. They state that they once dwelt on the hills now held by the Khyens. What this means, however, is uncertain. The Khyens of a forthcoming section lie south of the Koladyn on the Yuma mountains. If these, then, were the men who displaced the Kami and Kumi, the Kami and the Kumi, when they moved upon the Mrú, moved northwards. But this need not have been the case. Khyen is a name given to more populations than one; and the very Mrú of the last noticed are sometimes called Khyen. If so, it may have been from one part of the Mrú country that the Kami and Kumi moved against another part. I do not give this as history; scarcely as speculation. I only give it as a sample of the complications of the subject.

Word for word, I consider the Kami and Kumi to be neither more nor less than the name of the Khumia of Chittagong. I also think that Mrú is Miri.

The Kami (Kumi) of British Arakan amount to 4129 souls.

*The Sak, or Thak.*—The Sak, or Thak, are a small tribe on the river Nauf.

| English. | Mrú. | Kúmi. | Kami. | Sak. |
|---|---|---|---|---|
| *Head* | lú | a-lú | a-lú | a-khú |
| *Hair* | s'hám | s'hám | a-s'hám | kú-mí |
| *Eye* | min | me | a-mí | a-mí |
| *Ear* | pa-rám | ka-nọ | a-ga-ná | a-ka-ná |
| *Tooth* | yun | he | a-fhá | a-*tha*-wá |
| *Mouth* | naur | li-boung | a-ma-ká | áng-sí |
| *Hand* | rút | ka | akú | ta-kú |
| *Foot* | khouk | khou | a-kho | a-tar |
| *Skin* | pí | pé | a-phú | mi-lak |
| *Blood* | wi | a-thí | a-thí | thé |
| *Bone* | a-hot | a-hú | a-hú | a-mrá |
| *One* | loung | há | ha | sú-war |
| *Two* | pré | nhú | ní | nein |
| *Three* | shún | túm | ka-tún | thin |
| *Four* | ta-lí | pa-lú | ma-lí | prí |
| *Five* | ta-ngá | pán | páng-ngá | ngá |
| *Six* | ta-rú | ta-rú | ta-ú | khyouk |
| *Seven* | ra-nhit | sa-rú | ṣa-ri | tha-ni |
| *Eight* | rí-yát | ta-yá | ka-yá | a-tseit |
| *Nine* | ta-kú | ta-kau | ta-ko | ta-fu |
| *Ten* | há | hau | ha-suh | si-su |
| *Sun* | ta-nin | ka-ni | ka-ní | sa-mi |
| *Moon* | pú-lá | hlo | lá | *that*-ta |
| *Star* | ki-rek | ka-si | a-shi | *tha*-geing-*thi* |
| *Fire* | má-i | mhá-i | má-i | bá-in |
| *Water* | tú-í | tú-í | tú-í | mi (?) |
| *Bird* | ta-wá | ta-wú | ka-vá | wa-si |
| *Fish* | dám | ngho | moí | pan-na |
| *Snake* | ta-ro-a | pú-wi | ma-khu-í | ka-pú |
| *Stone* | ta-whá | lún-s'houng | ka-lún | ta-lon |
| *Tree* | tsing-dúng | din-koung | a-kún | púng-páng |
| *Mountain* | shung | mo-i | ta-kun | ta-ko |
| *River* | au | ka-wú | ka-vá | pi-si |
| *Village* | kwá | a-váng | váng | thing |
| *House* | kín | úm | ín | kyín |
| *Egg* | diú | dín | du | wa-tí |
| *Horn* | anáng | ta-ki | at-ta-ki | a-rúng |
| *Man* | mrú | ku-mi | ka-mí | lú |

*The Heuma*, or *Shendu*.—In 21° 15′ N. L. the Meeyk-young falls into the Koladyn from the east. It, of course, arises on some higher level, and this higher level is the watershed between it and the drainage of the Manipur rivers; the Manipur rivers being on the system of the Irawadi. And this watershed is the range of the Yeomatoung hills, the occupancy of a population with a like name; the occupancy of the Shendu, or, as they call themselves, Heuma. The hill-ranges themselves are low at first, but they soon arise mass upon mass, and tier upon tier, with jungle along their skirts, and deep, narrow water-courses down their sides.

What we know of the Heuma is from Captain Tickell, whose informant was one of their Aben, or chiefs, named Lebbey. Lebbey's village was on the Khoon (Khyen?) frontier. Its name was Búkí, and it consisted of 350 houses. Further to the north-east lay the following villages.

| | Houses. |
|---|---|
| 2. Thubban . . . . . . | 400 |
| 3. Lalyang . . . . . . | 100 |
| 4. Tumbú . . . . . . | 100 |
| 5. Rúngfe . . . . . . | 50 |
| 6. Yanglyng . . . . . | 250 |
| 7. Húthe . . . . . . | 240 |

The numbers, here, are inordinately and improbably, high. I give them, however, as they stand.

In shooting elephants the Heuma use the trap-bow, or rather a pair of them, so set that a line pulls both triggers and shoots the huge animal on each side. The use of the musket is superseding that of the ruder and more native arms.

Men may marry two sisters at once, but not more; may not marry their stepmothers. This the Khumia *may* do. All property goes to the eldest son; provided he be unmarried. Should he have settled himself in life the property is divided amongst his brothers. Daughters get nothing: widows as little. They bury their dead.

They regard the sun and moon as deities, and sacrifice pigs and cattle to them at the beginning of the rainy season.

| English. | Heùma. |
|---|---|
| *Man* | che-pa |
| *Woman* | che-noung |
| *Village* | kù |
| *Hill* | klo |
| *Forest* | roley |
| *Stream* | pevu |
| *One* | mé-kha |
| *Two* | mé-ny |
| *Three* | mé-thao |
| *Four* | mé-pullee |
| *Five* | mé-pá |
| *Six* | mé-churru |
| *Seven* | mé-sharree |
| *Eight* | mé-charia |
| *Nine* | mé-chùkru |
| *Ten* | mé-hra |

*The Mowtu and Tantang.*—These are the names of certain tribes occupant of the country beyond the Heuma boundary, as taken from the Heumas. They, probably, belong to the Yo country.

*The Khyen.*—I believe that most of the rude tribes of the Arakan and Burmese mountains are called Khyen, or Kho, by some one or other. The Khyens, however, who are now about to be brought under notice, lie south of tribes already noticed, occupants, however, of the same range of hills. They fall into two divisions, divisions which we expect *à priori*. The Khyens of the lower levels are nearer the centres of the Burmese power, and more amenable to Burmese influences. They have, consequently, unlearned something of their original rudeness, and live a life of comparative quiet and inoffensiveness. They pay taxes. They are liable to be called upon for a quota of soldiers. In short, they are Burmese subjects.

Not so, however, the Khyens of the hills and hill-tops. They acknowledge no Burmese, no native, sovereign, but live a life of democratic or patriarchal simplicity; after the manner of the Abor, the Mishmi, and the other rude tribes of Asam, in small and distant villages.

At one time, they say, their ancestors were the occupants of the fertile plains of Ava and the rich alluvia of Pegu. But strangers came down upon them, and drove them both northwards and eastwards. At first they kept up the appearance of friendship, but afterwards threw off the mask of dependence, and comported themselves as the lords of the soil. It was "contrary," said they, "to the dictates of nature for two kings to reign, or for two populations to live together." So they deposed the Khyen king, and banished the most powerful chiefs. These, along with others, fled to the hill-country, and, for a while, kept up a semblance of a sovereignty and a royal family. But the members of it died out, and now they have no one but their little village chiefs, captains, patriarchs, elders, or whatever they may be called. So that the republican principles of the Abors and Bor Abors prevail amongst the Khyens also; carefully observed, jealously defended.

In their religious matters their liberty and equality is somewhat less than in their secular. The Passin is the head of the Khyen Church. He resides on a mountain by the side of a river, and by his descendants in the male and female line the office of prophet, soothsayer, or priest, is continued. Passins officiate at weddings and funerals; expound doubtful points of law and custom; are the conservators of the traditions; are the exorcists in cases of sickness.

One of the objects of the simple worship of the Khyens is a thick bushy tree, bearing a small berry, called subri, and under its branches they assemble at certain seasons, with all the members of their family, and with their cattle, feasting and making sacrifices of pigs and fowls; just the animals that so many other rude tribes are in the habit of offering.

Another object is the thunderbolt, or what passes for such. When a storm occurs they watch the lightning, see what it strikes, and if it strike a tree or building, or can be seen to touch the ground, wait anxiously for the weather to become calm, and then dig for the thunderbolt. They are unfortunate if something in the shape of a stone is not found, and when found supposed to have fallen with the lightning from heaven. It is thus invested with supernatural powers—has a hog and a bullock sacrificed to it—is delivered to the Passin, and kept as a talisman.

The souls of those who have acted well are transferred, after death, to the bodies of oxen or pigs; so that the Khyen creed admits of a rude kind of metempsychosis. Yet they kill their cattle without compunction, but not without the leave of the Passin.

When any one dies a feast is held over his remains. If they be those of a poor man they are buried in the immediate neighbourhood. The burial-places of the wealthy, however, are the two holy mountains of Keyúngnatin, or Yehantoung, to one of which they are conveyed, even when the death takes place at a distance. From the summit of Yehantoung "the whole world can be seen." Near the tombs there constructed a hut is erected, in which a certain number of people are left for the purpose of defending it against malignant spirits. Over the remains a rude carving converts a log into a likeness of the deceased.

Marriages are just so far religious ceremonies that the Passin is consulted about them. The contracting parties ask his sanction. When given, the bridegroom sends presents to the parents of the bride. A feast follows.

But the bride may prove unfaithful; if so, the adulterer is fined, and the wife is restored to former favour, her reputation being as good as before.

With unmarried women the custom is different. Simple discovery is fined. The birth of a child creates a claim on the part of the female. The offender must either marry her or pay the fine over again, and take the child—the fine being a bullock. The damsel starts *de novo* as a damsel.

Unless she be the daughter of a chief, when the fine is tripled, other things being as before; but three bullocks instead of one being the mulct.

Cousins marry, but not brothers and sisters. Intercourse, however, between even these is possible and contemplated. The fine for it is a bullock to the father.

A divorce costs a bullock.

A murder costs ninety rupees; the valuation being got at by the following process. The murderer is seized by the village chief, who requires of him either three of his friends to be given up to the family of the sufferer, or thirty rupees a man for each. But he may escape. If so, he must be given up, or war ensues unless he be given up. Given up, he is committed to slavery; bloodshed for offences being forbidden.

Ordinary theft is not much punished. The stealing,

however, of corn is a felony. The culprit must either become a slave, or pay thirty rupees, *i. e.* the third of the price of a murder.

We know beforehand what the medical practice is. The thunderstone in the hands of the Passin will cure everything.

Are the Khyen hospitable? We are inclined to say yes; because hospitality is the virtue of rude tribes. We answer, however, *à priori*. So few strangers traverse their land that a precedent in the way of the reception of one is unknown. Those, however, from whom our authority (Mr. Trant) got his information, said that if a foreigner fell in with one of their nation "he would not be ill-treated; but that they did not remember such a visit having taken place."

Cotton grows in the Khyen country, and of cotton the Khyens spin enough to dress with and export. Black seems their favourite colour, or no colour. A black cloth, striped with red and white, is thrown across their shoulders. A black cloth goes round their loins. A black jacket is used occasionally. The women wear a black petticoat reaching the knees. Are they handsome? More so than they make themselves; for a story runs in the Khyen country that when it was overrun and conquered, the marauders, who drove the aborigines to the mountains, imposed upon them a tribute, in default of which they seized the most beautiful of their women, and laid them out before their king, who chose the flower of them for his harem. To save the race from extermination the men persuaded the maids to disfigure themselves. So they cheerfully complied, and tattooed their faces. We have seen something of this kind already in Tibet. It is as true as the story in the so-called Anglo-Saxon history of Edwin and Elgiva. In the natural history, however, of personal disfiguration, a natural history which beginning with the Pagan populations of these parts, and, after going through the nose-pieces and labrets of America, the leg bandages of Africa, the tooth operations of Australia, and ending with the ear-rings of London and Paris, is of importance. It is a sign of rudeness. It is a practice which the women keep up longer than the men. It is a barbarity which they explain away. As a general rule the explanation admits that what passes for an ornament is, in reality, a deformation.

The true and typical Khyen is the independent mountaineer of the central districts. Of the Khyen of the lower country some, as aforesaid, are under Ava. It may be added that others (those in the west and (?) south) are British subjects. All are described as a simple agricultural people; quiet, if left alone, though not without their quarrels amongst each other.

More important, more widely spread, and, to a certain extent, better known than the Khyen, but, like them, a wild, and (generally speaking) an independent race, are—

*The Karen.*—The ordinary way of speaking of the Karen is to call them a population of remarkable geographical extent, both vertically (or from north to south) and horizontally (or from east to west). In fact they are said not only to be found within the British, Burmese, Siamese, and Chinese frontiers, but to extend from 28° to 10° N. L., if not further. Then there are the Karens of the *eastern* part of Siam, separated from those of the Burmese, or western, frontier by the Valley of the Menam, and the great bulk of the native T'hay population. In Bowring's map this eastern branch occupies the parts about Korat, and the foot of the mountains that form the watershed of the Mekhong.

Now the evidence that these are true Karen is unsatisfactory. It consists of the name only. Different populations, however, may easily have borne it, especially as it is not native. Nevertheless, the fact may be what the term suggests, and true Karen may have an actual existence in Eastern Siam.

The evidence to the Karen of the north is better. Mr. Cross met with one from the Chinese province of Yunnan, from whom he obtained the following information. The Karen of the parts between the Burmese empire and China, although some of them lie within the Chinese province of Yunnan, are, upon the whole, independent, though not beyond the reach of attacks from the Burmese. They are agricultural, with a patriarchal constitution. They reckon themselves by families, not by cities or villages, nor yet by tribes. Each family occupies but one house, and this house may be large enough to contain three or four hundred individuals. Its floor is raised some six or seven feet above the ground, the material being bamboo, with mattings and a thatch of palm-leaf. Strong posts sunk firmly into the ground constitute its foundation and frame-work. A raised floor made of beams is attached to them, with a matting of split bamboo laid over them. The whole house—a court or covered village rather than a house—is divided into compartments, one for eating, one for sleeping, and so on, with a regular household discipline to match.

The continuity of the Karen area has yet to be proved; the only ascertained facts being that there are Karen in Tenasserim, and in *Western* Siam, that there are Karen in Yunnan, and that there is a population called by one or more of its neighbours by the name Karen in *Eastern* Siam.

With such a distribution as this we need not wonder if we find a multiplicity of doctrines respecting the origin of these remarkable tribes. Did they move from north to south, from east to west, or *vice versâ*? The primary divisions into which fall the hypotheses concerning their occupancies in Tenasserim are two—one embracing the opinion that they are aboriginal to their present seat, the other the notion that they are immigrants.

The reasoning which makes them aboriginal is based upon the so-called traditions of the Burmese and the Môn. That of the Burmese certainly makes them older than themselves; more than which cannot be said. But the Burmese themselves are of no great antiquity, either in Pegu or Tenasserim; on the contrary, they are intruders and strangers.

The Môn, however, of Pegu are actually, to all appearance, the aborigines of the land. Nevertheless, they, also, are said to make the Karen older occupants than themselves. I do not, however, find this in the actual narrative; which runs thus—when Gautama visited Pegu, Tavoy and Mergui were inhabited only by Nats and Belú. Now a Nat is simply a spirit or demon; whilst Belú means wild man. Why should these Belú have been Karen? The fact is, that nothing is commoner than a notice like the one under consideration when either Buddhism or Brahminism is introduced into a Pagan country. "All," say the historians, "was either devilish or barbarous." The Belú may have been unconverted Môn as easily as aught else. At the same time a statement of Mr. Mason's should be made known. He infers that the Belú were Karen, from the fact of an island south of Martaban being called, when first discovered, Belu, and at the same time exclusively occupied by Karen. *Valeat quantum.* The Karen may easily have been in Pegu, Tavoy, Mergui, and Tenasserim in the sixteenth century. Add to this, that any wild tribe may have so been called, and that Pulo (suspiciously like Belú) is the Malay for an island, and that the men who furnished the early navigators with the name of the island in question, were, very probably, Malays. Still, the question is an open one.

The doctrine that they are immigrants takes two forms. In one, they come from India—the evidence on this point being unsatisfactory. It may be found in Mr. Cross's paper.

Far, far more probable is the second doctrine, which derives them from the north. They "crossed" says one of their so-called traditions, "a river of sand." So the Chinese, and probably others, call the desert to the north of the Laos country. They did this before the Shans came into Zimmay; a statement which will be explained in the next chapter.

Their language points to the north. It is decidedly Burmese, with notable Singhpo affinities.

The Karen on and within the British frontier are the only ones described in detail. They are called the Red Karen from their dress; not from their complexion as has, occasionally, been stated. Such, at least, is the express statement of Mr. Cross, an American Baptist Missionary, to whom we owe a full account of them. The same authority connects the Kakhyen with them; a population to be noticed hereafter.

Some of the tribes are Buddhists; but the two described by Mr. Cross, which may fairly serve as a sample of the stock, are Pagan. They are the Sgau and the Pgho; the former being the more primitive. They are also smaller and lighter-coloured than the Pgho.

The term Karen is Burmese; the native name being *Pgha-Kenyau* = *man*.

Word for word Karen is Khyen; and so it is often sounded in Burmese.

Their government is patriarchal; but, besides the elders,

two classes of men exercise considerable influence, the *bukho* and the *wí*.

The *bukho* is, perhaps, a priest rather than a prophet, inasmuch as he rarely commits himself to the prediction of future events, but lin its himself to the regulation of feasts, and the conduct of ceremonials. He is also the great authority for magical formulæ. He is also, more or less, a physician.

The *wí*, on the other hand, is a shaman, capable of foretelling events, recalling departed spirits, seeing embodied ghosts—only, however, when in a particular physical condition. Of course, this is one of excitement into which the *wí* is capable, like the Sibyls and Pythonesses of classical antiquity, of working himself. He writhes his limbs, he twists his features, he foams at the mouth, he affects an epilepsy. When the fit, real or affected, is over, he delivers his prophecy. Many of these relate to the political condition of his countrymen, and (amongst the dependent Karens) predict a deliverance from the grinding tyranny of the Avans. Some of these either suit, or are fitted to, the political and missionary advent of the English and Americans. I give the following *wí* prophecies as I find them in Mr. Cross.

"If deliverance come by water, rejoice, for you will be able to take breath.

"When the Karens have cleared the horn-bill city happiness will arrive.

"When the Karens and white foreigners shall fight happiness will arrive.

"The white foreigners possess the word of God, and will one day restore it to the Karens who have lost it."

The local, personal, and individual *genii* of the Karens are called *kelah*. Every object has one. If the rice-crop look unpromising, the rice *kelah* is supposed to be away, and has to be called back. "O come, rice kelah, come. Come to the field. Come to the rice. With seed of each gender come. Come from the river Kho. Come from the river Kaw. Come from the place where they meet. Come from the West. Come from the East. From the crop of the bird, from the maw of the ape, from the throat of the elephant, come. Come from the sources of rivers and their mouths. Come from the country of the Shan and Burman. From the distant kingdoms come. From all granaries come. O rice kelah, come to the rice."

The human kelah may leave the body and wander about, in which case it has to be recalled. For this there are various formulæ, which it is the business of the wí to understand.

This is a sketch of the first series of ideas attached to the word kelah. There is a second. The kelah is supposed to possess seven existences, seven yet one. The first seeks to render the person to whom it is attached mad, the second produces reckless folly, the third shamelessness, the fourth anger, and so with the rest of our bad passions and infirmities. All kelahs of this kind are essentially bad.

The moral principle, however, is *thah.* It is thah rather than kelah, through whom we sin or act rightly. The following distinction is from a native Karen, though not (I imagine) an untaught one. "When we sin, or commit any offence, it is the *thah,* soul, which sins; and again, when we perform any good action, it is the *thah.* Praiseworthiness, or blame-worthiness, is attributed to the *thah* alone. By some the *kelah* is represented as the inner man, and with others the inner man is the *thah.* When the eyes are shut and in sleep, the reflective organs are awake and active. This is sometimes attributed to the *kelah.* Hence the *kelah* is the author of dreams."

Another deity, spirit, demon, or genius is named Tso. Tso resides in the upper part of the human head, and as long as he keeps his seat no kelah can do any mischief. But, in order for him to do so, the head must be attended to. Its owner must attire it handsomely. He must keep it, too, out of the reach of danger; away from roots that may fall in, or from trees that may break down.

The Karen vampires, goblins, *et hoc genus omne*, are named *kephoo*, *theret* (*theret thekah*), *tahmus* (or *tahkas*), *plupho* and *sekhahs*.

The kephoo is more of a raw-head-and-bloody-bones than aught else. It is the stomach of a wizard which prowls about at night to devour the kelahs of men in the shape of a human head and entrails.

The therets, too, feed on kelahs; the therets being the souls of men untimely slain, and malefactors, not wicked enough for a place in the seat of punishment, nor yet good enough for the full fruition of the region of bliss. Hence they wander about on earth.

The tahmus and tahkas are the spirits of pre-eminently wicked men, tyrants and Burmese most especially. After leaving the body they invest themselves with the forms of the lower animals; sometimes with that of a gigantic human being.

The sekhah is the spirit of an infant, or of an old man in his second childhood. Or it may be that of one forsaken by his *tso*.

Plu-pho is the occupant of Plu, which is Hades. In Plu the dead alive renew their earthy occupations. To go to Plu is the normal state for the deceased. To become a kephoo, theret, tahmus, tahkas, or sekhah is irregular and exceptional. The king of Plu is named Cootay or Theedo. He "holds his dominion in the country of *Plu*. When he comes to call our *kelahs*, our bodies die, and we become the inhabitants of *Plu*, and enter the dominions of *Cootay*. When he has called men, and they are under his dominion, if they by their endeavours please him, or are good, they are in due time dismissed to the region above, or heaven. But, on the contrary, if they are wicked, such as strike their fathers and mothers, they are delivered into the hands of the king of hell, and punished by being cast into hell."

Hell is called Lerah. It has two divisions, the Lerah of the milder, and the Lerah of the severer inflictions.

The tah-*nahs* or *nahs* (word for word the *nat* of the Burmese, &c.) are invisible beings, capable of taking the forms of animals, and endowed with a theret's appetite for kelahs. Some are worse, and more malignant than the others. The king of the more fiend-like nats is Mukauli.

Then there are the deities of the elements and atmospheric phenomena, the kelipho who create the winds with their fans, the tah-yumu, who cause eclipses, the cuda and laupho presiding over seasons. The dry season and the wet season fight for victory, each in its turn winning or losing.

The mukhas are worshipped with offerings. Though they are more gracious than malevolent, it is as well to keep on terms with them. Besides this there is a natural feeling of affection and respect for them, since they are the parents and ancestors of the Karens who have ascended into the upper regions, where they live under a king, in towns and cities. They are the creators of the present generation. The work that the mukhas themselves do is good; that of their king bad. He is too busy to allow himself time; so that the individuals which he sends into the world are lame, or ill-formed. The mukhas that preside over marriage take care the blood of the two producing parties is properly commingled.

Phíbí Yau sits on some lonely stump and watches the livelong day over the ears of corn as they ripen. She fills the granary, and is one of the best loved and the most beneficent deities of the Karen Pantheon.

A mother behaved herself so cruelly towards her daughters that they died; whereupon the mother repented of her harshness, and betook herself to a wí. The wí called to him first the spirit of the younger daughter, and entreated it to prevail upon the elder one to return. So they returned. But the mother kept on with the cruel usage that had before killed them, and, when they had died, again called upon the wí. This second time the younger daughter alone could be prevailed on. Nevertheless, she is cruelly treated for the third time. After this she retires to the world of shades, never more to be tempted by either the invocations of a wí or the ephemeral contrition of a cruel mother.

In revivifying the dead the wí operates upon, and through, the living; his first step being to catch the spirit of some person alive and to divert it to the dead one. The Karen thus robbed of his animating principle sickens and dies. But as he can be revived by a similar process inflicted upon some one else, his death is only temporary. Some one is killed off (ex-animated so to say) in order to restore him to life; and so they go on, ex-animating and re-animating, *ad infinitum*.

The wís are the chief poets of the Karens.

So much for the true and undoubted points of Karen paganism. The following extracts savour so much of a perverted Christianity, possibly introduced by some of the early Roman Catholic missionaries to Ava or Siam, that

I give them separate. I give them, however, in full and as I find them.

The name of the supreme deity is Ywah. The traditions concerning him run as follows:

"God is immutable, eternal. He was from the beginning of the world." "He is everlasting, and existed at the beginning of the world." "He existed in the beginning of time. The life of God is endless. Generations cannot measure his existence." "God is complete and good, and through endless generations will never die." Again, "God is omnipotent, but we have not believed him. God created man anciently. He has a perfect knowledge of all things to the present time." "The earth is the footstool of God, and heaven his seat. He sees all things, and we are not hid from his sight. He is not far from us, but in our midst"—showing that God was believed to be a spirit. More particular allusion to the specific work of the creation, and an almost exact resemblance to the Scripture history of it, is found in other traditions. "He created man, and of what did he form him? He created man at first from the earth, and finished the work of creation. He created woman, and of what did he form her? He took a rib from the man and created the woman." Again, "He created spirit or life. How did he create spirit? Father God said: 'I love these my son and daughter. I will bestow my life upon them.' He took a particle of his life, and breathed it into their nostrils, and they came to life and were men." "Thus God created man. God made food and drink, rice, fire and water, cattle, elephants, and birds." *

The evil deity is Nauk'plau; male or female as the case may be.

* Mr. Mason's translation.

"Nauk'plau at the beginning was just,
But afterwards transgressed the word of God.
Nauk'plau at the first was divine,
But afterwards broke the word of God.
God drove him out and lashed him from his place:
He tempted the holy daughter of God.
God lashed him with whips from his presence;
He deceived God's son and daughter."

The account goes on as follows. "Pa Ywah, our father God, spoke and said: 'My son and my daughter, I shall make for you a garden, and in the garden will be seven different kinds of trees, bearing seven different kinds of fruit. But among the seven different kinds of fruit there will be one which it is not good for you to eat. Do not eat of it. If you eat of it, sickness, old age and death will come upon you. Eat not of it. Consider, everything which I have created, all, I give to you. Select to eat and drink whatever you desire. Once in seven days I shall come to visit you. Hearken to all I command you, and take heed to what I say. Do not forget me. Worhip me each morning and evening as they return.'

"After this, Mukaulee" (the devil under another name, but the name principally in use to designate that being) "came and asked them: 'Why are you here?' 'Our father God placed us here.' 'What do you here find to eat?' asked the devil. To that they replied: 'Our father God has created for us food and drink, and our food is more abundant than we can eat.' The devil said to them: 'Permit me to see your food,' and the husband and wife both conducted him away to show it to him. The devil followed them to the garden, and they showed him the fruit and said: 'This is sweet, this is sour, this bitter, this astringent, this delicious, this pungent, this savoury. But this tree we do not know. Whether it is sour or sweet, we know not. Our father God commanded us, in reference to this tree: "You shall not eat of it. If you eat of it," said he to us, "you shall surely die;" and we have not eaten of it; and whether it is sour or sweet, we know not.' Then the devil said: 'Not so, my children. Your father God has no regard for you. The tree of which the fruit is most delicious and the sweetest, more delicious and sweeter than any other—he commands you not to eat of it. Not only is the fruit of this tree delicious and sweet, but if you eat the fruit you will become divine, and will ascend to heaven or enter the lower parts of the earth at pleasure; and will be able to fly. Your God has no love for you, and does not wish to make your lot agreeable. I am not like your God. Your God is unjust and envious. But I am just and not envious. I love you, and tell you all things. Your father God does not love you, and does not tell you all things. If you do not believe me, do not take the fruit. But if you will each of you take of it and eat, you will know.' The man replied: 'Our father God commanded us not to eat the fruit of this tree, and we will not eat it.' So saying, he arose and left the place. The woman, on the contrary, listened to the words of the devil, and was slightly pleased with what he said. Upon this the devil renewed his attempts, and at length she yielded to his varied solicitations, and raised her eyes upon him and said: 'Do you say that, if we eat, we shall be able to fly?' The devil replied: 'My son and my daughter, it is purely from my great love for you that I have spoken to you.' Then the woman took of the fruit, bit and ate. Upon which the devil laughed and said: 'My daughter, you have well and readily listened thus far to my words, but I will again speak. Go to your husband, and give him of the fruit to eat; and say thus to him: "I have eaten the fruit, and it is exceedingly delicious." Thus say to him, and, if he refuses to eat, you must entice till he eats. You have already eaten, and if you die you will die alone. If you become divine, you will become so alone.' As the devil said to her the woman did, and enticed her husband as he directed her. She repeated her enticements until finally he yielded to her, and took the fruit from the hand of his wife and ate it. When this was done, and her husband had eaten the fruit, she went and told the devil, and said to him: 'My husband has eaten the fruit.' Whereupon the devil laughed excessively, and said: 'Now, my son and my daughter, you have well done in listening to me.'

"But again, on the morrow after the day in which they had eaten the fruit, Ywah [Jehovah] came to visit them. But they no longer followed God, and met his coming with their songs and their hymns of joy. God came to them, and asked of them: 'The tree of which I said ye should not eat, have ye eaten of it? I commanded you. Why have you eaten of it?' But they were afraid to return any answer to God; and he cursed them and said: 'That which I commanded you, you have not heeded nor obeyed. The fruit of which I said: "It is not good to eat, eat it not," ye have eaten. You have disobeyed, and have eaten it. And now, old age, sickness and death shall come upon you. But it shall be in this way. Some of you shall sicken and recover, and some shall die. There shall be those among you who shall die after the life of a single day. There shall be those who shall live two days and die, three days and die. There shall be those among you who shall die in their youth—virgins and young men shall die. Women shall die when but half their births are finished, and others shall die when their bearing is passed. There shall be some among you who shall die when their locks are white, and others shall die when old age has come upon them.' Thus God commanded and cursed them, and God ascended up from them." *

The following lines give us the additional fact that it was in the form of a dragon that Nauk'plau effected his temptation.

> "Ywah in the beginning commanded,
> But Nauk'plau came to destroy.
> Ywah at the first commanded,
> Nauk'plau maliciously deceived unto death.
> The woman E-u and the man Thay-nai—
> The malicious fiend enviously looked upon them.
> Both the woman E-u and the man Thay-nai
> The dragon regarded with hatred.
> The great dragon deceived the woman E-u,
> And what was it that he said to her?
> The great dragon deceived them unto death,
> And what was it that he did?
> The great dragon took the yellow fruit of the tree,
> And gave it to Ywah's holy daughter.
> The great dragon took the white fruit of the tree,
> And gave it to Ywah's son and daughter to eat.
> They kept not every word of Ywah,
> Nauk'plau deceived them. They died.
> They kept not each one the word of Ywah,
> Then he deceived and beguiled them unto death.
> They transgressed the words of Ywah,
> Ywah turned his back and forsook them.
> After they had broken the commands of Ywah,
> Ywah turned his back upon them and left them."

Then follows an allusion to a flood.

"Anciently, when the earth was deluged with water, two brothers, finding themselves in difficulty, got on a raft. The waters rose and rose till they reached to heaven; when, seeing a mango tree hanging down, the younger brother climbed upon it and ate, but the waters suddenly falling left him in the tree.* . . ."

* Mr. Mason's translation.

"Men had at first one father and mother, but, because they did not love each other, they separated. After their separation they did not know each other, and their language became different, and they became enemies to each other and fought."

> "The Karens were the elder brother;
> They obtained all the words of God.
> They did not believe all the words of God,
> And became enemies to each other.
> Because they disbelieved God,
> Their language divided.
> God gave them commands,
> But they did not believe him,
> And divisions ensued."*

That the presence of missionaries, whose teaching might touch the Karen, is by no means a gratuitous assumption will be seen by the sequel.

*The Thoung-thú.*—If the Thoung-thú, a population of the Karen frontier be not actually Karen, it is one which, in language, at least, is closely allied.

| English. | Sgau. | Pgho. | Thoung-thoo. |
|---|---|---|---|
| *Sun* | mu | mü | mu |
| *Moon* | lá | lá | lu |
| *Star* | tshá' | shá' | hsa |
| *Fire* | mé'u | mé' | may |
| *Water* | thi | thi | htí |
| *Bird* | thó' | thő' | á-wa |
| *Fish* | nyá' | yá' | lita |
| *Snake* | gu | wgü | h'm |
| *Stone* | lu | lón | lung |
| *Tree* | thé' | thén' | thing-mu |
| *Mountain* | ka-tsű | khó'-lon | koung |
| *River* | thi-kló | thi-kló' | nhrong |
| *Village* | tha-wo | ta-wűn | dung |
| *House* | hi | yén | sam |
| *Egg* | di' | di' | de |
| *Horn* | ku-nu | nón- | nung |
| *Man* | pó-khwá | phá' | lan |

* Mr. Mason's translation.

| English. | Sgau. | Pgho. | Thoung-thoo. |
|---|---|---|---|
| *Head* | khó' | khó' | katu |
| *Hair* | khó-thu | khó-thu | tu-lu |
| *Eye* | me | me | may |
| *Ear* | ná | na | nau |
| *Tooth* | me | thwa | ta-gna |
| *Mouth* | thá-khó | nó | proung |
| *Hand* | tshü | tshu' | su |
| *Foot* | kho | khán' | khan |
| *Skin* | phi | phí | phro |
| *Blood* | thwi | tshü thwi | thway |
| *Bone* | ghi | ghwi | htsot |
| *One* | ta | ka du | ta |
| *Two* | khi | ni | ne |
| *Three* | thu | thün | thung |
| *Four* | lwi | li | leet |
| *Five* | ye | yei | ngat |
| *Six* | ghu | ghü | ther |
| *Seven* | nwi | nwi | nwot |
| *Eight* | ghó | ghó | that |
| *Nine* | khwi | khwi | koot |
| *Ten* | ta-tshi | ka-tshi | tah-sí |

Such is the notice of those members of the Burmese family with which the ethnologist most especially concerns himself, such the rude tribes of the hill and forest, always more important than the comparatively civilized men of the town or city; because they more truly exhibit humanity in its older and more primitive forms. Physical conformations, so long as the physical conditions of soil, climate, aliment and the like, remain the same, alter (if at all) but slowly. The same is the case with language. Religious beliefs, however, may be not only changed within the course of a few generations, but, when changed, modify the numerous characteristics that accompany them. It is as rare for one of the literate religions (by which I mean Christianity, Judaism, Mahometanism, the Parsi creed, Brahminism, and Buddhism) to be introduced into a country without carrying with it the alphabet by which its ritual is embodied, as it is for an alphabet to find its way into a country without a creed to attend it. Hence, the loss of a system of paganism is the gain of a literature; or, if not of an actual literature, of the means of creating one. When a population has arrived at this period of its development, foreign influences become rife and common, and actions and reactions take place between it and its neighbours. When this has gone on beyond a certain time, nine-tenths of the individualities of the primitive populations are abolished. Small and independent streams meet in one large plain and the wide expanse of a lake is the result of their confluence. Small and independent families become united to large and dominant nations; losing their characteristics; merged into uniformity.

As surely as rivers find their way to the sea will the Khyen and Kuki, the Karen and Luncta, become something not only different from their present selves, but something similar to one of the ruling populations. Let them lose a single characteristic, and the fusion begins. Let them lose them all, and it is complete. Let the characteristics be numerous, and the process of fusion will be slow. Let them be few, and it will be speedy. Most of the tribes under notice have nothing to lose but their pagan creed before they become ordinary Burmese; a little ruder, perhaps, than their fellows of Ava and Umerapura, but still ordinary Burmese. This is the case if Buddhism be the religion to which they become converts. That such, however, will be the case universally is, by no means, certain. Asam is Hindú, so is Sylhet, Tipperah, and Chittagong. Here are points whence Brahminism may diffuse itself; as it has done, as it will do. Munipúr is Brahminic in its creed; with an alphabet directly from the Devangari of India; and Munipúr, with much of its original rudeness remaining, is still in the category of

Arakan, Tipperah, and Ava itself—a civilized state. But much of its original rudeness remains. So it does elsewhere. So it does in Ava itself. Side by side with Buddhism, and (if we prefer the expression) underlying it, the worship of Nats, or Spirits, is to be found in the very metropolis itself, in the palace of the king—

"—— manent vestigia ruris."

Such is the case with Ava. Such the case with Siam. Such the case with China; old as its Buddhism, older as its philosophy is believed to be. Such the case with France and England—with all the world. In even the most purified creeds the last sparks of the original paganism have yet to die out.

That the alphabet, without being exactly that of either Southern India, or the neighbouring countries of Pegu, Siam, Laos, and Kambojia, belongs to the same class with all these, and is of Indian origin, is what we expect from the fact of the religion being Buddhist. The same applies to the language of the Scriptures. It is a learned tongue, the Pali; the same as that of Siam, Ceylon, and the Buddh countries in general. The native language, however, has its secular literature, lyrical, historical, and dramatic; no composition being of any high antiquity, and none of any notable merit. There are songs for lyrics; a mixture of pantomime and dialogue (more or less extempore) for a drama; a Buddhist chronology, and a short period of trustworthy narrative for a history. When does this begin? In the mind of the present writer very little earlier than the time of the first European visitors.

Then there are the laws; full of cruel and degrading punishments, even as the laws of Siam and China. And, then, there is the ceremonial—full of degrading obeisances and absurd circumlocutions. There is one set of words for equals, one for inferiors, one for superiors; even as there is in Siam, Java, and elsewhere. A difference between the language of politeness and rudeness exists everywhere. The phenomenon of a court dialect, as contrasted with the dialect of ordinary life, exhibits itself in the greatest prominence in the south-east of Asia.

The character of the Burmese drama, in respect to its decency or indecency, is a matter upon which there are two opinions. It has found defenders. The presumptions, however, are against its purity, the fact of a given writer having seen or heard nothing improper in a given number of performances being of no great weight against a single statement in evidence of indecorum.

The general character of the population has not been given in very favourable terms. Allowance, however, must be made for the class with which our embassies have come in contact. Residents of towns, and the official classes, are never safe representatives of a nation. The character of the rural population is probably that of the pagan tribes out of the like whereof they originated. Now these form a class that generally gets its due (and over-due) meed of praise. Where the mode of living is simple, there is no want of either courage or energy. Simplicity of living, however, is the exception rather than the rule with any one who can indulge in sensualities. The stimulants are those of the neighbouring populations, opium, bang, and the betel nut. The Burmese tattoo themselves, and they are, perhaps, (after certain Turks,) the most civilized men and women that do so.

It was in the middle of the last century that the Burmese power developed itself into that of a leading nation, and the hero of its development was the adventurer Alompra, the founder of the present dynasty. What Sivaji was *to* the Mahrattas, Alompra was to the Burmese. In the direction of Asam, in the direction of China, in the direction of Kambojia, Alompra conquered. This means that he annexed portions of territory from Munipúr on the north, and from Siam on the east. He also conquered Arakan and Pegu; since ceded, along with the Tenasserim districts, to Great Britain. The rule of the Burmese over the tributary populations is said to be hard and grinding.

A minute knowledge of the history of the countries of the Transgangetic Peninsula in general is necessary to enable us to fix, with any degree of accuracy, the relations of Ava to its neighbours as a military power. Its people seem to be warlike and brave, and to make good soldiers. Under Alompra the prestige was in their favour. Yet the very fact of Alompra being the conqueror he was, and the sudden development of the Burmese power, suggests the likelihood of the military history having once been different. And such was the case. The prominent place held by Ava, at the present moment, seems to have been held by no less than three other states in turn, Tipperah, Munipúr, and Pegu; all now on the low level of third or fourth-rate powers. The relative strengths, too, of Ava and Siam have been different; and Siam has at times been more superior than equal. When the T'hay populations come under notice, it will be seen that several petty districts, whose ethnological and geographical relations are Siamese, are subject to Ava. The Burmese call these the Shan part of their empire; and if the present work, instead of being ethnological, were political, the Shan states would find their place in the present notice. As it is, they will come before us in the next.

| English. | Burmese. | Rukheng. | Khyen. |
|---|---|---|---|
| *Man* | lu | youkkya | padau |
| *Women* | mairima | mingma | notau |

| English. | Burmese. | Rukheng. | Khyen. |
|---|---|---|---|
| *Head* | k'haung | yaung | lu |
| *Eye* | myitsi | myitsi | myik |
| *Mouth* | n'hok | kandwen | kako |
| *Sun* | na | ni | k'hu-n'hi |
| *Moon* | la | la | klau |
| *Star* | ke'nekkat | kre | ashe |
| *Sky* | moh | kaungkan | ane |
| *Fire* | mih | mi | mia |
| *Water* | re | ri | tui |
| *River* | myit | mrik | lik |
| *Sea* | pengle | panle | panlai |
| *Stone* | kyauk | kyauk | long |
| *Mountain* | toung | toung | song |
| *One* | tit | taik | pa-hat |
| *Two* | n'hit | n'haik | pa-n'hi |
| *Three* | thon | thong | pa-thong |
| *Four* | le | le | l'hi |
| *Five* | nga | na | n'hau |
| *Six* | k'hyauk | khrauk | s'houk |
| *Seven* | k'how-n'hit | k'hu-naik | shi |
| *Eight* | s'hit | s'hit | s'hat |
| *Nine* | ko | ko | ko |
| *Ten* | tase | tase | ho |

There is another family besides that to which the Shans belong, which, though other than Burmese, has its representatives in Ava. This is the Môn. Môn is the native name of the indigenæ of Pegu. The Burmese call them Talieng. The Siamese appellation is Mingmôn; apparently the native names in a state of composition. In the early Portuguese notices a still more composite form appears, and we hear of the ancient empire of Kalamenham, supposed to have been founded by the Pandalús of Môn or Pegu. Notwithstanding the recent annexation, some Môn are still Burmese subjects. They will be briefly noticed in the sequel.

## CHAPTER VIII.

The T'hay, or Siamese group.—The Khamti.—The Shans.—The Laos.—The Siamese Proper.

IT seems as if all our ethnology were centred in Asam; so numerous have been the notices of the different populations which occupy the mountain-ranges of its margin. We have already given a long list—Changlo Bhots, Akas, Doflas, Abors, Bor Abors, Miris, Mishmis, Singhpos, Muttuks, Jilis, Nagas, Mikirs, Kukis, Kasias, Borros, and Garos. *Necdum finitus Orestes.* There is still an addition to be made to the frontage. At the eastern extremity, on the Mishimi, and Singhpo frontier, dwell the Khamti; far north as 27° or 28° N. L.

*The Khamti.*—It is the Siamese stock to which the Khamti belong. The Siamese are Khamti, the Khamti Siamese. The Khamti and Siamese belong not only to the same stock, but, in speech at least, to the same division of it. Between the language as it prevails on the frontier of Asam, and the language as it is spoken at Bankok, the difference is simply that which exists between the English of Somersetshire and the English of Aberdeen. In Brown's tables ninety-eight per cent. of the words are identical. Such a fact as this is worthy of notice, because it exemplifies what may be called the *vertical* direction of a language, *i. e.* a direction from north to south as opposed to one from east to west. The Khamti creed and alphabet are Siamese; indeed, the whole population seems to be but a northern branch of a division of the T'hay group which has already been alluded to as—

*The Shan.*—I have little doubt but that Shan is a political, rather than an ethnological, term. It means a man of the T'hay stock who is a subject of, or tributary to the Burmese empire. Cross the frontier, and get into the Siamese dominions, and the name no longer prevails. Yet the population is essentially the same. So are the political relations. As certain petty chiefs are to the central government at Ava, so are certain petty chiefs to that of the metropolis of Siam. The authorities, however, of Bankok do not call them Shan, but Laos. Laos states are Shan, and Shan states are Laos, *mutatis nominibus.* If Shan, they are Burmese; if Laos, Siamese; in each case they are T'hay.

The Shans of the Burmese empire remind us of what we found in Bultistan. They fall into so many small states. What shall we call them? Kingdoms? Principalities? Rajahships? We cannot, perhaps, do better than take the local and national title of the chiefs, Tsawbwa, and talk of so many Tsawbwaships. The Shan Tsawbwaships are hereditary in certain families; but nothing more. The individual who takes one is appointed at Umerapura. It is only necessary that he belong to the right family. Doing this, he has a *locus standi*—nothing more. If the Tsawbwa be, in a small way, an Augustus, the Einshe Mon is a sort of Cæsar. He is the Tsawbwa *designatus*—a Prince of Wales to a King of Great Britain and Ireland. When he comes to his full honours he keeps a kind of court, and resides in a palace at his capital. Perhaps he builds, or patronizes the theatre, after the fashion of the small German potentates. At any rate, Captain Yule writes that the Tsawbwas appear in greater contrast to their subjects in the way of blood and its concomitant refinement than do the rulers of Ava, where there is little distinction of the kind. Good. Better, however, the statement that their domestic administration is really paternal, or as near an approach to it as any sovereign administration can be. More definite, too, the statement of Macleod, that the particular Tsawbwa of Kiang Tung was a fine, blind, old, noble gentleman. More definite, too, a comparison between a Shan Tsawbwa and the Hebrew patriarch, Boaz. In harvest-time the chiefs and their followers move into the fields, reside there in temporary sheds, and superintend the getting-in of the crops. The particular example is from the Zimmay states; but it very probably is Burmese also. At any rate, it is T'hay.

The number of the Shan Tsawbwaships, according to Captain Yule, is twelve; of which seven are on the west, five on the east of the Salwen. The further they are from Burma Proper, the more uncertain is their allegiance. Neither is their frontage a matter of unimportance. China has influence on the Chinese side, as we expect; besides which three of them are dangerously near the independent Red Karen. The nearest of these is Mobyé; and the Red Karen have so encroached upon its area as to have left the unhappy Tsawbwa little more than his dilapidated capital; a capital, which, in '37, contained no more than fifty-six houses. He sent to Ava for assistance; but in vain. So now he pays tribute, or black mail, to the Karen, barbarians and pagans as they are.

The next state of Mokmó does the same; at least to a great extent. The town of Mokmó contains about 350 houses.

Nyúng-yuwé, with a metropolis of about 150, and a population in all, of about 1000 houses, has been more flourishing than it is now; the Karen having done the mischief. So that of the Shan states of the east, there are three that are less exclusively Burmese than the heading of our notice suggests. Amongst the inhabitants of the valley Nyúng-yuwé is a colony of settlers whose traditions and language connect them with Tavoy. The traditions, however, are vague. They were to the effect that it was the ancient monarch Narapati-tsítsú who brought them; the date of Narapati-tsítsú being fixed by Crawfurd in the twelfth century. A town called Thatúng, on the frontier of the Karen, to whom it pays tribute, is of similar origin; at any rate, its inhabitants are from the west. The great king Nauratha-men-zau led them from a town of the same name in Martaban. I doubt whether this be a tradition. I think it is more likely to be a mere inference from the identity of name. Most traditions are only inferences of this kind in disguise. Again, I am by no means satisfied as to the historical existence of Narapati-tsítsú.

Conterminous with Nyúng-yuwé is the district of Myelat. It is under no Tsawbwa at all, but pays its revenue direct to the king.

Moné comes next. Of all the Shan states this is the most important. It is the one, too, in which the Burmese influence is strongest; indeed, it is the seat of the Burmese presidency, and the occupancy of many Burmese families. It extends to both sides of the Salwen; and is the largest of all the Shan capitals, a town about 2000 feet above the level of the sea, with as many as 8000 souls.

Of Legya and T'heinné I only give the names; remarking that, for area, T'heinné is the largest of the Shan Tsawbwaships, although not the most populous.

Mormeit and Túng-bain are in the predicament of Myelat, *i. e.* they are districts without any recognized Tsawbwa.

Beyond the Salwen to the north is either a single state,

or a confederacy of two—Kaingma-Maingmaing. It is but little known, and is believed to be in closer relations to China than Ava. The nature of this relation is made intelligible by the state of—

Maing-leng-gyé, which pays tribute annually to Ava, and triennially to China. It seems to be divided into petty chieftaincies, which practise private war against each other. The Lawa area lies in or on the frontier of Maing-leng-gyé.

Kiang-hung lies on both sides of the Mekhong, or Kambojia River. It sends tribute to Ava once in three years. In other respects it is Chinese; produces tea; is occasionally placed within the limits of the Chinese province of Yunnan in our maps; has the wild tribes of the Kakui on its frontier; and is divided into as many as twelve petty and subordinate Tsawbwaships, which quarrel amongst themselves, and practise private war as in Maing-leng-gyé.

With Kiang-tung and Kiang-khen the list of Shan states ends. It ends because we cross from Burma to Siam.

*The Laos, &c.*—On crossing the frontier we reach Zimmay, also spelt Chang Mai, and Xieng Mai. It is easily found, even in an indifferent map. It lies on the Menam between 19° and 22° N. L.; due north of Siam Proper, due west of the Burmese frontier.

A small territory, with a capital of about 12,000 inhabitants, is dependent upon Zimmay, and seems to have followed its fortunes. It is named Laphun. Another district, Lakhon, is (perhaps) in the same category.

The metropolis of Zimmay bears the same name as the kingdom itself. Standing at the foot of a high mountain, and rising from a wide plain, it contains a population of 50,000 inhabitants. On the top of the mountain is a print of Buddha's foot; a print which invests the hilltop with an atmosphere of sacro-sanctitude. It helps, too, to fill the city with talapoins; whose lives are said to be none of the purest. Then there is a large body of men from Siam, who have run in debt in their own country, and chosen a residence in another. I mention this to show that the Laos are anything but barbarians. The country is but little known, and, in the maps, seems destitute of inhabitants, and beyond the pale of civilization. Such, however, is not the case. The differences between them and the T'hay are, probably, less than those between the English and the Scotch. The language of the two is identical; the Buddhist creed is common to Bankok and Zimmay; probably the self-same form of it. The Laos, however, are the poorer population. Many of them visit Bankok in quest of work; where they have a good name, not only as labourers, but as musicians. Not a little praise has been bestowed upon the Laos songs and airs. On the other hand, debtors and other offenders (as aforesaid) from Siam find a refuge in Zimmay. Money is scarce. Salt the chief article of barter.

The history of Laos, if known in detail, would be of equal interest with that of Siam Proper. In the first place it is probable that, as the T'hay migration followed the course of the Menam, it was from Laos that the lower portions of the river were colonized. Secondly, Laos has been, at one time, an independent kingdom; and not only that, but, in all probability, the chief of the T'hay states. In its alphabet it still shows signs of having derived its Buddhism from a separate source. The Laos letters are less like the Siamese than is the language. The Laos letters are Kambojian rather than Siamese.

Between Zimmay and Bankok there are upwards of thirty waterfalls. This is a bar to navigation; helping to isolate the Laos, and to separate their civilization from that of the Siamese. They can make but little use of boats. When the valley of the Menam is cleared, it is all forest and mountain. This makes the elephant the chief beast of burden. In no part of the world are elephants used more exclusively than at Zimmay. Rice is the chief grain. The natives eat it. They distil it. They get intoxicated, very intoxicated, off the result of the distillation. They are good Buddhists withal; the town being full of pagodas. In 1843 a missionary tour was made by Mr. Grandjean. In Zimmay he was tolerated: in Laphun and Lakhon insulted.

Due west of Zimmay lies Nan, with its capital, Muang Nan, with a population of 60,000 (?), and, south of Nan, Phre, with Muang Phre (15,000 inhabitants) for its metropolis.

To the south-east lie Muang Loon, a small, and Muang Phre Bang, a large, state. It lies, not on the Menam, but on the Mekhong, on the frontier of Kambojia, with a capital of 80,000 (?) inhabitants. It just recognizes the sovereignty of Siam.

Of Phre Khiail, and Suvan-naphum we know little beyond the name. Korat, in the midst of a rude population, manufactures sugar, and works copper-mines. It is the capital of a district of about 60,000 souls. The Karen of Eastern Siam are placed in the neighbourhood of Korat.

In claiming for the Laos a civilization akin to that of the proper T'hay, I restrict the statement to the populations of the central portions of the Laos area, to the valley (perhaps the very bank) of the Menam and its feeders. Neither do I extend it to the northern frontier of the area so denominated, on the high lands in the direction of the Menam's head waters.

The Laos of the west are called Thaung Khao, or White Bellies, because they do not do what is done by the

Thaung Dari, or Black Bellies. The Thaung Dari, or Black Bellies of the east, tattoo themselves, the abdominal region more especially, and that with a black indelible ink. Hence the name. As the White Bellies are said to pay little respect to their idols and talapoins, we must suppose that there is some Buddhism amongst them—some, though not much. Their "character approaches that of the Chinese, and it would not be difficult to convert them to Christianity."

The Thaung Dari are more like the Siamese in temper, more bigoted to their Buddhism, less likely to be amenable to missionary influences. Their Buddhism, however, is imperfect; their native superstitions numerous.

Of the Laos superstitions, other than Buddhist, we know thus much: that certain genii and demons are, in reality, more respected than the Buddhist idols. The *Phi-phrai*, or wood-demons, are especially feared. Penetrate into the recesses of their forests, and you may never be heard of again. It is doubly dangerous to do so during the night. Your fate may be to be taken away from the earth altogether, and transported to an enchanted land, full of illusions, where you may live for years and years. At the end, however, of a certain time you escape from these supernatural scenes, shake off the magic influence, and find yourself at your own door-step, as altered as Rip Van Winkle; so altered that neither wife nor child shall recognize you. Sometimes these same *Phi-phrai* smite the trespasser on their grounds with fever.

The *Phi-lok*—the bugbears or bogies of Laos—delight in frightening men and women at the turnings of roads, and in sequestered parts of the forest. At night they haunt the neighbourhood of houses and gardens, making strange noises, putting on strange shapes.

The *Phi-pob* are gluttons. When one person wishes to

injure another he bribes a sorcerer to invoke a *Phi-pob,* who enters the body of the victim, feeds upon his intestines, and so kills him.

The *Thevada* are the tutelary deities who protect the hut, and watch over the family. They are more good than bad in the way of temper; yet require conciliation. They must be treated well, or the rice crop will fail, the family sicken, the undertaking fail. To gratify them do thus:—erect at one end of the hut a small pyramid, and attach to it some loose cotton threads. Let these blow into the house, and the *Thevada* will enter along with them. For the *Thevada* sits at the top of the pyramid, which is a good place for a look-out. From the top of the pyramid the *Thevada* keeps watch and ward against serpents and tigers, against *Phi-loks* and *Phi-pobs.* Every family recognizes his presence; and honours him with an altar, on which are presented to him wax-candles, scented woods, arrack, and rice—rice steaming hot. This is put for him every morning, and every evening. He does not eat it all; not always any part of it. It is the fragrant steam which he loves to inhale. He is jovial in his tastes, but jealous; unwilling to share the house with a guest. A stranger in a Laos house, after three days' reception, is often requested to depart for fear of offending the *Thevadi.*

*The T'hay of the Chinese Province of Yunnan.*—Some members of the T'hay family are to be found within the limits of the Chinese empire, in the province of Yunnan. It is needless to say that we know nothing about them. They are most likely Shans, or Laos, more or less modified by Chinese influences.

*The Siamese Proper.*—These are the occupants of the lower part of the Menam, a river which is T'hay or Siamese, in the same way that the Nile is Ægyptian. The occupancy of the Menam, as far as its course is known, is wholly, or almost wholly, T'hay; and it is on the alluvial soil of the Delta of the Menam that the T'hay civilization attains its chief development. As the tribes descended the stream they found a richer soil, a warmer climate, and access to the sea. The Laos people are less rude than the tribes to the north; the Siamese more refined than the Laos. The present metropolis is Bankok; but when Siam was first visited, Ayuthia, higher up the river, was the capital.

Founded in the fourteenth century (1351), it was abandoned in the eighteenth (1751), when it was devastated by the Burmese, and Bankok became the royal residence. Mandelsloe visited it about 1640, and described it. The king's palace was a town of itself. The temples, with gilt steeples, amounted to 300. 400,000 inhabitants dwelt within its impregnable walls; three leagues in circumference. Of these only the outlines remain. A new city has arisen near the old, but with curtailed proportions, containing, perhaps, some 40,000 inhabitants. The king visits it once a year; but his palace is meanly built of teak and bamboo. One sacred edifice of great height, half spire, half pyramid, represents its ancient glories.

That the stream of population ran from north to south is probable; other facts, besides the ordinary presumptions, favouring this view. One of these is the opinion of the Siamese themselves, who look upon the Laosas the older people. Another will be suggested in the sequel, when the languages of Pegu and Kambojia have been noticed.

The differences between the Burmese of Ava, and the Siamese of Bankok lie within narrow limits; the chief difference being that of language. No dialect of the T'hay is intelligible, or anything like intelligible, to a Burmese. The alphabets, too, differ, though in a less degree. The Buddhist creed and the Pali ritual are common to both. The Siamese cultus is, perhaps, somewhat the more priestly of the two. The Siamese habits may be somewhat more maritime and commercial. The contact with foreigners may, perhaps, be greater in Bankok than in Umerapura. The details of their dress and ceremonial may differ. Upon the whole, however, the essentials of their civilization are the same on both sides. Some writers have described the Siamese as having more than a Burmese share of the Chinese physiognomy and frame; which may or may not be the case. The chief difference, as aforesaid, lies in the language.

The Laos alphabet slightly differs from that of the Siamese Proper; more, perhaps, than does the language, which is spoken with remarkable uniformity over the whole T'hay area. From this I infer that the spread of the T'hay population is recent. Practically speaking, the Siamese Proper, the Laos, the Shan dialects, and the Khamti, so far, at least, as they are known, are one. Such being the case (philologically speaking) the T'hay is the only member of its group, the only genus of its order.

| English. | Khamti. | Laos. | Siamese. |
|---|---|---|---|
| *Man* | kun | khōn | khōn |
| *Hair* | phom | phom | phom |
| *Head* | ho | ho | hoa |
| *Ear* | pu | pu | pu |
| *Eye* | ta | ta | ta |
| *Blood* | lüt | leut | leut |
| *Bone* | nuk | duk | kaduk' |
| *Foot* | tin | tin | tin |
| *Hand* | mü | mü | mü |
| *Tooth* | khui | khiau | khiau |
| *Sun* | wan | kangwan | tawan |
| *Moon* | lün | deun | tawan |
| *Star* | nau | lau | dau |
| *Fire* | fai | fai | fai |
| *Water* | nam | nam | nam |
| *Stone* | pin | pin | pin |
| *Tree* | tun | ton | ton |

| English. | Khamti. | Laos. | Siamese. |
|---|---|---|---|
| *One* | nüng | nüng | nüng |
| *Two* | song | song | song |
| *Three* | sam | sam | sam |
| *Four* | si | si | si |
| *Five* | ha | ha | ha |
| *Six* | hok | hok | hok |
| *Seven* | tset | tset | chet |
| *Eight* | pet | pet | pet |
| *Nine* | kau | kau | kau |
| *Ten* | sip | sip | sip |

There is more foreign blood in Siam than in Ava. In the port of Chantaburi, the Chinese and Cochinchinese form a notable portion of the population. In the town of Meklong, containing 10,000 inhabitants, more than half are Chinese. Bongplasoi, a large fishing-town, is chiefly Chinese. Paklat is a colony of nearly 7000 men from Pegu. The Chinese generally marry Siamese women. Of Portuguese half-bloods there are many. Of French and Dutch blood there may be a little. Then there are the Malays and Kambojians of the frontier. The chief foreigners, however, are the Chinese. Pallegoix' table, based upon calculations which can scarcely be called satisfactory, gives us the following population. Whatever else it may do it shows the supposed number of the Chinese, and the vast proportion they bear to the natives.

| | |
|---|---|
| Siamese Proper | 1,900,000 |
| Laos | 1,000,000 |
| Chinese | 1,500,000 |
| Malays | 1,000,000 |
| Kambojians | 500,000 |
| Môn (from Pegu) | 50,000 |
| Karen, Khong, &c. | 50,000 |
| Total | 6,000,000 |

Like the Burmese, the Siamese have encroached on their neighbours. There has been a T'hay conquest of Asam. Kambojia pays tribute to both Siam and Cochinchina. In the Malay Peninsula, Ligore, Kedah, Patani, Perak, Kalantan, and Tringanu are, more or less, directly or indirectly, under Siamese control.

Of trustworthy history, in Siam there is but little. It may possibly begin about the middle of the fourteenth century, when the southern capital Ayuthia was founded. It pretends, of course, to a fabulous antiquity; the antiquity of a Buddhist chronology. Wars with Burmah, Pegu, and Kambojia, are what we expect and find.

The drama is, perhaps, inferior to that of Ava; the lyrical poetry superior.

Of the T'hay music Craufurd speaks favourably; as favourably, at least, as he speaks of anything belonging to the T'hay country. Bowring does the same in respect to the native airs of the Laos. Laos, or T'hay,—be it which it may—the music has commanded the approbation of more than one writer.

The sacred literature of the Siamese is in the Pali language; the profane in the native tongue. In this it is chiefly metrical; the epistolary correspondence of ordinary life being the only kind of composition which runs in prose. The songs are in verse; the romances in verse; the histories (such as they are) are in verse. The dramatic performances are based on the romances, the actors being left to improvise the dialogue. The Pali language is generelly called Bá-li or Pá-li, sometimes Pasa Makata or the language of Magadha (Bhasa Magadha). There is a medical literature, of some extent, in it.

Descending from the romance and drama to the lower amusements, we find the game of chess amongst the foremost; then puzzles with numbers, then gambling and betting on cock-fights, and other contests stranger still. A T'hay boy will fight crickets against each other, and bet on the result. Then there is a fighting fish; small in size, irritable in temper. He will attack a fellow fish with violence, bristling up his fins, and showing all the signs of ferocity and anger that so mute an animal can show. He will fight his own self, when seen in a looking-glass, and butt his own head against his own shadow. On fish-fights, then, the Siamese will bet; and they will ruin themselves at lotteries. All this is Chinese, Burmese, and Malay as well.

Like the Japanese they enjoy and support pugilism. They join, too, in boat-races; and delight in jugglery and feats of leger-de-main. Children take pleasure in flying kites, in which there is nothing remarkable. It is only remarkable that adults should find pleasure in the same childish amusement. So, however, they do; and when certain winds prevail kite-fighting comes into season. You entangle your kite with the kite of your adversary, pull it down if you can, and then, if you can, get possession of it.

As both the T'hay and Laos populations are Buddhist little is known concerning the original paganism of the Siamese. Of superstitions there is abundance. I do not, however, say that any are sufficiently characteristic to demand a lengthened notice. There are official astrologers attached to the Court. There is a class of *modu* or wise men who give professional advice on the ordinary transactions and events of common life. There is a widely-diffused belief in amulets and talismans; there is a strong partiality for odd numbers (much to the prejudice of anything like the decimal system); there is a trust in philtres and love-potions; there is a dread of ghosts and evil genii;

there are strange doctrines connected with the gestation of women, and the birth of children; and, lastly, there are traces of alchemy; Arabic, no doubt, in origin. La Loubere mentions one king of Siam who wasted 2,000,000 (*sic*) horses in pursuit of the philosopher's stone.

Magicians have the credit of being able to reduce buffaloes to the size of peas; which peas, after some unfortunate individual has swallowed them, resume their original dimensions, and burst his abdomen.

Servitude exists in several forms. There is the *corvée*, or forced labour. Every Siamese is bound to give one-third of the year to the service of the kings. Debtors, like the *nexi* of republican Rome, have to work out the extinction of their debts. Prisoners of war are absolute slaves. The language itself is ceremonial, or, rather, I should say, that there is a ceremonial language; a language of humility on one side and assumption on the other; but this we shall see more in Java and elsewhere. In China the left hand is more honourable than the right; in Siam the right more honourable than the left.

As the Nile is to Ægypt, so is the Menam to Siam. It rises to a certain height before it does its due amount of good. It sinks after attaining it; or else does mischief. The swelling of its waters is the occasion of more than one periodical ceremony.

The spirits of their ancestors are special objects of reverence to the Siamese; and it is probable that in the fact of their being so we find one of the most characteristic elements of their original paganism.

The following is a Siamese ode:—

Human tortures are not one hundred thousandth part equal to the tortures of hell. He who is condemned by the king of hell will be exceedingly tormented.

His sin has brought to pass that he is confined in a dungeon, bound to a beam with chains, on account of his sin in unmercifully binding others with fetters. They stretch him on a heated iron plate, they stab him, his blood gushes forth, he dies, and is born again seven times in a day.

Being greedy of rewards he feared not to lie; his tongue shall be plucked out, because he judged unjustly.

When he was a judge, he threatened in order to extort money; having received which, he held false evidence to be good. Assuredly, after his death he shall not escape punishment; he did not pronounce judgment in accordance with the truth, therefore will he be subject to hell for a long period.

He was blind to crime, he despised the institutions of his ancestors; therefore dogs as large as elephants, vultures, and ravens shall devour his flesh.

The Siamese described by one of themselves, a T'hay Theophrastus, are men of this fashion:—

"In the kingdom of Siam things are thus—viz. The men and women have a form three cubits high (near five feet), it is generally agreed. Some are three cubits and a half. A few are four cubits high; about one man in a hundred.

"Another subject: The complexion of the Siamese is a dark red. Some are light, and they dress after the same fashion. There is no difference. They make their teeth black. They take the shell of a cocoa-nut, burn it and take the dark water which comes out of the shell, and rub it on the teeth. The teeth then become black. When the teeth are well blacked, they take quicklime and spread it on seri leaf to be rolled up—they take of betel-nut quartered, one part, and one seri leaf rolled up—they take tobacco rolled up into a little ball about the size of the poot-sa fruit, and all being prepared, they eat, taking the tobacco to wipe the teeth, and then depositing it between the lips and the teeth.

"Again: the men smoke cigars. These cigars they carry behind their ears. Sometimes they also carry there a scented preparation made with fragrant materials, and a wreath of flowers is worn on the wrist.

"Another subject: They preserve long finger nails. In the cool of the day they take hog's fat to anoint the nails every day. Another way is to take garlic to rub their nails, and the nails grow long very fast. They take care not to do any labour—they only work at toys. The man who keeps long finger-nails is a man of dissolute mind. His heart rides on primpness. He is the master of harlots, and desires to deck himself that he may stroll about and talk with the women that they may have a heart to love him. Men of this sort are few; amongst a hundred men there will be about forty.

"At the present time, persons fancy pa-nungs. Chintz pleases the men. Pa-nungs of alternate stripes of silk and gold thread—also chintz of a very small blue and white check, with gold thread borders, please the women.

"Again: the men are pleased with pa-homs of black silk crape sewed together, and also silk crape of various colours If they wish them to make merit, they can. If they wish to go anywhere, they can. If they wish to go to transact business, they can. If they wish to visit their relations, they can, according as they fancy a pa-nung or a pa-hom. There is no particular choice. A pa-nung either dark, red, purple, green, light, or scarlet, with a silk crape pa-hom, answers the same purpose. There is particular choice.

"Again: the men cut off their hair. The shape of their hair is like the lotus flower. They cut that hair all around even with the edge of the hair on the forehead. On the back part they shave off the whole. They preserve only what is on the crown.

"As to the women, they cut their hair like the open lotus flower. They never shave, but preserve the whole head, trimming the forehead, the eyebrows, and a small circle around the crown. And they bore their ears, and insert ear-rings made with pure gold, set with jewels and precious stones. They also wear finger-rings made with pure gold, and set in the same way. They also wear guards—the strands being made with pure gold. They have girdles; they have sashes; they have bracelets; and their pa-homs are the same with those of the men mentioned above.

"Another subject: The children (male and female) dress themselves, preserving a bunch of hair—some, about a cubit and a half long—others, only a cubit; and it is twisted up into a knot on the crown of the head, and a gold pin is stuck in, and a wreath encircles the knot. Bracelets encircle the wrists, and anklets encircle the ankles. Strands of large beads also encircle the wrists. A large badge is worn about the neck. A double guard is worn athwart the breast, having a roll of gold sheeting strung on it. The pa-nung being put on, they take a girdle and gird the loins.

"All these ornaments which are used in the dress of children are made with pure gold, set with jewels, precious stones, and jet; different ones being made in different ways.

"Another subject: If one be a prince, he fares well. If one be the child of a prince, he fares well. If one be the nephew of a prince, he fares well. If one be the offspring of the royal family, he fares well. Would such visit any one, he can. Would he walk for pleasure in any direction, he can. Would he go anywhere, he has four men to carry him on their shoulders. He has an umbrella spread over him. He has men to attend him, and various marks of distinction—viz. a royal waiter, a royal goglet, and a royal betel-bag prepared according to the rank of princes.

"Again: public officers and the children of public officers act according to their several grades, agreeable to established customs.

"Another subject: Gardeners' and farmers' pa-nungs and pa-homs are different. They are vulgarly short, and they wear a jacket and a hat suitable to keep off the rays of the sun.

"We have a season in the first, second, and third months that is considered very cool. All the inhabitants of the exalted city put on jackets, because it is very cool. But in the hot season the men prepare themselves cloth of light materials, in width about two cubits, in length about two cubits and a half, and they dip this pa-hom in water.

"In this explanation respecting the kingdom of Siam, the manner of dressing is, in general, the same throughout the kingdom."

## Siamese Proverbs.

When you go into a wood, do not forget your wood-knife.

Place not your boat across the stream (in the way of the current).

An elephant, though he has four legs, may slip; and a doctor is not always right.

Go up by land, you meet a tiger; go down by water, you meet a crocodile—(Difficulties on all sides.)

Nobility is seen in the race; good manners, in the individual.

If a dog bite you, do not bite him again.

He who lives under the sky should not fear the rain.

Nourish no worms that eat timber: *i. e.* Be cautious in the selection of your friends.

I conclude with the following notices from two very competent authorities of a Siamese generation of individuals covered with hair. Craufurd, who describes the grandfather, writes: "Wallich and I took down on the spot the following account of himself and his history. His name was Shive-maong, and he stated himself to be thirty years of age. He was a native of the district of Maiyóng-gyé, a country of Laos. The chief of the country presented him to the king as a curiosity when a child of five years of age, and he had remained in Ava ever since. His height was five feet three inches and a half, which is about the ordinary stature of the Burmese. His form was slender, if compared with the usually robust make of the Hindoo-Chinese races, and his constitution is rather delicate. In his complexion there was nothing remarkable, although upon the whole he was perhaps rather fairer than the ordinary run of the Burmese. The colour of his eyes was a dark brown, not so intense as that of the ordinary Burman. The same thing may be said of the hair of the head, which was also a little finer in texture, and less copious.

"The whole forehead, the cheeks, the eyelids, the nose, including a portion of the inside, were covered with a about fine hair. On the forehead and cheeks this was eight inches long, and on the nose and chin about four inches. In colour it was of a silvery gray; its texture was silky, lank, and straight. The posterior and interior surface of the ears, with the inside of the external ear, were completely covered with hair of the same description as that on the face, and about eight inches long: it was this chiefly which contributed to give his whole appearance, at first sight, an unnatural, and almost inhuman aspect. He may be strictly said to have had neither eye-lashes, eye-brows, nor beard, or at least they were supplanted by the same silky hair which enveloped the whole face. He stated that when a child, the whole of this singular covering was much fairer than at present. The whole body, with the exception of the hands and feet, was covered with hair of the same texture and colour as that now described, but generally less abundant: it was most plentiful over the spine and shoulders, where it was five inches long: over the breast, it was about four inches long: it was scanty on the fore-arms, the legs, thighs, and abdomen. We thought it not improbable that this singular integument might be periodically or occasionally shed, and inquired, but there was no ground for this surmise. It was quite permanent.

"Although but thirty years of age, Shive-maong had, in some respects, the appearance of a man of fifty-five or sixty. This was owing to a singularity connected with the formation of the teeth, and the consequent falling in of the cheeks. On inspecting the mouth, it was discovered that he had in the lower jaw but five teeth, namely, the four incisors and the left canine; and in the upper, but four; the two outer ones of which partook of the canine form. The molares, or grinders, were of course totally wanting. The gums, where they should have been, were a hard, fleshy ridge; and, judging from appearances, there was no alveolar process. The few teeth he had were sound, but rather small; and he had never lost any from disease. He stated that he did not shed his infantine teeth till he was twenty years of age, when they were succeeded, in the usual manner, by the present set. He also expressly asserted that he never had any molares, and that he experienced no inconvenience from the want of them.

"The features of this individual were regular and good for a Burmese. The intellectual faculties were by no means deficient; on the contrary, he was a person of very good sense, and his intelligence appeared to us to be rather above than below the ordinary Burmese standard.

"He gave the following account of the manner in which the hairy covering made its appearance. At his birth, his ears alone were covered with hair, about two inches long, and of a flaxen colour. At six years of age, hair began to grow on the body generally, and first on the forehead. He distinctly stated that he did not attain the age of puberty till he was twenty years old.

"Shive-maong was married about eight years ago, or when twenty-two years of age; the king, as he stated himself, having made him a present of a wife. By this woman he has had four children, all girls; the eldest died when three years of age, and the second, when eleven months old. There was nothing remarkable in their form. The mother, rather a pretty Burmese woman, came to us to-day along with her third and fourth child. The eldest, about five years of age, was a striking likeness of her mother, and a pretty, interesting child, without any malconformation whatever, or, indeed, anything to distinguish her from an ordinary healthy child. She began to teeth at the usual period, and had all her infantine teeth complete at two years of age.

"The youngest child was about two years and a half old, a very stout, fine infant: she was born with hair within the anterior portion of the ear. At six months old it began to appear all over the ears, and at one year old on different parts of the body. This hair was of a light, flaxen colour, and of a fine silky texture. When two years of age, and not until then, she got a couple of incisor teeth in each jaw, but had as yet neither canine nor molares. Shive-maong assured us that none of his parents or relations, and, as far as he knew, none of his countrymen were marked like himself."

The complement to Mr. Crauford's notice of the father is Mr. Yule's of the daughter and the grandchild. "The whole of Maphons" (so she was named) "is more or less covered with hair. On a part of the cheek, and between the nose and mouth, this was confined to a short down, but over all the rest of the face was a thick silky hair of a brown colour, paleing about the nose and chin, four or five inches long at the alae of the nose, under the eye, and on the cheek-bone this was very fully developed, but it was in and on the ear that it was most extraordinary. Except the extreme upper lip no part of the face was visible. All the rest was filled and veiled by a large mass of silky hair, growing apparently out of every part of the external organ, and hanging in a dependent lock to a length of eight or ten inches. The hair over her forehead was brushed so as to blend with the hair of her head, the latter being dressed (as usual with her countrywomen) *à la chinoise.* It was not so thick as to conceal altogether the forehead.

"The nose, densely covered with hair as no animal's is as I know of, and with long, fine locks, curving out and pendant like the wisps of a fine sky terrier's coat, had a most strange appearance. The beard was pale in colour and about four inches in length, seemingly very soft and silky.

"Her manners were good and modest, her voice soft and feminine, and her expression mild and not unpleasing, after the first instinctive repulsion was overcome. Her appearance rather suggested the idea of a pleasant-looking woman masquerading than that of anything brutal.

"Her neck, bosom, and arms appeared to be covered with a fine pale down scarcely visible in some lights. She made a move as if to take off her upper clothing, but reluctantly, and we prevented it.

"Her husband and two boys accompanied her. The elder boy, about four or five years old, had nothing abnormal about him. The youngest, who was fourteen months old and still at the breast, was evidently taking after his mother. There was little hair on the head, but the child's ear was full of long silky floss, and it could boast a mustache and beard of pale silky down that would have cheered the heart of many a count. In fact, the appearance of the child agrees almost exactly with what Mr. Crauford says of the mother as an infant.

"This child is thus the third descent exhibiting this strange peculiarity, and in this third generation, as in the two preceding, this peculiarity has only appeared in one individual. Maphons has the same dental peculiarity also that her father had, the absence of the canine teeth and grinders, the back part of the gum presenting merely a hard ridge. Still she chews pawn like her neighbours."

When we remember the Siamese twins, it seems as if the valley of the Menam were prodigal of abnormalities. The distribution, however, of the several deviations from the ordinary standard of the human form over different countries has yet to obtain the attention it deserves. Considering how little we know of Siam at all, the prominence of wonderful men, women, and children in our accounts is remarkable. The country of the white elephants is also the country of strange human beings. Mr. Hunter describes an aquatic child:—

"Mr. Hunter sent for us to witness a sight which in more enlightened countries than Siam would be considered equally strange. It was a young child sporting in the water as in its native element, with all the buoyancy and playfulness of a fish. Its evolutions are astonishing, sometimes rolling over with a rapid motion and apparently no exertion, then turning round like a hoop by bending its face under, as it lies on its back, and throwing its feet under its head. It floats like a cork, with no apparent motion of any of the muscles; occasionally allows itself to sink till only half of the head is seen, dives, holds its face under water enough to alarm those who are ignorant of its powers, and yet appears to breathe as easily as though it had suffered no suspension of respiration. From its actions and countenance it is evidently delighted with the exercise, evinces no fatigue nor the least apprehension, and often cries when taken up. It is a singular object, both in and out of the water. It is three years old, very small, can neither speak nor walk, is very defective in sight, will take nothing but its earliest provision,—in fact, appears quite idiotic, and has exhibited the same fondness for the water, and peculiar feats in it, from the first year of its age, the first time that it was tried."

# CHAPTER IX.

## The Môn of Pegu.

The head-waters of the Irawadi are Burmese. So is the middle course. But not the Delta.

The Delta of the Irawadi is Môn; Môn being the name of the native population of Pegu and the provinces of Martaban. In both these districts there is a Burmese population. In both, however, it has the appearance of being foreign to the soil. The aborigines call themselves Môn. Their neighbours call them Talieng. The Môn, or Talieng, is the vernacular language of Pegu.

It is quite unintelligible to a Burmese; quite unintelligible to a Siamese. The alphabet, also, in which it is written is slightly different; though equally of Indian origin. Like the T'hay and Burmese it is essentially the alphabet of the Pali form of speech. Like all alphabets of this kind it embodies a Buddhist literature; of which, however, but little is known.

In the 16th century the king of Pegu seems to have been a powerful monarch; inasmuch as the T'hay histories speak of a Pegu invasion of Siam, and a Pegu conquest. Whether, however, the leading men in this event were actual Môn is uncertain. A conquest from the kingdom of Pegu may have been effected by Burmese.

The Môn are now British; Moulmein or Amherst having been ceded to us at the close of the Burmese war of 1825, and the remainder in 1853. The condition of the inhabitants under their previous rulers is believed, on fair evidence, to have been that of a very oppressed and misgoverned population.

| English. | Môn. | Thay. | Burmese. |
|---|---|---|---|
| *Man* | bani | manut | lu |
| *Head* | kadap | hoa | k'haung |
| *Eye* | mot | paned | myitsi |
| *Mouth* | pan | pak | n'hok |
| *Sun* | man-tangwe | p'hraatid | na |
| *Moon* | man-katok | p'hraachan | la |
| *Star* | nong | dao | ke'nekkat |
| *Sky* | taka | fa | moh |
| *Fire* | kamet | fai | mih |
| *Water* | dat | nam | re |
| *River* | bukbi | menam | myit |
| *Sea* | talle | talle | penglo |
| *Stone* | kamok | hin | kyauk |
| *Mountain* | tu | fukao | taung |
| *One* | mue | nung | tit |
| *Two* | ba | song | n'hit |
| *Three* | pai | sam | tong |
| *Four* | pol | si | le |
| *Five* | pasun | ha | nga |
| *Six* | ka-rao | hok | k'hyauk |
| *Seven* | ka-bok | chet | k'hown'hit |
| *Eight* | ka-cham | pet | s'hit |
| *Nine* | ka-chit | kao | ko |
| *Ten* | chok | sib | tase |

Word for word, the Burmese name of the Môn, *Talieng*, is *Telinga*. That an important and influential settlement was made in Pegu by certain Hindus of the Telinga districts is highly probable. More than this, in the way of a *direct* affinity between the Môn and Indians, cannot safely be asserted. The nearest relation to the language of Pegu seems to be that of the Kho, or Kamer, of Kambojia.

## CHAPTER X.

### The Kho, or Kamer, of Kambojia.

THE Môn occupied the Delta of the Irawadi; the Kho occupy that of the Mekhong. Pegu was the country of the Môn. The Kho are the natives of Kambojia. The Môn differ from the Burmese in language; agreeing with them in creed. The Kambojians do the same with the Siamese; the Kho and T'hay languages being mutually unintelligible. At the same time the alphabet of each is a modification of the Pali.

Lying between Siam and Cochinchina, the kingdom of Kambojia has had the ordinary history of areas similarly situated. When it has been strong it has struck its own blows; to the right and to the left. When it has been weak it has been stricken on both sides. When the Portuguese first discovered the country its power was at or near its zenith; and Siam, and Cochinchina were, at best, but its equals. At present they encroach upon it; yet, jealous of each other, leave it a modicum of independence. So that, with the parts to the east of the Mekhong under Cochinchina, and with the western side under Siam, there is still a central portion under the king of Kambojia, whose port is Kampot (whence the name of the country), and whose capital is Ujong, and whose four provinces are Potisat and Kampong Suai, in the interior, and Kampong and Kampot Son on the coast. The population of these is about 500,000, of which about 400,000 are of the Kho family, the rest being Chinese, Cochinchinese, Siamese, Malays, Portuguese, and half-bloods.

| English. | Kambojia. | Ka. | Khong. | Môn. |
|---|---|---|---|---|
| *Man* | manus | — | rum | bani |
| *Head* | kabal | tuwi | tos | kadap |
| *Eye* | panek | mat | mat | mot |
| *Mouth* | mat | boar | raneng | pan |
| *Sun* | tangai | tangi | tangi | man-tangwe |
| *Moon* | ke | kot | kang | man-katok |
| *Star* | pakai | patua | sum | nong |
| *Sky* | kor | krem | pleng | taka |
| *Fire* | plung | un | pleu | kamet |
| *Water* | tak | dak | tak | dat |
| *River* | tanle | dak-tani | talle | bukbi |
| *Sea* | sarmot | — | — | talle |
| *Stone* | tamo | tamoe | tamot | kamok |
| *Mountain* | pnom | manam | nong | tu |
| *One* | moe | moe | moe | mue |
| *Two* | pir | bur | bar | ba |
| *Three* | bai | peh | peh | pai |
| *Four* | buan | puan | pon | pol |
| *Five* | pram | chang | pram | pasun |
| *Six* | pram-moe | trao | ka-dom | ka-rao |
| *Seven* | pram-pil | puh | ka-nul | ka-bok |
| *Eight* | pram-bai | tam | ka-ti | ka-cham |
| *Nine* | pram-buan | chin | ka-sar | ka-chit |
| *Ten* | dap | chit | rai | choh |

The Ka and Khong (the Gueo of the Portuguese) are rude tribes either actually pagan or imperfectly Buddhist. Little or nothing is known concerning them, except that they are elephant hunters, and that the great epic poet of Portugal in his Lusiad describes them as cannibals; tattooed cannibals. That they coloured their own flesh is likelier than that they fed upon their neighbours'.

## CHAPTER XI.

### Cochinchina and Tonkin.

ALTHOUGH the exact details of the boundary between the Burmese and Siamese areas are unknown, I have little hesitation in committing myself to the doctrine that the two stocks are conterminous; by which I mean that of the numerous rude tribes of the hill or mountain, the forest or the jungle, there is none which cannot be referred to one of the two divisions. *Mutatis mutandis*, this is what will apply to the boundary between Siam and Kambojia; also to the boundary between Kambojia and Cochinchina.

The ethnology of Cochinchina is also that of Tonkin; the language, manners, and physical conformation of the occupants of the two countries being the same. The collective name for them is Anam, or Annam; whence we get the adjectives Anamese or Anamitic, as the name of the group, which is a section of the division to which the Chinese belong. The Chinese form of Annam is Ngannan. The Tonkinese call the Cochinchinese Kuang and Kekuang; names which are, probably, the same as Khyen and Kakhyen. The Cochinchinese, on the other hand, call the Tonkinese Kebak.

The Anamese are said to be the lightest coloured of all the tribes of the trans-gangetic peninsula; it being also stated that they are the most warmly and completely clothed. Their average height is low: a fact to which both Craufurd and Finlayson bear witness. The former considers them to be lower in stature than any people of Central Asia; the latter compares them with the Chinese, but makes their average height something less. The upper extremities are long, the lower short and stout, at least with the males; who, if squat and somewhat ill-favoured in aspect, are hardy and active. The women, on the other hand, are disproportionately fairer and handsomer than the men, for their extremities are well formed, and the carriage, even amongst the lower orders, is graceful. The form of the skull is more globular than square, the eyelids less turned than those of the Chinese. The mouth is large, the lips more prominent than thick, the mustache more abundant than the beard. Craufurd compares their features to those of the Malays, except that they bear none of the Malay expression of ferocity, but, on the contrary, exhibit good-humour and cheerfulness. And this seems to be their character. The lower orders are eminently lively, talking and laughing as if their government were as satisfactory and agreeable as it is despotic and oppressive. The higher classes, however, are solemn and decorous, after the manner of the Chinese. Their dress is that of the Chinese before they adopted that of their Mongol conquerors. It varies but little with the sex, consisting, with both men and women, of loose trousers, and a loose frock reaching half-way down the thigh. The sleeves are loose; and when the wearer has no need to labour, hang a foot or foot and a half over the fingers. The ankles and neck only go bare. The hair is worn long, and put up in a knot at the back of the head: this, too, being the old and original Chinese practice. A straw hat, which is sometimes in the form of an inverted basin and sometimes like a sugar loaf, which is of great breadth in the rim, and which is constantly worn out of doors, is a good fence against the sun. As to the materials of the clothing, they are generally of silk or cotton; oftener of silk than in any other country. Metallic ornaments are far rarer. White is the colour of the national flag — white is the colour for mourning: but the royal colour is yellow or orange.

The use of the cigar, and of the usual masticatories, is universal.

The government is despotic, and the punishments cruel; the religion is Buddhist, but latitudinarian, as in China. There is little vitality in any of their venerational feelings, save and except those which are so embodied in the respect shown towards the *manes* of their ancestors.

In all this they agree with the countries in their neighbourhood; with Siam, with Burmah, with China itself. The miserable fooleries of the medicine-man of the North-American Indians are not more American than Siberian (for where is the tribe of Northern or Central Asia that has not its shamans?), and not more Siberian than Anamitic. Buddhism should expel such follies. Yet the Buddhist countries, one and all, are full of them. The exorcisers in Tonkin and Cochinchina have "their books by which they pretend to find out the cause and result of all sickness, and never miss to tell the sick party that his distemper proceeds from the devil, or some water-gods, and pretend to cure it by the noise of drums, bassoons, and trumpets. The conjuror of this tribe is habited very antickly, and sings very loud, and makes hideous noises, pronouncing many execrations, and jumping and skipping as if the devil were really in him; and all this while there is a store of victuals prepared for an offering to the devil, but it is eaten by himself; and he will continue this sport for several days, till the patient be either dead or recovered, and then he can give an answer with some certainty. It belongs to them to dispossess such as are possessed by the devil, which is the ultimate of their conjuration, and is commonly effected in this manner :—They curse and most impiously invoke—I do not know what demon; and they paint the pictures of devils with horrible faces, on yellow paper, which is fixed to the wall of the house. Then they fall to bawling so terribly, and scream so loud, dancing and skipping as is most ridiculous, sometimes fearful to see and hear. They also bless and consecrate new houses; and if they be suspected to be haunted, they drive the devil out of them by their conjuration, and the firing of muskets."

Buddhism takes no cognizance of processions like the following; which form part of the ceremonies by which the new year is opened :—

"The King, general, and prince, with most of the mandarins of the court, on this solemn occasion, go before break of day severally to a place at the south end of the city, purposely built for this occasion, with three gates different from their other pagodas; neither are there any images in the house. Here they stay without in sundry apartments till daylight. The King, in the meantime, is to wash his body, and put on new clothes never worn before.

"About eight of the clock a piece of ordnance is fired; on which signal the general, prince, and mandarins repair to the King, to do homage, though it extends, as to the general and prince, no further than a bare point of formality. This compliment passes in silence, yet with much state and gravity on both sides; then immediately the second signal of a gun is heard, whereupon the King is accompanied to the gates of the said house, which are all shut; whereat he knocks, and is by the door-keeper asked who he is. He answers, 'The King,' and they let him in; but none may enter with him, that being contrary to their superstition. Thus he does three several times till he comes into the house, where he falls to his devotion and supplications, having kept a strict fast to his gods, after their mode; which done, he seats himself in a gilt chair, placed in the yard of the said house; and having paused a little, a plough with a buffalo tied to it, in the same manner as they use them for tilling the ground, is presented him, who, holding it by the place usually taken hold of when they work it, he blesses the country, and teaches the people, by this emblem, that none should be ashamed to be a husbandman, and that the diligent, industrious, and provident, especially in the culture of the ground, may certainly expect the enjoyment of their labour and pains.

"I am informed by some that at the same time the ceremony of the cups is used; others again contradict that, and affirm it to be on the day of installing the new King.

"Be it when it will, the manner is thus: on a bandesia or lacquered table stand several cups, with prepared victuals in them; and, among the rest, there is one with boiled white rice, another with yellow rice, one with water, and one with herbs or greens. All these cups are nearly covered with fine paper, and with starch fastened thereon, so that one cannot be known from another. One of these the King takes at adventure, which is immediately opened, and if he lights on the yellow rice there is great rejoicing, because it portends (as they believe) plenty in the land; if on the white rice, a good harvest; if water, an indifferent year; but the herbs or greens are extremely bad, denoting great mortality, famine and desolation; and so of the rest of the cups, every one hath its particular signification and augury, according to what their superstition and idolatry dictates.

"With this ends this grand ceremony."

It is not the only one. The agency of evil spirits is believed in throughout the whole length and breadth of the land; but it is also believed that some ceremonies will propitiate, and that others will frighten them. On a certain day towards the end of February, the general of the empire prepares himself for a grand demonstration. The procession is formed. Three blows are given to an enormous drum.

"On this signal the general comes from the arsenal to the place where the soldiers stand in order, and enters the house prepared for him. In a while after three other strokes are given on a great copper bassoon or gong, in the same manner as on the drum for distance of time; the general beginneth then to offer meat offerings to the criminal devils and malevolent spirits (for it is usual and customary likewise amongst them to feast the condemned before their execution), inviting them to eat and drink, when presently he accuses them in a strange language, by characters and figures, &c., of many offences and crimes committed by them, as to having disquieted the land, killed his elephants and horses, &c., for all which they justly deserve to be chastised and banished the country. Whereupon three great guns are fired as the last signal; upon which all the artillery and muskets are discharged, that, by their most terrible noise, the devils may be driven away; and they are so blind as to believe for certain that they really and effectually put them to flight.

"At noon every one may feast himself at his own cost, but the soldiers are fed with the offered meat."

More effectually to terrify the evil genii, the Tonkinese give their children strange names, changing them when they think that the children are old enough to be independent. They let six or seven tufts of hair grow to different lengths; this in honour of one idol, that to the glory of another. At the beginning of the year they set up hideous figures before their doors.

The first of these two ceremonies is called Bovidiyaw; the second Thekkydaw. The magicians, medicine-men, or shamans, fall into four classes; being either Thay-bu, or Thay-bu-twe; either Thay-bu-di-lye, or Bacote, the last named being the lowest of all. The name for either the shamans in general, the belief in them, or the believers is Lanzo.

Marriage takes place later than in most of the other parts of Asia; for if the rich sometimes marry at fifteen, the poor often remain single till thirty. The age of the female is from seventeen to twenty, at least in the lower orders. In no country—our own not excepted—is the date of the marriage more regulated by the ways and means of the parties contracting. A Cochinchinese marries as soon as he can; but his wife must be purchased. Marriages are indissoluble; but, as polygamy is habitual, the first wife has a pre-eminence over the others. Abortion is commoner than infanticide, and a violation of the laws of chastity amongst unmarried women commoner than either. Adultery, however, is an offence of the gravest nature, of which the legal punishment, though often commuted for milder penalties, is death. Without being jealously confined, as in the Turk and Persian parts of Asia, the Anamitic women are coarsely and often brutally treated. The infliction of corporeal punishment on an offending wife passes without comment, and as a matter of course.

Less industrious than the Chinese, the Cochinchinese are also less ingenious. Their arts, however, are the same in kind, though on a lower level of excellence.

| English. | Cochinchina. | Cochinchina. | Tonkin. | Chinese. |
|---|---|---|---|---|
| *Man* | nga'oi | danon | nguoi | nan |
| *Head* | dau | tu | drâu | t'eu |
| *Eye* | male | mok | mok | mu |
| *Mouth* | mieng | kau | kau | k'eu |
| *Sun* | mat-troi | nhet | nit | zhe |
| *Moon* | mat-tran | blang | blang | yue |
| *Star* | sao | sao | sao | sing |
| *Sky* | troi | bloei | bloei | ti'an |
| *Fire* | lu'a | hoa | hoa | kuo |
| *Water* | nu'oe | nak | nak | shui |
| *River* | song | sou | sou | kiang |
| *Sea* | bien | be | be | khai |
| *Stone* | da | ta | dra | shi |
| *Mountain* | nui | nui | nui | sham |
| *One* | mot | mot | mot | i |
| *Two* | hai | hai | hai | öl |
| *Three* | ba | teng | tam | san |
| *Four* | bon | bon | bon | syu |
| *Five* | nam | lang | lam | ngu |
| *Six* | sau | lak | luk | lu |
| *Seven* | bay | bai | bai | zi |
| *Eight* | tam' | tang | tam | pa |
| *Nine* | chin' | chin | chim | kui |
| *Ten* | mu'oi | taap | tap | shi |

The Anam analogues of the Ka and Chong, the rude tribes of the more impracticable parts, are the tribes of the Nguon, Moi, Romoi, Kemoi and, Diditsh (all unknown in detail), who occupy the mountain ranges between Tonkin and Cochinchina, and Cochinchina and Kambojia. The Tshampa will be mentioned in the sequel.

## CHAPTER XII.

The Chinese.—The Name.—Civilization.—Its Date.—Neither very Early nor Self-developed.—Moral and Physical Character of the Chinese.—Conditions of Soil and Climate.—Foreign Influences.—India.—Syria.

THE Chinese have no truly national name; the name by which they are described in the present and all other European notices of them being one which is unknown in China. Sometimes the inhabitants call their country by the name of the ruling dynasty; sometimes they give it some fanciful designation. They are, for instance, the people of the Celestial Empire, the people of the Central Empire, the people of the Flower of the Centre. If these be over complimentary, the terms under which they describe the populations of the rest of the world are anything but eulogistic. The Sifan of the Tibetan frontier, are the western, the English and other Europeans the outer, Barbarians. That the ideas conveyed by the original expressions are both less offensive on one side and less flattering on the other than they appear in the current translations is likely enough, for the genius of the Chinese language is far removed from that of the tongues of Europe. At the same time the absence of a definite common-sense name, with the use of an absurd circumlocution in its stead, is a fact which has always commanded the attention of geographers. It certainly stands out with greater prominence in China than elsewhere; though something of the kind may be found in most of the empires of the far East.

The name China itself, a modification of Sin, Tshin, Dzhin, and other allied terms, is probably Indian in origin; and, being Indian, it is Persian, Arabic, Malay, and European also. It is an old name, being, word for word, the Sinæ (Thinæ) of the classical writers. Whether this exactly denoted the Chinese in general, or any portion of them, is uncertain. It was a name by which the Indians, and other populations between Europe and the extreme East, denoted the occupants of certain countries beyond their own. Respecting the name, Seres, which many have applied to the ancient Chinese, I have elsewhere maintained that no such population existed; the argument being that the similarity between the word *serik* as the name for silk, and the adjective Σηρικὴ (*Serikê*), which would be the name for the country of the Seres, first engendered the local, and, after that, the national name—not as geographical facts, but as etymological deductions.

One thing is certain, that if the Chinese, during the flourishing periods of Greece and Rome, were a polished and powerful people, their power and polish were utterly unknown to the lettered nations of the West. They were not even a mystery to stimulate their curiosity and awaken their imagination. The Sinæ, or Thinæ, for all that is said to the contrary by any Greek or Roman writer, may have been amongst the rudest of the tribes of Asia. The Seres, as the men whose country produced so costly an article as silk, and who wore it on their persons, may have been held in higher estimation—though except in the later writers we have no proof of even this. But the Seres were not a population at all *eo nomine.* They were simply the occupants of the silk-producing country, wherever and whatever that was.

Of the notices of China in Indian compositions I can say but little. They may, or may not, occur in the earliest works on Buddhism. Let them, however, appear as early as they may, they are no evidence to that extreme antiquity which so many writers have attributed to the Chinese civilization, and which is sometimes supposed to transcend that of India itself.

It is clear, that if this be the case it must be a thorough homegrowth of the soil of China, developed out of itself, and independent of foreign influences. For whence could they have come? There is nothing in the history of Tibet, Siam or Ava which carries us back to any very remote period; less in that of Turkestan or Mongolia. India, on the other hand, was, at an early period, in continuity with countries like Bactria and Persia, which, in their turn, were continuous with Assyria, Phœnicia, and Greece.

If the civilization of China be older than that of India, or (if not older) independent of it, it gives us so remarkable a phenomenon in the history of the world at large that we may well ponder over, and wonder at, the intellectual constitution of the people who developed it. But this very fact raises a presumption against its being the case.

Add to this, as a second presumption against it, its stationary character. England passes for a nation in which progress is rapid; and so it is, inasmuch as many of the great inventions and discoveries which have accelerated our onward movements are quite recent. They were made. They were used. No time was lost in applying them. They bore fruit; and they bore it soon. Our reputation for progress is formed accordingly. But what, if steam were as old as the time of Alfred, printing a familiar process in the reign of Ecbert, and gunpowder known to the ancient Britons, the present conditions of our arts, science, and literature remaining as it is, neither better nor worse? In such a case we could scarcely be called progressive, though not without high claims to a civilization—very respectable and very stationary.

How long has the civilization of China remained as it is? Perhaps as long as 3000 years. If so, it is disgracefully remarkable for its immobility. Perhaps only 300. If so, it has gone forwards less rapidly than we expect *à priori*. Still, it has not sunk in absolute torpor. Between extremes of this kind there may be any number of intermediate points. It is only certain that where the absence of progress is so extreme as to simulate absolute immobility for a long series of years, the primary fact of its antiquity becomes questionable. There is a certain amount of presumption against all cases of antiquity, simply because things are oftener lost than kept. There is an additional amount of presumption against it when this antiquity is sterile, *i. e.* when early discoveries remain as they were at first, without developing themselves into anything better.

Still, it is only so much presumption after all—so much presumption which so much evidence on the other side may outweigh. Is this evidence forthcoming in the case of China? I answer this question, without hesitation, in the negative. That China in the time of the Athenian and Roman republics was, even in kind, the China of the nineteenth century I neither believe nor pretend to believe. That when Greece had its Thales, the Celestial Empire had its Confucius I hold to be improbable and unproven. That there was printing and gunpowder, and paper money in Pekin and Nankin, before there was printing, gunpowder, and paper-money in Genoa or Venice is incompatible with the general history of human civilization. The presumptions are against such being the case; and the testimony is insufficient to neutralize them. It is more probable that such things, though non-existent, should be imagined; more probable that they should be claimed by a vain nation unduly, and admitted by uncritical writers on insufficient evidence than that they should actually have had a *bonâ fide* real existence.

The main argument to the contrary rests upon the accounts of the Chinese themselves; accounts which have not, as yet, been submitted to more criticism than had the Epistles of Phalaris, before Bentley wrote, or the Epics of Ossian before Johnson had asked for the originals. Individually, I believe, that until Buddhism was introduced from India, the Chinese were in the condition of the Khyens, Nagas, and similar wild tribes; except in certain favoured localities along the alluvia of rivers. In these, there was probably a barbarous tiller of the soil, instead of a barbarous feeder of flocks and herds; an unlettered farmer instead of an unlettered grazier. Such, I hold to have been the imaginary cotemporaries of an unreal Confucius.

If the Chinese developed an independent civilization they differed from their neighbouring nations, not in degree but in kind. Denying that they did this, I by no means take exception to a moderate view of their superiority. As a political power, they are immeasurably more important than all the rest of their congeners put together. There is, probably, no art in which the Siamese or Burmese excel the rude tribes, in which they are not themselves excelled by the Chinese. Their industrial energy and commercial aptitude are generally recognized.

Politically speaking China is all in all. The area itself of China Proper is large; but to China Proper Tibet is a dependency. Though Ladakh at the present moment belongs to Ghúlab Singh and the East India Company, it was once Tibetan and (as such) Chinese. Though Bultistan is now Sikh, it was once a dependency of Ladakh; as such Tibetan; as such Chinese. China here, China there, China everywhere. From Nepaul the Chinese profess to have taken tribute. If they have not done this, they have been in intimate political relations. The Ghorka (Ku-ru-ka-li) were reckoned upon as auxiliaries in the last war; and they may possibly be looked to in the present. In Lin's report, the English are said to respect three hostile powers beyond the pale of China, viz. Russia, France, and the United States, and to fear four of the Chinese tributaries—Cochinchina, Siam, Ava, and Nepaul. Cochinchina carries with it a part of Kambojia, just as Ava carries with it Pegu. Now with Ava there is, at least, this much in the way of politics. The frontiers touch. Some of the Shan states pay tribute to both Ava and China. There are, then, between them wars, treaties, and standing agreements. I cannot say that what is done by Siam may not be done by the Burmese also. The Siamese pay *something* to China. What it is is a matter for diplomatists to decide. The Chinese call it tribute. The Siamese consider it a sort of licence to trade. It is, certainly, compatible with a practical independence. Again, the nearest approach to freedom of trade and intercourse that is permitted to any nation by the Japanese is permitted to China. The Dutch can do more with those cunning islanders than all the rest of Europe put together. But the Chinese can do more than the Dutch. Much of the civilization of Japan is Chinese in origin. So is that of Korea.

Bringing all these points together, bringing in also Mongolia and Chinese Turkistan (Chinese Tartary), we make up a whole world over which the influence of China is to be felt; and it may be added that it is felt where that of no other country is to be found. What does the little Tibetan either know or care about Siam? What is the Burmese of Ava to the Gurung or Magar? To each and all of these, however, China is a reality and a power. It is safe to say that what Turkey is to the Mahometan, that is China in the Buddhist, world.

With this it is, as nearly as may be, co-extensive. It extends up to its boundaries; and it extends but little further. Cross the Himalayas from Tibet; cross the Paropamisus; cross the Russian frontier. The decidedly Chinese characteristics either wane or disappear; and things are Hindu, Persian, Uzbek, or Moscovite, as the case may be.

The superiority of the Chinese in the art of war may possibly be denied. It is one which they may easily have lost for want of exercise. To which it may be added that, even here, the loss is apparent rather than real. If the soldiers have but few opportunities of exhibiting their valour, there is plenty of naval enterprise. Next to the Malays the Chinese are the most formidable pirates of the eastern seas; and where there is piracy there are skill and courage also.

In the arts of peace the skill of the Chinese is well measured by both their success as settlers at a distance from home, and the ease with which they displace or encroach upon the populations of their frontier.

In respect to the settlements beyond the sea the migratory habits of the people stand in strong contrast to the exclusiveness of their government. The Malay ports swarm with Chinese, and in Sincapore, Borneo, and the Philippines there are large Chinese colonies. So there are in Australia, in the West Indies, in the Sandwich Isles, and in California. In all these settlements the spirit of combination keeps them closely connected with each other. They settle their disputes as much as possible by arbitration amongst themselves, and form societies more or less secret. They send out remittances of their earnings home. They look forward to returning with a competence to

China. Most of their wives are the women of the country; more or less temporary, and liable to be left. The effect of this is that there are numerous half-bloods; Chinese on one side, Javanese, Malay, Hawaiian, Siamese, &c., on the other.

At the same time it is not all the Chinese that thus readily emigrate. When Mr. Fortune went with the special object of procuring a body of men skilled in the growing, sorting, and preparing of tea, he found the greatest difficulty in procuring them. He went to the tea-farms and found all the tea-growers attached to their tea-trees. He offered high wages if they would go with him. A sailor would have done so for half the money. The tea-growers, however, kept at home. They were as truly Chinese as the men of Canton and Fokien; the only difference being that whilst the one population was agricultural and inland, the other was in contact with the sea, and addicted to maritime pursuits. As a general rule the Chinese abroad are from the districts round the seaports. The English are migrants; but there is no part of England a hundred miles from the sea coast. The Norwegians are migrants; the Danes, the Sleswickers, and the Holsteiners the same. Hanoverians within the circles of Hamburg and Bremen are migrants; and all, in their degree, are maritime. For other reasons, poverty and bad government, certain Rhinelanders and Bavarians become migrants. As a general rule, however, the clinging to the soil is in a direct ratio to the distance from the sea. France colonized Canada. The *habitans*, however, of Canada are chiefly from the one province of Normandy.

Equally remarkable with the success with which a Chinaman holds his own in distant countries is the effective manner in which he extends his own frontier at the expense of the Mongols and Mantshus who lie beyond, and in contact with, it. How does he do this? Not by what historians are over-fond of calling the "inroads of barbarians;" not by that unproven piece of ethnological dynamics called a national migration; nor by processes like the invasion of Rumelia by the Ottomans, Hungary by the Magyars, or England by the Normans. For the analogues of these we look in vain. The closer parallel is that of the back-woodsman in America or of the annexationist in Texas. Closer still is that of the money-lender in England and Ireland. Closest of all is that of the British mortgagee. Huc saw much of this kind in the parts to the north of the great wall. The area was Mongol. The names of the localities were Mongol. The language of the country was Mongol. All the estates in these parts are encumbered, and the capitalist is a Chinese. The Chinese is the mortgagee; but on occasions, he must carry his life in his hand. The land is full of silver and gold; which the Chinese can find out, the natives cannot. Although there are severe penalties against working these mines, or diggings, the thing is done. Bands of Chinese marauders undertake the work. Innumerable vagabonds follow. In '41 a great mass of them were crowded together in a single mine. The Mongols blocked up the entrance. The cries of the wretched, starving, suffocated robbers were piercing and horrible. They were left, however, to starve and smother. Some escaped with life. These were taken to the king and had their eyes put out.

The town of Tolon-nor is walled, populous, and commercial. It is a depôt for the Kiakta goods from Russia. The workmen in its foundries are skilful in modellings and castings. The bells, vases, idols, and other metallic implements of Buddhism are made here. The large images are cast in several pieces and soldered together. The parts of a single statue seen by Huc loaded eighty camels. Besides its foundries Tolon-nor has a considerable trade. But it is all to the benefit of the Chinese. The Chinese make their fortunes, the Mongols are ruined. The whole place is one "monstrous pneumatic trough for producing a vacuum in Mongol purses."

The bearings of these notices are various. They show the aptitude of the Chinese for both head-work and hand-work, as well as the way in which he exercises them at the expense of his neighbours. In the physical history of mankind this is important; inasmuch as the amount of Chinese blood, either pure or mixed, beyond the area of China Proper is annually increasing. The pure Mantshus of the northern frontiers become, in certain localities, more or less Chinese. The pure Mongols, on the western frontier, do the same. In parts of Tumet the occupants are no longer nomads. They cultivate the soil, and that well. They look down upon the brethren of the camp and steppe. Many of them speak Chinese, and some of them nothing but Chinese. Their own native tongue they have wholly forgotten.

Again, on the very frontier of the Russian dominions, as well as on the side of independent Tartary, there are several convict settlements; settlements which bring Chinese blood into the very heart of Asia; far, very far, to the west of the most western part of China Proper.

The skin of the Chinese is yellow rather than brown, not unlike parchment in the matter of colour. Sometimes there is a maroon tint. The yellow-brown hue, however, predominates. The face is broad and flat; the cheek-bones projecting; the irides black; the eyes oblique; the beard scanty; the stature above that of the Malay and Tibetan, below that of the European. The crania of several Chinese have been examined and described; but the results are not very definite. Sometimes the occipital protuberance has been large, and given the head an elongated appearance; whereas, in other instances, it has been nearly wanting. I believe this inconsistency has puzzled that excellent anatomist Professor Retzius, whose division of skulls, as is well known, is into the brakhy-kefalic and dolikhokefalic—the short-headed, with a great diameter from side to side, and the long-headed with a great one from fore to aft. Both kinds are found in China. In Morton's collection there are eleven specimens (chiefly the skulls of murderers and pirates), the largest of which measures 98, the smallest 70 cubic inches, internal capacity. The mean is about 85.

As are the habits and appearance, (different in many notable details from those of the neighbouring populations,) so are the physical conditions of soil and climate. As opposed to the areas of Mongolians and Mantshú, China is one of the lands of the South. As opposed to Siam and Cochinchina it is a northern country. As opposed to Tibet it is a flat. As opposed to the steppes of Turkistan it is a broken tract of hill and valley; an undulating country at least. It has less of a seaboard than the kingdoms and principalities of the Transgangetic peninsula; and much less of one than either the Malay or the Japanese islands. On the other hand, it has large rivers. They run, as the Danube runs in Europe, west and east; and so doing lie under the same parallels during their whole course; there or thereabouts. This ensures to the alluvial soils on their banks a uniformity of climate which we should seek for in vain if streams of the same length ran from north to south. If the Hoang-ho did this its mouth would be within the tropics, and its source on the frontiers of Siberia. Cotton might be grown at its delta, barley might be starved at its head-waters. Let us say that the rivers of China run horizontally, rather than vertically. Whatever else such horizontal lines of water may ensure, they ensure to the country through which they run a certain amount of uniformity in the way of agriculture and industry. Now the uniformity of the Chinese civilization is one of its most prominent characteristics.

Though the details of the physical conditions under which Chinese civilization has been developed are interesting, they are still details. If it were necessary to enlarge on them the list would be a long one. There would be in it metals ; clay both for building and pottery ; gums for varnishes ; and a Fauna and Flora containing the silk-worm, the mulberry on which it feeds, and various kinds of tea. The land of silk and tea must, of necessity, have much that is peculiar to itself.

Of the Chinese civilization the basis is, to a great extent, agriculture ; agriculture, for which we have seen that the Tibetans displayed an aptitude, but which the inhospitable character of their country prevented from being carried to perfection. Where, however, there is an acre of alluvial soil in Tibet, there is a square mile of it in China ; not to mention the difference of climate and elevation.

Its basis is, to a great extent, trade. For this, too, the Tibetans have displayed an aptitude. Though Tassisudon and Tíshú Lúmbú were monasteries rather than commercial cities, Hlahsa was full of trade. The country, however, in general was unfavourable to its full development. Where were its ports and harbours ? In China they are numerous enough.

A notable portion of Tibet was occupied by nomad herdsmen. Their occupancies, however, were either a desert or the border of one. In China such localities form but a small part of the surface, so that, as far as our knowledge goes, herdsmen are rare.

Without undervaluing the numerous points in which China is thus favoured, as forces by which civilization is developed, I repeat the statement of my belief that they have not been sufficient, single-handed, to give the phenomena with which the Celestial Empire is too often credited, viz. an antiquity so remote as to transcend that of all other countries, and, so doing, exist as a self-developed, indigenous, and independent product of the soil and climate.

The complement to the conditions afforded by these agencies is the history of the influences from without. Of these, the most important, beyond all comparison, are those from India, as they have been the earliest. The Buddhist creed is, certainly, of Indian origin. Those who believe in the existence, or even the antiquity of great philosophers like Confucius and Mencius, at a time when Solon was giving laws to Athens, will, probably, make but little of it. They will merely see in it, so much dogma engrafted upon so much philosophy. They will see metal upon metal; one civilization upon another. They will merely see what they see in the relations of Greece and Rome. There is an early native culture. There is a foreign addition to it. There is a case of more or less in the way of ideas; a difference, not of kind, but of degree. There is possibly, in some respect, a retrograde movement, just as there would have been in Ionia if the philosophy of Thales had been disturbed by some strange piece of fire-worship from Persia. Those, however, who, sifting evidence, have doubts and something more on these and similar points of Chinese antiquity may, possibly, believe that when Buddhism was first introduced it fell upon a nation of savages and pagans; unlettered mountaineers in some cases (just like the Miaoutse at the present moment), unlettered lowlanders in other: men who were potters, after the fashion of the Fiji islanders, simply because a good kind of clay was ready to their hands; men who drank tea because the tea-plant grew in their country, and the infusion was easily made; men whose highest and most peculiar art was the rearing of silkworms and the spinning of silk—and a very characteristic art we must admit this to have been.

The next influence is from Turkestan; not that the tribes of that district had anything of their own to communicate. In the sixth and seventh centuries, they were, probably, what they are now; herdsmen for the greater, agriculturists for the smaller part of their area; carriers, too, in the way of commerce. Robbers they were as well, and, when united under some energetic captain, conquerors. Just now, however, we are looking at them as civilizers. Originators they were not. Propagators they were. Nestorian Christianity, which in the sixth century was rife and common in Persia, extended itself from Persia to Turkestan, and from Turkestan to China. The evidence that satisfied Gibbon upon this point may satisfy his readers. Here and there, indeed, he may have claimed for his Nestorian missionaries a tribe or two too many. He may have counted certain Kerait Mongolians as Christians at a time when they were not even Buddhists. He may have laid too much stress on the evidence of such a writer as Cosmas Indicopleustes. He may have introduced the suspicious name of the mythic Prester John. He may have spoken too favourably of the famous inscription of Siganfu. He may have erred in introducing the Christianity of the Chinese through the port of Canton; erred in making his missionaries seamen. But upon the whole his notice of the extent to which Nestorian Christianity prevailed amongst the so-called Tartars of Central Asia is true and unexaggerated. It is true that in "the sixth century Christianity was successfully preached to the Bactrians, the Huns, the Persians, the Indians, the Persarmenians, and the Elamites; the barbaric churches from the Gulf of Persia to the Caspian were almost infinite; and their recent faith was conspicuous in the number and sanctity of their monks and martyrs. The pepper coasts of Malabar, and the isles of the ocean, Socotra and Ceylon, were peopled by an increasing multitude of Christians. The missionaries of Balch and Samarcand pursued without fear the footsteps of the roving Tartar, and insinuated themselves in the camps of the Imaus and the banks of the Selinga. In their progress by sea and land the Nestorians entered China. Unlike the senators of Rome, who assumed with a smile the characters of priests and augurs, the mandarins, who affect in public the reason of philosophers, are devoted in private to every mode of popular superstition. They cherished and they confounded the gods of Palestine and of India; but the propagation of Christianity awakened the jealousy of the state, and after a short vicissitude of favour and persecution, the foreign sect expired in ignorance and oblivion."

The evidence of this has grown in strength since Gibbon wrote. The Mongol alphabet is that of the Oriental Turks; the alphabet of the Oriental Turks is Syriac and Nestorian. Klaproth has shown this; and it is one of the very best of his showings. For the "Huns and Bactrians" of Gibbon, read "Chinese Tartars." It was when Chinese Tartary was visited by the missionaries whom Gibbon celebrates that their language was reduced to writing.

We have carried, then, Christianity from Syria to the

very frontier of China. The evidence of its having penetrated into the country is less decisive. The presumptions are in its favour. A great deal of evidence, which a great many competent judges admit, is also in its favour. The phenomena for which it would account are numerous. Individually, I treat Christianity in China during the sixth and seventh centuries as a fact; Christianity on the frontier being one upon which no doubt can exist.

The third series of influences is modern Europe, that of the Jesuits being the chief.

It is to the learned men of this order that the great mass of our information concerning China is due; some of them having worked as missionaries at Pekin, others as closet students in Europe. The earliest materials were almost wholly of their collection; and, as they chiefly found their way to the Royal Library of Paris, a French school of investigators was developed. By these the current ideas respecting the value of the Chinese historians were introduced. A show of antiquity strikes the imagination, and warps the judgment. For a time it generally passes as a reality, inasmuch as criticism is in abeyance. Again; the newer a subject the greater the monopoly of those who possess a knowledge of it. Out of this grow an exaggerated appreciation of the thing known and a mischievous intolerance of dissentient judgments. The opinions that prevailed during the last century are best known to the English reader through the famous chapter (the 27th) of Gibbon, upon the manners and history of the nations akin to the Huns. All his authorities are French. Most of their opinions are adopted.

Since the date of the Decline and Fall, the stream of Chinese scholarship has widened itself. Without leaving France, it has spread over England, Holland, Germany, Scandinavia, and Russia. Yet the same acquiescence in an unproven antiquity prevails. The latest editor of Gibbon, indeed, no special Chinese scholar, but a critical judge of evidence in general, takes certain exceptions of his own, and rejects the date which Gibbon assigns to the commencement of the historical period in China. Nevertheless, he shows that the ablest Chinese scholars in Europe, men of the newest school and the most advanced opinions, men of great acquirements in philology at large, accept with little scruple what, after such authorities, few are inclined to reject, viz.—traditions instead of documents, inferences instead of traditions, *ex-post facto* narratives, improbable dates, doubtful eclipses, an unreasonable history, a suspicious astronomy. Remusat carries the history of China to the twenty-second century *before* our æra. Neumann admits an equal antiquity. Klaproth—as Klaproth—is a sceptic of the sceptics; I give his account of the origin and development of the Chinese school of history, as a sample of the extent to which acute men will shut their eyes to suspicious circumstances when they make against the value of a special study

The Chinese alphabet, according to Klaproth, is as old as the very germ of the empire; for when its founders consisted of no more than 100 families, those 100 families could read and write. Originally there was no more than 100 family names in China. Hence the inference that out of so few individuals arose so great an empire. Had China been a colony from India or Arabia, this accuracy in the way of pedigree might be probable. But China was not built or made. It grew; and, like all other growths, had approached maturity before its origin got thought about. If writing came to men as building goes to beavers, by an instinct, this contemporaneous origin of the state and alphabet would be natural. As it is, it requires proof.

But inscriptions exist as old as 800 B.C.; one, that of Yú, being earlier. This, however, may be but a transcript. Upon this I can give no opinion. I only know that, with our very imperfect knowledge of Chinese palæography, an inscription from the Hoang-ho of the date of the building of Rome requires an extraordinary amount of evidence to support it. The presumptions against its preservation have to be overbalanced, as well as the presumptions against its original production.

To continue—where writing exists, there exists history also; for without writing no record can become permanent. True. History without an alphabet is scarcely possible. An alphabet, however, may exist without being used by a historian.

From the earliest time the rulers of China registered the remarkable events of their reigns. They also made collections of laws, religious liturgies, ceremonial directions, old poems, and the like. In the sixth century B.C. these had grown to so unwieldy and inconvenient a bulk, that Confucius undertook to make an abstract of them. Doing this he composed—

(1.) The *Shu-king*; or, a history of China from the year B.C. 2357, to his own times.

(2.) The *Shi-king*, a collection of poems.

(3.) The *Li-ki*; or, book of ceremonies.

(4.) The *Yo-king*; or, a treatise on music.

(5.) The *Y-king*; a mystic work on transformations.

(6.) *Tshun-tsieu*; or, spring and autumn, a history of Lu, the district in which the author was born, from B.C. 723 to B.C. 479.

The first two dynasties lasted from B.C. 2205 to B.C. 1122; the third, that of Dzheu, from B.C. 1122 to the middle of the third century—also B.C. Vu-Vang founded the dynasty of Dzheu; and changed the constitution.

Before his time it was a pure monarchy. Under him, however, and his successors, it became feudal. As long as the king was strong enough to hold his feudatories in hand, the system of Vu-Vang flourished and the Dzheu dynasty ruled. But discontents set in, and in the eighth century as many as twenty petty kinglings quarrelled with each other, and disorganized the empire. They were, however, eventually coerced, and the dynasty of Dzheu was succeeded by

The dynasty of Tsin. Of the dynasty of Tsin the Emperor Shi-kwang-ti was the great ornament. His nobles, however, troubled him. They looked back to the feudal times of the Dzheu; hankered after lost powers and privileges; made inconvenient claims, and supported them by reference to the works on history, and the works on law. Whereupon Shi kwang-ti issued an order that all such books should be burned, especially the Shu-king and the Shi-king. What he ordered was done, but imperfectly. In a country where writing is general, it is difficult to destroy all the copies of all the books, especially when they are written, or scratched, on so incombustible a material as bamboo. So writes Klaproth, not without simplicity.

Now any one at all conversant with the history of fiction can write the forthcoming narrative *à priori*. There is the loss and the gain; the wreck and the salvage; the fire and the preservation. A new dynasty will succeed the old one; and a king will come who will sigh with sadness over the hasty folly of Shi-kwang-ti. He will try to undo the harm that has been done. He will search for odd and scarce copies: perhaps he will offer a reward for them. Failing this he will have recourse to the oldest inhabitants, and the longest memories. He will, of course, be successful; and the result will accurately coincide with the conditions required for an old-new history; a history in which we must expect imperfections, and yet find facts. The fire accounts for the first; the reconstruction for the second.

So about B.C. 200, when Fabius Pictor and Nævius were founding a literature in Rome, the first of the kings of

The dynasty of Han begins to rule. He restores the feudal system of the Dzheu, and attempts to restore the books on which their claims were based. An old man knows the Shu-king by heart, from whose dictation the work, as we have it at present, is written down. Other works were similarly reconstructed; sometimes with the commentary as well as the text; for, so advanced were the subjects of the Dzheu, and Tsin, that they had not only original authors, but critics also.

B.C. 100, lived Vu-ti, the Liberal; Vu-ti held out rewards for any one who would discover, and produce, an old manuscript; and many were the applicants unto Vu-ti.

Vu-ti was the patron, Szu-ma-tan the artist. Szu-ma-tan compiled, abridged, and arranged the MSS. that Vu-ti's premiums brought forth. Szu-ma-tan, however, died during his work, and was succeeded in the editorship by Szu-ma-tsien, his son.

Szu-ma-tsien's history (Szu-ki as it is named) begins with Kwang-ti, who reigned B.C. 2637, and with the Tsin dynasty; in other words, it ranges from the earliest times to those of the author, a fact which gives us Klaproth's opinion in the following statement, viz. that history of some kind, uncertain history, begins as early as B.C. 2637; certain history as early as B.C. 782.

The text of Szu-ma-tsien, on grounds which satisfy all who can read it, is believed to have come down to us.

It has not, however, been translated into any European language; though notice of its contents is given by Abel Remusat in more than one of his valuable contributions to oriental literature. We should remember, however, that Abel Remusat believes not only in Szu-ma-tsien; but in a history 2000 years older than Szu-ma-tsien.

If the unlearned critic has no means of getting at the exact text of Szu-ma-tsien, he has easy access to that of the Shu-king of Confucius, which is translated by Deguignes, into French. The following is a translation of a translation. Making allowances for this, the reader may form from it a notion of what the so-called history of the early Chinese actually is. Of this it is a favourable specimen, being taken from the end of the book, and, consequently, giving us the times nearest those of the author. Ping-vang, who reigned about B.C. 900, is the king. The following is the account of his reign; nothing being added, nothing been taken away. Can any one pretend to mistake it for history? It is simply a piece of morality that would suit any king, of any country, at any time, and, *mutatis mutandis*, might be called the reign of Numa Pompilius, Alfred the Great, Charles V., or the King of Yvetot. It is *locus communi*; neither more nor less :—

"Yho, Ven-vang, Vu-vang were once famous. They followed exactly the laws of reason. The splendour of their virtue reached the sky. Their fame spread over the whole kingdom. The sovereign Khang-ti placed them on the throne. Illustrious subjects, full of capacity and zeal, served these princes. In all that they undertook, great or small, they followed justice and reason. It is to this sage conduct that the prosperity which our ancestors enjoyed is due. 'How I am afflicted at mounting the throne! I see that Heaven has ceased to favour the people that have submitted to our yoke. The Yong have reduced my kingdom and my family to the last extremity. My ministers are no longer the old men renowned for prudence. I can do nothing by myself. Who shall stand beside me like my father and my grandfather? Could I see any one who would serve me faithfully, I should believe that my crown was safe.

"'O my father, Yho; thou comest to give a new lustre to the memory of the chief of thy branch. Thou hast retraced the image of the times when Ven-vang and Vu-vang founded the kingdom. Thou hast established me as their successor. Thou hast shown that thou art the equal of thy ancestors in filial piety. Thou hast helped me in my affliction. Thou hast strongly supported me in all my dangers. I cannot but load thee with praises.

"'O my father, Yho!' said the prince, 'examine the subjects of thy state. Make peace and union reign amongst them. I will give thee a vessel full of the wine of Kutshang, a red bow with 100 red arrows, a black bow with 100 black arrows. I will also give thee four horses. Depart then. Make thyself obeyed by those who are afar. Instruct those who are near. Love the people and put peace amongst them. Avoid pleasure and amusements. Prove and love the people of thy royal city, and give to all the world a great example of virtue.'"

The contrast of these not unfavourable samples of the supposed sources of Szu-ma-tsien's history are the accounts of early writers other than Chinese, of which the date is known, and the conditions, under which the information was attained, intelligible. That the classical writers give us little or nothing has already been stated. What a Chinese Buddhist saw in India, in the sixth century, is to be found in the translation, by Stanislas Julien, of his narrative. This, however, is an account of Hindostan, not China. It shows, however, that China produced Buddhists, observers, and writers at an early period, *i. e.* as early as the reign of Justinian; provided the date be accurate. In this there is nothing very improbable; the reign of Justinian being the date of the introduction of silk into Europe.

The work, however, is no description of China. Of these the earliest is the work translated by Renaudot, and known as the Travels of the Two Mahometans. It is referred to the eighth century. It re-appears in Masudi, who wrote in the tenth, running thus:—

"The money of the Chinese consists, for the most part, of copper and brass coins.

"This city became the residence of the kings of China. The name of it is Ankû, and it is three months' journey distant from the Abyssinian sea. They have another large town called Madú (Amid) in the north-west of their empire towards et-Tubbet. Madú and et-Tubbet keep up a constant warfare, without either party being conquerors or conquered. Order in the affairs of the empire, good government, and prosperity continued under the successors of this king; justice was everywhere exercised, and injustice was banished from their country. They followed the regulations made by the former kings, whom we have mentioned; and they kept up the wars with their enemies. Their frontiers were well guarded by soldiers, the armies received their pay regularly, and merchants flocked there, by land and sea, from all parts of the world. They were of the ancient faith, the Samanean religion, which is about the same as the belief of the Koraïshites before Mohammed. They worshipped symbols, towards which they turned their faces in praying. Persons of intellect addressed their prayers to the Almighty, and they considered the images of idols and other symbols merely as objects to fix their eyes upon; whilst the uneducated and ignorant confounded these symbols with the Almighty, and worshipped them both (God and the symbols) together. The adoration of the idols brought them nearer to God, although the notions expressed in their religious service were too concrete to be adequate to the sublimity, greatness, and majesty of the divinity. The service which they performed to these idols was nevertheless an expression of obedience to God, and it brought them nearer to Him.

"This continued until speculations and sectarianism grew up in China. Then rose the Dualists, and those who believe on a time without limits. Previous to these innovations, they had worshipped images like the higher and lower classes in India. These religious quarrels caused a complete revolution. They had not been without speculation, but they had referred in all questions to the ancient sacred laws.

"The Chinese empire borders on the kingdom of the Taghizghiz, and it was from them that they received the doctrine of Manes, of a god of light and darkness. Previously they had been in ignorance, and had the same system of worship as the various Turkish hordes, until a satan of a Manichean came to them, and preached to them in flowing phrases of the discord which prevails in this world; the opposition of life and death, health and illness, rich and poor, light and dark, separation and union, continuity and division, rising and setting, existence and non-existence, night and day, and other things which are opposite to each other. He named to them the different pains and frailties to which all animals are subject, both those endowed with speech and those deprived of this faculty; and by which even children, and persons not possessed of their mental faculties, are tortured, adding, that as God the Almighty did not stand in need of their sufferings, they must be ascribed to a powerful opposite principle, which was active in contaminating what is good and moral; and that this was in God. Far be from God what he professed! for He is the Exalted, the Great. Manes misled by this and similar theories their reason, and they believed them. When the king of China was a Samanean he sacrificed animals, and was constantly at war with Jikhân the king of the Turks, but when he had turned Manichean, they became on terms of friendship.

"The kings (and governors) of China follow different sects and religions, and they are at variance in their faith. But they are not biassed so as to abandon the laws commanded by reason, and sacred by usage, in making regulations and passing sentences. The laws of reason are acknowledged by all sects. The Chinese are divided into tribes and branches, like the tribes and families of the Arabs. They bestow great care upon the preservation of their genealogies, and some persons can name fifty ancestors; many know them as far back as Abûr. Persons of the same family do not intermarry; so, for instance (referring for an example to Arabia), a man of the Modhar tribe would marry a woman of the Rabiah tribe, and a man of the Rabiah would marry into the Modhar tribe, or a Kahlan man would marry a Himyarite woman, and a Himyarite a woman of the Kahlan tribe. They are of opinion that the children of such a match will be of a good constitution; and, indeed, this law contributes to public health and longevity."

The opinions of the Chinese as to their relations with the rest of the world are collected from the following continuation of Masudi's account.

"He asked him further, what was the gradation in dignity of the kings of the earth? 'I do not know,' replied the Arab. The king ordered the interpreter to explain to him. 'We count five great kings; the most powerful of them is he who is in possession of el-Irak; for this country is in the middle of the world, and is surrounded by all other kingdoms. We give him, since ancient times, the title of king of kings. After him ranks this our king, to whom we give the title of king of men (mankind). No government is better than ours, no monarch more absolute and firm in his power than our king, nor do the subjects of any other monarch yield such strict obedience as we to our king. We are the kings of men. After ourselves follows the king of the lions, this is the king of the Turks, our neighbour. They are men-lions. Next to them ranks the king of the elephants; that is to say, the king of India, which has with us the name of the kingdom of wisdom, for the Hindus have invented philosophy.

"'Then follows the Byzantine king, whom we call the king of men; for no men on earth have better constitution or finer countenances than the Byzantines. These five stand at the head of kings; all others are beneath them.'"

Upon these extracts we may remark that, even if the date assigned to Szu-ma-tsien be, at one and the same time, correct and too early for the art of writing in China to be considered as an introduction of Buddhism from Tibet or India, there is still the earlier religion of the fire-worshippers, the religion of a lettered nation, to account for such elements of civilization as transcend the Christian era; if any actually do so. With this notice I leave the subject; which I have treated only as an ethnologist. If Chinese civilization be as ancient as it is supposed to be it must be self-evolved; self-evolved and independent of foreign influences, for all of which it is too old. If self-evolved, it is so remarkable an instance of a difference on the part of the Chinese, in respect to their moral and mental constitution, from all the surrounding populations as to simulate a difference of species. Are those who uphold this antiquity prepared to maintain that Chinese differ from Mongolians and Tibetans, as hares from rabbits, or as dogs from foxes?

The Chinese system cannot always have been so exclusive as it is. When the bounds of the empire were narrower, when the imperial treasury was poorer, when a moderate number of soldiers and officials was all that could be supported, the accessibility of the country must have been neither more nor less than that of the rest of the world. At any rate, exclusion was a matter of some difficulty; and when exclusion was the exception rather than the rule, the influences from without must have been greater than at present.

| English. | Mandarin. | Canton. | Tibetan. |
|---|---|---|---|
| *Head* | te'u | te'u | *m*go |
| *Eye* | mu | mok | mig |
| *Ear* | öl | y | sa |
| *Nose* | pi | pi | nawa |
| *Mouth* | ke'u | hou | ka |
| *Tongue* | shi | shit | *b*dzhe |
| *Hand* | sheu | sheu | lagha |
| *Foot* | kio | koh | *r*kangha |
| *Blood* | khiue | hiut | khrag |
| *Sun* | zhi | yat | nyima |
| *Moon* | yue | yuet | zlava |

| English. | Mandarin. | Canton. | Tibetan. |
|---|---|---|---|
| *Star* | zing | zing | *s*karma |
| *Fire* | kho | ho | me |
| *Water* | shui | shoi | chhu |
| *Tree* | mu | mok | *l*jonshing |
| *Stone* | shi | shap | *r*do |
| *One* | i | yik | *g*chig |
| *Two* | ny | y | *g*nyis |
| *Three* | zan | zam | *g*sum |
| *Four* | szu | si | *b*zhi |
| *Five* | ngu | ong | hna |
| *Six* | lü | lok | druk |
| *Seven* | tsi | tsat | *b*dun |
| *Eight* | pa | pat | *b*rgyud |
| *Nine* | kieu | kou | *d*gu |
| *Ten* | shi | shap | *b*chu. |

## CHAPTER XIII.

The rude tribes of China.—The Miaoutse.—The Gyami dialect.

THAT the civilization of China is, by no means, uniformly spread over the whole country has long been known. It has also been known that the nationality may, possibly, be as little uniform as the civilization. Have we not seen that on the Tibetan frontier there were the tribes of the Sifan, who, although for the most part actual Tibetans, may also have had offsets in China? Have we not also seen that in the province of Yunnan there were Karens and Shans? In both of these cases we had populations which were other than Chinese in blood and language at least. They were not, however, the so-called aborigines of China.

Now whoever the so-called aborigines of China may be, they are a population of more than ordinary interest to the generality of investigators. The Chinese themselves are old—very old—even in their ordinary condition; at least such is the current doctrine. How primitive then, and ante-diluvian, and primeval, and Ogygian and the like are men who are their aborigines; who stand to them, with their own wondrous antiquity, as the Welsh do to the English! Such aborigines the Miaoutse are said to be. That they have stimulated curiosity is true; but that the stimulus has led to much is doubtful. How are they accessible? They belong to those parts in which aborigines most especially delight, the hillier parts of the more retired areas. We have no first-hand account of them, no vocabularies, no minute or trustworthy notices. They are probably (but by no means certainly) Chinese in blood. They are probably not so much the aborigines of China as the Chinese in their aboriginal state. It is not likely that they have any general name for themselves. It is not likely, then, that the name Miaoutse is native. Chinese in origin, it is, nevertheless, convenient.

There are the White Miaoutse and the Black Miaoutse; so named according to the difference of their complexion. I do not know the evidence of this. It may only be an inference. The names of colours are not always what they appear to be. There is a White Russia and a Red Russia. There is a White Wallachia and a Black Wallachia; for so the Turks call Moldavia. There are White Croatians—all the names being applied without any regard to the colour of the skin. The Red Karen were one of the populations of the Burmese empire. Some said that they were named from the colour of their cheeks. Others said they were named from the colour of their breeches. All we know, then, about the Miaoutse is, that there is a Black and a White division of them.

One tribe (occupant of the Ping-sha-shih hills) has the following custom. When a man marries he sticks five small flags into a bundle of grass, bound together by seven bands. Of this he makes a sort of idol, kneeling before it. Meanwhile his friends fold their arms and bow. After this they feast. At the death of a parent the eldest son remains at home without washing his face for forty-nine days. Having done this he sacrifices to Tang-kwei. Tang-kwei is the Miaoutse Mercury.

Another tribe (Hea-king by name) offer the head of a tiger to their chief deity when a friend is sick. The head is placed on a dish or platter, with a sword, with three incense-sticks and two candles behind it, and three cups of wine in front. Before this they cross the arms and bow.

Another tribe (name unknown) when they wish to propitiate the good-will of the demons of the weather, appoint ten companies of young men and women, who, after dressing themselves in robes of felt, and binding their loins with an embroidered girdle, dance and play the (?) organ. This is done for three days and three nights, and ensures a plentiful year. A father, when his son is ten years of age, sacrifices a white tiger, and names the child.

Another tribe (Chung-king), when they mourn for their dead, kill an ox, and place the head and feet upon an altar, with basins filled with food, lighted candles, and cups of wine.

Another tribe (name unknown) solemnize the marriage by sacrificing a dog.

Another (name unknown) in the middle of autumn offer a sacrifice to the founder of their race. Having fed an ox, they sacrifice, and feast on it; drinking a liquor distilled (*sic*) from rice. This is done by one of the western tribes.

Another (name unknown, but of the Miaoutse division) keep an ox ready fattened for sacrificing to the honour of their founder on such occasions as may demand a festival.

Another (name also unknown, but remarkable for the purity of its manners) kindle a vast bonfire at the funeral of their friends.

Another (name also unknown), when a man is about to marry, knock out two of his teeth with a hammer. This is remarkable because we shall see the custom repeating itself in Australia.

*The Gyami.*—One of the languages which Mr. Hodgson treats as Sifan, or as the language of one of those tribes of China which are, at one and the same time, occupants of the western frontier, and either really or apparently ruder than the rest of the population, and which he calls Gyami, is certainly more Chinese than Tibetan, more Chinese than T'hay, more Chinese than Burmese, more Chinese than aught else.

It has also an affinity with a vocabulary of Stralenberg's which has perplexed Klaproth. Stralenberg gives a short list of words which he says belong to the language of the Mantshu Tartars who were once the vassals of the Mongols. Yet it is not, as Klaproth remarks, Mantshú; but rather Chinese. It is certainly Chinese in its numerals; at the same time ten (about half) of the other words "exhibit not the least likeness to any Asiatic language known to me (*i. e.* Klaproth)." Now both this vocabulary of Stralenberg's, and the Gyami of Hodgson agree in adding *-ko* and *-ku*, or *-go* to the numerals. One of the Mishmi dialects does the same. The Chepang adds *zho*.

| English. | Gyami. | Chinese. | Strahlenberg. | Karen. | T'hay. | Tibetan. |
|---|---|---|---|---|---|---|
| *Man* | rin | nan, zhin | oydzha | pokwa | —— | mi |
| *Head* | thau | têu | nedo | kho | hon | go |
| *Hand* | syu | sheu | —— | tshu | me | lango |
| *Foot* | chyaa | kio | —— | kho | tin | kango |
| *Sun* | rethau | zhi | —— | mu | let | nyima |
| *Moon* | yoliang | yue | —— | la | leon | dawa |
| *Star* | singshu | sing | —— | tsha | lao | karma |
| *Fire* | akkha | kho | —— | meu | fai | me |
| *Water* | shiu | shui | —— | thi | nam | chhu |
| *One* | iku | i | ygà | ta | ning | chik |

| English. | Gyami. | Chinese. | Strahlenberg. | Karen. | T'hay. | Tibetan. |
|---|---|---|---|---|---|---|
| *Two* | liangku | ol, ny | hanga | khi | song | nyi |
| *Three* | sangku | sang | sanga | thu | sam | sum |
| *Four* | siku | szu | shygga | lwi | sy | zhyi |
| *Five* | wuku | ngu | ugæ | ye | ha | gna |
| *Six* | leuku | lu | higæ | ghu | khok | thu |
| *Seven* | chhiku | zi | szygæ | nwi | dzhea | dun |
| *Eight* | paku | pa | baye | gho | ped | gye |
| *Nine* | chyaku | kieu | dzhugæ | khwi | kau | guh |
| *Ten* | issha | shi | shy | tatshi | sib | chu |

It is probable (nothing more) that the Miaoutse and Gyami are in the same category in respect to their language.

## CHAPTER XIV.

**Population of unexplored districts.—Bibor.—Kulta.—Lawa.—Lolo.—Moy.—Kwantong.—Tshampa.**

Thus far the populations which have come under notice, with the exception of Miaoutse, whom we have (possibly upon insufficient grounds) considered as Chinese, have been known to us by specimens of their several languages; so that, as far as speech is concerned, they have been classified. I do not say that the blood and the language always coincide. I only say that the latter is *primâ facie* evidence of the former.

But the populations whose languages are thus known are, by no means, the whole of the occupants of south-eastern Asia. Several large districts are either imperfectly explored or wholly unknown.

The parts due south of Upper Asam are in this predicament. So are the parts due north thereof. Who succeed the Bor Abors, the Mishmi, the southern and eastern Naga? Who touch the Khamti, and the Singpo on the east? Where does the Shan family end? Where does the Chinese begin? What are the details of the southern frontier of Manipúr? What those of northern and eastern Siam? Where do the Kambojians begin and end? Where the Anamese?

The populations to the north and east of the Abor and Mishmi localities are, when other than Tibetan or Chinese, in all probability, allied to the known mountaineers of the

Asam boundary; being like them rude, more or less independent, more or less pagan. Of these the Bibor may be the least, the Kulta the most, Indianized.

*The Bibors*, called Barkan by the Abors of the Subanshiri, tattoo their lips.

*The Jubars* lie three days' journey beyond them.

*The Kulta*, or *Kolita*, are more civilized, having received a tincture of Brahminism, and having been at one time sufficiently powerful to effect a conquest of part of Asam. They dwell to the north-east of the extremity of the Asam Valley.

Beyond the Kulta country lies that of the Yam Sinh Rajah, whose subjects are independent and warlike; famous, too, for their horses; also for their trowsers, or breeches, which are somewhat after the European fashion. In this respect more than one tribe (or if not this the same tribe under a variety of names) has commanded notice. Captain Yule heard of the same article of dress being used on the northern eastern frontier of Burma.

The Bibor, Jiobar, and Kolita are on the drainage of the Brahmaputra. But, besides the Brahmaputra, there are the great rivers that run from north to south, the head-waters of which are, one and all, unexplored. There is the Irawadi, which is more especially Burmese; the Siamese Menam; the Kambojian Mekhong, the longest and the least known of all. Then there are the rivers of Cochinchina and Tonkin; running from west to east, rather than from north to south, of less length than the one previously mentioned. There are the rivers and the water sheds between them; the banks being alluvial, and fit for cultivation, the watersheds being either hilly or mountainous, woods or forests. Such is the difference in the physical geography. In ethnology the difference is— we need scarcely say what it is. We anticipate its nature.

The plains will be occupied by the more civil, the hills by the ruder, race. The more civil tribes will be Buddhist; paganism being a *non inventum.* The ruder will be more or less pagan; sometimes wholly so.

*The watershed of the Irawadi and Menam.*—On the watershed between the Irawadi and the Menam, and on the frontier of Siam and Ava, common, in all probability, to both empires, lie the Lawa.

In Bowring's map they are placed due north of the Karens and due west of the Laos. It is only for the sake of making assurance doubly sure that I notice them here; having but little doubt as to their being T'hay. Word for word Lawa is Lao, Lau, or Laos. Still, as the name may be applied to more populations than one, there is a shade of doubt over their exact ethnological position.

The same applies to the Khong. The name is generic. Some of the tribes to which it applies are certainly Kambojian. These have already been noticed. Whether *all* are so is a question upon which further evidence is wanting.

*Watershed of the Upper Menam and Mekhong—Valley of the Middle Mekhong.*—Here we find the names Kakui and Kakua applied to the occupants of both sides of the Mekhong, the Mutsa being near them. Word for word Kakui is the name of certain tribes, already noticed, of the Singpho area. The criticism that applies to the term Lawa and Khong applies here.

That the Lilun, the Laulan, and Lolo are populations bearing one and the same name, I have little doubt. They lie (some of them at least) east of the Mekhong, being Buddhist in creed.

That Pulai and Paloung are one and the same words I have little doubt; holding also, that they may, possibly, be Lilun and Lolo as well. The Yem, the Dumu, and

Duner lie in their neighbourhood, *i. e.* on the drainage of the Mekhong, and in a tea-growing district.

Lastly, comes a series of names beginning with *ka;* viz. Kali, Kapin, Kalau, Kadam, Kamu, Kamet. The populations which bear them seem to lie to the west of the ones just enumerated, on the frontier of Siam and Ava rather than on that of Siam and China. They may be Karen. They may be Shan.

*Watershed of Mekhong, and the rivers of Cochinchina and Tonkin.*—In the south, between Kambojia and Cochinchina, reside the Moy; to the north, on the frontier of Tonkin, the Kwantong. The Moy are said to be very dark-complexioned. The Kwantong are said to be a lettered nation. They are, probably, in the same category with the Lolo; the Moy being either Anamese or Kambojian.

*The Tshampa.*—The *coast* between the mouth of the Mekhong and the frontier of Cochinchina is in the occupancy of a population called Tshampa. The only known vocabulary for these parts is Malay. Whether this represent the language of true Tshampa is a question upon which we desire further evidence.

| English. | Tshampa. | Malay. |
|---|---|---|
| *Man* | orang | orang |
| *Head* | akoh | ulu |
| —— | —— | kapala |
| *Eye* | mata | mata |
| *Mouth* | chabui | mulut |
| *Sun* | naharai | mata-ari |
| *Moon* | bulan | bulan |
| *Star* | bintang | bintang |
| *Sky* | langi | langit |
| *Fire* | apoi | api |
| *Water* | aya | ayar |
| *River* | sungai | sungi |
| *Sea* | laut | laut |
| *Stone* | batao | batu |

| English. | Tshampa. | Malay. |
|---|---|---|
| *One* | satu | satu |
| *Two* | dua | duwa |
| *Three* | klao | tiga |
| *Four* | pak | ampat |
| *Five* | limo | lima |
| *Six* | num | anam |
| *Seven* | tuju | tuju |
| *Eight* | dalapan | dalapam |
| *Nine* | samilan | sambilan |
| *Ten* | plu | pulu. |

This list is from Craufurd, who took it from a merchant trading to Sincapore.

# CHAPTER XV.

Islands.—The Mergui Archipelago, Formosa and the Nicobars.—The Mincopi of the Andamans.

ALL the populations hitherto noticed belong to the Continent; indeed the class to which they belong is pre-eminently a class of lândsmen. As a general rule the islanders of both the Indian Ocean and the Pacific are Indians (like the Cingalese of Ceylon), Japanese (like the Luchu), or (like the natives of Sumatra and Borneo) Malay. At the same time, there are the following exceptions:—

Hainan is, as we expect from its contiguity to the mainland, Chinese.

The Mergui Archipelago and Formosa, wide apart as they lie, are in the same category, with each other, and with the Tshampa district. The known specimens of their language are, more or less, Malay; it being, however, doubtful whether they represent the aboriginal form of speech.

Of the Silong, or wandering fishermen of the Mergui Archipelago, the number amounts to about 1000 souls.

| English. | Silong. | Malay. |
|---|---|---|
| *Man* | mesa | orang |
| *Head* | atak | ulu |
| —— | —— | kapala |
| *Hair* | autak | rambut |
| —— | —— | bulu |
| *Eye* | matat | mata |
| *Ear* | tengah | talinga |
| *Tongue* | klek | lidah |
| *Tooth* | lepadn | gigi |

| English. | Silong. | Malay. |
|---|---|---|
| *Hand* | langan | tangan |
| *Foot* | kakai | kaki |
| *Sun* | matai-alal | matar-ari |
| *Moon* | bulan | bulan |
| *Star* | bituek | bintang |
| *Fire* | apoi | api |
| *Water* | awaen | ayar |
| *Stone* | batoe | batu |
| *Tree* | ki | kayu. |

*Formosa.*—The western coast of Formosa is occupied, to a great extent, by Chinese, recent settlers. But the interior is the residence of more than one rude tribe. These it is whose language is supposed to differ from that of the only known specimen, which is as follows :—

| English. | Formosan. | Malay. |
|---|---|---|
| *Man* (*irr.*) | paraigh | laki |
| —— (*homo*) | aulong | orang |
| *Eye* | matta | mata |
| *Ear* | tangira | talinga |
| *Head* | bungo | ulu, kapala |
| *Mouth* | mutaus | mulut |
| *Tooth* | ualigh | gigi |
| *Tongue* | dadila | lidah |
| *Hair* | waukugh | rambut, bulu |
| *Hand* | rima | tangan |
| *Foot* | rahpal | kaki |
| *Blood* | amagh | darah |
| *Sun* | uai | mata-ari |
| *Moon* | waunat | bulan |
| *Star* | attatalingahei | bintang |
| *Fish* | tung | ikan |
| *Fire* | apœi | api |
| *Water* | ralaum | ayar |
| *Sea* | waungh | laut |
| *Tree* | parannah | kayu |
| *Stone* | watto | batu |
| *Hill* | waukein | bukit, gunung |
| *Earth* | nai | tana, bumi |
| *House* | tallag | rumah |
| *One* | saat | satu |
| *Two* | rauha | duwa |

| English. | Formosan. | Malay. |
|---|---|---|
| *Three* | tauro | tiga |
| *Four* | hpat | ampat |
| *Five* | rima | lima |
| *Six* | nnum | anam |
| *Seven* | pytto | tuju |
| *Eight* | kauyphpa | daiapar |
| *Nine* | matauda | sambilar |
| *Ten* | kytti | pulu |

*The Nicobar Islanders.*—The natives of the Nicobar islands are described as an ill-looking population, with dark skins, yellow scleroticas, flat faces, and scanty beards, whose chief aliment consists in hogs, poultry, and cocoa-nuts, whose deities are the *Ividi*, or genii of the hills and woods, and whose priests are called *Malains*.

In northern islands—Carnicobar, Shovra, Teressa, Nankovry, and some others of less importance, differ from the Great and Little Nicobar in being volcanic rather than coralline, and in their occupants being somewhat better shaped, and somewhat less wild. In the interior of the Great Nicobar a population ruder than that of the coast is said to reside.

Crawfurd's notice of the Nicobar language is founded upon the vocabularies of Hamilton and Fontana, the former representing the language of the most northern, the latter that of the most southern of the islands. Such being the case, the extent to which the two forms of speech differ, seems considerable. No wonder, then, that the following list of the fourteen words common to the two vocabularies should suggest the suspicion that the Carnicobar and the Nicobar were "two distinct languages."

| English. | Carnicobar. | Great Nicobar. |
|---|---|---|
| *Man* | kejonia | enkoñi |
| *Woman* | kekana | enkana |
| *Child* | chu | keñu |

| English. | Carnicobar. | Great Nicobar. |
|---|---|---|
| *Fowl* | hayam, m | toföak |
| *Hog* | hüon | not |
| *Dog* | tamam | ham |
| *Fire* | tamïa | henu |
| *Rain* | kumra | hame |
| *House* | alhanum | ñi |
| *To laugh* | ayelaur | hethai |
| *To eat* | na | hanino |
| *To drink* | ok | püum |
| *To sleep* | lumlum | etqja |
| *To weep* | püing | höum |

Again—the vocabularies to which alone Mr. Crawfurd had access gave very few Malay words ; a fact which led that writer to the statement that the base of the language they represented was other than Malay. Since this opinion was published the whole group has been visited in detail by the Danish exploring expedition under Steen Bille, and our philogical *data* have been increased thereby. Of these it may fairly be said that they help to break down the broad line of demarcation both between the northern and southern dialects, and the language of the group in general and the Malay. The little islets, compared to which even such small blocks of land as the main islands assume a continental magnitude are called by the Malay name *pulo*.

| English. | Carnicobar. | Teressa. | Nancowry. |
|---|---|---|---|
| *Man (homo)* | ——— | bayu | dzhubayu |
| *Head* | ——— | goseh | ——— |
| *Hair* | kheui | hehok | ——— |
| *Eye* | olmat | ——— | ——— |
| *Ear* | ——— | nang | ——— |
| *Nose* | ehelme | mhang | moah |
| *Mouth* | monoi | ——— | meno |
| *Hand* | ——— | ——— | genâs |
| *Foot* | gundron | ——— | ——— |
| *Blood* | mam | ——— | vhoa |
| *Sun* | ——— | huik | ——— |
| *Moon* | tingaat | hahæ | khaæt |

| English. | Carnicobar. | Toressa. | Naucowry. |
|---|---|---|---|
| *Fire* | ——— | pala | ——— |
| *Water* | mak | ——— | ——— |
| *Stone* | ——— | ——— | manghæ |
| *Egg* | laal | ——— | ——— |
| *Demon* | ——— | pivi | ——— |

*The Mincopie of the Andaman Islanders.*—The Andaman islanders are mentioned as early as the twelfth century, *i. e.* by the two Mahometan travellers of Renaudot. These write, that beyond the Nicobar Islands "lies the Sea of Andaman. The people on this coast eat human flesh quite raw; their complexion is black, their hair frizzled, their countenance and eyes frightful; their feet are very large, and almost a cubit in length, and they go quite naked. They have no embarkations; if they had, they would devour all the passengers they could lay hands on." Marco Polo writes equally unfavourably—"Angaman is a very large island, not governed by a king. The inhabitants are idolaters, and are a most brutish and savage race, having heads, eyes and teeth resembling those of the canine species. Their dispositions are cruel, and every person not being of their own nation, whom they can lay hands on, they kill and eat."

A paper, by Lieutenant Colebrooke, is the chief source of our knowledge concerning the Mincopie, the author being indebted to his predecessors Major Kyd and Captain Blair, for some of his facts. He describes them as plunged in the grossest ignorance and barbarity; barely acquits them of the charge of cannibalism; and unhesitatingly affirms that they are guilty of the murder of the crews of such vessels as may be wrecked upon their coast. Does he do this on the strength of his observation or his reading?

The late Sir Charles Malcolm, who had had one of the natives aboard-ship with him, took considerable pains to dilute the charges that lay against this ill-famed population, and spoke in strong terms as to the gentleness and docility of the individual with whom he thus came in contact.

| English. | Andaman. |
|---|---|
| *Man* | kamolan |
| *Hair* | otti |
| *Head* | tabay |
| *Eye* | jabay |
| *Ear* | kwaka |
| *Mouth* | morna |
| *Arm* | pilie |
| *Nose* | melli |
| *Finger* | mornay |
| *Hand* | gonie |
| —— | monie |
| *Blood* | kotshengohi |
| *Belly* | napoi |
| *Teeth* | mahoi |
| *Breast* | kah |
| *Tongue* | talie |
| *Bone* | gitongay |
| *Chin* | pitang |
| *Foot* | guki |
| *Knee* | ingolay |
| *Leg* | tshigie |
| *Fire* | mona |
| *Water* | migway |
| *Sky* | madamo |
| *Sun* | ahay |
| *Moon* | tabie |
| *Star* | tshelobay |
| *Wind* | tomjamy |
| *Wood* | tanghi |
| *House* | beaday |
| *Bird* | lohay |
| *Fish* | nabohi |
| *Black* | tshigiuga |
| *Cold* | tshorna |

The Mincopie are skilful in shooting fish with their arrows. They take, however, but little pains to cultivate the soil; feeding on what they find or kill. They are fond of singing and dancing; ignorant of the art of working in metal; but not unskilful in the management of their canoes. These are hollowed out of the trunks of trees by means of fire, or instruments of stone. Sometimes they use rafts of bamboo. Their bows are remarkably long. Hand-nets, wicker-baskets, and a few specimens of pottery-ware have been seen amongst them.

## CHAPTER XVI.

The Tungús Stock.—The Mantshu or Tungús of China.—Tungús of Siberia.—Horse; Reindeer; Dog.—Lamuts.—Daurians.—Application of the European Alphabet to Siberian Languages.—Shamanism.—Tshapodzhirs, Tungús, &c.

TUNGUS is a general name, current amongst ethnologists for a population common to Siberia and China; a population of vast area and varied manners, a population, however, whose physiognomy connects it with the tribes of Northern Asia in general, whose history links it to China, and whose language forms a transition between the monosyllabic and agglutinate forms of speech. It approaches inflection nearer than any of the dialects hitherto enumerated; recedes from it more than any that are likely, for some time at least, to be mentioned in the sequel.

I have little doubt that the name means, or, originally meant *man*, and that it is a word which we shall find frequently appearing and re-appearing in Asia, in Europe, and still more frequently, in America. In some respects it is a native name; in others not. For the family at large there is no general name at all. There is only a series of names for the several divisions of it. One of these is *beye*, which we know means *man*. Another is *donki*, which I suppose is the word out of which Tungús arose. In Chinese this becomes Tong-chu. This the Russians adopt from the Chinese, the ethnologists adopting it from the Russians.

The Tungús area is of vast extent in every direction. It touches, or, at least, approaches, the Arctic Ocean on the north. It extends to the frontier of China on the south; not to mention the Tungús who, under the name of Mantshus, constitute the dominant population of China itself. The court of Pekin is, more or less, Tungús. East and west it reaches from the Yenisey to the Pacific Ocean. No wonder, then, if the nations, families, tribes, stocks of divisions of the Asiatic populations with which the Tungús come in contact be numerous. No wonder, too, if the frontier be irregular. We shall find several cases where its outline is deeply indented, and where populations other than Tungús interrupt its continuity.

*The Tungús of China—Mantshu.*—The political division of the Tungús stock is convenient, and, by no means, very unnatural. The tribes of Siberia are under Russia. The tribes of Mantshuria belong to China. The Mantshuria of the maps is, there, or thereabouts, the water system of the river Amur or Sagalin; Amur as it is called by the Russians, Sagalin, or Sagalin Ula (Black River), as it is called by the Mantshu. The whole, however, of the river is not Tungús. The parts about the mouth are occupied by members of the Aino family. The peninsula, too, of Korea is other than Mantshu. Thirdly, in the parts due north of Pekin a long process, or offset, from Mongolia cuts-in, and well-nigh separates the true Tungús part of Mantshuria from China. The Mongols, however, of this district are intrusive.

The Tungús of China—and it must be remarked that there are Tungús only in the way that an Englishman is a German and that the designation is purely technical—are in a very different predicament from their congeners of the more ungenial climate of the north. The valley of the Saghalin, a district of which the geography is imperfectly known, seems to present free undulations of hill and valley, to have a large surface of productive land, and to be fertilized by a moist atmosphere. In its latitude it coincides with Northern Germany; but it is a Germany without either a Baltic on its north, or a Mediterranean on its south; *desiderata* which must be carefully remembered when we speculate upon the causes which have determined the difference of the two civilizations. All the tribes of Mantshuria are not on the same level with the Proper Mantshu: for the Proper Mantshu are a lettered population; though neither their literature nor their alphabet is of any great antiquity; the latter being a mere modification of the Mongol. They are more or less agricultural and industrial, occupants of valleys and villages. They are conquerors; for the present dynasty of China is Mantshu. And this suggests a division. There are the Mantshus of Mantshuria and the Mantshus of China. Of course they are numerous in this latter country, where there is a court and a government, and where official aptitude leads to honour and emolument. The rewards, however, of this kind are chiefly monopolized by Chinese. Still, the dynasty is Mongol, and some portion of the bureaucracy is the same; though the extent to which it is so is unknown. The army, on the other hand, is Mantshu to an inordinate extent; and as the European practice of quartering the soldiers of one country on the soil of another is also that of China, there are Mantshu soldiers everywhere but in Mantshuria. There are Mantshu soldiers in Mongolia; Mantshu soldiers (far outnumbering the Chinese) in Tibet. The Kumaon frontier, as we have already seen, is kept by a Mantshu garrison. By this means Mantshu blood is propagated far and wide, and Mantshu half-bloods must be common in garrison towns.

Well clothed, warmly lodged, and with an environment of civilization, many of the Mantshus of China have changed their physiognomy no less than their habits. Sir

John Barrow saw both men and women of Mantshu blood who were "extremely fair and of a florid complexion; some had light blue eyes, straight or aquiline noses, brown hair, immense bushy beards, and had more the appearance of Greeks than of Tartars." Whatever intermixture may account for in this description, it will not explain the beards. Who were the bearded nations to supply it? The Chinese are nothing of the kind. Still less the Mongols.

The Mantshu of China are inconveniently called Tartars and the Mantshu dynasty a Tartar dynasty. The Bhot of the Himalayan frontier of Tibet are also so called; as are the Turks of what stands in the maps as Chinese Tartary; by which we mean the countries of Khoten and Yarkend, or Little Bokhara. The less we use the equivocal term Tartar, Tahtah, or Tatar, the sounder will be our ethnology.

The Mantshu call

| | |
|---|---|
| China | *Nikan.* |
| The Mongolians | *Monga.* |
| The Russians | *Oros.* |
| Nertshinsk | *Niptshi.* |
| The Giliak* | *Fiaka.* |
| Korea | *Solgo.* |

This last name is remarkable because the Mantshu tribes of the Upper Sagalin are called Solon; and because there is evidence of other kinds that a portion, at least, of what is now Mantshuria, was once Korea.

| English. | Mantshu. | Korean. | Aino. |
|---|---|---|---|
| *Man* (*vir*) | ——— | sand | okkai |
| *Man* (*homo*) | beye (?) | saram | ainu |
| ——— | ——— | ——— | gura |
| *Eye* | yasa | nuon | shigi |
| *Head* | udzhu | mati | shaba |
| *Hair* | funieke | muri | numa |
| *Ear* | shan | kui | kisara |

* A branch of the Aino, or Kurilian stock.

| English. | Mantshu. | Korean. | Aino. |
|---|---|---|---|
| *Nose* | okoro | ko | idu |
| *Mouth* | anga | yip | paru |
| *Tongue* | veikhe | hie | ai |
| *Tooth* | ilengu | ni ' | nimaki |
| *Hand* | gala | sun | tegi |
| *Foot* | betkhe | pal | kima |
| *Sun* | shun | peng | tshukf-ramo· |
| *Moon* | bia | oru | tshukf |
| *Star* | uzhikha | peru | nodzi |
| *Fire* | tua | pol | undzhi |
| *Water* | make | mu | raka |
| *Tree* | moo | nan | nü |
| *Stone* | vekhe | tu, tol | shioma |
| *Egg* | umkhan | al | nuku |
| *Fish* | nimakha | koki | zepf |

The tribes that, collectively, constitute the Mantshu division amount to more than sixty; so many names, at least, are to be found in Klaproth's list.* The Mongols call them either Uzun Dzurtshit or Angga Dzurtshit. Tshurtshut, Zhudzhi, Nyudzhi, Geougen, and Nyudzhri are the same word under different forms. A list of Nyudzhi words from a Chinese narrative is shown by Klaproth to be Mantshu.

The Nyudzhi, or Mantshu conquest of China, A.D. 1644, under Taidzu, from whom the reigning emperor of China is descended, is a definite piece of history, to which we shall do well in giving due prominence; inasmuch as the details of the several, real or supposed, Tungús invasions of earlier date are by no means sufficiently established. Chinese and Mantshu scholars may, perhaps, be satisfied. If so they should have better grounds for being so than those which they have made accessible to the general reader. The editor, for instance, of Castrén's posthumous work on the Altaic populations allows himself to believe that this same tribe of Nyudzhi, Zhudzhi, or Yutshi are mentioned, *eo nomine*, as a Tungús tribe of the eleventh

* See page 287.

century *before* the Christian era; concerning which we learn thus much, viz., that they paid tribute to China in arrows made of a sort of wood called *pu*, the heads of which were of stone. It is these Yutshi who have been identified by respectable writers with the Goths, and converted into the Germans of North-eastern Asia. If Yutshi be Goth, why may not Nyutsh be Deutsch? That certain Chinese writers describe certain Tungús tribes as rude Nyudzhi, or Zhutshi, or the like, I believe. I only demur to the doctrine of these being anything more or less than the tribes of the sixteenth century so denominated.

From the time of these early Nyudzhi to the year 263, A.D., no notice of anything Tungús is to be found. So runs the continuation of the statement in Castrén. It means that during the tenth, ninth, eighth, seventh, and subsequent centuries of the times B.C., the times of the Trojan war, the Homeric poems, the rise of Athens, &c., &c., there was no one in China who has given us any account of Mantshuria. I believe it; only wishing that the rest of the early history of China and the neighbouring countries were equally satisfactory. Let those who over-love antiquity limit themselves to negative statements. This, however, is not done; so that, A.D. 263, another tribe of Mantshuria emerges. The Yleu or Yliu send in that year a tribute of bows, arrows, and sables to the emperor of the Goey dynasty, then sitting on the throne of China. The land of the Yleu was cold and hilly; susceptible, however, of agriculture. The Yleu themselves had neither prince nor chief, but lived under the direction of their elders in small villages, the houses of which were underground holes. In these the rude and miserable occupants passed the winter, smeared with lard, and clothed in garments of hogskin; for, though sheep and oxen were wanting, swine were numerous. In summer the Yleu ran naked. They had no iron. Nor yet salt. For this they used wood-ashes. As to their meat they thawed it, when frozen, either by stamping or by sitting on it. The bridegroom bought his bride. At funerals a pig was buried along with the corpse. Their arms were the bow and arrow.

A break again (and, be it remembered, that every break increases suspicion,) until the fifth century—when, again, under the dynasty of the Goey, we hear of the Mu-ky, Mokh-o, or Mo-ho. Their country lay on the banks of the Songhari. It is strange to find how like the description of the Mokho is to that of the Yliu. They dwelt underground; had no flocks and herds; ate pork; could till the soil, and (what is not said of the Yliu) could brew an intoxicating liquor out of corn. At a Mokho wedding the wife brought her jacket and petticoat; the husband a dress of hogskin. Mark the re-appearance of these hogs. They point to the Nyudzhi. The head-dress, however, of the bridegroom was the tail of a tiger or leopard. If a woman were accused of adultery so openly as to make it impossible for the affair to be hushed up, or winked at, the husband struck her dead on the spot; then and there, when and where the news was told. They shot with bows, and their arrows were poisoned. So strong was the poison that to open a quiver and smell at the cover was death. Die in the summer or spring, and you will be buried on a hill with a building on the spot where you lie. Die in winter, and your frozen body goes to the foxes and polecats.*

The Chinese who describe these nations call them foul

* Urina in lotum adibebatur. Nuptâ virgine, pro primitiis, mammæ à marito sugebantur. Multa de nigritudine mammarum apud Samoyedas scripsere historici. Olim credidi aut gravidas aut fusciores visas fuisse. Quid si hæc mammarum stupratio causa nigritudinis fuerit?

and filthy. So far Chinese history is right. I give what I find (at second-hand) as it comes. It is worth something as Chinese geography. It is worth something as actual ethnography. As chronology it is vain and foolish. There were certain barbarians, whom, at a certain time, the Chinese justly described as barbarians. What this time was is another question. It is not likely to have been 200 A.D. Still less is it likely that it was 1000 B.C.

The period which begins with the Mokho and ends with the Nyudzhi Mantshu is, more or less, historical. It will be considered more fully when the Mongols and Turks have been noticed.

Even in the ordinary Mantshu conquest there are mythological elements. Huc found in the capital of the Chinese province Setshuan a kind of Euhemeric worship of one of the Mantshu captains. Of the present emperor he also gives the following genealogy :—"Ten generations," said his informant (who was he?), "ten generations have now passed away since three young girls descended from the skies to bathe on the banks of the Songai; their names were Argila, Changula, and Fégula. Some magnificent red fruits, coming they knew not whence, were found on the banks by the river close by Fégula's tunic, and she perceiving them, and admiring their beauty, ate of them. Her two companions, after rising from the stream, reascended into heaven, but Fégula could not follow them. She had become pregnant, and had no longer power to quit the earth. She gave birth to a beautiful male child, suckled it, and then placed it in a little island formed by the waters of the river. She directed it to await there the coming of the person who was to be its guardian, and who would, ere long, come to the island to fish; and having said these words, she arose up into the sky whence she had descended.

"It happened as Fégula had foretold. The child grew up into a prodigiously strong and valiant man. He had sons and grandsons, who by degrees became powerful in the land. After five generations, a terrible war broke out, which annihilated them; they were all put to death with the exception of one, who fled across the desert. When overpowered by weariness, and unable to continue his journey, he sat down on the ground, at the risk of dying by the hands of his pursuers.

"But the divine Fégula was watching over him. She directed the flight of a magpie, which perched on his head. The enemy, thinking that the magpie was perched on the trunk of a tree, departed; and thus, by the help of heaven, was rescued the heir of that race which Fégula had brought into the world. He became the progenitor of the Mantchu Tartar nation, and from him descended in a direct line the founder of the dynasty which now fills the imperial throne of Pekin."

The division into tribes is Mantshu and Tungús, and in Mantshuria there are tribes, and sub-tribes. Does this exist in China as a Chinese institution? Mr. Daa of Christiania, whose opinions on all matters connected with those dubious points whereon ethnology and the history of the development of society meet, are of the highest value, has laid great stress on the fact of there being traces of a tribual constitution in China. Individually, I should as soon expect to find them (in the towns) as in England. He states, however, that families of a different name do not intermarry. This may be the case. It may occur on the soil of China. Still, it may or may not be Chinese. It may simply be Mantshu. Let future observers decide. Masudi's statement has already been noticed.

The Russians call the Nyudzhi Deutsheri. Before we

have passed from Siberia into Europe we shall find a Ugrian tribe that calls the Russian Dyutsh. No wonder (I repeat it) that the Yutshi have been made Goths. Yet they are simply Tungús.

There may possibly, and not improbably, be a few independent Tungús tribes in the Tshuktshi country, the only part of Northern Siberia which is not Russian. Roughly speaking, however, all that is not Chinese is Russian.

| English. | Tungús of Amur. | Mantshu. |
|---|---|---|
| *Man (homo)* | —— | beye |
| *Head* | topti | udzhu |
| *Hair* | nurikta | funiekhe |
| *Eye* | yesa | yasa |
| *Ear* | syen | shan |
| *Nose* | ongokto | okhoro |
| *Mouth* | ommün | anga |
| *Tongue* | ini | ilengu |
| *Tooth* | ikta | veikhe |
| *Hand* | nyala | gala |
| *Foot* | adbigi | betkhe |
| *Sun* | delesa | shün |
| *Moon* | bega | bia |
| *Star* | ohikta | uzhikha |
| *Fire* | toho | tua |
| *Water* | mu | muke |
| *Stone* | dsholo | vekhe |
| *One* | mu | emu |
| *Two* | dyul | dzhelo |
| *Three* | ela | elan |
| *Four* | duye | diun |
| *Five* | tonsa | sundzha |
| *Six* | nyuyu | ninggun |
| *Seven* | nada | nadan |
| *Eight* | tshapku | dzakun |
| *Nine* | khuyu | uyun |
| *Ten* | dzha | dzhuan |

I add the following tables, believing that the history of Mantshuria will have to be worked out to a great extent, through its dialects. Chinese geography is like the lovers in Martinus Scriblerus. Annihilate time and space and it would be happy. Give it dates and longitudes and it would be useful.

| English. | Middle Amur. | Mouth of Sangara. | Mantshu. | Kisi. |
|---|---|---|---|---|
| *One* | amun | omu | amoa | omu |
| *Two* | dyuo | dzur | dzhoua | dyul |
| *Three* | elan | ela | gilang | ela |
| *Four* | diyin | duye | tuye | duye |
| *Five* | tonsya | tonga | sundzha | tonsa |
| *Six* | nunyun | nyungu | nyunguen | nyungu |
| *Seven* | nadan | nada | nadang | nada |
| *Eight* | dzabkun | dzhakfo | tsakoi | tshapku |
| *Nine* | yögin | huyu | uyen | khuyu |
| *Ten* | dzhan | dzhoa | dzhuyen | dzha |

*Tungús Proper—The Tungús of Siberia—Russian Tungús.*—The ordinary division of the Tungús of the Russian empire is founded upon the names of the animal with which the different sections chiefly come in contact. In Dauria it is a horse, in the middle districts a reindeer, on the east a dog; so that Horse Tungús, Reindeer Tungús, and Dog Tungús are the denominations. The Horse Tungús approach the Mongolians, the Reindeer the Koriak, the Dog the Kamskadals and Eskino. The Forest Tungús is a sub-division; possibly a cross-division. The Steppe Tungús the same. The Foot-going Tungús the same also. Let a Tungús of any kind live in a steppe or a wood, and his habits are modified. Let a rich man become poor, and he goes on foot instead of driving or riding. Ermann gives a saddening and sickening account of a poor Tungús and his daughter, in a lone hut, desolate, and isolate. They had simply lost their cattle and hunted, apart from their fellows, in solitude. A Bushman who has lost his herds is a Tungús without his dogs, reindeer, or horses, and the history of an afflicted family in the south of Africa is, *mutatis mutandis*, the history of an afflicted family in the north of Asia.

*The Lamut.—Lamu*, or *Lamut*, means *Sea*, and the Tungús of the coast of the Pacific are the Tungús of the Sea. They lie between the watershed of the Aldan, &c., and the Ocean. They are Dog Tungús; for they are near the great dog country, Kamtskatka. Their language connects them with the Mantshú. The parts about Okotsk are their chief locality and the Okota is their chief river.

| English. | Lamut. | Kamskadal. | Koriak. |
|---|---|---|---|
| *Head* | del | kobbel | lavut |
| *Hair* | nyurit | tsheron | katshugui |
| *Eye* | esel | elled | lalat |
| *Ear* | korot | ilyud | vyilut |
| *Nose* | ongata | kayako | enigytam |
| *Mouth* | amga | tshkylda | zekiangin |
| *Tongue* | ilga | dydzil | gügil |
| *Hand* | ngal | tono | myngakatsh |
| *Sun* | nyultan | koatsh | tykete |
| *Moon* | bekh | quinganakuletsh | geilygen |
| *Star* | otshikat | ezhingin | lelapitshan |
| *Fire* | toh | pangitsh. | milugan |
| *Water* | mu | i | mimal |
| *Tree* | mo | oo | uttepel |
| *Stone* | dzholo | kual | guggon |

*The Tungús of Dauria.*—The Lamut lie north and north-east of Mantshuria; the Daurian north and north-west. In language they are connected. The Tungús grammar of Castrén represents the language of the Urulga and Manikov tribes, whose dialect is less pure than those of many others inasmuch as it contains a great number of words from the Buriat dialect of the Mongol.

| English. | Nertshinsk. | Buriat. | Yakut. | Yeniseian. |
|---|---|---|---|---|
| *Man (homo)* | boie | kun | —— | hit |
| *Head* | deli | tulgai | baz | takai |
| *Hair* | nyurikta | nokhon | az | khingayang |
| *Eye* | isal | nidu | kharakh | tesh |

| English. | Nertshinsk. | Buriat. | Yakut. | Yeniseian. |
|---|---|---|---|---|
| *Ear* | zin | tshikin | kulgakh | klokan |
| *Nose* | ongokta | kabar | murun | an |
| *Mouth* | amga | ama | ayak | hohui |
| *Tongue* | ingni | kylyn | tiz | alup |
| *Hand* | dzhalan | gar | ili | —— |
| *Foot* | bokdil | kull | —— | pulang |
| *Sun* | shivun | nara | kun | oga |
| *Moon* | biga | khara | ui | shui |
| *Star* | oshikta | odun | zulus | alak |
| *Fire* | togo | gall | wot | hat |
| *Water* | mu | ugun | u | ul |
| *Tree* | mo | modun | maz | atsh |
| *Stone* | dzhalo | tsholo | taz | shish |

*Russian Tungús.*

| | | | |
|---|---|---|---|
| In the Yakut Districts . . . . . . . . | | | 13,550 |
| „ Circle of Gishiginsk . . . . . . . | | | 500 |
| „ Neighbourhood of Turuchansk— | Males | 1,011 | 1,981 |
| | Females | 970 | |
| „ Circle of Kirinsk . . | Males | 826 | 1,695 |
| | Females | 869 | |
| On the Baikal Lake and in the Sayanian Mountains . . . . | Males | 890 | 1,706 |
| | Females | 816 | |
| In the Circle of Verkneudinsk . | Males | 1,252 | 2,395 |
| | Females | 1,143 | |
| „ Circle of Nertshinsk . . | Males | 7,060 | 13,791 |
| | Females | 6,731 | |

The Tungús language being now, for the first time, exhibited in a grammatical form and treated as a lettered lánguage, we are induced to ask the question, what is its alphabet? Native letters there are none. The only member of the group which has long been reduced to writing is the Mantshú. Doubtless, the letters which suit the Mantshú will also suit the Tungús. They are, however, both inconvenient in form, and limited in application. They embody the scanty literature of the Mongols, from whom they were derived. They embody the scantier literature of the Mantsúhs themselves. Besides this they are connected with China rather than

Western Asia and Europe; with China rather than Muscovy. A Mantshú alphabet might, possibly, have been a convenience to such missionaries as had begun with a knowledge of the Mongolian. To the Russians, in general, it would have been useless. So it would have been to the literati of Europe.

It is in the ordinary Roman alphabet that Castrén's Tungús grammar is drawn up; the author having preferred this to the Russian. This latter would, indeed, have fitted the language well, being both more copious than the Roman, and being already applied to more than one language of Northern Asia. More than this—one of Castrén's own grammars (that of the Ostiak language) is Russian in respect to its letters. Nevertheless, the Tungús orthography is Roman. The grammar itself is in German; and the fact of its being addressed to the readers of the German language has probably determined the character of the alphabet. Whether Russian missionaries, and Russian officials, whose views in the matters of writing and reading are practical rather than theoretical, may confirm the choice is another question. As a general rule, the Slavonic alphabet and Greek Christianity go together. They do this even in Wallachia and Moldavia, where the language is of Latin origin.

The introduction of the European alphabets into Russian Asia is a point which we may advantageously contemplate; inasmuch as the principles by which it has been regulated are, if not unexceptionable, at least laudable.

These alphabets are two; the Russian and the Roman. The former is the easier to handle; the easier by far. By this I mean that when an unwritten language has to be written, and the elementary sounds of that unwritten language are new and strange, so that the question of their representation becomes difficult, the Russian orthography can be applied with greater ease than any other in Europe. There are three reasons for this. One is, the fact of its consisting of a full and sufficient number of simple single signs for the expression of its sounds. The second is, that of the sounds themselves being numerous. The third and the most important, is the freedom with which it has already been treated. It was originally the old Slavonic; closely akin to the present Servian. To become Russian it took four new letters. It was extended to the writing of the Rumanyo of the Danubian Principalities. Here, the existence of two peculiar sounds called for the addition of two new letters. In England, France, or Germany, two old ones would have been combined. We, of Western Europe, are chary of adding new letters to an old alphabet. In Eastern Europe there is no such prejudice. A new sound calls for a new sign, and obtains it. Of the previously-unwritten languages the following have, within the last few years, been embodied by means of the Russian alphabet.

1. The Aleutian of the Islands between Kamtskatka and America.

2. The Osset of Caucasus; the application being made by Sjögren.

3. The Ostiak; the application being made by Castrén. This was in 1849. The adoption of the Roman letters took place later.

4. The Yakut; the application being by Middendorf and Botlinck.

The Roman alphabet—what have been its applications, what the principles on which those applications were made? To the Fin of Finland it had been applied from the beginning, introduced along with the introduction of the Gospel. For the Fin of Finland it was as natural and current as it is for the English or French; Finland having, until 1812, been Swedish. On the other hand the Ziria-nian and Permian languages are written in Russian. But, then, the Estonian and Magyar are Roman. So that, on the whole, it is not too much to say that the Roman is the alphabet for the Fin family.

In 1830, the great Danish philologue, Rask, found his attention directed to the Georgian and Armenian languages; each with an alphabet one-third longer than our own, and each with strange sounds for those alphabets to express. However, they *did* express them; having signs, or letters, to match. These signs did Rask transliterate into Roman; and that, upon a principle, which, though negative rather than positive, is worthy of imitation as far as it goes. He avoided the expression of simple sounds by complex combinations. If a new sound appeared a new sign was excogitated. It might be wholly new. It might be an old letter modified. The former gives us the better and bolder, the latter the more usual and easier, plan. However, in the proposed alphabet the Georgian runs thus—

a, e, i, o, u, p, f, v, ꝑ,
t, d, þ, k, g, ꝁ, ɼ, q, x,
s, z, ś, ż, c, ȝ, ʒ, ć, ǯ,
ʒ̇, j, h, ħ, l, m, n, r, ɧ.

The Armenian thus—

a, e, é, ë, i, o, u, p, b, u *or* w
v, ꝑ, t, d, þ, k, g, ꝁ, ɼ *or* ł
x, s, z, ṡ, ż, c, ʒ, ʒ, ċ,
ǯ, ʒ̇, l, m, n, r, ṙ, j, h.

ꝑ, þ, and *k*, were sounded as the *ph*, *th*, and *kh* in ha-*ph*azard, nu-*th*ook and in-*kh*orn; the original alphabets having thus compendiously expressed three pairs of compound sounds. If it were not for this the combinations of *p*, *t*, *k* and *h* would have sufficed. The ɼ was, nearly or exactly, the Arabic غ, a variety of *g*. The corresponding variety of *k* is expressed by *q*, compared to the Arabic ق. Another guttural was expressed by *x* (Arabic خ). For two varieties of *h* were proposed ħ and ḫ; for the sibilants *s'* (*sh*); *z'* (*zh*); *c* (*ts*); *c'* (*tsh*); ȝ (*dz*); ȝ̇ (*dzh* or the English *j*). Then, for a pair of sounds described as approaching *dhz*, and *dhzh*, ȝ and ȝ̇. The Armenian transliteration had the additional signs ó, ë, t, and ṙ.

Previous to the work in which these two alphabets were proposed the author had been engaged on the Lap of Norwegian Lapland, and had published a grammar on it in which the signs ȝ and ȝ̇ were introduced; as well as ŋ for the *ng* in *king*, *sing*, &c.

Though Castrén's Ostiak grammar, published in 1849, is in Russian, his Zirianian grammar, published 1844, is in Roman letters; these being those of Rask, except that for ȝ and ȝ̇ he used *dz* and *dź*. The Samoyed was the next sound-system he found it necessary to investigate. Here there were two modifications of *l*, viz.: *ɫ*, ɫ, and ɼ; the sound of the *gn* in French words like Boulogne, along with similar modifications of *d*, *t*, *s*, *z*, and *c*; which were written *dy*, *ty*, *sy*, *zy*, *tshy*—there or thereabouts.

Lastly, the Tushi alphabet of Schiefner contains x̣, ḥ, k̇, ǵ, ċ, ç, ç̇, ȝ̇, ṡ, ż, t, ṗ, ḷ.

All this, though exceptionable in many respects, is better than the system too much in vogue amongst ourselves of making combinations, which have generally no other merit than looking as if they were pronounceable in a foreign tongue because they were unpronounceable in our own.

The creeds of the Tungús coincide with their political distribution. Those of China, as has been stated, are Buddhists; those of Russia Christians of the Greek Church or pagans. That their Christianity is little more than nominal is easily believed. The details of their paganism are obscure; which is to be regretted inasmuch as the Siberian mythologies in general have a common character, and this of the Tungús is the first that comes under our notice.

The ordinary term for them is Shamanism. The exact details of the application of this name are obscure. It originated in India; and, in 295 B.C., Megasthenes, in his embassy from Seleucus to Sandracottus (Chandragupta) divided the philosophers of that country into two classes, the Brakhmans and the Sarmans, Sramans, or Samans. Of these latter the most famous were those who lived a life of asceticism in the woods, clothed in the bark of trees, and feeding upon seeds and fruits. The modern Shaman is something of the kind. He affects a peculiar intimacy with the divinities of the stream, cave, and forest. He acts as the medium between them and the dupes who put their trust in him. He fashions rude images of what he calls deities. He works himself into a strange mixture of trance and epilepsy. We shall, however, see more of their behaviour as we proceed.

With the Shaman as the adviser and go-between, the objects of a Siberian *cultus* are not likely to be of an exalted kind. The immediate wants of life determine them, success in hunting, success in fishing, success in journeys being the specialities most definitely requested. Of a system of rewards and punishments after death there are traces, definite and undeniable; but the punishments are grotesque and impossible, the rewards coarse. Of a God separate from his works, above nature, and not himself a natural object, the ideas, whatever may be said to the contrary, are of the very faintest and loosest kind; neither do they pervade the whole of those mythologies in which they appear. A vague feeling of awe is suggested by the contemplation of the heavens, a feeling of fear by the storm, a feeling of loneliness by the solitude of either the forest or the steppe; and these find their exponent in the personification of things unseen, and the attribution of mysterious powers to any object, natural or artificial, which may exhibit any peculiarity of either form or properties. Let a stone or tree of irregular shape depart from the ordinary type of trees and stones,—still more, let it resemble some living object, and it becomes the object of a Siberian *cultus*. The families in the neighbourhood will make humble offerings to it. Tribes from a distance will visit it. They do this in Lapland, they do it on the shores of the Pacific, they do it on the banks of the Obi, the Yenisei, and in all the interjacent localities.

Nor must it be imagined that Shaman is a mere European name, a term adopted and applied by the learned men of the West and speculating critics. So far is it from being a word of this kind that there is the express evidence of Stralenberg that the Yakuts of the Lena, a Turk population in respect to their language at least, a Turk population, notwithstanding their Arctic locality, call the name by which they designate their highest divinity *Saman*.

The chief deity of the pagan Tungús is Boa, or Bugi, the Genii being called Agei, or (oftener) Buri. Garan is the Buri of the waters; Dorokdi, or Kongdorokdi, of the earth. Shuro takes cognizance of thieves; and Atshintitei is the god of flies. The greater the influence of Christianity the worse the character of the Buri. Originally mere genii, good or bad as the case might be, they are now evil-minded devils; the sense of the word Buri being more and more unfavourable as the original paganism wanes. The symbols representative of the divinities are various. Dianda, like Garan, a god of the waters, is represented under the figure of a boat. The sun has the face of a man. The moon is a semi-circle; the stars little rings; the earth a four-cornered piece of metal. Sokyovo, whose function it is to look after reindeer, has the form of that animal. The images, or symbols of the domestic deities, which are made by the Shamans, are of wood or metal, ornamented with fur, tinsel, or coral. Georgi calls them Shovokoi. Castrén found them named Hargi—this on the Yenisei. The Han and Shonan are varieties of these holy images.

The first of the following lists represents the eastern rather than the western dialect of the Tungús; the column headed Yakutsk meaning, not the true Yakut of the Sokhalar Turks (of which more will be said in the sequel), but the Tungús of the Yakut country.

The second gives us the Tungús of the west rather than the east.

| English. | Nertshinsk. | Yakutsk. | Lamut. |
|---|---|---|---|
| *Man (homo)* | boie | boye | bye |
| *Head* | deli | dyll | del |
| *Hair* | nynrikta | nyuritta | nyurit |
| *Eye* | isal | eha | esel |
| *Ear* | zin | zen | korot |
| *Nose* | ongokta | ongokto | ongata |
| *Mouth* | amga | hamun | amga |
| *Tongue* | ingni | ingni | ilga |
| *Hand* | dzhalan | nggala | ngal |
| *Foot* | bokdil | halgan | bodan |
| *Sun* | shivun | ziguni | nyultan |
| *Moon* | biga | boga | bekh |
| *Star* | oshikta | haulen | otshikat |
| *Fire* | togo | togo | toh |
| *Water* | mu | mu | mu |
| *Tree* | mo | mo | mo |

| English. | Nertshinsk. | Yakut. | Lamut. |
|---|---|---|---|
| *Stone* | dzhalo | dzholo | dzhola |
| *One* | omon | ômukon | ömin |
| *Two* | dzhur | dzhur | dzhur |
| *Three* | ilan | elan | elan |
| *Four* | dygin | dygin | dügün |
| *Five* | tȯngna | tonga | tọngau |
| *Six* | nyungun | nyungun | nyungun |
| *Seven* | nadan | nadan | nadan |
| *Eight* | dzhapkun | dzapkan | dzhapkan |
| *Nine* | yagyn | jagin | uyun |
| *Ten* | dzhan | dzhan | men |

| English. | Yenesei. | Tshapodzhir. | L. Tunguska. | Mangascia. |
|---|---|---|---|---|
| *Man (homo)* | boya | boyo | boya | boyo |
| *Head* | dil | dyl | dil | dil |
| *Hair* | nyurikta | nyurikta | nuriktah | nyurikta |
| *Eye* | osha | esha | öhsah | esha |
| *Ear* | shin | shern | syen | shen |
| *Nose* | nigsha | oiokta | onoktah | ongokto |
| *Mouth* | amga | amga | amga | ammungah |
| *Hand* | hanga | nali | ngala | ngala |
| *Foot* | halgar | bodol | khalgan | halgan |
| *Sun* | shiggun | dylega | delatsha | delyadzya |
| *Moon* | byega | ——— | bäga | beya |
| *Star* | oshikta | oshikta | oshikta | oshikta |
| *Fire* | toggo | togo | toggo | togo |
| *Water* | mu | mu | muh | mu |
| *Tree* | mo | mo | mo | mo |
| *Stone* | dishollo | zhyulo | hysha | dzyollo |
| *One* | ummukon | omukon | mukon | ommukon |
| *Two* | dzyur | dzhur | dyur | dyur |
| *Three* | illün | ilän | ilan | illen |
| *Four* | diggïn | dygyn | degenn | diggin |
| *Five* | tungya | tunga | tonga | tõngna |
| *Six* | nyungun | nugun | nungun | nyungun |
| *Seven* | nadan | nadan | naddan | naddan |
| *Eight* | dzyapkun | dzhamkun | dzhapkul | dzapkun |
| *Nine* | yegin | yegin | iyogyin | yögyin |
| *Ten* | dzyan | dzhan | dyann | dzhan |

Bell, who, by the way, errs in saying that the Tungús took their name from the river Tonguska (the converse being the case), gives the following description of the Tshapodzhir.

"The Tongusy are the posterity of the ancient inhabitants of Siberia, and differ in language, manners, and dress, and even in their persons and stature, from all the other tribes of these people I have had occasion to see. They have no houses where they remain for any time, but range through the woods and along rivers at pleasure, and where-ever they come they erect a few spars, inclining to one another at the top; these they cover with pieces of birchen bark, sewed together, leaving a hole at the top to let out the smoke. The fire is placed in the middle. They are very civil and tractable, and like to smoke tobacco and drink brandy. About their huts they have generally a good stock of rein-deer, in which all their wealth consists.

"The men are tall and able-bodied; brave, and very honest. The women are of a middle size, and virtuous. I have seen many of the men with oval figures like wreaths on their foreheads and chins, and sometimes a figure resembling the branch of a tree, reaching from the corner of the eye to the mouth. These are made in their infancy by pricking the parts with a needle, and rubbing them with charcoal, the marks whereof remain as long as the person lives. Their complexion is swarthy. Their faces are not so flat as those of the Kalmucks, but their countenances more open. They are altogether unacquainted with any kind of literature, and worship the sun and moon. They have many shamans among them, who differ little from those I formerly described. I was told of others whose abilities in fortune-telling far exceeded those of the shamans at this place, but they lived far northward. They cannot bear to sleep in a warm room, but retire to their huts, and lie about the fire on skins of wild beasts. It is surprising how these creatures can suffer the very piercing cold in these parts.

" The women are dressed in a fur gown, reaching below the knee, and tied about the waist with a girdle. This girdle is about three inches broad, made of deer-skin, having the hair curiously stitched down and ornamented, to which is fastened, at each side, an iron ring, that serves to carry a tobacco-pipe, and other trinkets of small value. Their gowns are also stitched down the breast, and about the neck. Their long black hair is plaited, and tied above their heads, above which they wear a small fur cap, which is becoming enough ; some of them have small ear-rings. Their feet are dressed in buskins made of deer-skins, which reach to the knee, and are tied about the ancle with a thong of leather.

" The dress of the men is very simple, and fit for action. It consists of a short jacket with narrow sleeves, made of deer-skin, having the fur outward ; trowsers and hose of the same kind of skin, both of one piece, and tight to the limbs. They have besides a piece of fur that covers the breast and stomach, which is hung about the neck with a thong of leather. This, for the most part, is neatly stitched and ornamented by their wives. Round their heads they have a ruff made of the tails of squirrels, to preserve the tips of the ears from the cold. There is nothing on the crown, but the hair smoothed, which hangs in a long plaited lock behind their backs.

" Their arms are a bow, and several sorts of arrows, according to the different kinds of game they intend to hunt. The arrows are carried in a quiver on their backs, and the bow always in their left hand. Besides these they have a short lance, and a little hatchet. Thus accoutred, they are not afraid to attack the fiercest creature in the woods, even the strongest bear ; for they are stout men, and dexterous archers. In winter, which is the season for hunting wild beasts, they travel on what are called snow shoes, without which it would be impossible to make their way through the deep snow. These are made of a very thin piece of light wood, about five feet long, and five or six inches broad, inclining to a point before, and square behind. In the middle is fixed a thong, through which the feet are put. On these shoes a person may walk safely over the deepest snow; for a man's weight will not sink them above an inch. These, however, can only be used on plains. They have a different kind for ascending hills, with the skins of seals glued to the boards, having the hair inclined backwards, which prevents the sliding of the shoes, so that they can ascend a hill very easily; and in descending they slide downwards at a great rate.

"The nation of the Tongusy was very numerous, but is of late much diminished by the small-pox. It is remarkable that they knew nothing of this distemper till the Russians arrived among them. They are so much afraid of this disease that, if any one of a family is seized with it, the rest immediately make the patient a little hut, and set by him some water and victuals, then packing up everything they march off to the windward, each carrying an earthen pot with burning coals in it, and making a dreadful lamentation as they go along. They never revisit the sick till they think the danger past. If the person dies they place him on a branch of a tree, to which he is tried with strong wythes, to prevent his falling. When they go a hunting into the woods they carry with them no provisions, but depend entirely on what they are to catch. They eat every animal that comes in their way, even a bear, fox, or wolf. The squirrels are reckoned delicate food; but the ermines have such a strong, rank taste and smell, that nothing but starving can oblige them to eat their flesh. When a Tongusy kills an elk or deer, he never moves from the place till he has eat it up, unless he happens to be near his family, in which case he carries part of it home. He is never at a loss for a fire, having always a tinder-box about him. If this should happen to be wanting he kindles a fire by rubbing two pieces of wood against each other. They eat nothing raw but in great extremity.

"The sables are not caught in the same manner as other animals. The fur is so tender that the least mark of an arrow, or ruffling of the hair, spoils the sale of the skin. In hunting them they only use a little dog and a net. When a hunter finds the track of a sable upon the snow he follows it perhaps for two or three days, till the poor animal, quite tired, takes refuge in some tall tree; for it can climb like a cat. The hunter then spreads his net around the tree and makes a fire. The sable, unable to endure the smoke, immediately descends, and is caught in the net. I have been told by some of these hunters that, when hard pinched with hunger on such long chaces they take two thin boards, one of which they apply to the pit of the stomach, and the other to the back, opposite to it; the extremities of these boards are tied with cords, which are drawn tighter by degrees, and prevent their feeling the cravings of hunger.

"Although I have observed that the Tongusy in general worship the sun and moon, there are many exceptions to this observation. I have found intelligent people among them, who believed there was a being superior to both sun and moon, and who created them and all the world.

"I shall only remark further, that from all the accounts I have heard and read of the natives of Canada, there is no nation in the world which they so much resemble as the Tongusians. The distance between them is not so great as is commonly imagined."

Notice may now be taken of some of the Tungús names.

The Mantshú tribes are :—

Zukzukhu Aiman
Zargu
Giamukha
Dzhar
Vanggia
Elmeri
Dzhakumu
Zakda
Zuan
Donggo
Yarkhu
Andarki Aiman
Varka
Fui
Zzakhaltsha
Dzhoogia
Mardun
Onggolo
Antu Gualgia
Khunekhe Aiman
Tomokho
Dzhanggia
Barde
Dzhaisian
Dunggia
Olkhon
Dung
Dshusheri
Neien
Fodokho
Zibe
Antshulaku
Akiran
Khezikhe
Omokho Soro
Fenekhe
Khuifa
Khuye
Namdulu
Suifun Niggudu
Urgutshen
Muren
Dzhakuta
Ula
Uzui
Yaran
Zirin
Ekhe Kuren
Gunaka Kuren
Sakahan ni Aiman
Indakhun takuraragolo
Noro
Zirakhin
Yekhe
Gualtsha
Uzuri
Khingan
Khuntshun
Kuala
Nimatsha.
Dzhetshen ni Aiman

Mark the word Aiman.

The Mantshú call all the tribes other than Mantshurian Orotshong. Orotong is what the Tungús of the Lower Tunguska call themselves.

The native name for the tribes to the north and east of Lake Baikal is Ovön, or Ovönk. This is, perhaps, but another form of the root Tong.

The Mongolians call the Tungús Khamnoyon.

The Tshapodzhir are tattooed. So are many other

Tungús tribes. The Tshapodzhir, however, are in contact with tribes who do not tattoo themselves. I think (for reasons given* elsewhere) that their name is derived from the practice, and that it is a name used by their Turk neighbours rather than by the Tshapodzhir themselves.

As the Mantshú language appears to differ from the other Tungús dialects more than they do from each other, the division, suggested above, into Mantshú and Non-Mantshú, or Orotong, is, probably, natural. If so, the class stands thus—

TUNGÚS.

| Mantshú Division. | Orotong Division. |
|---|---|
| Zukzukhu Aiman | Orotong Proper |
| Zargu, &c. | Tshapodzhir, &c. |

Solon, Solo, or Solong, is the name of one of the tribes of Mantshuria, on the Mongol frontier. It will be noticed in the sequel.

* *Native Races of the Russian Empire.* In the notice of the Yukahiri.

## CHAPTER XVII.

The Mongolians.—The Mongolians Proper.—The Kalka.—The Buriat.—The Ölöt, Torgot, Durbet, Khoshot, Dzungarians.—Kalmuk of the Volga, &c.—The Aimâks of Cabul.

Now comes the notice of the Mongolians, agreeing in many respects with that of the Chinese, Mantshú, and Tungús, but, at the same time, exhibiting several peculiar characteristics. The chief Mongol occupancy is Mongolia or Mogulistan, a vast area of elevated steppe and desert to the north and north-west of the Great Wall of China. Save and except some portions of the frontier, and a few outlying isolated ramifications, the great Mongolian stock is Chinese in its political relations, and Buddhist in creed. But it has not always been either. In the time of the Tshingiz-khan, the Mongols were not only independent of all the world, but the conquerors of a great part of it. They were, too, but partial and imperfect Buddhists; some being pagans, others Christians, some, perhaps, Fire-worshippers, and (as such) akin to the Parsís.

Again—the successors of Tshingiz-khan conquered China, and ruled over it under the name of the Yuans or the Yuan dynasty. In 1367, however, they were ejected, and the Ming dynasty ruled in their stead. The Mongol title for their kings or chiefs is khan, and when the Yuan dynasty is broken-up the history of Mongolia is the history of so many khanates; some large, some small; some wholly independent of their neighbours, some more or less united with them; some comparatively isolate, some consolidated; some friendly, some hostile to China; some, perhaps, tributary; the Chinese title of a Mongol khan being *wang*. The *wang* in Mongolia is the Tsawbwa of the Shan, or the Gyalpo of the Bulti states, his power being territorial.

More important, however, because more truly Mongol than the division of the land into khanates, or wangdoms, is the distribution of the population into tribes; for, in no part of the world, Arabia itself not excepted, is the tribual system more developed than in Mongolia. The connection between the members of a tribe is that of blood, pedigree, or descent; the tribe itself being, in some cases, named after a real or supposed patriarch.

The tribe, by which term we translate the native name *aimauk*, or *aimâk*, is a large division, falling into so many *kokhúm* or *banners*.

If the khanate, or wangdom, exactly coincided with either the kokhúm or aimauk, it would be a matter of indifference whether our division was territorial or genealogical. The two principles would coincide. This, however, is not the case. The political division frequently traverses the tribual, and *vice versâ*.

*The Kalkas.*—The population to which the name Kalka applies falls into divisions and sub-divisions. In exhibiting these I follow the phraseology of Timkovski, who writes about "the tribe of the Kalkas." I imagine, however, that some of its divisions are also tribes. Be this as it may, the Kalka country is of vast extent, and comprizes the greater part of Mongolia, being bounded on the north by the Russian governments of Irkutsk, Yeniseyisk, Tomsk, and Tobolsk, and on the south and south-west by Chinese Turkestan and Dzungaria. It falls in four *Lou* (provinces), or *Yam* (*ways, marches*). These are best named after the title of their khan, wang, or chief—the title not the name. As a general rule, the Kalka districts belong either to the great central steppe, or to the water-system of the rivers that fall into Lake Baikal. The eastern division, however, is at the head-waters of the Amúr or Sagalin. This is the country of—

*The Tsetsen-khan.*—Its chief encampment is at the foot of Mount Undúr-daba on the Kerúlen. In some of the maps it is marked Baras, or Bars-khota = Tiger-city. The number of banners is twenty-one or twenty-two, the most eastern of which are in contact with the Mantshú Solon. In 1688, when the chief of Tsetsen-khan submitted to China, he had about 100,000 subjects. On the western frontier of the Tsetsen-khan country lies that of—

*The Tushitu-khan,* with twenty banners. Urga (town), or Kúren (encampment), belongs to this province. Still more to the west—

*The Dzassaktú-khan,* on the southern side of the Kangai mountains, commands nineteen banners.

*The Sain-noyon* government, with twenty-four banners, is on the river Orkhon.

*Kalkas of Wings.*—Of the Kalkas of what are called the Right and Left Wings the ethnological relation differs from the political. Both are more directly under China than the other members of the division. The first belonged originally to the Túshetú, the second to the Dzhasaktú, Khan.

*Kalkas of the Koko Nor.*—Of the twenty-nine banners of the Koko Nor, or Blue Lake, one is Kalka.

*Kalkas of the Russian Empire.*—A few of the Kalka are Russian, viz. the tribes (or parts of the tribes) of Dzongol, Ashekhabat, Tabunggut, Sartol, Atagan, and

Khatshagan, their occupancies being the banks of the rivers Selenga, Uda, Khilok, Tshikoi, Dzida, Onon, and Ingoda, to the south of the Lake Baikal.

Along with the sections now coming under notice the Kalkas form the proper Mongol division of that great stock of which the Buriat and the Olöt are the other two primary branches.

*The Sunid.*—East and south of the Kalka lies the country of the Sunid, Sunites, or Sounites, on the road from Kiakta to Pekin. So lying, it has been crossed more than once by the members of the Russian mission. It belongs to the Desert.

The Sunid tribes, which fall into two divisions, the Eastern and the Western, are, like their land, poor; a land with few streams, and with brackish water in many of the wells, the lakes being actually salt. In the beginning of summer the Sunid prays for rain; which, if denied, causes drought and death to his cattle; whilst in the winter they are chilled and starved. In 1815 the whole steppe was so terribly afflicted with murrain and mortality that some proprietors of 500 horses had only twenty left, and others only saved four out of 200. The account of this heavy visitation was given to the Russian mission in 1820, at which time the tribes had yet to recover from their loss. In many places the ground is white with salt; sometimes at the edge of an existing lake, sometimes in spots where lakes have once been. The face of part of the country at least is broken and undulating, and more than one mountain is invested with a halo of sanctitude. A pointed hill named Karbatu, or the Mountain of Archery, is sacred to a deified hero, Ghessur Khan, who is believed to have set up his mark on the Karbatu, whilst he himself stood on a similar mountain, fifty miles off. He shot and shot, and never once missed.

As his target stands in the Sunid country, Ghessur Khan must be more especially a Sunid hero; such, at least, is our conclusion when we localize the scene of his exploits. They may, however, have other points of attachment. His fame fills Mongolia; and the Kalmuks as well as the Buriats delight in the narrative of his exploits. Whatever may have been the origin of the legends concerning him, they have been greatly complicated by the Buddhist creed. Pallas tells us that his spirit inhabits the body of the present Dalai Lama; having, previous to its incarnation in Ghessur himself, been that of Burkhan Aria Balu. It was also incarnate in the form of a servant, or shieldbearer; also in that of a horse; in both of which capacities it served Ghessur Khan. If so, it was servant and master at once. Such the spiritual view. Klaproth's is diametrically opposite; reducing the legend to a simple piece of euphemism. According to this:

Ghessur Khan was a captain or general, who lived in the third century of our era. He was born near the Koko Nor (Blue Lake), between China and Tibet. He was commander-in-chief of the army which revolted from the last emperor of the Han dynasty; was taken prisoner; commanded the admiration of his captor, the imperial general; was tempted to join the Imperialists, but withstood the temptation; was again taken prisoner, and executed. The Chinese, however, believe that he is not dead, but living amongst the demigods; and the Mantshú look upon him as their tutelary genius, saint, or patron. He is generally represented sitting with his son on his left, and a black-faced shieldbearer on his right, hand. Sometimes he sits on a bay horse. The Chinese call him Kuan yu tshang; the Mantshú, Kuang tshing ti kuin. The following extracts from a work on his exploits in the Mongol language increase the confusion; since the prominence given to Kurmusta, or Ormuz, points to the times when fire-worship was the dominant creed of Mongolia; whilst Koubilgan is Kubilai-Khan. Or was he a Mantshú, a Chinese, or a Tibetan demigod?

Bogdo Ghessur Khan, born for the destruction of tho roots of the ten Evils, and reigning in the ten parts of heaven, arose like a lion, and conquered with the strength of a Koubilgan, Mangoucha, an evil spirit with twelve heads, seized on his wife Aroula, and took possession of his golden palaces.

Aroula, whose mind was filled with resentment, one day presented a philter to Ghessur, inviting him to taste it. Scarcely had the khan, who knew everything, drank it, than he forgot all that had passed.

The Bogdo resided for twelve years in the palace of the twelve-headed Mangoucha. During this period, his possessions were invaded by three khans of Sharagol, his empire destroyed and his subjects dispersed. Then the three blessed sisters of this sovereign looked down from heaven, and with sorrowful hearts spoke as follows:

'The enchanted beverage has vanquished him who was always invincible; thou hast raised thyself with the might of a Koubilgan, to the throne of the twelve-headed Mangoucha, and there thou hast forgotten everything.' They wrote a letter on the shaft of an arrow, and sent it to the sovereign; he read it and began to recollect past events. But the wicked Aroula soon gave him the fatal potion, and the Bogdo again returned into a state of oblivion.

The three sisters descended to the palace of Mangoucha, to reanimate the spirits of Ghessur. They succeeded in delivering him from his enchantment; the remembrance of the past returned; his voice, which was like that of a lion, was heard; the earth trembled, and a torrent of flame having enveloped the golden palaces eighty-eight times, and the walls of the city three times, the whole was consumed. The conqueror mounted his enchanted bay courser, and returned to his empire.*

Having raised himself to a dignity a thousand fold that of a Koubilgan, he devastated all the country of Sharagol, delivered his pious wife from her imprisonment, and re-established the throne in the city, which had twice thirteen temples, and a hundred and eight large fortresses.

This sovereign of the ten parts of heaven, seeing Tsarghin, a warrior eighty years old, and the sons and daughters of this hero, vanquished by the khans of Sharagol, uttered a deep sigh. His afflicted soul beginning to recollect the heroes, his companions in arms, he exclaimed:

'O thou rapid vulture, who with a generous heart wast ever foremost

* In the Mongol temples, Ghessur Khan is represented on a horse of this description, made of wood.

in the fight, Sesse Shikher, my dear brother, where art thou? Where art thou, haughty Shoumar, an eagle among mortals, and fearless like an elephant crushing everything in thy way? And thou, falcon among men, where art thou, my Bouiantik, who, endowed with a heart of adamant, dedicated thy strength to me at so early an age?

'Lion's claw of the sovereign, thou who like a falcon didst never miss thy prey, thou the conqueror of eighty nations, where art thou, my youthful Nanson? And thou, my hero with thy rocky heart, Bars, the irresistible conqueror, where art thou?' Thus speaking of his warriors, he raised his voice, and the walls, agitated by the whirlwind, turned three times.

The sovereign commanded his bay-horse to be saddled, in order to repair quickly to the places where his heroes had been overcome. Behind him Tsarghin spurred his piebald courser. When he arrived on the field of battle the Bogdo uttered dreadful cries, and when he saw the skeletons of Bouiantik and Bars, he fell on the earth insensible. But the soul of Nanson having passed into the body of a lion, and that of Shouman into that of an elephant, the sovereign recovered. He embraced the elephant and the lion, and addressing the gods of all the ten parts of heaven, exclaimed sorrowfully:

'O, my incomparable heroes, Nanson, Shoumar, and thou, my beloved brother, Sesse Shikher, and thou, Bars, who rushedst with fury upon the enemy! you who have fallen so prematurely in my defence; you were the bright torches which dispelled the gloom of my night! Thou, faithful Bouiantik, and you, all my heroes, my priests, and my people, you opposed the enemy, immoveable as a rock of granite. Yes, I am the reigning Bogdo, but after I had vanquished the twelve-headed Mangoucha, I was myself subdued by the enchanted potion of Aroula.'

Like the thunder produced in the heavens by dark blue dragons, resounded the lamentations of the sovereign. The souls of the heroes in the forms of elephants, tigers, and wolves, approached, and went three times round the monarch, uttering plaintive moans.

The three sisters hearing the lamentations of the sovereign, descended from their celestial habitations to give him repose; but finding Ghessur inconsolable, they returned to Kourmousta, their father, chief of the thirty-three Tengheri, and the supreme protector of the earth. Kourmousta opened the book of fate, and read the following words: 'Ghessur Khan left the empire of the Tengheri, at the head of his heroes, but fate has decreed that they should perish before their master. However, Ghessur Khan, before he fought his last battle, had nine times conquered the three wicked Tengheri, who, under the form of three powerful Khans, had once succeeded in overcoming him.'

Kourmousta, surrounded by a crowd of Tengheri, appeared before Bouda, and said respectfully: 'Master of the Gods, your envoy upon earth has lost thirty of his heroes. The war is concluded, but their valiant chief laments over the remains of his warriors.'

The master of the gods listened with a complacent smile; and in the presence of a thousand Bourkhans, took a black *badin*,* with arshan, filled a *boumba* with it, and presented it to Kourmousta, saying:

'Send this arshan to him who has terminated his combat. As soon as he has shed a drop of it upon the body of his heroes, their souls will be restored to them: the third drop will entirely recall them to life. Then let them drink the arshan, and their protecting angels, returning to them, will endow them with extraordinary virtues.'

Kourmousta took the arshan, and delivered it to the three sisters, with these words: 'Say to him who has terminated his combat: What has befallen thee? The gods of the ten regions of heaven guard thy head; thy breast is defended by the valiant Tengheri, and thy steps are protected by eighty-eight powerful Bourkhans; an hundred and eighty goddesses guard thy girdle, O Ghessur Khan! thou commandest in the ten regions of heaven; thou, the descendant of Kourmousta! if thou hadst not been separated from thy heroes, thou wouldst not now lament their death.'

The three sisters descended from the clouds amidst dreadful claps of thunder, like the bellowing of twenty dragons. Ghessur Khan, after having prostrated himself nine times before the master of the gods, and nine times before his father Kourmousta, took the arshan, and by means of this miraculous beverage the thirty heroes were restored to life, and resumed their original forms.

Returning to his country after so many combats, the monarch assembled his heroes, and the three tribes of his people. Cries of joy resounded on all the coasts of the sea, incense ascended in clouds from the altars, lilies of extraordinary beauty rose from the ground, by day they were invisible, but at night they served as brilliant torches. Defended by inaccessible ramparts the heroes prostrated themselves before their sovereign. After three months' fetes and rejoicings, every one returned to his own home. The lion-strength of the monarch had reanimated his heroes. The destinies being accomplished, Bogdo Ghessur Khan lived in profound peace.

The Chinese authorities seem to presume on the poverty and weakness of the Sunid; for Timkovski especially states that they treat them with less consideration than either the Tshakar or the Kalka; indeed, that they oppress them heavily, and with impunity. Their taidzi or nobles are numerous, proud, pretentious, and poverty-stricken, the last of a line of princes. A taidzi of the

* A sacred vase, with which the principal Bourkhan is generally represented among the Mongols.

first class has, in addition to a certain amount of land, eighteen labourers; a taidzi of the second class, twelve; a taidzi of the third class, eight; of the fourth, four. The taidzi of the fifth class are scarcely taidzi at all; but are ranked with the ordinary population.

A taidzi, when he visits Peking, must present the Emperor with a live sheep. Should it be accepted, the offerer receives in return about double its value in money, two measures of rice, and four pieces of nankeen If refused, no nankeen, one measure of rice, and halt the amount of money is equivalent. This custom, established when the Sunid were formidable, is going out of use.

Chinese hats are worn during the summer by some of the Sunid; not being worn by the Kalkas, who despise the foreign fashion.

In 1634, when the Tshakar were subdued, the Sunid submitted also. The name appears (and that prominently) in the time of Tshingiz-khan. Considering that *pi* is no part of the original word, but only an affix, it is probable that, word for word, the name of the famous old Sienpi and the name of the modern Sunid is the same; the Sienpi districts appearing to have lain near the Sunid part of Mongolia.

The Sunid seem to be well within the desert. To the east and south, however, the physical conditions change. To the east lies a range of mountains, in which numerous streams that fall into the Pacific, either as small rivers or as feeders of the Sagalin, take their rise. In these less inhospitable districts, on the Sunid frontier, lie—

The Abaga;

The Abakanar;

The Udzhumutshi; each with two banners.

Under the dynasty of Yuan, the Abkhanar, or Abaganar, made part of a Chinese province, which was conquered by the Mongols, under the dynasty of the Ming, and by the Mantshú, about A.D. 1640.

Conterminous with the Sunid, by which they are bounded on the east and north, lie—

*The Dürben Keuked,* in Chinese Szu tsu pu lu, in Mantshú, Dúin Dzhusé, and in English the Four Sons, with one banner, and with an encampment to the north-west of the town of Kalgan.

*The Khaotshit,* or Khagotshit, in contact with the Ud-zhimutshi, has two banners.

*The Tumet of Koko-khoto,* or the Tumet of the Blue Town, are one of the banners whose country touches the Great Wall, where the Great Wall bounds the province Shansi. The Durben Keuked lie to the east, the Ortú to the west of them. They belong to the drainage of the Yellow River. So do

*The Maomingan,* with one banner. And so do

*The Orat* or *Urad.*—Orat means artizan. The three banners of the Orat occupy a country full of the signs of an earlier population, earlier than the present Orat, and more settled; for the ruins are those of ancient cities and celebrated temples. It was here that the Thui-kiu (? Turks) assembled for their attacks upon China. Also on the Yellow River lie

*The Ortú,* with seven banners. It is in the Ortú country that several of the earlier Chinese pieces of history (so-called) find their venue. It is in the Ortú country that the ancient city of Súfang, built under the Han dynasty, before the Christian era, is supposed to have stood. It was in the country of the Ortú that the Emperor Ngan, of the Sui dynasty, built the palace of Yulinkúng, in the city of Tshingtsheú. The Hiúngnú, whom so many investigators believe to have been the ancestors of the Huns of Attila, were occupants of the Ortú country. The Ortú country, in the tenth, eleventh, and twelfth centuries, belonged to the kingdom of Hia, or Tangút, which was one of the earliest conquests of the Temuginian Mongols, or the Mongols of Tshingiz-khan. In 1550 the tribe of Ghinang, or Dzinang, settled in it, the head of the tribe assuming the title of Tsetsen Khan; a Kalka designation, as we have already seen. After the death of this Ghinang, his seven sons divided the population amongst them, and formed an army of 100,000 men. After this the territory fell under the Tshakar dominion, and the name Ortú was attached to it.

It was one of the first to submit to the Mantshús.

So much for the tribes which belong either to the drainage of the Yellow River, or the edge of the desert; east of which the streams grow broader, and the country more favourable. Here lies valley after valley of the southern feeders of the Sagalin. Here, too, lie those of the Sira muren or the Yellow River of the North; the Yellow River of Mongolia, with its Mongol name, as opposed to the Yellow River of China or the Hoang-ho. The banners of this area, which more than one geographer has compared, in respect to its soil and climate, to Northern Germany, and which is doubtless well watered both by rain and rivers, are—

*The Durbet*, with one banner, in 47° N. L., and on the frontier (as aforesaid) of the Solones. South of them—

*The Tshalet* or *Dzalaid*, and

*The Khorlos* or *Gorlos*, with two, and—

*The Aru Khortshin*, or Kortshin of the north, with one banner, and

*The Dzharot* with two.

*The Barin.*—The Barin, or Bagarin, are occupants of a district in close and especial connection with the history of the Liao dynasty. Puthu, an ancestor of its founder, was born in the Barin country, Mount Bardan being his birth-place. He was born in the Barin country and buried there as well. The metropolis of his successors, the ancient city of Ling-huan-tshing, was also Barin in respect to its locality. Twenty-five cities were dependent on it. It is remarkable that none of their ruins are to be found, and that their sites are uncertain. There are the remains of both dwellings, and burial-places in the Barin country; but they are not the remains of the Liao dynasty; a dynasty of the tenth century.

*The Naiman.*—One banner.

*The Dokhan.*—One banner.

*The Kharatshin* or *Kartsin.*—Three banners. The Kharatshin country is full of the remains of ancient cities, viz.: of the

| Chinese. | Mongol. | English. |
| --- | --- | --- |
| Thsing tsheú | Khara khoto | Black City |
| Hoei tshú | Tsagan khoto | White City |

and others.

*Tumet.*—Two banners.

*Uniot.*—Two banners.

*Gesikten.*—One banner.

The Uniot and Gesikten countries are pre-eminent amongst the countries of the generally treeless Mongolia for the luxuriance of their woods and forests. The Chinese, however, clear the ground by felling them, and the climate is said to be notably affected thereby. The natives, too, recede; sometimes to become paupers, sometimes to become robbers, after the manner of banished men in general. Sain Ula ill deserves its name of the Good Mountain. Its occupants are bad amongst the bad for their brigandage.

They are Buddhists; with decided traces of their original paganism. They adore the spirit of one of their more conspicuous mountains, Mount Obo. A cairn of stones is the sign of their adoration. At the base is an úrn of granite for incense. On the top of the heap is a mass of dry branches hung with relics—bones, or scraps of paper with pious sentences written on them; some in Mongolian, some in Tibetan. The more devout adorers give not only incense but money; bending and kneeling before the urn and cairn. The Mongolians do this and leave a few coins when they go away. The Chinese do the same, except that they pick up and pocket the coins which the Mongols have left.

*Tshakar.*—Timkovski and Klaproth decidedly commit themselves to the doctrine that the word Tshakar, in Mongol, signifies a frontier country. If so, it is a word like the German March. If so, it is a word like the Slavonic Ukraine. On the other hand, Schmidt, a more special Mongol scholar than either, maintains that this is a wrong translation.

Under the dynasty of the Ming, writes Timkovski, the name of the territory of the Siao-vang-tsu, or the Little King, a descendant of the Yuan, was Tsagan. In 1530, the powerful chief Butsi took possession of it, his tribe taking the present name, Tshakar, from their forming a March, or frontier to China. Under Butsi's successor the Tshakar khanate became powerful; indeed Tshakar was the chief kingdom of Mongolia. The Mantshús, however, reduced it in 1632. In 1675, the Tshakar khan Búrni revolted, was subdued, and (along with his brother) put to death. Many of his subjects were transplanted elsewhere.

Again—when the Emperor of China was at war with Galdan and his Olöt, the Tshakars assisted him. When the war was over, several Kalka and Olöt companies were joined to them. This has mixed the population; indeed the division seems to be, as its name suggests, political rather than ethnological. Its divisions are military, eight in number, and named thus :—

1. The plain yellow banner ;
2. The bordered yellow banner ;
3. The red banner ;
4. The bordered red banner ;
5. The white banner ;
6. The bordered white banner ;
7. The blue banner ;
8. The bordered blue banner.

Each banner has its district ; each district its chief From the eight chiefs a captain general is chosen. Tshakar is eminently the *Land of Grass,* as more than one district of Mongolia is called. The 365 herds of the Imperial horses graze it. Each herd contains 1200 (or more) horses. For these the Mongol at the head is responsible. Should he lose one he replaces it.

*Department of Tshing-te-fú.*—To the north-east of Pekin lies the least Mongolian of the Mongol districts—the department of Tshing-te-fú—originally, according to the Chinese accounts, the occupancy of two rude tribes, the Shan Dzhung and the Túnghú (word for word Tungús). It is in Tshing-te-fú that the Emperor most especially diverts himself with hunting. In Tshing-te-fú is the chief imperial summer residence ; along with numerous temples. In Tshing-te-fú the Chinese population amounts to more than half a million of souls ; this being the fact which renders the district less Mongolian than the districts around. These, however, are all, in their degree, invaded by the Chinese. There are Chinese settlers in Bagarin, in Uniot, in Tshakar, and in many other provinces besides.

| English. | Kalka. | East Mongol. |
|---|---|---|
| *Man* | ere | ere |
| *Head* | tologoi | tolokhai |
| *Hair* | usü | usü |
| *Eye* | nidu | nüdu |
| *Ear* | tshikè | tshiki |
| *Nose* | khamar | khamar |
| *Mouth* | ama | ama |
| *Tongue* | kolè | kele |
| *Hand* | gar | khar |
| *Foot* | küll | gül |
| *Sun* | narà | naran |
| *Moon* | zara | zaran |
| *Star* | odo | odon |
| *Fire* | gal | gal |
| *Water* | uzu | uzu |
| *Tree* | modo | modon |
| *Stone* | tsholo | tsholon |
| *One* | nege | nige |
| *Two* | khoyir | goyer |
| *Three* | gurba | khurban |
| *Four* | dürba | dürban |
| *Five* | tabu | tabun |
| *Six* | dzurga | dzirkhokhan |
| *Seven* | dolo | dolokhun |
| *Eight* | naima | naiman |
| *Nine* | yuzu | dzhisun |
| *Ten* | arban | arbau |

*The Olöt, Ulut, Eleut, Kalmuks.*—The chief authorities treat the words Olöt and Kalmuk as synonyms. They denote the tribes to the west and south of the Kalka, the tribes of the Turk frontier, the tribes of the very centre of Asia, the tribes of Dzungaria, and that district of small lakes and blind rivers (rivers with either no outlet, or falling into inland seas) which lies to the north of Khoten and Yarkend. The valley of the Ilí, falling into the Balkash Nor, belongs to this district. There are, however, Olöt occupancies elsewhere. It has already been stated that some of the Mongols of Tshakar are Olöt.

Then there are the Mongols of the Volga; who are, certainly, more Olöt than either Kalka or Buriat. Upon the whole, the Olöt division is irregularly distributed over a discontinuous area.

The Chinese form of Olöt is Wala; the Tata, or Tartars, and the Wala being clearly and decidedly separated from each other. In a geographical work of the Ming period it is stated that "the land of Tata is bounded on the east by that of the Uliangkhai, and on the west by that of the Wala." Again; the Tibetan name is Tnsa; the name for the other Mongols being Sok. This shows that the division is natural. The Kalka are one branch; the Buriat another; the Olöt a third. This is indicated by the nomenclature. It is also indicated by the language. The Mongol of the Kalmuk of the Volga is more akin to the dialects of the Ili and Koko Nor than to either the Buriat or the Kalka.

*Olöt,* according to Klaproth, means *separate*. This statement would be unexceptionable were it not that Timkovski deduces the Olöt of Tsoros from a prince of the Yuan dynasty named Olutai; complications of this kind being common in Asiatic ethnology. The import of the word is, by no means, clear. It seems to me to have two interpretations. There are certain tribes who are, *eo nomine*, Olöt; being called, and calling themselves Olöt of the Koko Nor (Blue Lake), Olöt of the Alashan, Tsoros Olöt. Here the appellation is specific. On the other hand, however, there is Olöt, a generic name, for the Durban Oirad, or four tribes, viz. the Durbet, the Torgod, the Dzungar, and the Khoshot. These are, certainly, somewhat different from the Olöt Proper in the restricted sense of the word. I first notice

*The Khoshot.*—Having no specimen of the Khoshot language, I am unable to say whether or not it belongs to the Olöt group of dialects. I should not, however, be surprised to find it Kalka. This is because, according to Klaproth, "the Khoshot are, from one of their old royal families, named Kalka;" this being a statement that suggests the probability of the present arrangement being political rather than ethnological.

*The Dzungar* are the Mongols of Dzungaria, a geographical, rather than an ethnological, term; one, however, which gives us true and undoubted members of the Olöt group, as is shown by the dialect. The etymology of the word is said to be *dzun* = *left*, and *gar* = *hand*; which may, or may not be the case. I think it possible that it is another form of Tshakar or March. The nucleus of the Dzungar division is the drainage of the Ili, and those numerous lakes, which appear on the frontier of what is called Chinese Tartary, under the native or Mongolian name of Nor; *e.g.* the Lob Nor, the Balkash Nor, and others. Here the population is pure. In the parts about Ulan-kum, however, the sixty banners that constitute the population are only partly Dzungar; some being Durbet, other Khoit.

*The Torgod.*—Four banners of the Torgod are in the Koko Nor district; one on the frontier of China; others on the Volga, associated with the Durbet.

*The Durbet.*—Some of the Durbet are associated with the Dzungar; some with the Torgod of Chinese Mongolia; some with the Torgod of the Volga.

*The Olöt Proper.*—Of the Mongols of the Koko Nor the great majority is Olöt—twenty-one banners.

Of the Olöt united with the Tshakar the number of banners is eight.

The Tsoros Olöt (of the Koko Nor and Mount Alashan) give three banners.

The Tsoros Olöt, the Dzungar, and the Durbet seem to be most especially and most closely connected. That the Khoshot genealogies pointed towards the Kalka has been already stated. The Torgod have a particular patriarch Mahatshi Mengho. But the Durbet and Dzungar have a common ancestor, Olinda Budun Taidzhi, who was exposed under a tree, but nourished by the juice of its twisted and crooked *tshoros*, or branch.

*Other Mongols of the South and West.*—One of the banners of the Koko Nor district is named Khort, another Tsagan Nomon Khan.

Another banner is that of the Dzakhazin.

The Mongols of the North of Tibet are called Hor (or Horpa) and Sok (or Sokpo). Some call themselves Siragol or Sharagol, which seems to mean neither more nor less than Yellow River.

All these are probably allied to the Olöt. I cannot, however, give their exact relations.

*The Tsiken.*—Besides the Mongols of the different banners, there dwelt, under the Ming dynasty, on the frontier of the Chinese province Shensi, the Tsiken Mongols. Klaproth is unable to say whether these exist at the present time as a separate tribe, or whether they are undistinguishably mixed up with the others.

| English. | Dzungarian. | Kalmuk. |
|---|---|---|
| *One* | nege | nigen |
| *Two* | khoyur | khoyur |
| *Three* | gurba | gurban |
| *Four* | dörbö | dörbön |
| *Five* | tabu | tabun |
| *Six* | surga | surgan |
| *Seven* | dolo | dolon |
| *Eight* | naima | naiman |
| *Nine* | yezu | yezun |
| *Ten* | arba | arban |

*The Buriat.*—The Buriat, to the amount of about 190,000 souls, live in Russian Siberia, divided into tribes, and are, as compared with the other Siberians, civilized.

The majority of them is Buddhist. Still there are amongst them some Pagans, some Christians of the Greek Church, and some few Mahometans.

Their area touches that of the Mantshú on the east; and the parts about Nizhni Udinsk on the west; where it comes in contact with that of the Tungús of the Tusguska, the Yeniseians, and certain Turk tribes. Castrén divides them, according to their dialects, into the Buriat of the Kuda, the Lena, the Akhon, the Ida, the Alari, and the Tunka rivers; to which he adds the Bolagan of the left bank of the Angara; all of which lie on this side of Lake Baikal. Beyond, and to the south or south-east of that great inland sea, lie the Khorin Buriat, and the Bargu Buriat, the former the more numerous, and consisting of eighteen tribes, the latter on the river Barguzin.

Due south of the lake, the Kudarin are an offset of the Buriat of the Kuda.

The Selenga Buriat of Castrén are the Zongol and their allied tribes, which Klaproth (as has been stated) makes Kalka.

The Buriat of the parts about Nizhni Udinsk, the Buriat of the extreme west, call—

| | |
|---|---|
| Themselves | *Buriat* |
| The Russian | *Mangut* |
| — Tungús | *Kaldzhak-shin* |
| — Katshintsi Turks | *Kat-kum* |
| — Kot | *Kotob-kum* |
| — river Birus | *Byr-hu.* |

The chief difference between the Buriat and the Kalka seems to be political. Neither is it quite certain that Castrén's divisions between the Buriat of this side of the Baikal, and the Buriat beyond the Baikal, is natural.

The Selenga forms of speech approach most closely the written or literary language. They also approach the Khorin dialects.

| English. | Khorin. | Nizhni-Uda. | Tunkin. | Selenga. |
|---|---|---|---|---|
| *Man (vir)* | ere | ere | ire | ere |
| *Man (homo)* | khung | kung | kung | khung |
| *Head* | tarkhi | tologoi | tologi | tologoi |
| *Hair* | uhun | uhung | uhung | usu |
| *Eye* | n̈yudeng | nyideng | nyudeng | nyude |
| *Ear* | shikheng | shikeng | shikeng | shikhe |
| *Nose* | khamar | kamar | khamar | khamar |
| *Mouth* | amang | amang | amang | ama |
| *Tongue* | kelen | keleng | khelengn | khele |
| *Hand* | gar | gar | gar | gar |
| *Foot* | khol | köl | köl | khul |
| *Sun* | narang | narang | narangn | nara |
| *Moon* | hara | hara | hara | sara |
| *Star* | odon | odong | odong | odo |
| *Fire* | gal | gal | gal | gal |
| *Water* | uhan | uhung | uhungn | oso |

*The Pelu.*—From the Japanese encyclopædia, known in China as *Kho-khan Zan-zai-tu-khuy*, completed A.D. 1713, Klaproth gives a specimen of a Mongol dialect entitled *Pelu*; adding that *Pe* means *north* and *lu* means *western barbarians*. If so, the Pelu are the north-western barbarians.

| English. | Pelu. | Mongol. |
|---|---|---|
| *Man* | kore | ere |
| *Woman* | khoton | khatun |
| *Father* | kozike | etshige |
| *Mother* | koke | eki |
| *Brother* | teuge | dagu |
| *Girl* | oka | okin |
| *Sky* | tengri | tangri |
| *Sun* | nara | nara |
| *Moon* | zara | zara |
| *Star* | khuton | odon |
| *Sea* | talai | dalai |
| *River* | murun | muran |
| *Water* | uzo | uzu |

Such are the divisions of the Mongols of Mongolia, or Mongolistan, arranged, as much as possible, according to their tribual affinities; affinities which are by no means clear and patent, and which correspond much more definitely in books than in nature. They are evidently traversed by political and other complications. The great steppe of Gobi, or Shamo, exhibits itself so prominently in our maps that it looks as if the Mongolians were pure nomads of a desert. The extent to which this view is inaccurate may be inferred from the notices of Tumet, Tshakar, and Gesikten.

At the same time the Mongolians are as nomad as any nation in the world. Few are exclusively so.

Say that the Sunid, who (by the way) are more especially the occupants of a steppe than any tribe of which we have a description of any notable fulness, represent the average Mongolians, and the following is a notice of them. Their country is stony rather than sandy, and undulating or broken rather than flat. It is also stony rather than clayey. It abounds in nitrous, and other saline, scurfs. The wells are from six to ten feet deep. Yet streams are by no means wanting. If Mongolia were in Africa it would be a desert full of oases. The industry, however, such as it is, is nomadic rather than agricultural. Wheat will grow. Flax grows wild. Millet, however, is the chief object of cultivation. So uncertain and severe are the seasons that, out of flocks of 1000, no more than eighty have, in certain seasons, been preserved. Metallic wealth may or may not exist. It is only known that the Mongols have as little taste for mining as for agriculture. Gold, too, probably, is to be found. Yet there are few or no washings and diggings. One thing especially favours the breeding of cattle. There are few or no tormenting insects. Of wood there is little. The framework of the tents is osier. The chief fuel is camel's dung. This is the case with the steppes. Yet on the Russian frontier wood is abundant, and in Eastern Mongolia wheat is grown and agricultural habits are developed. The trade is done by the Chinese. A few Mongols act as merchants, and sell their goods in China. Numerous Chinese make profitable journeys to different parts of Mongolia. On the eastern edge of the desert there is no want of rain; of rain irregularly distributed. The droughts are frequent; yet the rainfall is considerable. More fish is to be found in the rivers; more game is to be found in the plains, than the inhabitants use as food; the greater part of which is supplied by the flocks. Of domestic animals the horse, camel, ox, sheep, and dog are the chief. The cat is scarce. To have husbanded a few stacks of hay is a great fact in Mongolian economy.

Under conditions like these a dense population is impossible. For a single herd and single flock a large tract of land is needed. There must be a winter pasture, and a summer one. There must be locomotion from place to place; and places to match. The population is thin. It is doubtful whether the Chinese officials themselves have a true census. Each Mongol prince, when he submitted to China, declared the number of men he could bring into the field. Each Dsarsak, or noble, must bring to the field from three to twenty-three companies, squadrons, or regiments; each consisting of 150 horsemen. Taking thirteen of these as average, and multiplying them by the 49 banners of the Southern Mongols, and the 84 of the Kalkas, Timkovski gets 260,000 men; without the eight banners of the Tshakar, calculated at 241,000 men. This estimate, however, applies to the end of the seventeenth century, after the struggle between China and the Dzungarians. Since then, there has been peace, with no need for a *levée en masse*. Under peace, however, population increases. The present estimate is 500,000 tents, or 2,000,000 souls.

The desert is the country where the primitive habits are best preserved. In Tshakar and the neighbouring khanates or wangdoms there is a great loss of the original simplicity; Chinese practices being largely adopted.

The dress, in the east at least, is of nankeen, cloth, fur, and leather; a nankeen robe, a cloth vest, a leather girdle, leather boots, fur trimmings. Of the women coral is the favourite ornament. The bow and arrow, with a short sword, is the chief weapon. Powder, shot, and muskets are obtained from China. The tents are of felt; containing, over and above the ordinary utensils, some copper idols. In the list, however, of ordinary utensils chairs find no place. The Mongol sits on the ground cross-legged.

Pure water is drunken but rarely. Brick tea is the ordinary beverage—beverage and food as well; for it is thickened with butter, milk, and salt. In every tent there is a kettle full of it; of which the passing stranger is free to partake. Arrak is made from the milk of the cows and sheep; kumiss from that of the mares. Hunting, horseracing, wrestling and archery are the chief games. I find no notice of boxing; though a boxing-match is a favourite spectacle in Japan. Again; Timkovski never heard of a Mongol dance. Amongst the closely-allied Tungús we hear of many.

Story-telling and singing are the usual accompaniments to tea, arrak, and kumiss. The songs remind us of what the Romans believed to have been the custom of their ancestors. A boy takes down the lyre from the peg; the lyre being a violin with three strings, made out of a goat's horn. He then hands it to the master of the feast, who passes it to the Tulholos, minstrel, or bard. The

Tulholos begins often with an invocation to Timur. "O divine Timur, will thy soul be soon born again? Come back! Come back! we await thee, O Timur." Yet Timur was no Mongol, but a Turk. The great Mongol was Temudzhin or Tshingiz-khan, from whom Timur and a whole Timurian family deemed it an honour to be derived. But of this more hereafter.

Till the time for marrying, children of both sexes live with their parents. The time, however, for separation comes early. The bridegroom receives from his father some cattle and a separate tent; the portion of the bride consisting chiefly of clothes, and household utensils. When a couple is thus settled its residence is generally within the same district as that of the parents; as near as the pasturage permits. First cousins marry. Two sisters may successively marry the same man. Pedigrees are kept so carefully that the *yasu*, or degree of affinity, between two individuals is rarely lost sight of.

Before a marriage is concluded the stars have to be consulted. One star rules another. The woman born under such a star would rule the husband. This is to be avoided. If the woman be born under the ox, or the mouse, and the man under the dragon or the serpent, the marriage is allowed; but if one be born under the mouse, and the other under the horse, it is forbidden. Other signs, also, are hostile; *e. g.* the tiger, the hen, the horse, the hog, and the ape.

The signs, themselves, are twelve; corresponding with the twelve months.

| | | |
|---|---|---|
| 1. The mouse. | 5. The dragon. | 9. The ape. |
| 2. The ox. | 6. The serpent. | 10. The hen. |
| 3. The tiger. | 7. The horse. | 11. The dog. |
| 4. The hare. | 8. The ram. | 12. The hog. |

The preliminaries are carried on by proxies, or negotiators; strangers, very often, to the parties most concerned. The father of the man visits the relations of the bride. The negotiator attends him. They take a sheep ready dressed and cut up, some arrak, and some *khaduks*, or consecrated pocket-handkerchiefs. These are placed before the image of the Burkhan along with lighted tapers. Then follow prostrations; then a feast; then a largess. This is called the *tabil tabikhu;* succeeded by the bargaining part of the business. What will you give for the girl? How many head of cattle? When will you deliver them? Will you pay at once or by instalments? When the parties are rich these points are understood rather than discussed.

Another feast, the *khorun khurgeku*, finds place when the bridegroom receives presents, and consults the priests about fixing the day. Let it be a lucky one. The mother sets these inquiries afloat; the mother of the bridegroom. But where is the bride? Not at the feast; not with her intended. From the day of the betrothal neither of the elect sees each other. The bride must live secluded. Her lover is the very last person for her to consort with. She may not see him. She may not see even his parents. After marriage the same restraints prevail. For a certain time (a week, ten days, or a fortnight) the bride's mother, who accompanies her daughter, lives in the tent. As long as she does this, husband and wife (if so they may be called) know nothing of each other.

The Mongols were a lettered nation soon after the death of Tshingiz-khan, their alphabet being that of the Uigur Turks. How far it was used is another question. Two circumstances prevented its developing itself into a literature. First, there was the natural character of the Mongols themselves, a character which, combined with the conditions under which it was evolved, inclined them to war rather than peace. Secondly; there were their conquests in the east, the south, and the west; in China, in Persia, and in Turkey. In all these countries the intruders adopted the higher civilization of the natives. The descendants of Kublai Khan became Chinese; the Holagu dynasty Persians; the descendants of Tshagatai and Dzhuzhi Turks and Indians. There is a Mongol alphabet as early as the fourteenth century. There is no pure Mongol literature equally old. But there is a notable amount of authorship in a Persian and Turkish dress.

The earliest, perhaps the only classic, whose work is in the language of his tribe, and that tribe one of Mongolia, is Sanang Seetsen, of the country of the Ortu, and of real or supposed royal blood; in other words, a descendant of Tshingiz-khan. He lived early in the seventeenth century, and wrote soon after the establishment of the Mantshú dynasty in China. Translated into German by the learned Schmidt, it is, under the title of The History of the Eastern Mongolians (Geschichte der Ost-Mongolen), an accessible, if not an interesting, work. It begins with the Creation, and ends with the Mantshú conquest. Tibet, however, in the earlier part of the work, is much more prominent than Mongolia. The Mongols derive their royal line from Tibet; the Tibetans from India. From Tibet, too, came the Buddhist creed to the Mongols; India having given it to Tibet. Now the whole work of Sanang Seetsen is eminently Buddhist; so much so that it is a religious history rather than a political one. It is difficult to praise it. Even its editor admits that it is faulty. A sad want of accuracy, and a sadder want of discrimination is apparent throughout. The language, however, is simple, and the narrative brief; in this respect, unlike the majority of Asiatic compositions.

Preliminary notices, like the history of the Tibetan

Buddhism, take up about one-fourth of the book, and must be waded through before we arrive at the times of Tshingiz-khan; the notice of whom is very lax and unsatisfactory, though it fills another quarter of the volume. This is followed by a very short sketch of the Yuan dynasty. The most historical portion of the work is what now follows. The dynasty of the Ming, which succeeded that of the Mongols, is characterized by the vindictive zeal with which it destroyed all the literary records (what were they ?) of the hateful foreigners; so that the condition of the ex-rulers between the time of their ejection from China and the Mantshú conquest is one of the very darkest of the numerous dark questions of Asiatic history. This, however, Sanang Seetsen gives. Without going too minutely into the question of his authorities, we may take a general view of his account; which is to the following effect. There was first a state of anarchy, during which the very existence of the Buddhist belief was in jeopardy. There was war, and there were its barbarities and barbarisms, and, whilst these were in operation, a reaction towards the old paganism set in. The Shamans revived for a while, and confronted the Buddhists. More than one speech of the Kami (Shamans), made during these controversies, is given. However, an approach to order was effected; the descendants of Dayan Khan formed a dynasty, and Buddhism was re-established. This brings us to the Mantshú conquest and the conclusion of the work; in reading which we must remember that the author was an Ortu, and that the Ortu are among the most eastern of the Mongolians. Hence, he tells us but little of what took place westwards. The Religions of the Eastern Mongolians—this is Sanang Seetsen's work, a work which, from its unique character, we may easily overvalue, but which is, nevertheless, one of no little importance. It is a history of the countrymen of Tshingiz-khan in the language of their great emperor.

The Mongols of the twelfth and thirteenth centuries were formidable conquerors. Because they were this their military organization is of interest. Fortunately it has been described. Their chief weapon was the bow; as it was that of the conquerors of Hungary. It was the weapon at which they were the most expert; the weapon which the very children loved to practise themselves in. The next was the iron mace; the next the spear. This was somewhat exceptional: "their arms are bows, iron maces, and, in some instances, spears." The ox supplied the defensive armour. Ox-hides, dried by fire, and so made hard and strong, served as a defence to their bodies. Was it shields or breastplates into which it was made? We are only told that it was made into defensive armour.

Such the individual. The system of the army was truly and pre-eminently decimal. To every ten men an officer; to every ten of these lower officers a centurion; to every ten centurions a chiliarch; to every ten chiliarchs a commander of 10,000. A company of 100 was called a *tuk*. Ten *tuks* made a *toman*.

When a march is to be made, a company is drafted from the main body and sent two days in advance, other companies being stationed upon the flanks and in the rear to prevent surprises. When one horse is tired, another is mounted. Eighteen horses to one man is the average allowance. Under the pressure of an extreme scarcity the horseman bleeds his horse and drinks the blood as it flows warm from the veins. In sight of the enemy, he fights after the fashion of the old Parthians, hovers about him at a distance, affects a flight, shoots arrows as he rides away, makes a sudden turn, and wins a battle.

All the chiefs of the family of Tshingiz are buried in

the same place; on the side of a lofty mountain named Altai. So writes Marco Polo; but, as Altai is the name of a range rather than any particular mountain, the exact locality is undetermined. Wherever they may chance to die, it is on the Altai that they are buried. Thither they must be borne even though the journey last 100 days. During the removal, sacrifices are made of horses and of men. The best of the stud is killed in order that, in the next world, his master may have the use of it. Any one who is met on the road is killed, in order that he may help to form an escort to the deceased. The bearers and attendants of the body kill him, saying, "depart for the next world, and there attend upon your deceased master." When the corpse of a particular prince named Mongù was followed to the Altai burial-ground no less than 10,000 persons, whom fanaticism, or fate, or bad luck threw in the way, are said to have been killed.

The Mongol huts are of felt, round, and well-made, easily taken down, easily set up, easily packed up and moved about. The waggon on which they are carried is four-wheeled, drawn by oxen or camels. The women attend to them. When the tent is pitched its entrance faces the south. The women work. The women trade. The men hunt and hawk. The dogs and the falcons are of the best. Whatever the hunters take they eat; sometimes they eat the dogs themselves, sometimes the camels, sometimes the horses. Camels' flesh is eaten at the present time. Huc, who tasted it, reports unfavourably. The preparation of mare's milk which they drink now they drank in the time of Marco Polo; and they called it by its present name—*kemurs* or rather *kumiss*.

The women work; being industrious and well-behaved as well. No females in the world excel them in chastity.

This cannot always be said of them at present. In Polo's time, however, infidelity was the most heinous of crimes. Neither was rudeness of speech permitted. Offensive language (frequent at the present time amongst all the nomad tribes) is never heard (they now call a spade a spade), so busy are they, and so exclusively attentive to their domestic employments. And the men are as steady as their wives; of which (by the way) they are specially stated to take as many as they choose; some having ten, some twenty. The expense of such establishments is moderate. A wife not only earns her keep, but has to be purchased; the *kalim* system being thus old, and, doubtless, much older. When a husband marries he pays a dower to the wife's parents. The one first espoused has a sort of supremacy over the rest. She is the true wife. The rest are concubines. When the father dies, the son may take to himself all the wives left behind, save and except his own mother. Upon the death, too, of one brother the others may marry the widow. Is this done at once, or in succession?

The chief object of worship was Natigay. Every Mongol had an image of Natigay in his house. This was covered with cloth or felt. To this they made humble offerings of morsels of food and lumps of fat; never eating a meal without greasing his lips, and at the same time those of his wife and children. For Natigay has a family, the different members of which have also their images. These are associated with that of Natigay himself; the wife on the left hand, the children in a reverential posture round about him. When the lips of the Natigay family have been greased some of the liquor in which the meat has been cooked is thrown out of doors. This is for the other spirits—the spirits of the open air as opposed to those of the domestic hearth. Until all this has been done, the real meal has to begin. The Natigay first; then the spirits out of doors; then the masters of the feast—this is the order. When all has been done, the family eat and drink without further ceremony.

The worship of Natigay is intelligible. It is conducted after the manner of the Siberian tribes in general; with all of whom the analogues of the Italian Lares and Penates, the domestic deities, are objects of affectionate veneration. The worship, too, of the gods outside the tent is intelligible. The remainder of the notice, however, may be criticised. It is to the effect that, over and above these minor godheads, the Mongols believed in a single deity whose nature was sublime and heavenly. To him they burned incense. To him they offered prayers for bodily health and moral excellence. This may have been the case. The idea, however, of such a deity may have been no native offspring of the Mongol intellect. It may have been due to the early Christianity of some of the Tartar tribes. Or the fact itself may be overstated. There is some danger of this being the case. A great deal of what Marco Polo describes, he has seen; but a great deal which he tells us is either drawn from second-hand accounts or rests upon inference. The "original manners," he says, "are much corrupted. What we see now is other than original. The Tartars at Ukaka have forsaken their old laws, and worship idols. The Tartars of the eastern provinces have adopted the manners of the Saracens." Yet it is the original manners which he professes to describe.

Of the present superstitions we have anything but a full, systematic, and trustworthy account.

Atkinson witnessed the immolation of a ram. An assistant killed it. The priest himself turned towards the east, chanted a hymn, beat a tambourine, and prayed for a large increase of cattle. The victim was then flayed, the skin hung aloft on a pole; the flesh cooked and eaten. Meanwhile the priest chanted, and the tambourine went on being beaten. This was in the valley of the Tshurish, in the Yabagan steppe, amongst the Olöt.

The specimens given by Castrén of the Buriat language supply a complement and expansion to this notice of Atkinson's. From them we learn that the *sacalga*, or libation, is accompanied by the following song or invocation :—

There ! there ! go on ! speaking in a whisper;
There ! strewing, speaking aloud ;
There ! lord of the sky, expanded ;
There ! space of earth, stretched out ;
There ! ninety princes of the south-west ;
There ! nine grey-haired old men ;
There ! Buriat and Bulgat ;
There ! throw the millet even ;
There ! spout out like a spring ;
There ! Bukha Noyan, our father ;
There ! call on him ;
There ! I pray to thee ——*
There ! thy father's tribe was ——*
There ! thy mother's tribe was ——*
There ! thy father was ——*
There ! thy mother was ——*
There ! that was thy name ——*

At the third libation, the song or invocation is again taken up :—

There ! in the beginning was the king of men ;
There ! then was the king of the earth ;
There ! then were the princes of the hills ;
There ! then were the gods of the greenswards ;
There ! advancing with the echo of high hills ;
There ! advancing the roar of wide seas.

The brandy is then poured, drop by drop, upon the fire, the invocation continuing thus :—

Father ! father ! Malan Tengri ;
Mother ! mother ! Yoren Tengri ;

* Giving the names of the person prayed to, &c.

Youngest son of the father Malan Tengri;
Old man Sagadai, wife Sakhalu,
Lying and blowing, gnawing and kindling
The fire Bului-khan, his wife Gulyi,*
With the covering of grey lambskin,
With the offer of a lamb a year old;
At bed-time like a hill,
At rising like a greensward;
May he be rich in herds,
Rich in heritage.

The *kerek*, or solid sacrifice, consists in the offer of a sheep. The Shaman who kills it wets his staff, whirls it round his head, and sings:—

For the life, a compensation;
For the body, a gift;
Kinsman here, evil hence;
Cry wrong, blame the Shaman;
Minister wrongly, blame the ministers;
Cry right, minister right;
The Gods go away,
Blame yourselves.
Lighter than a feather,
Swifter than an arrow.

When the ecstacy is over, and the spirit which entered into the Shaman has left him, he prays for his employer, the founder of the feast or sacrifice:—

Ho! ho! here! here!
I call on the king of the wide-spread sky,
The king of the wide-spread earth;
The ninety princes of the south-west;
The nine white-haired old men;
Our father Bukhu Noyan,
The body of our mother Budan Khatun,
For good fortune and prosperity,
For long life,
Lasting luck,
A skin a span thick,
A body like iron,
We pray for.

* Brass.

The operation of the offerings,
The defence of life,
We pray for.
The cure of sickness,
The healing of ills,
We pray for.
Riches and cattle
We pray for.
A numerous posterity
We pray for.

Bukhu Noyan was the husband of Budan Khatun, and the two together were the first beings in the human shape, and the makers of the rest of the human race. These they cut out of paper, and placed in a yurt. In the wall of the yurt was a hole, and at the door of the yurt was a dog. The dog watched, to guard the men in the yurt against the evil spirit. The men were all covered with hair; the dog had no hair at all. The men slept; the dog did so too. The evil spirit entered through the hole in the wall. He maimed and defiled the new-made men. When Bukhu Noyan and Budan Khatun knew this, they knew not what to do; but arose in a hurry, and laid their hands upon a shaving-knife. With this they shaved the men until they were bare of hair, except in certain parts of their bodies. The dog they punished for his heedlessness by clothing with the foul hairs.

Much in favour of either the solemnity or beauty of the Shaman's invocation cannot be said. Neither are the other Buriat specimens of any literary value.

1.

From the prince has come a board sprinkled with black marks;
The chief holds all the people together:
From our lord has come a paper marked with diverse-coloured marks;
All these our lord supports,
Ever pitying us all.

2.

The hoof of the horse crashes
The white stone of Agi.
The sorrow of the heart
Vexes the distant friend.

3.

The willows of Kemnikhe* wave here and there;
Khulebaksen,† the brandy warmed my body;
In the midst of seventy or eighty horse is a red nag;
Father! take him; thy son is on horseback.
In the front tent, on the stand, is a strong red breast-plate;
Mother! take it; thy son is on horseback.
On the right side, in the box, is a harness;
Father! take it out; thy son is on horseback.

4.

On the bottom of my quiver
Are three-and-twenty arrows;
Uncle! take them.
Sege Mergen I.
Go into yon land.
On the bottom of my box
Are thirteen arrows,
Uncle! take them.
Sege Mergen I.
Go into yon land.
In the bottom of my chest
Are many arrows;
Uncle! take them.
Sege Mergen I.
Go into yon land.

5.

Yo! yo! galde! to-day I am drunk;
Yo! yo! galde! to-morrow I will be drunk
Yo! yo! galde! the day after to-morrow I'll be drunk;
Yo! yo! galde! to the feast I will go;
Yo! yo! galde! I will be drunk.

The following samples, less rude than the preceding, represent the poetry of either the Kalkas, or the Eastern

* Name of a place. † Name of a person.

Mongolians. The first is theological, or moral; the second, heroic; the third, convivial.

1.

Dzungkaba, the prince of the law, is the powerful king of all that exists. Oh! happy people, born in the country of the gods! We beg you to carry us beyond the great river; that our souls may freely soar towards the abode of Outar Khan. And you, perverse men, who trouble the repose of your fellow-creatures, know that there is a judge for good and evil; the equitable Eerlik Nomoum Khan. The Lamas teach us the dogmas of the faith; our parents good manners: let us endeavour to profit by their lessons; for, wandering at random in an obscure valley, we cannot walk securely, or penetrate the thoughts of the man who lives with us; but if the intercession of the Delai Lama is favourable to us, we shall escape the snares of our enemies, and our secret faults will be pardoned by the three Bogda.

2.

A troop of warriors is going to issue from the territory of the Tsetsen Khan; it is composed of three thousand warriors, with the brave Tseden Beilé at their head. Among the horsemen of the court, Kounkoun Taidyi has been chosen; the valiant Beile Dordji Djonom, and Bauba Bouissoun noin, guided by their own inclination, will soon join their companions. The extraordinary valour of these heroes has already beeh felt by the enemy in the sanguinary battle on Mount Kangai; and when the august master (the Emperor), in his clemency, shall have put an end to our labours, we will pass, on our return to our own country, by Euketala, the thick and verdant grass of which will serve as food to our excellent coursers.

3.

What a delicious beverage is the generous archan, the gift of the Emperor; it is as sweet to us as honey; let us drink it, then, in our own social meetings.

The immoderate use of it causes stupidity; but he who drinks of it in moderation enjoys supreme pleasure.

Hail! to health, strength, and youth! as chance seldom unites us, let us enjoy together the delicious beverage; a banquet among brethren is the greatest of pleasures.

Dzungkaba is the Dalai Lama, of whom notice was taken in the account of Tibet; Utai Khan is a holy mountain of China; Irlik Khan, the Erle-khan of the Turks, is (I think) the Erle-king of Göthe's well-known ballad—

"Wer reitet so spät durch Nacht und Wind," &c.;

a fact which is probably new to the commentators, and was, I think, unknown to the author. It generally passes as a Danish ballad. The three Bogda are the Dalai Lama, the Bantshan Erdeni, and Kutuku Ghegen, the *august three* Buddhist dignitaries of the first class.

Riddles are to be found in the literature of most rude nations. Friis gives a collection for Lapland. Schleicher one for Lithuania. Amongst those of the Mongols of the Selenga we find that of our friends the Sphinx and Œdipus.

*Question*—Uglo durbo, edur dunda khoyir, udesi gurba? Morning, four; noon, two; evening, three.

*Answer*—A man.

There is Buddhism in the paganism, and paganism in the Buddhism of the Mongols. There are also traces of an intermediate creed—fire-worship. Khormusta, the name of a deity of frequent occurrence, has been identified (by Schmidt) with the Persian Oromasdes.

Okodil, according to Georgi, is the chief of the devils—the Obersatan as that writer calls him. Details concerning him would have been welcome. So would anything further concerning the terms Tengri, Burkhan, Esan, Ongon, Nogit, and Illmetshetshin. So they would concerning Irlik-khan, notwithstanding the appearance of his name in a poem. He is Turk as well as Mongol; as will soon be seen. Okodil occurs twice in Sanang Seetsen, where it means a corpse.

Tengri means sky or heaven; then (according to Castrén) the God of Heaven; then any minor deity.

Burkhan, by Castrén, is identified with Buddha; as I imagine word for word. I am much more inclined to make it, word for word, Perkunos, the Lithuanian deity;

who is not only Lithuanian, but Fin as well. I also make it the Scandinavian Fiorgyn. It seems, in the present state of Buddhism under which the Mongols live, to mean God; being often accompanied by a qualifying prefix, and becoming Tengri Burkhan, or Oktorgoi Burkhan, meaning Sky God.

Esan and T'tsen are the same word. They denote the little domestic tutelary gods, or the images.

Ongon has much the same meaning as Esan; and

Nogit is an Esan, or Ongon, painted. Nogit, perhaps, means the representation rather than the person; Esan and T'tsen (for they mean lord, or master) the person rather than the representation.

Imegiltshin is an image (or deity symbolized by it) made more especially out of lambskin than aught else; lambs and cattle being the especial objects of Imegiltshin's attention.

Another name for Okodil is Tshitkyr.

Over and above the Mongols of Mongolia, there are the Mongols of more than one area other than Mongol. The most important of these are the

*Torgod and Durbet of the Russian Empire.*—These are best known under the name of Kalmuk. A Tartar in Russia is a Turk; a Kalmuk a Mongol. The whole of the seventeenth century was a period of danger and disturbance; so much so that more than one division of the Mongols placed itself under the protection of China or Russia. About 20,000 families of Kalkas sought the Buriat country.

But the Olöt movements give the greatest results—two migrations and (to coin a new word) one *re*-migration.

The first migrants were of the Torgod tribe; the date of

their migration being A. D. 1630. Worsted by the Dzungar and Koshot they moved westward; reached Astrakan, attacked it, and were repulsed with the loss of their khan, whose attempt cost him his life. His son succeeded him, setled the horde, ruled over it for a time as an independent potentate, but eventually acknowledged the Russian dominion.

A. D. 1700–1703 a second movement took place; the majority of the migrants being, as before, Torgod, but some being Durbet.

Aiuki Khan, who died A. D. 1724, was a warrior of many battles. He defeated the Nogays. He assisted Peter I. in his war against Persia. He sent, in the reign of Elizabeth, 30,000 men to the Crimea, the descendants of whom still exist as colonists in that peninsula. Aiuki, however, was the last of the khans whose power was real. His immediate successors were but puppets under a Russian president. His successors, too, always had their title ratified from Petersburg.

Discontents arose. A.D. 1771 saw the withdrawal of 70,000 families. These were led by their khan Ubakha, and they forced along with them the Russian Captain Duden and a hundred soldiers. They were not pursued in any earnest, but they were harassed, and robbed, and killed by the tribes of their route; by the Kirghiz, and the Turcomans of Independent Tartary. They lost, indeed, 20,000 families by the way. They reached, however, the Chinese frontier after a journey of eight months —miserably distressed, diminished by nearly a third, and half-starved.

This was the *re*-migration; and, as real migrations are great rarities in history, though common enough in books, it deserves attention. The remnant that reached China was kindly and honourably received.

Fifteen thousand families were left behind; the ancestors of the present population, which amounts—

| | |
|---|---|
| In Astrakan to . . . | 87,556 |
| ,, Caucasus . . . | 20,591 |
| ,, Saratov . . . . | 692 |
| ,, Stavropol . . . | 10,223 |
| Total | 119,162 |

To which add, some in the Don Kosak country, in Orenburg, in Samar, and also an offset in the Crimea.

Their simple polity is regulated by a committee in Astrakan, consisting of two Kalmuk deputies, and two Russian judges under a Russian president.

The social constitution is that of their brothers in Mongolia. There is the head of the horde, or *ulus;* the heads of its divisions; some commanding 100, some 150, one more than 4000 tents. These are called Zaizans. There is also the Lama for the Buddhist majority; and a few priests, or missionaries, for the Christian minority. The nobles are called White, the commonalty Black, Bones. The wealth of the former is in their sheep and horses.

I imagine that the Kalmuks of Orenburg are those to whom Georgi devotes a short chapter, describing them as the Mahometan Mongols. A. D. 1753, there or thereabouts, they were received in their present localities by the Bashkirs, and in 1783 (when Georgi wrote) resided in three villages in the Government of Orenburg and in the district of Tset, to the number of fifty families. They intermarried with the Bashkirs, who are specially stated to have given them, on their arrival, both pastures and wives. Their children, though of Turk blood on the mothers' side, are still Mongol in appearance—flat-faced, big-eared. In the winter they reside in fixed dwellings. In summer, they move from pasture to pasture in tents.

There are a few Mongols in Bokhara; traces, real or supposed, of some in India; the same in Persia and Syria; the same in parts of Russia and Tartary. A true settlement, however, of greater importance than all these put together, is that of—

*The Mongols of Caubul and Persia.*—There are a few Mongols near Herât. In the king's body-guard is a regiment of Kalmuks (so-called even in Afghanistan), introduced from Balkh towards the end of the last century. But it is not these who are most especially under notice. The Mongolians of Caubul and Persia are the

*Tshehar Aimâk and the Hazara.*—On each side of a line, drawn from Herat to Caubul, lies, to the north of the proper Afghan, and to the south of the Uzbek and Turcoman, frontier, a great range of undulating country, often mountainous, almost always hilly, well-watered in some parts, bleak and rough in others. This falls into a western and an eastern division, with an important watershed between them. From the west flow the Murghab, the Tejend, and the Furrarud; from the east, the Helmund, the south-eastern feeders of the Oxus, and the north-western feeders of the Caubul River.

The former of these districts, lower and less mountainous, is the occupancy of the Tshehar Aimâk; the latter that of the Hazara;—names that require notice, because, unless we guard against it, confusion may arise in the use of them. Aimâk is our old friend, the Mongolian word for tribe; a word, however, which, though more Mongolian than aught else, seems to be Mantshu and Turk as well. Tshehar is the Persian for four; so that Tshehar Aimâk is a hybrid phrase, half from one language, half from another. Hazara, though there is a difference of opinion as to its actual meaning, is no proper name, but a common term. Say that it means soldier, regiment, horseman, noble, military frontier, or anything of the same kind, and it is clear that you may have Hazaras in more places than one. More than this, the word may in one place be used specially, or as the name of a single tribe or sub-tribe; whilst it may be used elsewhere as a general denomination for a collection of tribes, sub-tribes, clans, septs, families, or whatever we may call them. This is the case here. A special sub-section of the Tshehar Aimâk (Durban Aimâk it would be if the whole phrase were Mongol) will be called Hazara, and Hazara will also be the collective name for all the tribes of the other division.

Both are noticed in Elphinstone's Caubul: both are placed in the same category. The only doubt in the mind of the author is as to the nature of the class that contained them. He hesitates to make them Mongols. They generally spoke Persian. A sample of the language, since published by Lieut. Leach, settles the doubt—for the speakers of it, at least:—

| English. | Aimak. | Kalka. |
|---|---|---|
| *Head* | ekin | tologoi |
| *Ear* | tshakin | tsike |
| *Nose* | kabr | khamar |
| *Eye* | nuddun | nidu |
| *Tongue* | kelan | kolè |
| *Hand* | ghar | gar |
| *Fire* | ghar | gal |
| *Water* | ussun | usu |
| *Tree* | darakt* | modo |
| *Stone* | kuri | tsholo |
| *One* | nikka | nego |
| *Two* | koyar | khoyin |
| *Three* | ghorban | gurba |
| *Four* | dorban | dürba |
| *Five* | tabun | tabu |

How many members of the Aimâks thus show their origin in their language? What tribes are even more

* Persian.

purely Mongol than the speakers of the Mongol dialect—if any? What, if any, are less so? What are most Persian? What most Turk? I raise, rather than answer these questions. The Aimâk and Hazara areas are but little known and imperfectly described.

*The Four Aimâks.*—We know from the name the number of the primary groups. We anticipate their division and sub-division. The primary groups are:—

(1) The Timuni, divided into (*a*) the Kiptshak, and (*b*) Durzye.

(2) The Hazara, containing (*a*) the Jumshidi and (*b*) the Firuzcohi; the latter lying east, on the watershed, and on the frontier of Hazara (in the general sense of the word) division.

(3) The Zuri; and—

(4) The Timuri.

The Keri lie to the south of Meshed, far to the west of the others, and are doubtful Aimâks.

The Timúri and Hazara lie beyond the boundaries of Caubul, and, consequently, are subject to Persia. The former have long been where they are. The latter originally lay on the Timuri frontier; but a border quarrel caused their removal by Shah Mahmud. In dress, feature, and manners, the Hazara are more Uzbek than any other of the Aimâks, just as some are more like the Persians.

The tents of the Aimâk in general are Turk rather than Afghan; those of the Timuri, however, are Afghan rather than Turk.

As contrasted with the Afghans, the Aimäk (and, it may be added, the Hazara also) love a despotic rather than a free government; their princes being powerful and uncontrolled. They carry on the government in the name of the Shah of Persia or the Amir of Caubul, as the case may be; but are never controlled in the management of their own tribes, within which they have the power of life and death. They live in well-fortified castles, not without pretensions to comfort. They eat horseflesh, and mix the flour of an oily sort of nut, called khundzhik, with that of their wheat.

A few Persian villages are found in the Aimâk country. The date of the introduction of the Aimâk themselves is the thirteenth century; Manku Khan, the grandson of Tshingiz, having settled them. Elphinstone fixes their number at 400,000 or 450,000, without, however, pretending to accuracy.

As he only gives the primary divisions, we are not surprised to find, in the notices of the few travellers who have been in their country, new names. Ferrier names the tribe whose occupancy lay nearest to Herat, Zeidnat. Martial in habits, and yet not wholly averse to industry, it possesses the district of Kaleh-nuh, on the head-waters of one of the southern feeders of the Murghab. Here it is where it comes in contact with the Afghans of the Khorasan frontier. Here it is where the powerful chief Kerimdad Khan commands the efficient services of 5000 horsemen and 3000 foot. In case of need, the cavalry can be trebled, for the number of tents is 28,000.

Two other Zeidnat districts are governed by his two brothers—the districts of Pinjdeh and Murghab. A third brother resides in honourable exile at Herat, as a hostage in the hands of Yar Mohamed Khan for the fidelity of the other three. Nor is this precaution needless. The only doubt is as to whether it is effective. Kerimdad Khan, active, brave, intriguing, has twice been coerced, and twice shown that the coercion was insufficient. He was, at first, an ordinary plunderer, ravaging the districts to the south, and selling his captives to the Uzbeks. Then he was forced to acknowledge the sovereignty of

Herat, in evidence of which he sent an annual tribute of a few horses to Yar Mohammed, and received in return more than their worth of Herat valuables.

The Aimâk are, doubtless, a very free and independent population.

*The Hazara.*—The Hazara lie East; the Aimâk, west. The Hazara live in houses rather than tents; the Aimâk in tents rather than houses. The Hazara are Shia, the Aimâk, Sunnite, Mahometans. There are few or no Tadzhiks in Hazara. These are the chief points of difference.

The Aimâk have been described by those who knew them in their westernmost, the Hazara by those who have seen them in their easternmost localities—*i. e.* in Ghorbund, and Bamian. They are said to lend their wives to their guests. The tribes are as follows:—

| Names. | No. of Families. | Names. | No. of Families. |
|---|---|---|---|
| Da Murda . . . | 2000 | Da Murda . . . | —— |
| Durbi Ali . . . | 1000 | Dal Timur . . . | —— |
| Ism Tunun . . | 1000 | Deh Kundi . . | —— |
| Dia Zingi . . . | 5500 | Durghan . . . | —— |
| Doulat Pai . . | 2000 | Jakuri . . . . | —— |
| Marak . . . . . | 1000 | Naur . . . . . | —— |
| Kuptseom . . . | 2600 | Baddaws . . . | —— |
| Yarkhana . . . | 500 | Syud Dan . . . | —— |
| Zhalek . . . . | 200 | Tazak . . . . | —— |
| Tejuk . . . . . | 100 | Sugh Pah . . | —— |
| Die Murza . . | 300 | —— . . . | —— |
| Deh Zingi . . . | 5000 | —— . . . | —— |
| Sheek Ali . . . | 3000 | —— . . . | —— |
| Tatar . . . . . | 1000 | —— . . . | —— |
| Jurghai Burjeghai | 1000 | —— . . . | —— |
| Diah Pollah . . | 2000 | —— . . . | —— |

The first list gives the eastern, the other the western tribes—as far, at least, as they were known to our informant, Lieut. Wood; who puts the whole population at about 156,000 souls. Some are subject to the Uzbek Khan of Kunduz.

Many of the foregoing names are very suggestive. The word Hazara will appear and reappear again. The Jumshidi remind us of the Persian Jamshid. Then there are the Kiptshak — Turk and Mongol. Then there are the names Timur, Tshingiz, and Tartar. Durbi (or Durbi Ali) is, probably, the Mongol *durbet*.

The story about the laxity of Hazara females, and the carelessness of Hazara husbands, is found in both Elphinstone and Wood; in the latter, with the additional statement that the evidence is Afghan, and that the particular tribe of the Jakuri is most obnoxious to the charge. Let us hope that this frees the rest; though, by any one conversant with the extreme amount of coarseness which mixes up with the jealousy of rude nations, the fact must be pronounced credible.

The influence of the Mongols upon the world's history is so mixed up with that of the Turks, that the notice of it must stand over for the present. The colossal figure, however, of Temudzhin, or Tshingiz-khan, is purely Mongol. For his earlier history during the time when he was taking his first steps towards the consolidation of his power as a Mongol, it is clear that, with all his imperfections, Sanang Seetsen is our only approximation to an authority. For conquests in Persia, Turkestan, Armenia, or Europe, Europeans, Armenians, Turks, and Persians, are available. What, however, could they know of small additions made to a small nucleus; that nucleus being divided from the nearest of them by a third of the breadth of Asia?

Of Sanang Seetsen's account thus much seems trustworthy; that the original tribe of Tshingiz was in the north-east; not far from Lake Baikal; that (as far as the divisions are natural) it was Kalka, or Buriat, rather than Olöt; that the first blows were struck against the tribes of the north-east; that the Oerad Buriat, who were Mongols, submitted to him; that he attacked the Dzhurtshid and Solongos, who were Mantshurian Tungus; that Tangut and Tibet were afterwards reduced. In none of these conquests do we find the Mongols far from home. They simply extend their frontiers at the expense of their neighbours.

Upon the name of one of these we may pause. In the thirty-seventh year of his age Tshingiz sent a message to Ong Khan of the Kerait, saying, "At the time that I married my chief wife Burte Dzhenshin thou sentest to me a congratulatory gift, presented me with a robe of sable-skins, and behaved as a father. Let us be friends, even as father and son." But Ong Khan was distrustful; and assembled his men, and attacked Tshingiz unawares. Tshingiz, however, won the battle, and conquered the famous khan of the Kerait; famous, because of all the Mongolians he was the first who had a European reputation. Ong Khan was neither more nor less than the famous Prester John.

When we turn from the special to any general historian, we find a decided confirmation of the doctrine that the reputation of Tshingiz as a conqueror is beyond his actions. He consolidated the Mongols; and this is his chief work. He founded, rather than wielded, a power. Besides the conquests noticed by Sanang Seetsen, he conquered the northern part of China (but not the southern), and overran Kharismia and northern Persia.

Far beyond the bounds of Mongolia Tshingiz-khan

never went. His generals and successors it was who spread the terror of the Mongol name over Asia and Europe. They were the Alexanders. Tshingiz, the Philip of Mongolia, organized, rather than effected, distant victories. His special injunctions were that China should be conquered. This was done by his grandson. The captain, however, who led the Mongols round the Caspian from Bokhara to Dzungaria was, not Tshingiz, but Holagu.

Kubilai Khan, the grandson of Tshingiz, conquered China, and it is at the court of his grandson, Kubilai Khan, that we find our best informant for the Mongols of the fourteenth century, Marco Polo. By A. D. 1367 the native dynasty of the Ming had succeeded that of the Yuan, and little importance thenceforward attached itself to the once formidable name of Mongol.

Small heroes of more than one inter-tribual war, unsuccessful and successful insurgents against China, with captains who lent their swords to their former subjects, are all that history supplies. The Mantshú are now the conquerors. Galdan, prince of the Dzungarian Olöt, in the middle of the eighteenth century effected, partly by arms and partly by policy, an imperfect consolidation of the western tribes. His kingdom, attacked both by Russia and China, broke up after his death. Next, however, to Kubilai and Tshingiz, though by a long interval, Galdan is the greatest historical character of the Mongols. His field, however, was only Mongolia.

When Blumenbach published his celebrated Decads of human crania, those of the Mongols and Kalmuks exhibited characters so prominent, decided, and palpable, that he took them as the types of their class; much the same being done by more than one of the distinguished writers who have since illustrated the physical and natural history of Siberia and Central Asia. The accessibility of the Kalmuk country has had something to do with this. The main reason, however, lies in the undoubted and undeniable fact of the Mongol features being more strongly contrasted with those of either an ordinary European or an African than those of any other population equally well known. "It is easy," says Pallas, as quoted by Prichard, "to distinguish by their traits of physiognomy the principal Asiatic nations, who rarely contract marriage except with their own people. There is none in which this distinction is so characterized as amongst the Mongols. If the colour be set aside, the Mongol has as little resemblance to other people as a negro has to a European." There is some exaggeration in this statement, excellent observer as is its author. There is some exaggeration in it, but of such does a great deal of our ethnology consist. There is exaggeration; but it is not altogether useless. It helps to give prominence to a fact upon which the use of a very common term now rests. Mongolian physiognomies, Mongolian crania, Mongolian eyes, the Mongolian division of the human species, are phrases which few writers are cautious enough to use with either moderation or discretion. Hence it is as difficult to dispense with them altogether, as it is inconvenient to use them too freely.

The face of the Mongolian is broad and flat. This is because the cheek-bones stand out laterally, and the nasal bones are depressed. The cheek-bones stand out *laterally*. They are not merely projecting, for this they might be without giving much breadth to the face, inasmuch as they might stand forward. The cheek-bones of the African do this. Not so those of the flat-faced populations. A ruler laid across the face of a Mongol (or an Eskimo) is said to pass from cheek to cheek without touching the nose, so flat, snub, or depressed is that usually prominent organ. I consider this to be a somewhat extreme illustration. The distance between the eyes is great; the eyes themselves being oblique, and their carunculæ being concealed. The eyebrows form a low and imperfect arch, black and scanty. The iris is dark, the cornea yellow. The complexion is tawny, the stature low. The ears are large, standing out from the head; the lips thick and fleshy rather than thin; the teeth somewhat oblique in their insertion; the forehead low and flat; the hair lank and black.

With such elements the approach to beauty on the part of a Mongol must needs be distant and rare. Yet there are recorded cases of it. "Round and pretty faces, fine and regular features,"—so writes Pallas. The former are more likely to be of frequent occurrence than the latter. The rarity of personal deformities is a more definite characteristic. So is the rarity of fat people. What else do we expect with a population that lives an out-door life, and leaves the children to nature? Exceptions, however, lie against the lower extremities, to which continual exercise on horseback, beginning early and ending late in life, imparts an ungraceful curve, impairing the nutrition and development of the calves.

The well-trained eye of the Mongol discerns and distinguishes objects at a distance which surprises a European. It is a refinement, however, to refer this to any congenital peculiarity of the retina. The ordinary avocations of the life he leads call the senses both of sight and hearing into constant play; add to this that he is used to the atmosphere through which he sees.

The following description of the Kalmuks of the Don Kosak country is from Dr. Clarke. "Of all the inhabitants of the Russian empire, the Calmucks are the most distinguished by peculiarity of feature and manners. In their personal appearance, they are athletic, and very forbidding. Their hair is coarse and black; their language hoarse and guttural. They inhabit the countries lying to the north of Persia, India, and China; but from their vagrant habits, they may be found in all the southern parts of Russia, even to the banks of the Dnieper. The Cossacks alone esteem them, and intermarry with them. This union sometimes produces women of very great beauty; although nothing is more hideous than a Calmuck. High, prominent, and broad cheek-bones; very little eyes, widely separated from each other; a flat and broad nose; coarse, greasy, jet-black hair; scarcely any eyebrows; and enormous prominent ears compose no very inviting portrait."

The inter-parietal diameter of a Mongol skull, as compared with the occipito-frontal, is very great, the occipital protuberance so inconsiderable as to give the back of the cranium a truncate appearance, the zygomata curved outwards.

Behind the meatus auditorius the head swells out laterally; so as to present a remarkable broad base, and, at the same time, to look round and globular. The bones, too, are smooth and glabrous. Blumenbach writes of a Kalmuk cranium that it had *habitus quasi tumidus et inflatus*; and Dr. Meigs finds the only Kalmuk skull of Morton's collection to be *tumidus* and *inflatus* also. He quotes Blumenbach's epithets. The largest collection I have myself seen, that of the Berlin Museum, verifies them. The base of some of the Buriat crania, and the truncation of the occiput, are, in some cases, inordinate. Morton's specimen measures ninety-three cubic inches internal capacity.

If anything, the Tungús physiognomy is an exaggeration of the Mongolian Proper. So, at least, writes one of the most competent of our authorities, Pallas. The face is flatter and bigger than the face of a Mongol. It is Samoyed as much as Mongol. The beard is pre-eminently scanty; next to no beard at all.

Blumenbach, having written before the occipital protuberance and the ratios between the side-to-side, and the fore-and-aft diameters had taken their present importance, places, decidedly and without circumlocution, the Tungús skulls in the same class with the Mongolian, notwithstanding the fact that the particular specimen before him was eminently long-headed. He noticed the circumstance. He measured the longitudinal diameter. It was as much as nine inches. His view, however, has been refined on, in the mind of the present writer, needlessly.

# CHAPTER XVIII.

The Turk Stock.—The Kirghiz.—The Karakalpak.—The Barama, Baraba, or Barabinski Tribes.—The Tshulim, Kuznets, Abintsi, Katshalar, Yastalar, Boktalar, Kaidin, Beltyr, Birgus.—Teleuts.—Tubalar.—The Sokhalar or Yakut.—Turks of the Khanates, of Siberia, Kazan, Astrakan, the Crimea.—Basian.—Karatshai.—Kumuk.—Chunsag.—Nogays.—Bashkirs.—Meshtseriak.—Teptyar.—Tumuli, &c.—Uzbeks.—Turkman.

In the details of the Turk name, it is convenient to begin with the Kirghiz, whose occupancy is the northern and eastern part of that portion of our maps which is denominated Independent Tartary, but which would, more properly, be called Turkestan. As for its independence, the less prominence given to it on paper the better for historical accuracy. The land is more or less Russian, and more or less Chinese. At the same time, a large though decreasing portion of it is actually what its name denotes. The Uzbeks of Khiva are independent. The Turkomans of the Persian frontier are independent. Some of the Kirghiz themselves are independent.

Word for word, I believe that *Kirghiz* is *Tsherkes*, or *Circassian*, the exact details in the history of its application to the mountaineers of Caucasus being unknown. It is an old term, and appears in Menander's account of his embassy to the Khan of Fergana or Bokhara, in the reign of Justinian. With the Tartars under notice it is neither the native name exactly, nor yet a wholly strange one, as will soon be seen.

The adjectives applied to the three divisions, containing the Kirghiz of the *Great*, the Kirghiz of the *Little*, and the Kirghiz of the *Middle*, Horde, mislead us.

The *Great* Horde is by no means what its name indicates. Though not the most numerous, it contains the most dangerous and savage of the Kirghiz; either plunderers of every caravan that passes through their country, or levyers of black-mail as the price of passing it unpillaged. Its area lies eastward, on the frontier of Mongolia and Chinese Turkestan, its line of frontier being irregular and indented. Far to the east of the boundaries of what is marked Dzungaria, and even in the parts where the lakes are called (in our maps, at least) by the Mongolian term *nor*, Mr. Atkinson describes his interviews with various Kirghiz sultans. The whole district was divided between a number of them, all being but petty chieftains of limited areas—so many lords of so many valleys; differing but little in the style of their insignificant presidencies; differing more in habits, temper, and intelligence. One was a dangerous robber, who, whilst you were a guest in his tent, would not allow himself to be tempted to an injury, but who would waylay you on your way back. Others were men of only average dishonesty, others friendly and intelligent. One, especially, was more so than any Kirghiz Mr. Atkinson had met with. Silk, from Bokhara, entered somewhat largely into their dress. The curtains, too, of their sleeping-place, and the other hangings of their otherwise rude *yurts* were of silk. Neither was expense spared on their arms and accoutrements, nor yet care in the breeding of their horses. Falconry, in its noblest form, was their amusement and exercise—falconry, with eagles for hawks, and with deer for the quarry. In Scind, Lieut. Burton saw a gazelle killed by a falcon. On the edge of Great Cobi Desert,

Mr. Atkinson saw a stag struck down by an eagle—a bearcoot as he calls it. No dogs are taken out when the hunting is with the eagle, who would assuredly kill them, as he kills foxes (in the way of sport) and (as the Kirghiz say) even wolves. The deer and antelope never escape, but the fox, if he be near a hole, occasionally contrives to cunningly run into it.

It is safe to say that, as early as the time of the Yuan dynasty in China, a population bearing the name Kirghiz was to be found upon the Upper Yenisey, the name under which they are noticed by the Chinese geographers being Kilikiszu. A. D. 1606, these eastern Kirghiz, along with the Barabinski, submitted themselves to Russia, though not for a permanence. Sometimes they affected an imperfect independence, sometimes they contracted alliances with the Olöt Mongols. About the beginning, however, of the following century, they moved southwards, and attached themselves to the Great Horde—the Great Horde which calls itself Brut Erdena, or Burut. Burut was the name of the Kirghiz of the Yenisey; the exact import of which denomination I am unable to give—*i. e.* I am unable to say whether it be or be not a sign of relationship to the Mongols so called. The other two divisions call themselves Kasak, Kirg Kasak, and Kirghiz Kasak, which does not seem to be done by the members of the Great Horde.

*The Middle Horde of the Kirghiz Kasak.*—The Horde on the head-waters of the Ishim and Tobol consists of the following tribes:—

1. Atagni;
2. Naiman;
3. Argin, containing the Tshak-tshak, Tshartshid, Türtül, Karaul, Karakisak, Kandzhagali, Atshai, Tarakli, Kultshan-argin.

4. Uvak-girei ;

5. Kiptshak, containing the Kundelen, Usun, Tanabuga, Karabalyk-kiptshak.

In the winter they resort to the Lake Balkash.

*The Little Horde of the Kirghiz Kasak.*—The following are the divisions of the Little Horde :—

| | | |
|---|---|---|
| Alatsha | Boibat | Usen-bemer |
| Baibakte | Koshai | Diagus |
| Adoi | (?) Bersh | Kitai |
| Kaselgurt | Tazeke | Karakitai |
| Mashkar | Kensalban | Tshumankai |
| Serkesh | Moat | Tshiklin |
| Tana | Kartmalat | Tukmer-adoi |
| Tasdar | Balaksha | Dzhilgan-bailin. |
| Taibysh | Diemenei-karash | |
| Aslan | (?) Bersh | |

Levshen's calculations make the numbers of

| | |
|---|---|
| The Great Horde . . . | 100,000 |
| The Little Horde . . . | 190,000 |
| The Middle Horde . . . | 500,000 |
| | 790,000 |

The skin of the Kirghiz Kasak is a deep brown, heightened by dirt and smoke ; the colour being as much the effect of the heated atmosphere of their tents in winter, as of the dry heat of the summer sun. In habits they are idle ; in temper, fickle and uncertain. Between China and Russia they have contrived to play a part which makes them distrusted on both sides ; and until the strength of the latter kingdom was unmistakably felt, the Kirghiz wars and the Kirghiz inroads were formidable. On the other hand, the men are temperate, hardy, and dirty. Add to this, that they are thoroughly hospitable. When they have come in contact with the Russians, and applied themselves to smith's or carpenter's work, they have proved quick and docile.

The Kirghiz of Pamer are in immediate contact with Chinese Tartary, the political relations being with Kokan. To the ruler of this Uzbek State they acknowledge allegiance and pay tribute. With China and Tibet they are in a chronic state of border warfare. Their relations to the little States of the Upper Oxus are but little less hostile. It was from these that Lieutenant Wood heard his exceedingly unfavourable character of them—that they were cowards as well as robbers, and faithless as well as cowardly. That they robbed even of each other, tribe from tribe, encampment from encampment—their Bais (Beys) having but little power to restrain them even if they had the inclination. His own experience of them was less unfavourable.

They were small men. Out of seven that were measured the tallest stood 5 feet 5½ inches, the shortest 5 feet 2 inches—a height somewhat above that of the Ladaki Tibetans. Their "countenance is disagreeable; the upper part of the nose sinks into the face; leaving the space between their deep-seated and elongated eyes without the usual dividing ridge; the brow immediately above the eye is protuberant, but stands back more abruptly than in Europeans; the cheeks, large and bloated, look as if pieces of flesh had been daubed upon them; a slender beard covers the chin, and with those individuals who have a more luxuriant growth of hair, both beard and whiskers have a close natural curl; their persons are not muscular, and their complexion is darkened by exposure in all weathers rather than by the sun." This smacks of the language of Jornandes in describing the Huns, with whom the face was "offa magis quam facies." The women, on the other hand, were better-looking, and resembled the Hazara females in their comparative delicacy of frame and figure. They went quite unveiled, and seemed to enjoy full freedom, were attentive to their domestic duties, busy with the needle, unreserved, and dressy, wearing, as their chief ornaments, beads of black coral, beads of red coral, beads of glass, rudely-set gems, brass nick-nacks, hollow brass buttons, and mother-of-pearl decorations, &c.; all obtained from China. A daughter is more valued than a son; the price of the former being 40*l.* English money. On a husband's death the widow goes to his brother, or next of kin. Failing this she returns to her father. If a stranger take her a blood-feud results. Slaves are somewhat uncommon amongst them. The chief domestic animals of the Kirghiz are the horse, the sheep, and the camel. Kumiss is made from the mare's milk, and the enemies of the tribe say that when the kumiss feasts take place their encampments are scenes of the grossest intoxication, and the most unrestrained and sexual indulgence. The wild herds of Pamer are all objects of the chase, and the horns serve many of the purposes of iron. They serve, for instance, as stirrups; and even as horse-shoes, a Kirghiz horse-shoe being but a semicircular piece of horn fixed on the fore part of the hoof, and requiring to be renewed once a week. In summer the hordes split up in small encampments, and spread themselves over the higher levels of their mountains and table-lands; no spot being more visited by them than the lake out of which the Oxus takes its source—the Sir-i-kol 15,600 feet above the level of the sea. As winter comes on they move with the water-fowls, and as they depart the Kirghiz descend. Many of them encamp about the town of Kokan.

Till the beginning of the seventeenth century the

Kirghiz were pagans. They are now Sunnite Mahometans—with many pagan observances and superstitions.

The Kirghiz seen by Lieutenant Wood had ascended into the region of the yak, and rode the animal just like the Himalayans and Tibetans. Their hardiness was proverbial even amongst the hardy Wakhani.

| English. | Kirghiz. | Uzbek. | Turkman. | Baraba. |
|---|---|---|---|---|
| *Head* | baz | bash | bash | bash |
| *Hair* | tshatsh | zatsh | zatsh | tshatsh |
| *Hand* | kol | al | kol | ——— |
| *Foot* | ayak | ayak | ayak | ——— |
| *Eye* | kus | kyus | küs | kos |
| *Ear* | kolak | kulak | klak | kulak |
| *Tooth* | tiz | tish | dish | ——— |
| *Blood* | kan | kan | kan | ——— |
| *Day* | kündus | kündus | kyondos | ——— |
| *Sun* | kün | kyonash | koyash | kyosh |
| *Moon* | ai | ai | ai | ai |
| *Star* | dzhildzhis | yoldos | yoldos | oldar |
| *Fire* | ut | ot | ot | ut |
| *Water* | zu | zu | zu | zuu |
| *Tree* | agatsh | agatsh | agatsh | agaz |
| *Stone* | taz | tash | tash | tash |
| *One* | bir | bir | bir | bir |
| *Two* | oke | iki | iki | ike |
| *Three* | utsh | utsh | utsh | ytsh |
| *Four* | tyort | dyort | durt | tyort |
| *Five* | bez | bish | bish | bish |
| *Six* | alty | alty | alto | alte |
| *Seven* | dzhede | edi | edi | sette |
| *Eight* | zikus | zigus | zikis | zogus |
| *Nine* | tokus | tokus | tokos | togus |
| *Ten* | on | on | on | on |

Russia has pressed steadily upon the Kirghiz frontier, upon which it has encroached, and is encroaching. The Buriat of the Yenisey, the most eastern population of the name, and, perhaps, the most northern also, felt the sword of the earliest Siberian immigrants. About the beginning of the eighteenth century the independence of the Little Horde was invaded. The time was one of turbulence. The Dzungarian Mongols were exchanging their independence for submission to China. Their movements affected the whole area. Abulkhair, the khan of a great part of the Little Horde, called in the protection of Russia; several tribes of the Middle Horde doing the same. In 1732, Abulkhair and Shemyaka, another khan, took the oath of allegiance to the Czar. Disturbances, however, continued. There were Kirghiz inroads upon the Baskir districts; and Kirghiz inroads upon the Kalmuks of the Volga. Then Abulkhair died, and factions arose about the succession. The Chinese, too, now masters of Dzungaria, intrigued. The caravans to Bokhara got plundered more than ever. The remedy for all this was a change in the constitution, which took the power away from the khan, and distributed it amongst the secondary elders or nobles. The chief scene of this division was the Little Horde, which now ran a risk of being broken-up. Some of its tribes joined the Middle; some went over to the Uzbek Khanate of Khiva; some, probably, joined the Turkomans on the south; finally, a division of 10,000 families, under the headship of Bakei, son of Narali, and grandson of Abulkhair, made its way into the Government of Astrakan, settling itself on the left bank of the Volga. In 1812 Bakei was declared their khan, and has since been succeeded by his son.

In 1823 the Middle Horde, at the request of some of its Sultans, prevailed upon Russia to protect it. At first it paid no tribute at all; afterwards a certain number of cattle.

*The Karakalpak* (*Black Caps*).—There are a few Turks thus called in

(1.) The Governments of Perm, Orenburg, and Astrakan. Others more numerous in

(2.) The parts to the east of Lake Aral.

Common opinion connects these two divisions, deducing the latter from the former, so as to make the eastern Karakalpaks recent occupants of the present area. I cannot say how this may be; it being clear that wherever there is a population with black caps there is also a place for the name Karakalpak.

The eastern Karakalpaks, settled during the winter but migratory during the summer, partly belong to Khiva, and partly lie under the protection of Russia. Some may be wholly independent. They are but little known; passing for one of the rudest and most imperfectly Mahometan tribes of the Turk name.

The northern Kirghiz may truly be called Siberians, so thoroughly do they belong to the northern slope of the great Asiatic table-land and the drainage of the rivers which, falling into the Obi, finally find their way to the Arctic Sea. I follow the prolongations of these areas, beginning with those that run eastward. It would, perhaps, be more systematic to take the Uzbeks, and Turkomans next to the Kirghiz, with whom they divide Independent Turkistan—the Kirghis holding the northern, the Uzbeks and Turkomans the southern half of that vast steppe. The dialects agree. The histories, however, differ.

So the northern line is preferred. In this we must remark two layers or strata. Some of the Turks are *in situ*, by which I mean that they belong to their respective areas as the Kirghiz belong to theirs, viz. from times anterior to history. Others, however, are Turks of the Kiptshak, a term which will be explained in the sequel. Between the two there is this difference. The Kiptshak Turks are Mahometans; the older tribes are pagans, or, if not pagans, recent converts; sometimes to Mahometanism, sometimes to Christianity. I am not aware that any are Buddhists; though, from contact with the Mongols, this may be the case in a few instances.

The old occupants are the only ones which will, for the present, be noted. Of these the first are the

*Barama, Baraba,* or *Barabinski.*—The termination *inski* is Russian. In Fin *ma* means *land.* Hence, the very oldest occupants of the Bara-*ma* or Bara-*land* may have been Fins or Ugrians. The Barama Turks live in the Barama, or Barabinski, steppe. In summer they dwell in tents and encampments; in winter in huts and villages. They may amount to 3500 individuals paying *yasak* or tribute, Russia being the power that holds them tributary. They call

| | |
|---|---|
| The Russians . . . | *Urus* |
| „ Kirghiz . . . | *Kasak* |
| „ Kalmuks . . . | *Kalmuk* |
| „ Ostiaks . . . | *Ishtak* |

With the Ostiaks they come in contact on their northern frontier. They fall into the following Aimâks; this Mongol term being the one I find in Klaproth.

| In Turk. | In Russian. |
|---|---|
| 1. Langga. | Tanuskaya Volost. |
| 2. Lubai. | Lubanskaya Volost. |
| 3. Kulaba. | Turashkaya Volost. |
| 4. Barama. | Barabinskaya Volost. |
| 5. Tsoi. | Tshaiskaya Volost. |
| 6. Terena. | Tereninskaya Volost. |
| 7. Kargala. | Kargalinskaya Volost. |

Their features are Mongol, or Mongoliform; their habits pastoral, though not exclusively so. A little agricultural industry is to be found amongst them. Christianity is making way amongst the Barabinski. Bell describes their Shamanism.

"Baraba is really what its name signifies, an extensive marshy plain. It is generally full of lakes, and marshy grounds, overgrown with tall woods of aspin, alder, willows, and other aquatics; particularly many large birch-trees, having their bark as white and smooth as paper. The lakes abound with various kinds of fishes, such as pikes, perches, breams, eels, and particularly a fish called karrass, of an uncommon bigness, and very fat. These the inhabitants dry, in summer, for winter provisions, which are all the food to be found among them. I have eat of it often, and thought it not disagreeable. In winter they use melted snow for water. They are very hospitable; and desire nothing in return of their civilities; but a little tobacco to smoke, and a dram of brandy, of which they are very fond. The dress, both of men and women, consists of long coats of sheep-skins, which they get from the Russians and Kalmucks, in exchange for more valuable furs. As they wear no other apparel, nor even skirts, they are very nasty. Their huts are most miserable habitations, and sunk about one-half under the ground. We were glad, however, to find them, as a baiting place, in such a cold season.

"The Barabintzy, like most of the ancient natives of Siberia, have many conjurors among them, whom they call Shamans, and sometimes priests. Many of the female sex also assume this character. The Shamans are held in great esteem by the people; they pretend to correspondence with the shaytan,* or devil; by whom, they say, they are informed of all past and future events, at any distance

* Word for word, Satan.

of time or place. Our ambassador resolved to inquire strictly into the truth of many strange stories, generally believed, concerning the Shamans, and sent for all of fame in that way in the places through which we passed.

"In Baraba we went to visit a famous woman of this character. When we entered her house, she continued busy about her domestic affairs, without almost taking any notice of her guests. However, after she had smoked a pipe of tobacco, and drunk a dram of brandy, she began to be more cheerful. Our people asked her some trifling questions about their friends; but she pretended to be quite ignorant, till she got more tobacco and some inconsiderable presents, when she began to collect her conjuring tools. First, she brought her shaytan; which is nothing but a piece of wood, wherein is cut something resembling a human head, adorned with many silk and woollen rags of various colours; then a small drum, about a foot diameter, to which were fixed many brass and iron rings, and hung round also with rags. She now began a dismal tune, keeping time with the drum, which she beat with a stick for that purpose. Several of her neighbours, whom she had previously called to her assistance, joined in the chorus. During this scene, which lasted about a quarter of an hour, she kept the shaytan, or image, close by herself, stuck up in a corner. The charm being now finished, she desired us to put our questions. Her answers were delivered very artfully, and with as much obscurity and ambiguity as they could have been given by any oracle. She was a young woman, and very handsome."

| English. | Barama. | Ostiak. | Samoyed. |
|---|---|---|---|
| *Head* | bash | og | ollo |
| *Eye* | kos | zem | sai |
| *Ear* | kulak | pel | ka |

| English. | Barama. | Ostiak. | Samoyed. |
|---|---|---|---|
| *Nose* | murun | nel | putsh |
| *Mouth* | aus | lul | ak |
| *Hair* | tshatsh | upat | apte |
| *Tongue* | tel | nalem | she |
| *Hand* | kol | ket | uten-el |
| *Sun* | kyosh | khat | tsheled |
| *Moon* | ai | tilesh | ireda |
| *Star* | eldas | khuz | kysheka |
| *Fire* | ut | tut | tu |
| *Water* | zuu | ying | it |
| *Tree* | agaz | yokh | po |
| *Stone* | tash | kiv | po |
| *One* | bir | it | okkur |
| *Two* | ikke | katn | shiddega |
| *Three* | ytsh | khulym | nagur |
| *Four* | tyort | nyelle | tyetto |
| *Five* | bish | net | zomblag |
| *Six* | alte | chut | muktotn |
| *Seven* | sette | lazat | zeldzhu |
| *Eight* | zogus | nulle | shittetshan-gutköt |
| *Nine* | togus | irani | okurtshan-gutköt |
| *Ten* | on | yang | köt |

*The Tshulim.*—Tshulim is the name of a feeder of the Obi. Word for word, it seems to be Kolyma. If so, the oldest occupants may have been Ugrian. The Tshulim features, are, more or less, Mongol. The language is said to contain many Mongol words. It is also said to approach the Yakut. More pastoral than agricultural, the Tshulim tribes are also more Christian than Mahometan, more pagan (perhaps) than either. They number about 15,000. Like the Baraba, Barama, or Barabinski, they have been described by Bell.

"In summer, the banks of this river are inhabited by a tribe of Tartars, called by the Russians Tzuliminzi, from the name of the river, who live by fishing and hunting. We found several of their empty huts as we went along. In autumn, these people retire from this inhospitable place towards the south, near to towns and villages, where they can find subsistence.

"The 20th, we arrived at a Russian village called Meletsky Ostrogue, where we staid a day to refresh ourselves and horses. In the neighbourhood of this place, we found many huts of the Tzulim Tartars, who seem to be a different race from all of that name I have yet mentioned. Their complexion is indeed swarthy, like that of most of the other descendants of the ancient natives of Siberia; but I have seen many of them having white spots on their skins from head to foot, of various figures and sizes. Many imagine these spots natural to the people; but I am rather inclined to believe they proceed from their constant diet of fish and other animal food without bread. This, of course, creates a scorbutic habit of body, which often breaks out in infants; and the scars falling off, leave that part of the skin as if it had been scalded, which never recovers its natural colour. I have, however, seen several children with these spots, who seemed healthy.

"The Tzulim, like other Tartars, live in huts half-sunk under ground. They have a fire in the middle, with a hole at the top to let out the smoke, and benches round the fire, to sit or lie upon. This seems to be the common method of living among all the northern nations, from Lapland eastward to the Japanese ocean.

"The Tzulim speak a barbarous language, composed of words from many other languages. Some of our people, who spoke Turkish, told me, they had many Arabic words which they understood. They are poor, miserable, and ignorant heathens. The Archbishop of Tobolsky in person came lately hither, and baptized some hundreds of them, who were inclined to embrace the Christian faith. As they are a well-disposed and harmless people, probably in a short time they may be all converted."

| English. | Tshulim. | Kuznetsk. | Yakut. | Tobolsk. |
|---|---|---|---|---|
| *Head* | bash | bash | baz | pash |
| *Eye* | kos | kus | kharakh | kus |
| *Ear* | kulak | kulak | kulgakh | kulak |
| *Nose* | murun | mondu | murun | parun |
| *Mouth* | agus | aksy | ayakh | auus |
| *Hair* | tshatsh | tshatsh | az | tsats |
| *Tongue* | til | til | til | til |
| *Tooth* | tish | tish | tiz | tish |
| *Hand* | kal | kol | ili | khak |
| *Sun* | kun | kun | kun | kun |
| *Moon* | ai | ai | ui | ar |
| *Star* | yoldus | tshlitis | zulus | yoldus |
| *Fire* | ot | ot | wot | ot |
| *Water* | su | su | ui | su |
| *Tree* | agats | agatsh | maz | yagats |
| *Stone* | tash | tash | taz | tash |
| *One* | bir | pir | bir | bir |
| *Two* | ike | iki | iki | ike |
| *Three* | itsh | utsh | uz | itsh |
| *Four* | dyort | dort | tirt | dört |
| *Five* | besh | bish | vez | bish |
| *Six* | alte | alty | alta | alty |
| *Seven* | sette | setti | seta | siti |
| *Eight* | zegus | segys | agys | segis |
| *Nine* | togus | togus | dogys | togus |
| *Ten* | on | on | on | on |

Their tribes, which are called Dyon or Yon, are—

| | |
|---|---|
| Kursu Ayen | Kitshi Kurnatshi |
| Bilek | Ulu Terena |
| Bura | Tshibi |
| Tutal (Obek) | Temerzi (?) |
| Kitshi Tardegi | Yatshin |
| Yaseu Boshi | Kamnar I. |
| Uye | Bilet |
| Ulu Buru | Bagasari |
| Yazi | Ulu Yeshi |

| | |
|---|---|
| Kueruk | Anggas |
| Tutal | Shus |
| Kitshi Pushku | Atshig |
| Ulu Pushku | Kamnar II. |
| Kitshi Argun | Kisil Ashi |

They are fishers as well as herdsmen. They were once called Tutal; a term which is now restricted to two of their tribes. They call the Tshulim Tshum (Kem ? Tom ?). The occupants of the towns call them Uriankhai.

The *Verkho-Tomski* tribes, lie above Kuznetsk. *Verkho* means *Upper*, so that the Verkho-Tomski tribes are the tribes of the Upper Tom.

*The Abintsi* are a portion of the Verkho-Tomski. The Tsumush, the Kondoma, and the Mrasa are their rivers.

The *Katshlar, Katshtalar*, or *Katshintsi* lie beyond the unimportant watershed that separates the drainages of the Obi and the Yenisey, and occupy the *Katsha*, whence their name, a feeder of that river.

The *Yastalar* or *Yastintsi* (the form in *-lar* is Turk, that in *-tsi* Russian) are mixed with the *Katshlar*.

The *Bokhtalar* (*Boktintsi*) are on the Kom, to the east of the Yenisey, below Abakansk.

The *Kaidin* are on the same side, above Abakansk.

The *Beltyr*, on the right side of the Abakan, number about 150 tribute-payers.

The *Biryus*, on the river so-called, originally occupied the banks of the Kondama, a Kuznetsk locality. To each of their four divisions—Kobin Aimâk, Kargin Aimâk, Kain Aimâk, and Shaskin Aimâk is a Chief, Bashlik, or Head (*bas* = *head*). They are all poor; the last the poorest, and the occupants of the highest levels. They have a few horses and oxen, and grow a little rye.

*The Teleut.*—Abulgazi calls the Teleut (in Mongol Telengut) Uriat, a name which implies that they were Kalmuk Mongols. At the time of the Russian conquest they were called white Kalmuks. Their looks are Mongol. They were, and are subjects to the Mongols. Their language, however, is Turk.

| English. | Teleut. | Osmanli. | Mongol. |
|---|---|---|---|
| *Head* | bash | bash | tologoi |
| *Eye* | kus | gos | nüdün |
| *Ear* | kulak | khulak | tshakin |
| *Nose* | muran | buran | khamar |
| *Mouth* | ous | aghes | aman |
| *Hair* | tshatsh | satsh | üsün |
| *Tongue* | til | dil | kele |
| *Hand* | kol | el | gar |
| *Sun* | kun | gyun | naran |
| *Moon* | ai | ai | sara |
| *Star* | yiltis | yildis | odun |
| *Fire* | ot | od | gal |
| *Water* | su | su | usun |
| *Tree* | agash | agatsh | modo |
| *Stone* | tash | tash | tshulu |

For "Mongol" read "Samoyed" and, *mutatis mutandis*, the history of the Teleuts is the history of the

*Tubalar, Tubintsi,* or *Tuba,* tribes—Occupants of the banks of the Tuba. Turk in language, though, probably, Samoyed in blood. They are sometimes called Kyrgislar, *i. e.* Kirghiz.

And here we may pause, for the Teleut and Tuba Turks (if so they may be called) have introduced a new question. The blood and language differ. The lineage is Mongol or Samoyed, the speech Turkish. Such being the case, it is better, when the evidence is sufficient, to speak of certain Samoyeds or Mongols who have lost their own language and adopted that of their neighbours, than of certain Turks whose blood is Mongol, Samoyed, or aught else. The blood, lineage, pedigree, genealogy, descent, or affinity is the primary ethnological fact. The language is the evidence in favour of it. This may be conclusive, or the contrary. It is rarely conclusive when it stands alone.

Members of, at least, two different stocks, other than Turk, are reasonably believed to speak Turkish. Certain Mongols are reasonably believed to do so. So are certain Ugrians. The same may, probably, be said of certain Tungús. The Ugrians that have thus taken a Turk character belong to the Samoyed and Yeniseian divisions; to these certainly, probably to others. It is sufficient, however, to name these two; adding, that when the Soyot, the Matar, the Koibal, the Kamass, and the Karagass Samoyeds come under notice, they will all be said to use a Turk form of speech; adding, too, that the Arin, and other Yeniseian populations, are, *mutatis mutandis,* in the same category.

And may not some of the populations, already mentioned, the Baraba, the Beltyr, and the like, be less Turk than we have made them? They may. In saying that one group of Siberian tribes is other than Turk in blood, though Turk in tongue, I, by no means, claim pure Turk blood for each and all of the others. Of the Baraba, Tshulim, and the like, I have only said that the occupancy of their respective areas transcends the historical period. I think, with others, that they were preceded by certain Ugrians, having drawn my conclusion after the method of the geologist, rather than after that of the historian.

The name Sayan is given to that part of the Altaic range which contains the head-waters of the Yenisey, and is the occupancy of the populations under notice—populations which are conveniently called the Sayanian Turks; Sayanian Turks from the north-eastern parts of the

Kirghiz area; Sayanian Turks who are not the oldest occupants of the Sayanian range, but who seem to have thrust themselves in between Mongolians and Samoyeds, Samoyeds and Yeniseians, Yeniseians and Tungús. In the circles of Minusinsk and Nizhni Udinsk representatives of all these groups may be found, a fact which makes them one of the most interesting ethnological areas of all Asia. Mongolia lies to the south of them, but in North Mongolia there are Samoyeds. The Yeniseians touch both the Turks and Ostiaks. A little beyond the Yeniseians, the Tshapodzhirs represent the Tungús family. Ostiaks, Samoyeds, Tungús, Mongolians, pagan Turks—all these lie within a comparatively small compass in the Sayanian part of the Altai.

Of these pagan Turks but little is known, and that little is due to Castrên, who made his inquiries on the spot. The most prominent term in their mythology is *Aina*, which means three things. It means a *spirit*, and it is with the Aina that the Shaman puts himself in relation when the aid of a spirit is wanted. His dwelling is under-ground. What his own proper form may be I cannot say. He can change it, however, for that of men and certain animals, transforming himself into a human being, a bear, a fox, a snake, or a swan—a swan most especially, and by preference. Hence, all such animals are more or less holy, and the swan is the holiest of them all. Its value is that of a good horse. The fowler that kills a swan does not keep it himself but takes it to his nearest neighbour, presents him with it, and takes his best steed in exchange. The late owner of a good steed, but now the fortunate possessor of a valuable bird, repeats the process, and makes a similar good bargain with *his* neighbour, who does the same with the next, and so on. In this way the swan passes from hand to hand until it will keep no longer, when the last owner, who has given for it a horse has to throw it away or bury it, having got nothing in return. A swan, then, may be an Aina in disguise.

The gewgaws and gimcracks that ornament the Shaman's robe are called Aina, being, in many cases, made of the skin of some Aina animal.

Thirdly. The rude stone busts that, sometimes on the sites of ancient graves, and sometimes in localities not known to be sepulchral, are spread over the great Sayanian steppe, are Aina. Concerning these, the tradition runs thus:—They were once living men and women, heroes and heroines, whom Kudai had endowed with certain superhuman powers, and placed upon earth as his lieutenants or representatives. They presumed, however, on their strength, skill, and privileges, and their presumption so exasperated Kudai that he converted them into lifeless images of stone. As such they are *Aina* and objects of worship. To smear their stony lips with gobbets of flesh and fat is to show them honour—this being done at the present time.

The larch is amongst trees what the swan is amongst birds. With some tribes it is usual, when a child dies, to hang its body on the larch-tree bough.

A strange story, far too long for insertion, but which may be found in Castrén, gives us a view of the invisible world of these Sayanian Turks, the world of the Irle-khans and Talai-khans. The realm of the dead is presided over by nine Irle-khans, one of whom is the lord, prince, or Ataman (Hetman) over the others. Over his fellow Irle-khans he presides, and over a vast number of visible and invisible spirits besides. One of these is a nine-headed monster named *Dzhilbegan*, who rides on a beast with forty horns. One day he visited the upper world, where a hero named Komdei-mirgan was hunting a black fox, but broke his leg during the hunt. Whereupon Dzhilbegan cut off his head, and took it with him to his home below—the region of the departed, the realm of the Irle-khans. Komdei-mirgan's sister, Kubaiko, follows Dzhilbegan; her adventures, successful in the end (for she got back her brother's head), constituting the story just alluded to.

*Kudai*, above-ground, was what the great Irle-khan was below. "It is useless to shoot at me," said the latter to Komdei-mirgan, "since I am here what Kudai is on earth, and neither can, nor am to, be killed."

Then there is the legend of *Ai-kyn*. The Ainas, in general, only raise half their body above the earth's surface; so that their visible form is like that of the monumental busts of the steppes, it probably being these that suggested the imitation. One, however, named Ai-kyn (sun-and-moon) raised the whole of his body, and stood upon the earth with his feet. He stood upon the earth with his feet, and showing his full dimensions, challenged to single combat Ainas, heroes, and men. None attempted it. The seven Kudai, however, knew of a being who could conquer Ai-kyn. This was a certain three-year-old child. To it they sent an embassy, the seven Kudai and seventy heroes, begging its aid, which was granted. The two fought long and fiercely, until, at last, Ai-kyn was thrown down and bound hand and foot. Bound, however, as he was, he was sword-proof; at least, no amount of mutilation could kill him. This was because he carried his life, soul, or spirit, in the body of another object—a snake, which he kept in a sack which lay on the back of his horse. This snake had twelve heads. Now when the child of three years found out this, he left off hewing at Ai-kyn, and killed the snake. Whereupon Ai-kyn died.

*The Sokhalar* or *Yakut.*—But there are Turks beyond the Yenisey, and the Turkish language, at least, is spoken in the parts about Lake Baikal. And the valley of the Lena, in language at least, is Turk. So are the parts within the Arctic circle. So are the shores of the Polar sea. The government of Yakutsk takes its name from the Yakut or Sokhalar; Sokhalar as they call themselves, Yakut as they are called by the Russians.

One of the Sayanian tribes is called Sokha.

The word Baikal is Yakut; meaning Great Lake.

In Stralenberg's account, the Sokhalar are divided into the following ten tribes, (1) Boro Ganiska, (2) Baitungski, (3) Badys, (4) Yok Soyon, (5) Manga, (6) Kangalas, (7) Namin, (8) Bathruski, (9) Lugor, (10) Bologuir, in all about 30,000 men, calling themselves Zacha, after an ancient prince of that name. This prince we may fairly look upon as an eponymus, unhistoric, unreal. The name of the chief who headed them when they left the parts about Lake Baikal, and separated from the Brath, with whom they formerly made one nation, was Deptsi Tarkhantegin. Tarkhan is a name which frequently occurs in Turk narratives. The Brath were, probably, the Buriats. They are especially said not to worship "Bullwans, or idols carved in wood, like the Ostiaks and Tungús," but to "offer sacrifices to one invisible God in heaven. Yet they have a type or image of that deity stuffed out with a monstrous head, eyes of coral, and the body like a bag. This they hang on a tree, and round it the furs of sables and other animals. Each tribe has one of these images."

What then, we ask, as we read this account, is the difference between the Yakut and the Tungús? The Yakut priests have drums like the Laplanders; *i. e.* like all Shamanist nations. They worship the Invisible under three names, Ar-toygon, Shugo-toygon, and Tangara. At the funeral of a prince the oldest servants used to be buried alive with the master; a practice abolished by the Russians. The cultus of trees is common. A fine tree gets hung with iron, brass, and other gewgaws. The New Year begins in April, or, at least, in the spring, with its sacrifices. A green spot, shaded by a tree, is sought out, and horses and oxen sacrificed. The heads are then hung up on the boughs. Those of the horses keep the skin on. Of the kumiss, of which on these occasions they drink freely, they sprinkle, some in the air, some in the fire.

In February and March, as the sap begins to rise in the trees, they have a bast harvest; bast meaning the inner bark of the young fir-trees. This they collect, carry home, and beat into a fine powder; which they mix with fish, also dried and powdered, and boil in milk. This, and anything else edible, they feed upon most voraciously; pork only being the exception. From this they abstain, though not Mahometans, as do the Votiaks of the Government of Vologda. Horse-flesh they eat greedily. The tale in Strahlenberg of four Yakuts having eaten a whole horse, merely shows the credit they have, as a nation, for a large appetite. Similar tales are told of the North-American Indians of the same latitude. Cold and uncertainty of food are at the bottom of all this. Doubtless, they gorge themselves enormously, and that without taking harm. They smoke tobacco, which they buy (by barter) of the Russians. Their winter houses, for they shift their dwellings with the season, are built of planks and beams; their summer ones, which are round, and conical, are made of the bark of the birch-tree. This is ornamented with the tufts of dyed horse-hair. They are buried by choice near fine trees, and when the corpse is interred some of the valuables of the deceased are interred along with it. Sometimes however, the dead body lies above ground, in a box, supported by posts, with a few hides thrown over it. Sometimes there is no funeral rite at all; but the body is left in the hut, and the hut shut up. Those who die in the streets of the town of Yakutsk are left to the dog.

Each tribe looks on some particular animal as sacred, and abstains from eating it.

| English. | Yakut. | Osmanli. | Tungûs. | Yeniseian. |
|---|---|---|---|---|
| *Head* | baz | bash | dyll | tshig |
| *Eye* | kharakh | gos | cha | des |
| *Ear* | kulgakh | khulak | zen | okten |
| *Nose* | murun | burun | ongokto | olgen |
| *Mouth* | dyakh | aghis | hamun | ko |
| *Hair* | az | satsh | nyuritta | tshonga |
| *Tongue* | tyl | dil | ingni | ei |
| *Tooth* | tiz | dish | ikta (?) | —— |
| *Hand* | ili | el | ngala | togan |
| *Foot* | atakh | ayakh | halgan | toigon |
| *Sun* | kun | gyun | zIguni | i |
| *Moon* | ui | ai | bega | khip |
| *Star* | zulus | yildis | haulen | kugo |
| *Fire* | wot | od | togo | bok |
| *Water* | ui | su | mu | ul |
| *Tree* | maz | agatsh | mo | oksa |
| *Stone* | taz | tash | dzholo | tshugs |
| *One* | bir | bir | omukon | khus-em |
| *Two* | ike | iki | dzhur | uk-em |
| *Three* | uz | utsh | ilyan | dong-em |
| *Four* | tirt | dort | dygin | si-em |
| *Five* | ves | besh | tongo | gag-em |
| *Six* | alta | alty | nyungun | ages |
| *Seven* | seta | yedi | nadan | onse |
| *Eight* | agys | sekis | dzhapkun | —— |
| *Nine* | dogys | dokus | yagin | —— |
| *Ten* | on | on | dzhun | khogem. |

Such are the Turks who spread themselves over Siberia as pagans. The later layer was Mahometan. I believe that before the dawn of history (and, be it remembered, that, for the parts now coming under notice, this dawn is pre-eminently early), the parts between the Volga and the Don were Turk. Over the dreary steppes that lie between Astrakan and the Crimea, the Skoloti of Herodotus, Scythians as they are more usually called, must have passed in their way to Europe. Nor is there any reason to believe that they passed over them *sicco pede*. Some of them stayed in the way, and became occupants of the present governments of Astrakan, Caucasus, and the Don Kosaks. In other words, the Turk population from the Caspian to the Danube was continuous; not, perhaps, regularly distributed, but still continuous. To the north of the area thus occupied lay the frontier of the southernmost Ugrians, to the south that of the most northern Circassians. The intermediate populations I hold to have been displaced by the Scythians or Turks, who, without being the absolute aborigines of the land, were early, very early, intruders into it. Nor is there any evidence of their having ever ceded the possession of it to any one except its present masters, the Russians; themselves strangers to the soil, and only half occupants of it. In the third, fourth, and fifth centuries the name of the occupants was Alani, a name which (I think) occurs in Herodotus, in disguise, *i. e.* as Hellenes. Be this, however, as it may, the Alani of the time of Attila were Turks.

In the times immediately preceding the Mongol conquests the Alan country, along with, perhaps, much besides, was called the Kiptshak; and Kiptshak was the name it retained under the Mongols. It was not Mongol, though often treated as such. The Mongols found, but did not make, it. The name occurs in writings anterior to their time. It was a Turk area; with Ugrians to the north, Circassians to the south; some of whom were, probably, Turk tributaries.

That the Kiptshak, already Turk, may have been made more so by the Turks of the Mongol army is likely enough. I only object to the doctrine that it was the Mongol conquest which made it Turkish.

It is likely, too, that the court and the army were Mongol. I object, however, to considering the Kiptshak as a Mongol country. The Kiptshak was Mongol only as Lombardy is Austrian.

Mr. Erskine, in his history of India under the house of Timur, writes as follows:—"When Dzhindzhiz deputed his sons or generals to govern any of the conquered countries, and in this policy he was imitated by his successors, he sent along with them an uluus, or tuman, or some Moghul tribe, or division of a tribe, to overawe the conquered. The Moghul tribe so employed received an allotment of country, and placed themselves, with their families and flocks, in the pasture-range of the tribes amongst whom they were sent. By the inevitable intercourse that takes place between persons living under the same government, near to and in habits of intercourse with each other—by intermarriages—by traffic, and in other ways, a considerable mixture of the two races took place, which showed itself both in their language and in their features and bodily appearance." The doctrine that Mongol features imply Mongol intermixture will be considered in the sequel; considered and objected to.

The eldest of the sons of Tshingiz was Dzhudzhi, who died prematurely, when his portion was transferred to his son Batu. He it was who conquered Russia, and made his way so far westwards as Silesia.

By A. D. 1375, all was confusion in the Kiptshak; and when Timur had risen to power in the parts beyond the Oxus, he found that two rivals, Urus and Toktamish, were quarrelling for the dignity of Khan of the Kiptshak.

The latter being worsted, appealed to Timur for help; who gave it and seated him on the throne of Serai, on the Volga, and then proceeded to favour further discord, by raising successively, as Anti-khans, Timur-Kutk and Kaurtshik. Civil war, and such help as Timur's, soon broke the family of Batou and Dzhudzhi, and, though a Great Khan was nominally acknowledged, it was only in name that he was a khan at all.

Four khanats were developed out of the break-up of the Kiptshak; viz:—

1. The khanat of Siberia.
2. The khanat of Kazan.
3. The khanat of Astrakan.
4. The khanat of the Crimea.

The khanat of Siberia, to a great extent other than Turk, and where it is Turk, pagan rather than Mahometan, received settlers from the south and west. These are the so-called Tartars of Tobolsk, the Tom, the Tura (Turalinzi), and the Yenisey rivers—Mahometan in creed and with a language like that of Kazan and Astrakan.

The western parts, to which Russia, Poland, and Lithuania belonged, became European.

The central parts fell into the khanats of Kazan and Astrakan.

The Turks of the Kazan division are distributed not only over the Government of Kazan, but, in the following numbers, over those of—

| | |
|---|---|
| Permia . . . . | 17,271 |
| Viatka . . . . | 57,944 |
| Simbirsk . . . . | 87,730 |
| Orenburg . . . . | 230,080 |
| To which add in Kazan, itself . . | 308,574 |

The present town of Kazan is either the most Asiatic

of European or the most European of Asiatic cities. Of a population of more than 50,000, two-thirds are Russian, one-third Turk—the later living apart and in the so-called Tartar town. No longer the metropolis of a khanat, it is still a town full (comparatively speaking) of trade, industry, and intelligence. Its University is the great seminary for missionaries and propaganda agents for the religious and political designs of Russia in the direction of the east. For hemp, flax, and corn, it is a mart; and for curriery and tanning, a manufacturing town. The province, too, is the centre of the oak-tree district of Russia; the zone between 53° and 56° N.L., being the tract where that tree preponderates—preponderates to the exclusion of the firs and pines of the north, the pines of the south, and the beeches of Caucasus. Kazan is the great imperial forest for the Russian navy.

All travellers speak well of the Kazan Tartars—or Turks, as the ethnologist loves to call them. In the towns they have wholly sunk their originally nomadic character; and are as truly industrial as so many Jews, Armenians, or Anglo-Saxons. In the country, some of the old characteristics keep their ground. Yet, in the country, they are hard-working farmers—though shepherds and bee-masters also. In both they are zealous and sincere, though not intolerant, Mahometans; less sensual, because less wealthy and dominant, than the Osmanli of Constantinople, circumspect in business, and it may be, sharp in practice and suspicious—though more so to Russians than to others. In dress, they are rapidly accommodating themselves to that of the Russians, with whom, in their domestic architecture, and their ordinary mode of life, they are favourably contrasted; and still more so when compared with the Tshuvashes, Tsheremis, and Mordvins.

If the memory of their former power be extinct—of which, it should be added, we have no evidence—the daily experience of the feeling of being a subordinate population irritates them; so does the Russian ascendancy in matters ecclesiastic.

In respect to their physical appearance, they fall into two divisions; are referrible to two types. Of these the Osmanli of Constantinople, in his most European form, gives us one extreme; the flat-faced Mongolian of the Wall of China, the other: the one with an oval contour of face, prominent features, not inexpressive eyes, and a fine manly beard; the other with a broad and flattened nose, prominent cheek-bones, and glabrous skin.

That each of these physiognomies is to be found amongst the Kazan Tartars, we learn from the evidence of most observers. Some praise the beauty of both the men and women, and put their physical good qualities on the creditable level of their moral ones. Others compare them with the Mongols. A third line of criticism indicates the likelihood of a change for the better, having gone on since the time of the earlier observers, one of whom, Herberstein, writes—"Tartari sunt homines statura mediocri, lata facie, obesa, oculis intortis et concavis, sola barba horridi, cetera rasi. Insigniores tantum viri crines contortos eosque nigerrimos secundum aures habent."

I am not aware of any important details by which the khanat of Astrakan is separated from that of Kazan. To the khanat, however, of Astrakan must once have belonged

*The Turks of Caucasus.*—Of these;

(1.) *The Basian* are but recent occupants of their present area. So are—

(2.) *The Karatshai.*—Not so, however—

(3.) *The Kumuk.*—Klaproth specially calls them an

"old" Turk tribe. They stand in contrast to the Basian, who were introduced into their present localities in the fifteenth century. They live under a number of petty chiefs, who are often at war against each other; but who are, nevertheless, Russian subjects. They cultivate the soil, breed cattle, and fish the rivers of their hilly occupancy. Their dwellings are lightly constructed of wattles and mud—huts rather than either houses or tents. The White River or Aksu, the Koisu, and the Zundzha water the land of the Kumuk; on the drainage of which we find the Kara-bulak, the Kara-kaitak, and, doubtless, other Turk denominations. The Kaitak on the Caspian speak Turkish. The Karabulak use a Tshetshentsh dialect, and it may be that they are Tshetshentsh in blood. Their name, Turk as it is, only proves that they are in a Turk neighbourhood. The Kasi-kumuk, as a language, is Lesgian. Word for word, however, the latter part of the name is Kumuk. Surely, this is Koman, Cuman, or Cumanian. The Middle pass, that of Dariel, near the Russian fortress Vladikaukasus and the town of Dariel, is the *porta Caucasica*, or *porta Cumana* of the Latin writers. In the Arabic notices this is the Bab-al-Lan of Bellad Allan, or the Gate of the Alan land; a fact in favour of the Alans and Cumanians being identical or allied populations; also in favour of the Kumuk being the present representatives of the Alan or Cumanian branch—some of them retaining their original language, others speaking that of their neighbours.

Alan was a Greek as well as an Arab term, and we learn from Constantine Porphyrogeneta that in the tenth century the Land of the Alans—Bellad Alan—lay beyond Caucasus, *i. e.* to the south of Circassia. In 1346 Barbaro mentions an Alania. Earlier still Carpini speaks of the

Alans. Whether, however, either Alan or Cuman was a native name is doubtful. The Greeks used it. The Arabs used it. The Italians used it. But what said the Alans themselves? They called themselves As—"*L'Alania,*" writes Barbaro in the passage just alluded to, "*è derivata dai popoli detti Alani, liquali nella lor lingua si chiamono As.*" The evidence of Carpini is to the same effect. The early Russian writers notice the Yas.

Let us call them As, and go a little further in their history. Klaproth gives two accounts of them, both Georgian, the latter Iron as well.

(1.) In the year of the world 2302, the Khazars, who then occupied the parts north of Caucasus, invaded Georgia and Armenia. The khan who led them had a son named Uobos; to whom he gave all the prisoners from the parts between the Kur and Araxes. He also placed him over certain districts on the Terek. The settlement thus effected is the present Oseti, or land of the Osi; the name being Georgian.

(2.) At the beginning of the thirteenth century, the Osi were spread over the whole country from Circassia to the Don, when the Mongol conquest reduced their area. Batu-khan drove them from the open land to the mountains.

Klaproth, who supplies this account, adds that Ptolemy places a population called Ossilii at the mouth of the Don.

The distinction between the name by which a population designates itself and the name by which it is designated by its neighbours, always important, is of preeminent consequence in the ethnology of the Alans, or Osi; as will be seen when the Iron come under notice.

| English. | Kumuk. | Kuzzilbash. |
|---|---|---|
| *Head* | bash | bash |
| *Eye* | gos | gos |
| *Ear* | kulakh | kulakh |
| *Nose* | burun | buruni |
| *Mouth* | aus | aghis |
| *Hair* | sadzh | sadzh |
| *Tongue* | dil | til |
| *Tooth* | dish | dish |
| *Hand* | kol | el |
| *Sun* | gun | gun |
| *Moon* | ai | ai |
| *Star* | yoldus | yuldus |
| *Fire* | ot | oth |
| *Water* | su | su |
| *Tree* | terek | dyadzh |
| *Stone* | tash | dash |

The Kuzzilbash is spoken in Northern Persia.

*The Cumanians of Hungary.*—In A. D. 1770, an old man, named Varro, died in the Chunsag districts of Hungary. He was the last man who spoke the Comanian Turk of a country so far westwards as Hungary. Reasons for connecting this with the Kumuk of Caucasus will appear when the Lesgians come uuder notice.

The Cumanians, or Chunsag (mark the name), are Turks in blood, other than Turk in speech.

The Tubalar, &c., were Turk in speech, other than Turk in blood.

Kazan was reduced by Russia A. D. 1552, Astrakan two years later.

Before the time of the Kiptshak the khanat of Kazan was, more or less, the kingdom of Bulgana.

Before the time of the Kiptshak the khanat of Astrakan was, more or less, the kingdom of the Khazars.

*The Crim Tartars (so-called) of the khanat of the Crimea.*—The history of the Crimea is that of Kazan and Astrakan, with the difference that it became Osmanli before it was Russian. Indeed, it was not incorporated with the dominions of the Czar until the end of the last century.

After the break-up of the Mongol dynasty it became a khanat, the change being due to the conquests of the time of Timur. If so, the first century, at least, should be either a period of independence or one of vassalage, more or less close, to some one of the Timurian empires—to some one of the Timurian empires as opposed to that of the Amuraths, Bajazets, and Mahomets, who ruled in Rumelia and Constantinople. It should, at any rate, be other than Osmanli. Perhaps, it was so at first. On the other hand, however, I find that the earliest notice which occurs in so full and voluminous a writer as Von Hammer, in his history of the Ottoman (Osmanli) Turks, is in the first third of the sixteenth century, under the reign of Selim I., who is made to speak of the Tartars of the Crimea as formidable enemies, but, at the same time, as tribes, more or less, acknowledging his suzerainty. At any rate, he nominates their khan. The history of the times between the obliteration of the House of Tshingiz and this notice of a state of sovereignty and vassalage between the Porte and the Crimea, I am unable to give, and would willingly see investigated. I can only say, that by the beginning of the fourteenth century, the Crimea, or Crim Tartary, had ceased to be Mongol, and that by the middle of the sixteenth it was more or less Osmanli. The fragments of its history that I find, are the notices of so many murders, chiefly fratricides; and its details are bloody and revolting even for those of an Oriental dynasty. The usurper, the pretender, the unscrupulous minister, the renegade, play more than their ordinary parts. The authority of the

Porte is a see-saw—now up, now down—now strong enough to carry out its mandates with a high hand, now but nominal. As we approach our own times, the complications of modern state-craft set in—and there is diplomacy on the parts of Austria, of Poland, and (last and most effective) of Russia; diplomacy not unbacked by military demonstrations; diplomacy and menace, diplomacy and intrigue. The penultimate stage is one of Russian protection, the ultimate, one of Russian domination.

It was in 1778 that peace was concluded between Turkey and Russia, and the independence of the Khan of the Crimea of the Ottoman empire recognized. Upon this, no fewer than 30,000 Greeks and Armenians emigrated to the country of the Don Kosaks, where they now occupy several villages between the Don and the Benda.

In 1783 the second of the two changes took place, and the khanat of the Crimea, from being independent of Turkey, became subject to Russia. On this event, such Tartars as chose were allowed to emigrate, and Anatolia and Rumelia were the countries that vast numbers of them sought. During ten years lasted these emigrations; and in 1784 alone no less than 80,000 Tartars left their country.

It is not easy to take the exact value of these evictions, inasmuch as the calculations of the numbers of the Tartars before the peace of 1778 vary; Georgi making the number of both sexes between 330,000 and 400,000; whereas Pallas raises it to 500,000.

But the census of 1796 was inaccurate, and had to be taken over again. The highest number, however, that it gave was 90,000. In 1800 it had increased to 120,000. At present it is (as seen from the figures) more than twice as much. These give (less the Slavonians) for the whole peninsula—

| | |
|---|---|
| Tartars | 275,822 |
| Germans | 22,324 |
| Gipsies | 7,726 |
| Greeks | 5,426 |
| Karait Jews | 4,198 |
| Talmudic Jews | 4,110 |
| Armenians | 3,960 |
| Bulgarians | 1,234 |
| Mordvins | 340 |
| | 325,140 |

The Crimean Tartars on the hills live as shepherds and herdsmen, rather than as tillers of the ground. In the plains they exercise a moderate but not discreditable amount of agricultural industry, in a country where the soil is grateful and the climate mild, where tobacco thrives, and where the grape ripens into a vinous flavour. The representatives of some of the great families still retain their own lands,—lands held under feudal or quasi-feudal conditions; but the family of the khan himself removed to Asia Minor on the conquest of his khanat. There are a few unimportant points of difference between the Tartars of the hill-country and the Tartars of the plains—the herdsmen and the cultivators. Upon the whole, however, the Crimean civilization, creed, and speech are those of the Kazan and Astrakan Tartars. This is as much as will be said of them at present.

*Tartars* (*so-called*) *of Esthonia, Lithuania and Podolia.*—In the central parts of European Russia we find no notice of any Tartar population whatever—no notice of any

Tartars in such Governments as Vladimir, Tula, Kaluga, &c., the Governments where the true and typical Russian population of Great Russia presents itself in its fullest and most exclusive development. So that we lose them as we go westwards. Not, however, for good. When we reach Esthonia they re-appear, increasing in numbers in the Lithuanian provinces. The so-called Tartar census runs as follows: for the Governments of—

| | |
|---|---|
| Esthonia | 12 |
| Kovno | 415 |
| Grodno | 849 |
| Vilna | 1874 |
| Minsk | 2120 |
| Podolia | 46 |
| | 5316 |

*The Nogays.*—In the beginning of the seventeenth century the Nogays occupied the country between the Tobol and the Yaik. From the Government of Astrakan Peter the Great transplanted the majority of them to the banks of the Kuma and the Kuban.

To the north of the upper part of these rivers, between Georgievsk and Stavropol, the Nogay tribes of the Kasbulat, the Kiptshak, the Mang-gut, the Yedi-san, the Dzham-bulat, the Yedi-kul, and the Navrus reside; with the Mansur-ogli on the other side of the Kuban.

The Zhukan-Kangli and the Kabil-Kagli-Agakli lie to the north of the Black Sea. Thirdly, we have—

The Budziaks in Bessarabia; and fourthly, a tribe with a peculiar and separate history, viz.

The Kundur, on the Aktuba, one of the mouths of the

Volga. These are called by the Russians the Kundur Tartars. They change their residence with the season. In the winter they resort to the town of Krasnoyarsk, and dwell in houses: in the summer they occupy the ordinary felt tent of so many Turk populations. These Kundur were the Nogays who remained behind in the Government of Astrakan when Peter the Great effected the removal of the others.

Orenburg is full of traces, real or accredited, of the Nogays; tumuli, earthworks, and the like.

In the Crimea there is a Nogay colony; of which the members present a striking contrast to their nomadic brethren of the steppe between the Don and Caspian. The Crimean Nogays are truly stationary. So far from their being impracticable, migratory, and unsteady in their industry, so far from their preferring the tent to the village, and showing a repugnance to farming-work, the very converse is the fact. "The Nogais are, alas! the least numerous of the Tartars of the Crimea. They combine the taste for a nomadic life with the cultivation of the soil. They are the best agriculturists in the Crimea, and they now begin to settle in villages and to deal in cattle. It is a pity that this laborious and agicultural population is too small for the cultivation of the steppes." (*Mémoires de l'Academie de St. Petersburg. Serie vi., tom. i.,* p. 36.)

The Nogays are what is called Mongolian in physiognomy. I am not aware, however, of any proof of intermixture.

*The Bashkirs.*—The Government of Orenburg is the great Bashkir district. But besides the Bashkirs it contains Mordvins and Tsherimis, besides numerous Tshuvashes. The following tables give us the amount of the different populations, other than Russian, in the Government of Orenburg :—

| | |
|---|---|
| Bashkirs . . . | 332,358 |
| Tartars (so-called) . | 230,080 |
| Meshtsheriak . . | 71,578 |
| | 634,016 |
| Mordvin . . . | 5,200 |
| Tsheremis . . . | 2,626 |
| | 7,826 |
| Tshuvash . . . | 8,352 |

To these add a few Germans, Gipsies, Votiaks, Teptyars, Kalmuks, and Poles.

The Bashkirs of the present century are as truly Turk both in language and features as the Kirghiz. They are breeders and feeders of cattle, rather than tillers of the soil, or occupants of towns; but they are bee-masters even more than they are shepherds and herdsmen.

In religion they are Mahometans, like so many of the other Turkish populations.

Bashkir is the name by which they designate themselves. The Kirghiz, however, call them Ishtaki, a form of the name Ostiak.

A. D. 1555, three years after the battle which broke the power of the Tartars of the Volga, the Bashkirs submitted themselves to Russia and her victorious Czar Ivan Vasilievitsh. He is said to have ruled them gently, to have protected them well, and to have laid upon them a tribute of skins far lighter than the one they paid to their old masters.

Since 1741 the Bashkirs have themselves taken-on

more or less of the character of the Kosak, and submitted to a military organization. Instad of paying the tribute of peltry, they serve as soldiers; sending an annual relay of 1500 men to act with the Kosaks to the Yaik.

The ancient nobility is broken, so that the leading individuals in the different *volosts* (*lodges, encampments*) are the *starshin* (*judges, captains*). With these, the fountain of honour springs in Russia; in other words, they are officials. They decide disputes; they take the command of the detachments sent on military service; they promulgate the ukases. Russia appoints and the Bashkirs pay.

The numbers of the Bashkirs are—

| | |
|---|---|
| In Orenburg . . . . | 332,358 |
| — Permia . . . . | 40,746 |
| — Samar . . . . | 15,351 |
| — Viatka . . . . | 3,617 |
| | 392,072 |

*The Meshtsheriak.*—The Meshtsheriak are Turk in speech, and occupy—

| | |
|---|---|
| The Government of Orenburg to the number of . . . . | 71,587 |
| ———— Perm . . | 5,783 |
| ———— Saratov . . | 2,580 |
| ———— Penza . . | ? |
| | 79,950 |

They appear to be an increasing population.

They are Turk in speech, and Mahometan in creed, though considered to be Ugrian in blood. They are, probably, too, immigrants—their original locality being on the Oka, in the neighbourhood of the Mordvin and Tsherimis.

In the Bashkir rebellion the Meshtsheriak kept on the side of Russia, and were rewarded by being freed from their previous tribute, and having the privileges of the Kosaks extended to them.

| English. | Kazan. | Bashkir. | Meshtsheriak. | Nogay. |
|---|---|---|---|---|
| *Head* | bash | bash | bash | bash |
| *Hair* | tshatsh | zaz | tsats | zatsh |
| *Hand* | kol | kol | kul | kol |
| *Eye* | kus | kyus | kus | gyos |
| *Ear* | kolak | kulak | klak | kulak |
| *Tooth* | tyesh | tish | tish | tysh |
| *Tongue* | tyel | tel | til | til |
| *Blood* | kan | kan | kan | kan |
| *Day* | kyun | kyun | kun | gün |
| *Sun* | kuyash | kun | kuyash | gyon |
| *Moon* | ai | ai | ai | ai |
| *Star* | yaldus | yuldus | yuldus | ildis |
| *Fire* | ut | ut | ut | ut |
| *Water* | zu | zu | zu | su |
| *Tree* | agatsh | agatsh | agatsh | agatsh |
| *Stone* | tash | tash | tash | tash |
| *One* | ber | ber | ber | bir |
| *Two* | ike | ike | ike | iki |
| *Three* | utsh | ysh | uz | utsh |
| *Four* | dürt | dört | dyört | dört |
| *Five* | bish | besh | besh | bish |
| *Six* | alty | alty | alty | alty |
| *Seven* | yedi | yedi | idi | siti |
| *Eight* | zigis | zigis | zigis | zegis |
| *Nine* | tokus | togus | togus | togus |
| *Ten* | on | on | on | on |

*The Teptyar.*—When the khanat of Kazan became Russian, a mixed multitude of Turks, Tsherimis, Votiaks, Tshuvash, and Mordvins, fled to the east of the Ural. Out of these has arisen a population which the Turks call *Teptyar*—a population which, like the Meshtsheriak, kept to the side of Russia during the Bashkir rebellion, and became a privileged population accordingly.

They are Mahometan rather than Christian, and (probably) Pagan rather than Mahometan. Their habits in general are those of the Bashkirs. Some of them are employed as carriers in the salt trade between Orenburg and Kazan.

The underground monuments of the northern Turks, indeed of the Siberian tribes in general, deserve greater attention than they have found. They are spread over a vast area. Bell describes those of the valley of the Tom, a locality originally Ugrian:—

"About eight or ten days' journey from Tomsky, in this plain, are found many tombs and burying-places of ancient heroes, who, in all probability, fell in battle. These tombs are easily distinguished by the mounds of earth and stone raised upon them. When, or by whom, these battles were fought, so far to the northward, is uncertain. I was informed by the Tartars in the Baraba, that Tamerlane, or Timyr-ack-sack, as they call him, had many engagements in that country with the Kalmucks, whom he in vain endeavoured to conquer. Many persons go from Tomsky and other parts every summer to these graves, which they dig up, and find among the ashes of the dead considerable quantities of gold, silver, brass, and some precious stones, but particularly hilts of swords and armours. They find also ornaments of saddles and bridles, and other trappings for horses, and even the bones of horses, and sometimes those of elephants, whence it appears, that when any general or person of distinction was interred, all his arms, his favourite horse and servant, were buried with him in the same grave; this custom prevails to this day among the Kalmucks and other Tartars, and seems to be of great antiquity. It appears from the number of graves, that many thousands must have fallen on these plains; for the people have continued to dig for such treasure many years, and still find it unexhausted. They are sometimes, indeed, interrupted, and robbed of all their booty, by parties of the Kalmucks, who abhor the disturbing of the ashes of the dead.

"I have seen several pieces of armour and other curiosities that were dug out of these tombs, particularly an armed man on horseback, cast in brass, of no mean design nor workmanship; also figures of deer, cast in pure gold, which were split through the middle, and had some small holes in them, as intended for ornaments to a quiver, or the furniture of a horse.

"While we were at Tomsky, one of these grave-diggers told me, that once they lighted on an arched vault, where they found the remains of a man, with his bow, arrows, lance, and other arms, lying together on a silver table. On touching the body, it fell to dust. The value of the table and arms was very considerable."

Atkinson writes that in the northern part of the Kirghiz steppe the tombs are built of rough stone, with a base from ten to twelve feet square, and about eight feet in height. On the top of this is a small pyramid. In the cemeteries formed by a collection of these structures, one is, generally, larger than the others; as if the chief had been laid in the grave of honour, and his followers ranged around him. The present graves are much less elaborate. A shallow grave, with a few stones over it, suffices.

The fuller account of Müller divides the tumuli into two classes, one of which is generally believed to indicate a much higher antiquity than the other, and it also states that in the older the ornaments and implements that reward the toil and trouble of the investigating excavator, are of gold or copper, not of iron.

Now this distinction between the old and new is not the distinction of the Russian traveller or the English antiquarian, but, on the contrary, one drawn by the Kirghiz themselves. The burial-places which the present nomad assigns to his own people, are definitely separated from the older ones, to which he assigns an unknown origin. The labourer of an English parish knows all about the graves of the village churchyard. The barrow of the neighbouring field he attributes to the Romans, the Danes, Oliver Cromwell, or the devil. And so it is with a Kirghiz of Independent Tartary. He knows what belongs to his own times and the memory of man, in the way that a sexton knows a parish grave, and he leaves unknown what belongs to a time anterior to his own, just as the same sexton leaves unknown the history of a Roman, Saxon, or British tumulus.

The sepulchral memorials of their own ancestors, the analogues of the parish grave, the Kirghiz call *Uba*.

The sepulchral mounds of a pre-historic period, the analogues of the barrow or cairn, he calls *Moly*.

No one has yet classified the Moly and Uba with anything like the necessary minuteness, or rather, no one has taken much pains to ask how far they are susceptible of classification, and, assuming that they are so, to ask what any classification leads to. We only know that they vary both in form and construction, possibly as much as our own barrows. They are sometimes mere earthworks; sometimes earthworks *plus* a stone walling, and stone pillar. They are commoner on the eastern than the western side of Tartary. They extend into Mongolia (in the notice of which area they might have been mentioned), and they extend into several districts yet to be described.

But the Moly and Uba are not the only antiquities

of the Kirghiz. Their area supplies us with monuments above ground, as well as with records below. The walled town, the moated fortress, are, doubtless, exceptional, improbable, and, loosely speaking, impossible phenomena in a steppe. Yet approaches to them may have been effected by ancient populations. Ruins remain. There is, at least, one building of stone, walling-in a space of twenty-eight feet square within the limits of Kirghiz Tartary, not far from the Mongolian frontier, an object of superstitious reverence to the tribes around. There is this, at least; possibly others. Let us take it, however, as a sample or specimen of a class of remains, which may or may not be a large one. The like of it appear and re-appear elsewhere, far beyond the area under notice. The Mongol country has its tumuli in abundance; and of architectural ruins not a few. Mantshuria has, at least, tumuli. The Bashkir country has both tumuli and ruins. So has the Crimea. So has a large portion of the remainder of Siberia. We shall hear of them under different names. The monuments themselves, however, will be substantially the same.

The older graves are believed by the Kirghiz to have been constructed by a nation named *Myk*,—query *Magi*.

Besides the tumuli, there are the earthworks of numerous old encampments. One of the barrows, measured by Mr. Atkinson, was 200 feet in diameter, and 40 feet high, with a trench round it twelve feet wide, and six feet deep. A circular hollow on the top was ten feet deep. On the west side were four circles of large stones. Respecting this the tradition ran thus—a certain nation which once dwelt in these parts resolved that all the men, women, and children, of which it was composed, should be put to death. They were to destroy each other. Before they began to do this, they raised the barrows in which they were to be buried. The father killed his wife, and also his children; all except the eldest. The eldest killed his father first, and himself afterwards. The name of this people was the Self-slaughterers.

So runs one tale.

Another, belonging to the parts about Zaisan Nor, runs thus:—"Two mountains, the one called Kolmack Tologuy, and the other Sarte Tologuy, stood in the Tarbogatai chain; and two heroes or giants, father and son, engaged to carry Kolmack Tologuy to the rocky shores of the Irtish, and place it on the plain where the town and fortress of Oust Kamenogorsk are built, for the purpose of damming up the river. At a certain distance from the Karagol mountains, the heroes were to pass the night. Having put down their load, the son asked the father's permission to go and visit his bride, who dwelt on the broad steppes extending along the shores of Zaisan Nor. 'Remember,' said the father, 'that the *kalim* is not paid, and that you cannot stay with her in the right of a husband.' The son proceeded to the aoul of his bride; but was so charmed with her beauty, that he forgot his father's strict injunctions, and remained till sunrise, when the stern old man, growing impatient of his son's delay, had already raised his side of the mountain. On resuming his labour, the young giant found, notwithstanding all his efforts, that he was utterly unable to move his portion of the load. Enraged by this proof that his injunctions had been disobeyed, the old man ordered him to place himself under the mountain; when he remorselessly let go his hold, and the enormous mass fell, crushing both.

"The mother anxiously awaited the return of her husband and son; at length, tormented by painful uncertainty about their fate, and feeling a presentiment that some misfortune had befallen them, she determined to follow on their track. She at last recognized the mountain, now the monument under which her husband and son lay buried. The bereaved widow and mother sobbed bitterly—absolutely, according to the best authorities, shedding tears of blood. She mourned her loss for a long while, and would not be comforted. Finally, the blood-drops ran dry, and when she wept again, her tears were pure and transparent as a spring. The rocks were the silent witnesses of her misery, and have preserved the proofs of her sorrow and devotion; the tears of blood and drops of crystal having become petrified and transformed into layers of argil and quartz, which can be distinguished from a great distance by the colours of red and white. This mountain of quartz is about five versts south from Kolmack Tologuy. It is named by the Kirghiz, Ac-tas, or white stone, and is held by them in great veneration."

The extensions of the Turk area from the north have been sufficiently considered for the present. It has been convenient to give them in detail before we move southwards. It has been, perhaps, more convenient than systematic. If, on starting with the Kirghiz, we had merely looked for their nearest congeners, we should probably have taken the Uzbeks and Turkomans of the southern half of Independent Turkestan before the Baraba and Sokhalar; the latter being an extreme and outlying member of the group. Beyond doubt, the closer affinities with the central Kirghiz lay nearer home.

| English. | Uzbek. | Turkoman. | Kirghiz. |
|---|---|---|---|
| *Head* | bash | bash | baz |
| *Hair* | zatan | zatsh | tshatsh |
| *Hand* | al | kol | kol |
| *Foot* | ayak | ayak | ayak |

| English. | Uzbek. | Turkoman | Kirghiz. |
|---|---|---|---|
| *Eye* | kyus | küs | kus |
| *Ear* | kulak | klak | kolak |
| *Tooth* | tish | dish | tiz |
| *Blood* | kau | kan | kan |
| *Day* | kündus | kyondos | kündus |
| *Sun* | kyonash | koyash | kün |
| *Moon* | ai | ai | ai |
| *Star* | yoldos | yoldos | dzhildzhis |
| *Fire* | ud | ot | ut |
| *Water* | zu | zu | zu |
| *Tree* | agatsh | agatsh | agatsh |
| *Stone* | tash | tash | taz |
| *One* | bir | bir | ber |
| *Two* | ike | iki | oki |
| *Three* | utsh | utsh | utsh |
| *Four* | dyort | durt | tyort |
| *Five* | bish | bish | bez |
| *Six* | alty | alto | alty |
| *Seven* | edi | edi | dzhede |
| *Eight* | zigis | zikis | zikes |
| *Nine* | tokas | tokos | tokus |
| *Ten* | on | on | on |

Whether the language represented by these lists be that of the oldest occupants of the land is doubtful. It is only certain that it is much more akin to the Kirghiz than was the Yakut.

The Uzbek is spoken in the eastern, the Turkoman on the western, side of the parts between the Caspian Lake and the Chinese frontier.

*The Turkomans.*—A little to the south of the town of Bokhara, the river of both that city and Samarcand, a northern feeder of the Oxus (from which it is only artificially cut off), after having been held up by the dam of Karakul, ceases to irrigate and fertilize the otherwise barren soil, and stops or stagnates in a lake which the Turks call a sea (denghiz). Where the face of the country changes, the population changes also. The Uzbeks end and the Turkomans begin—the particular

Turkoman tribe, occupant of the parts around the Denghiz, being the Ersari.

The Ersari Turkomans are settled subjects to the khan of Bokhara, the greater part, if not the whole, of their area lying within the recognized limits of that kingdom.

They are one of the nine great divisions under which Sir A. Burnes, who was amongst them, classes the 140,000 families of the Turkomans, *e. g.*

| *Tribe.* | *Locality.* | *Families.* |
|---|---|---|
| Ersari | Bokhara | 40,000 |
| Sakar | Middle Oxus | 2,000 |
| Saruk | Merve | 20,000 |
| Salore | Shurukhs | 2,000 |
| Tuka | The Tejend | 40,000 |
| Goklan | The Gurgan | 9,000 |
| Yamud | Asterabad | 20,000 |
| Ata | Balkhan | 1,000 |
| Choudur | Mangusluk | 6,000 |
| | | 140,000 |

The Goklan fall into nine divisions, which encamp apart from each other, and are probably subdivided.

If a Turkoman slave-holder let his love of beauty prevail over his love of money, he may marry his prisoner, and have issue by her. But the sons or daughters thus born will ever be but as imperfect Turkomans. The pride of blood, potent throughout the whole population, will keep them down, not, indeed, as slaves, though with the name of such, but as half-casts. A Turkoman can liberate his captive; but his offspring by his captive he cannot liberate. The mother may be free; the son unequal to a freeman. The name for these half-blood half-casts is *kul*, and it is a name which a long line of descendants is insufficient to throw off. It is kept up by the common habits of conversation; for a full Turkoman in addressing a half-blood, says Kul-i-Otaboi, Kul-i-Tlgi, &c., as the case may be, not meaning much of an insult, but still using a title of inferiority. The value, too, of a *kul's* life is less than that of an *ig*, or full-blooded Turkoman. Kill an *ig*, and a blood-feud will follow. He belongs to a tribe, and his tribesmen must avenge his death. Kill a *kul*, and he has no tribe that either owns or avenges him.

*The Trukhmen.*—Word for word, Trukhmen is the same as Turkoman, except so far as it has come to us through a Russian rather than a Persian channel. It applies, however, to a different locality, and to a somewhat different population.

The Turkomans occupy the parts due north of Persia, and harass the Persian frontier from the south-eastern extremity of the Caspian Sea to the confines of Caubul.

The Trukhmen are distributed as follows: in

| | |
|---|---|
| Astrakan to the number of . . | 1,600 |
| Stavropol . . . . . . | 5,271 |
| Taurida . . . . . . | 450 |
| | 7,321 |

*The Uzbeks.*—The Uzbek physiognomy is Mongol; decidedly so. The men are short and stout, with broad faces, scanty beards, and small eyes. They occupy the countries due west of Chinese Turkestan, and seem to have been projected into them as intruders and conquerors at no very distant period. In one respect they resemble the Osmanli Turks in Europe—*i. e.* in being strangers in the land. In most of the Uzbek countries there is, side by side with the ruling nation, a subordinate population of older occupants. These are Persians in language, and, doubtless, in blood also. They are strongly contrasted with their lords; being occupants of houses, agricultural and industrial in their habits, and submissive in temper. They are submissive in temper where the Uzbeks have encroached. In some few districts where they have preserved their independence, they are bold and high-spirited. Some of them are to be found in Chinese Turkestan; but here we may suppose that it is the Tajiks (for that is what they are called) who are the immigrants. In the Uzbek countries, however, they are the older population. They are found in countries other than Turk; but this is a point of Persian ethnology.

In a certain number, then, of Tajik countries, and some which can scarcely be called Tajik, the Uzbeks are dominant, continuing, as a fixed population, the habits and organization of an army. The people are nothing. The power of the chiefs is broken. The sovereign is as absolute as in Constantinople. The country in which they settle is divided into districts, whose officers are appointed by the king. These have other officers below them; and it is not till we reach the head man of the village that we find any approach to independent or constitutional government. In the villages, however, the influential men have a voice in the recommendation of their head. Again, the Ulema, or Church, has a controlling, and, sometimes, a commanding, influence. In all the Uzbek States the Sunnite form of Mahometanism exhibits itself in all its bigotry. Bokhara and Morocco are, perhaps, the two most intolerant countries of all Islam.

With these premises, and with the repetition of a statement that, as a general rule, whatever is Uzbek in respect to the ruling powers, is Tajik in respect to the subordinate population, we may give the details of the Uzbek name.

Balk is Uzbek; Balk Proper, or the parts immediately round the capital.

Kunduz is Uzbek. In Khost, however, and Inderaub, which are mountainous countries, the population, although the districts are annexed to Kunduz. is wholly, or almost wholly, Tajik.

Taulikhaun is Uzbek; the population of Tajiks being, nevertheless, great.

Huzrut Imaum, along with Khullum, to which it is annexed, is Uzbek.

Meimuna, Andkhu, and Shibbergaun, further to the west, are Uzbek; though here there are independent Turkomans intermixed.

Bokhara is Uzbek. Kokan, or Fergana, is Uzbek. Khiva is Uzbek.

Of the Turks beyond the Turk area, the most important are :—

(1.) *The Ilyat of Persia.*—These are the nomads of Persia, occupants of tented encampments or imperfect villages. They will re-appear when Persia is investigated.

(2.) *The Turkomans of Asia Minor*—

(3.) *The Turks of Syria.*—Each of these is best noticed in the sequel.

(4.) *The Osmanli*, or *Turks of Turkey, whether in Europe, Asia*, or *Africa.*—Historical notices, which find no place just now, but which will find place ere long, best precede the notice of these.

So much for the representatives of the movement westward. India on the east and south-east has been conquered, more or less completely or incompletely, more than once. So has Caubul. So has China. Turks, however, *eo nomine* or *eâ linguâ*, no longer exist as a separate element of the population. Hence, the notice of the Turk influence in these parts must stand over.

One movement, however, eastwards, must be mentioned. I say "movement" because, hypothetically, Independent Turkestan (or Tartary) is our centre. It is possible, however—barely possible—that the parts in question may be the cradle of the stock. If so, no movement is needed. They start from it to go elsewhere.

*Chinese Turkestan* (*Tartary*).—Chinese Turkestan, Chinese Tartary, or Little Bokhara, is bounded on the north by the Mongols, on the east and south by the Tibetans, and on the west by other Turks, and the all but unknown populations akin to the Kafirs of Kafiristan. The minutiæ of the boundaries are unknown; the tract in question belonging to China, and being (as such) a *terra incognita*.

The countries of Khoten and Yarkend are the occupancies of this branch, countries traversed by rivers that have no outlet to the sea, and which, from their relation to the mountain-ranges of Tibet, are probably steppes, imperfectly watered by small rivers and unimportant lakes. Conditions like these favour a nomadic life modified by occasional opportunities for agriculture. They also favour an imperfect commerce; in which case the inhabitants are carriers and merchants rather than producers. Such is, probably, the case with a large proportion of the Chinese Turks. In religion they are Mahometans—Mahometans under a rule of tolerant or indifferent Buddhists.

In one respect the populations of these parts have a great historical importance. They were a lettered nation at an early period. The Mantshú alphabet was derived from the Mongols; that of the Mongols from the Uighur

Turks. The Uigur alphabet was of Syriac origin, though, perhaps, derived directly from Persia. The influence of the Nestorian Christians has already been noticed. These it was who, along with a Christianity now replaced by Mahometanism, introduced the alphabet in question; perhaps as early as the seventh century of our era.

My reasons for differing, unwillingly, with Mr. Hodgson, and considering a population called Hor, or Horpa, to be, in language at least, Tibetan rather than Turk, have been already given. I do not, however, deny that the Hor may be more Turk in blood than in speech. It has already been stated that they call themselves Igur.

Again, I can so easily believe that the word Chorbad, a name for one of the districts of Little Tibet, is Horpa, that I am ready to place the Chorbad Tibetans in the same category.

I find, too, that the Keris of Tibet may also be of Turk blood, though other than Turk in language.

| English. | Uigur. | Mongol. | Tibetan. | Bokhara. |
|---|---|---|---|---|
| *Head* | bash | tologoi | go | tser |
| *Hair* | zatsh | üsü | ta | mui |
| *Hand* | ilik | gar | lango | dest |
| *Foot* | adakhi | küll | kango | pai |
| *Eye* | kusi | nüdü | mik | tshesm |
| *Ear* | kulak | tshike | amtshuk | gush |
| *Sun* | kün | nara | nimo | aftab |
| *Moon* | ai | sara | oula | mah |
| *Star* | yaldus | odu | karma | sitara |
| *Water* | zuv | usu | chhu | ab |
| *Stone* | tash | tsholo | doh | tsenk |

*The Tshagatai.*—We are dealing with the Turks *eo nomine* or *eâ linguâ;* with the populations decidedly and directly akin to the Kirghiz Uzbeks and Turkomans—the central populations as they exist in a definite form. For this reason I give the Tshagatai a place here. The Mogul dynasty was Tshagatai, and certain Tshagatai are its fallen representatives. Yet these are no longer Turk, but Persian or Indian. Many of the Caubul families are Tshagatai, just, perhaps, as certain English families are Norman. Yet what distinguishes them from the Afghans? There is Tshagatai blood in Mongolia. Yet this is not a population of Tshagatai. At the same time I have read of Tshagatai Turks in books written by living men, though the details and *differentiæ* of a Tshagatai locality with a Tshagatai population I have yet to find. These are in Caubul, India, or Kokan (Fergana) if anywhere.

The family of Timur was Tshagatai. The conqueror of India, Baber, was a Tshagatai. The countries he ruled over and (what is better) described were, more or less, Tshagatai.

Ferghana fell, in the time of Baber, into seven districts, two of which lay to the north, and five to the south of the Jaxartes. Of these, Andeján, the district of the capital, seems to have been the most Turk, for, says Baber, the inhabitants are "all Turks," and "there is no one in the town or market who does not understand the Turki tongue."

Asfera, on the other hand, was pre-eminently Persian, Tajik, or Sart; as was, also, Marghinân. Of Asfera, writes Baber, "the inhabitants are all mountaineers or Sarts." In Marginân, too, "all the inhabitants are Sarts; the race are great boxers, noisy and turbulent, so that they are famous all over Mâweralnaher for their blustering and fondness for boxing, and most of the celebrated bullies of Samarkand and Bokhâra are from Marginân."

In the other four districts I imagine that the population was more mixed, partly Turk and partly Persian, though in what proportions I am unable to say.

It is clear that, however little we may know about

the existing Tshagatai, we know a good deal about the historical ones. Baber's Memoirs is the autobiography of a Tshagatai prince; besides being the most natural piece of regal life, regally written, in existence.

Which makes it clear that the Tshagatai of Baber's time were no illiterate barbarians, but readers and writers. This brings us to the consideration of the relations between the two old lettered, or classical, languages of the Turk stock. Were they the same? Was Tshagatai Uigur, and Uigur Tshagatai? They may or may not have been this. Whatever, however, was the case as to the language, the external conditions of form and time were different.

An Uigur literature (if there be such a thing, and if all truly Uigur compositions be not irretrievably lost, which hope rather than knowledge leads us to believe is not the case) must be the literature of the sixth, seventh, or eighth centuries of our era, Christian in origin as far as the alphabet is concerned, and in a character borrowed from Syria, and lent, or given, to Mongolia.

A Tshagatai literature is Persian in alphabet, and, to some extent, Persian in spirit. That such existed is beyond doubt. Baber wrote his own life. He quotes Turki, and Tshagatai, or, perhaps, Uigur, poets. He knew the Tshagatai Turk as a lettered, literary language. Yet Baber's life, as we have it in English, is a translation from the Persian, and the evidence that the so-called Turki originals are not also translations is less satisfactory than the means of making them so allow. There is more than one translation of a Persian translation from the Turki. There is more than one Turkish scholar in England who could translate from the Tshagatai direct. Yet Tshagatai texts and Tshagatai translations, at first hand, are rarities, to say the least.

And now let us look back upon our details, especially the philological ones. The forms of speech converge as we approach Independent Turkestan. They diverge as we move from it. The two extreme forms are

(1.) For the east, the Yakut and Uigur.

(2.) For the west, the Comanian and Osmanli.

The Yakut and Comanian are from the north, the Uigur and Osmanli from the south, of the central region.

Again let us look back on our details. They are numerous. Yet they represent less than half of the ethnological importance of Turks. Why they do this will appear anon.

Enough, however, has been written to show that the attempted analysis of the Turk population, and the separation of its primary, secondary, and tertiary layers is a subject on which error is excusable. What was Tshagatai in Baber's time, may or may not have been Uigur as well. It is certain that it is now Uzbek.

## CHAPTER XIX.

The Ugrian, or Fin, Stock.—The Fins, or Finlanders, of Finland.—The Hämalaiset and Kiriolaiset.—The Kwains of Norway and Sweden.—The Fins of Ingria.—The Auramoiset, Savakot, and Izhor.—The Tshud, Vod, and Vesp.

THE group that now comes under notice is named Fin or Ugrian. The Finlanders of Finland are its chief representatives. Ugoria, or Ugria, was the name of the parts on each side of the Uralian Mountains, the occupancy of more than one tribe akin to the Fins of Finland.

The Ugrian both agrees and differs with our last three classes; the chief points of agreement being physiological. Whatever may be meant by the term Mongolian, as applied to the anatomy of the human subject, it is certain that nine authorities out of ten have agreed in making the Ugrians Mongol. In the general character, also, of their languages, the Ugrians, Turks, Mongols, and Tungús agree; the Ugrian being, in some of its forms at least, liker to the Turk than to the other two. On the other hand, it approaches the Lithuanic.

The details of the difference are somewhat more complex. In the first place, the value of the class termed Ugrian is far higher than that of the other three. Possibly it is as high as all the three put together. All the Tungús, and all the Mongol forms of speech, are mutually intelligible. Whether an extreme form of the Yakut could be understood by an Osmanli or an Uigur is doubtful. It is certain, however, that the more distant forms of the Turk are less unlike each other than many of the nearest congeners of the Ugrian. This may be seen by comparing the Ostiak and Vogul, or the Fin and Lap, on one side, with the Uigur and Yakut, or the Yakut and Osmanli, on the other. Similarity in Ugria is difference in Turkestan.

In the way of religious belief, no Ugrians are Buddhists like the Mongols and Mantshú. Few, like the great majority of the Turks, are Mahometans. They are, for the most part, either Christians or Shamanist pagans. The Christians belong to either the Eastern or the Western Church; those of the latter being Protestants when they are in contact with Sweden and Norway, and Romanists when in contact with Austria. The recent proselytes from paganism are of the Greek Church, all being occupants of either Russia or Siberia.

That the Turks and Mongols were nomads rather than agriculturists has been made transparently clear in the foregoing notices. Many would say as much of the Ugrians. The writer, with whom, of all others, I most unwillingly differ, Mr. Norriss, in his edition of Prichard,* commits himself to the doctrine that "even the stationary Fin is little more than half reclaimed. The Fin of the large towns is rather a Scandinavian than a Ugrian." In confirmation of this view, the Russian ethnological map gives a special colouring, and a special name to the Fins of Abo, Helsingfors, and the southern half of the sea coast in general. It makes them "Swedish Fins." Nor can it be denied that, in these parts, the industrial and intellectual influences are of Swedish origin. *Mutatis mutandis*, this applies to the Magyars of Hungary.

* Vol. i. p. 201.

They have large towns; but it is Slavonic soil on which they stand, and German civilization with which they come in contact. I admit, then, that we have no conclusive evidence of any Ugrian population having ever, single-handed and *proprio motu*, built anything larger than a village. Yet the Permians and Bulgarians must have had emporiums, and Ugrian hands may have had much to do in construction of them. Residence in the tent rather than the hut, residence in dwellings of felt and skin, residence after the fashion of the Mongols and Turks, has always been, in Ugria, the exception rather than the rule.

Of Ugrian agriculture there is plenty. Compare it with that of either modern Germany or ancient Italy, and it is rude; no ruder, however, than that of the ancient Germans. The agricultural Fin is the destroyer of the forest. He burns for himself a clearing, and sows oats on the ash-manured soil till it is exhausted. He then goes on burning again. The Fins of the Norwegian settlement in Finskogen did this to such an extent as to provoke the legislature, bringing down laws upon themselves to the effect that no such burnings should be allowed. Yet the Norwegian himself often effects them. To clear woods, to sow oats and rye, and to milk cows, is to be agricultural; and this is what the Ugrians do, wherever the face of the country allows them. Many of them are nomads, with the reindeer instead of the cow. Where they are, the face of the country constrains them.

Lest the influence of this be undervalued, let us remember that the Turk and Mongolian steppes are amongst the most treeless parts of the world; whereas a great portion of the Ugrian area is a forest. The Government of Vologda, the occupancy of the Zirianians, has nine-tenths of its surface in wood. Again, the mineral wealth of the Ugrian area is far greater than that of the Turks. Again, the Mongols and Turks are essentially inlanders. The Fins and Estonians, at least, possess a sea-board, and exhibit nautical aptitudes.

In its greater amount of wood, in its sea-board, and in its climate, Mantshuria is more Ugrian than is either Mongolia or the Turk area; and it is probable that if we knew more of the details of the Mantshú population, we should find numerous points of resemblance. Like conditions give like results.

The tribual system is Ugrian, though only to a limited extent. The signs of it will be indicated as they occur. This they will most especially do in the Votiak and Ostiak districts.

The ruder members of all the four groups mistake disfiguration for ornament, and tattoo themselves. The Ugrians and Tungús do it most; the Turks and Mongols least.

The reindeer, as a domestic animal, was strange to the Turks and Mongols. The camel is strange to the Ugrians. All three populations use the horse; the Ugrians, however, use it but little. I cannot quite commit myself to the statement that, whilst both the Turks and Mongol enjoy its flesh, no Ugrians are hippophagi. I am only sure that if any of them are so, they are so to a very slight extent.

As originators of ideas and inventions the Ugrians have as little to boast of as the Turks, the Turks and Mongols of as little as the Mantshús.

As physical or material influences in the world's history, the Turks hold the foremost place; and that by a long interval. The notice, however, of their comparative conquests and settlements belongs to a later chapter.

The area occupied by the Mongols is eminently compact and continuous, *i. e.* regular in outline, with few offsets, and not many outlying districts. Of these the most important were those of the isolated Aimâk and the isolated Kalmuk. The Turk area, more irregular and more discontinuous than the Mongol, is, nevertheless, far more continuous and regular than the Ugrian; which, in some parts, has no continuity at all. Many of its occupants are quite isolate, separated from their nearest congeners by Russians, Tungús, or Turks. This implies that the Ugrians are a population upon which others have encroached. The Turks are eminently one that has encroached upon others. In short, the Ugrians belong to a broken-up, fragmentary, and ever diminishing family. Their occupancies extend from Norway to the neighbourhood of Behring's Straits, and from the North Cape to the Lower Volga. Yet the population amounts to less than eight millions. Of these half are in Hungary; and a fourth in Finland. The other two millions (there or thereabouts) are Laps, Ingrians, Estonians, Liefs, Zirianians, Permians, Votiaks, Tsherimiss, Tshuvash (?), Mordvin, Voguls, Ostiaks, Samoyeds, Yeniseians, and Yukahiri. Some of these divisions contain only a few hundred individuals; the largest numbers less than 400,000.

It is convenient to begin with

*The Finlanders* or *Fins proper*.—The Finlanders proper amount to about 2,000,000 individuals, speaking a lettered language; the alphabet being Roman, introduced along with Christianity, from Sweden. Like the Swedes, the Finlanders are Lutherans, with the exception of some few members of the Greek Church.

Many of the Finlanders are, more or less, Swedish in blood. Still more speak the Swedish language. Until A. D. 1809, their political relations were with Sweden.

Since then, they have been subject to Russia. Their civilization, however, so far as it is European, is essentially Swedish.

The nearest approach to a name, at once general and native, is Suomelaiset, meaning swamp, morass, or fen people; the term Fin and Finlander being of foreign origin. Two divisions, however, are recognized—by the learned at least.

(1.) *The Hämalaiset.*—Hämalaiset the plural of Hämalaine,* is the name for the Finlanders of the south-west, especially those of the parts about Tavastahus. Hence Tavastrian is another term for them. A difference of dialect is the chief characteristic of the Tavastrians, or Hämalaiset, as opposed to—

(2.) *The Karelians* or *Kirialaiset.*—The great block of land, more or less square in outline, and coinciding in respect to its physical geography with the table-land of the duchy, is the area of the Karelians. Here the surface of the earth lies high, and the rivers empty themselves into innumerable lakes, rather than directly into the sea.

The latest ethnologists for Finland lay great stress upon the difference between the Tavastrian and Karelian branches, and take considerable pains with the analysis of the sporadic populations of Fin blood in localities beyond the frontier of Finland. They take considerable pains to ascertain which is Karelian, which Tavastrian. I give their results as I find them, beginning with the Karelians.

*The Kwains* or *Quains.*—The Kwains or Quains are

* Suomelaiset was, in like manner, the plural of Suomelaine. This remarkable termination is an instrument of criticism. It indicates a Fin gloss. For this reason the name *Rhoxolani* in Tacitus has been looked upon as the Ugrian *Ruotsalaine.*

held to be Karelian rather than Tavastrian. They are the Finlanders of the north-western parts of the duchy. Their country lies along the coast of the Gulf of Bothnia from Tornea southwards, and they come in contact with the Swedes and Laps of Scandinavia. The name is native, East Bothnia being the land of the Kainu-laiset, a word of which the singular form is Kainulaine. Currency has been given to it by the Scandinavians; the old Norse form being Kœnir, and Kvœnir. As early as the time of Alfred, the Norse name was sufficiently common to have found its way into the Anglo-Saxon writings of that royal geographer, and Finland is the land of the Cvenas, or Cvena-land. But *qvinna* is Swedish for a *woman*, the same word as the English *queen* and *quean*, different in their degrees of courtesy as the two words are. Now, it is by no means improbable that when a nation of Cvenas was heard of, a nation of women (*qvinnas*) was suggested. Out of this would come a nation "ruled by a woman" (*queen* or *quean*).

This confusion is not merely a likelihood; it is, in three parts out of four, a fact. The land of the Sitones, over which Tacitus is satisfied with making a woman a ruler, becomes, when we get to Adam of Bremen, a land of Amazons—"hæc quidem insula" (Estland) "terræ *feminarum* proxima narratur."

Again—"circa hæc littora Baltici maris ferun't esse Amazonas, quod nunc terra feminarum dicitur, quas aquæ gustu aliqui dicunt concipere. . . . Hae simul viventes, spernunt consortia vi^r^vorum, quos etiam, si advenerint, a se veriliter repellunt."

Such is the history of a blunder; of which there are many to mislead the ethnologist.

The present population of Finland is roughly put at 2,000,000. In a paper of Koeppen's, read before the

Academy of St. Petersburg in 1846, the exact numbers are—

| | |
|---|---|
| Fins (pure) . . . . . | 1,102,068 |
| Swedes . . . . . . | 136,612 |
| Fins and Swedes (mixed) . | 129,520 |
| Russians and Fins (mixed) . | 43,752 |
| Germans . . . . . | 363 |
| | 1,412,315 |

In Norway the term more especially requires attending to; not only because the Kwains in that country are numerous, but because the word Fin has a very different meaning. It denotes a Laplander. Hence, to call a Kwain a Fin is an error of no slight importance. There are two Fin localities in Norway, one in Finmark, one in Solöer. The first is certainly Kwain; the latter may be, more or less, Tavastrian.

*The Kwains of Finmark.*—They are an increasing population, as may be seen from the comparison of the two following censuses.

| Parish. | 1845. | 1855. |
|---|---|---|
| Ibestad | — | 25 |
| Tranö | — | 7 |
| Lenvik | — | 10 |
| Maalselven | — | 80 |
| Tromsö parish | 22 | 91 |
| — town | 82 | 38 |
| Karlsö | 29 | 45 |
| Lyngen | 436 | 721 |
| Sjærvö | 426 | 858 |
| Alten | 863 | 1107 |
| Hammerfest parish | 50 | 26 |

| Parish. | 1845. | 1855. |
|---|---|---|
| Hammerfest town | 118 | 150 |
| Kistrand, &c. | 154 | 195 |
| Næsby, &c. | 205 | 276 |
| Vardö parish | — | 14 |
| — town | 8 | 14 |
| Vadsö parish | 129 | 259 |
| — town | 134 | 353 |

In the second of these two censuses, account is taken of half-bloods, whether Kwain and Norwegian, or Kwain and Lap. Only those, however, are enumerated whose father or mother was a pure Lap, or a pure Kwain; the further offspring being considered as Norwegian. This is to be regretted, as the results of a series of marriages between half-bloods would have been a valuable contribution to the physiology of the mulatto, mestizo, sambo, and other mixed races.

| Parish. | Kwain and Norwegian. | Kwain and Lap. |
|---|---|---|
| Tranö | 11 | 4 |
| Lenvik | 43 | — |
| Maalselven | 21 | 5 |
| Tromsö town | 8 | 3 |
| Sjærvö | 107 | 167 |
| Alten | 283 | 63 |
| Loppen | 34 | 9 |
| Hammerfest parish | 29 | 2 |
| — town | 1 | — |
| Kistrand | — | 8 |
| Kautakeino | 6 | — |
| Vardö parish | 5 | — |
| — town | 3 | — |
| Vadsö parish | 12 | — |
| — town | 27 | — |

The intermixture is stated to be, as a general rule, the result of legitimate marriages. Of the pure Kwains, 186 are landed proprietors.

*The Finlanders of Finskogen.*—These belong to the south rather than the north of Norway, and are old occupants of their present occupancy, which is on the Glommen, in the district of Solöer. They are far less of a separate people than the Kwains of the north. Most of them speak Norwegian. They may amount to 2000; the parishes of Grue and Hof being their localities. Finskoven, or Finskogen, means the wood (shaw) of the Fins.

The Fins of Finskogen entered Norway A. D. 1624 from Sweden. At first, they were spread over many parishes, in which they are now no longer to be distinguished. They cleared the forest by burning, and sowed their rye or oats. They used, and use, the steam-bath.

As the district of Solöer is on the boundary of Sweden and Norway, there are Kwains in the former country as well as the latter. I am unable, however, to give the details of the

*Finlanders of Sweden.*—I only note the fact of there being some.

We may now pass to the other extremity of the Duchy, and consider the parts about the metropolis of Russia. These lie in the Government of St. Petersburg; but, as this name is political rather than ethnological, the older term is the more convenient one. This is Ingria, Ingermannia, or Ingermannland, as we find the word in the Latin, the Swedish, and the German. In this the root *igr-* is, doubtless, the same as the *ukr* in the word *Ukraine*; *Ukraine*, as is well known, meaning a boundary, or limit, and corresponding most closely to our word mark, or march. In this case, Ingria and the Ukraine are the Slavonic analogues of the Welsh and Scottish marches—the occupancies of Borderers, Marchmen, or Marcomanni.

If this be the meaning of the name, it is not difficult to ascertain the area of which it represented the Marches. On the south and west were the Germans of the Baltic provinces; on the north, the Fins and Swedes of Finland. Towards the interior, extending far eastwards and far southwards, lay the Slavonians of Novorogod and Moscow; and these it was who gave the name.

I enlarge upon this, because the same root will appear over and over again—almost as often as we find a Slavonic frontier, either actually in existence, or reasonably inferred.

That Ingria was originally wholly Ugrian is obvious from its situation and history. It is partially Ugrian now.

*The Auramoiset, Savakot,* and *Izhor.*—In the Government of St. Petersburg are three populations, other than Russian, and decidedly Fin, called Auramoiset, Savakot, and Izhor. They are clearly separated, by these names, as well as by other minor details, from each other.

How far are they Karelian? Should this seem too much of a verbal question, let us put it in a real form, and ask whether they are aboriginal to the soil or decidedly recent settlers? Or are they intermediate in character; less ancient than the one, not so modern as the other would be? The Auramoiset and Savakot have most of the appearance of recent settlers. They lie most to the north, and, consequently, nearest to Finland Proper. Some of them stretch into the district of Viborg. They are closely allied to each other; the Savakot being somewhat the less rude. In some of their localities the two populations are intermixed. Other forms of the word Auramoiset are, Akramoiset and Agramoiset. Now in 1623 a portion of Viborg called Agrepää was ceded by the Swedes to the Russians, and it is believed that when this was done, the ancestors of the Auramoiset, or Agramoiset, migrated into their present seats.

When Agrepää was ceded, Savolax (another district of Viborg) was ceded also; and it is believed that when this was done, the Savakot did the same as the Auramoiset. All this is highly probable. I am not aware, however, that it is received as an actual historical fact. As an inference from the similarity of name it is by no means unexceptionable. The root *Agr*, may have originated within the government of *Ingr*-ia.

The Izhor have the most of the appearance of aborigines. They call themselves (for Izhor is the Russian name) Ingrikot. This connects them with the name of the district—Ingria. On the other hand the Vod call them Karelians.

NUMBERS IN 1848.

*Auramoiset.*

| | |
|---|---|
| Of the Government of St. Petersburg | 29,344 |
| ——————— Novogorod . | 31 |

*Savakot.*

| | |
|---|---|
| Of the Government of St. Petersburg | 42,979 |

*Izhor.*

| | |
|---|---|
| Of the Government of St. Petersburg | 17,800 |

*Isolated or Sporadic Karelians.*—South of those parts of the Duchy of Finland and the Governments of Archangel and Olonets, which constitute the proper occupancy of the Karelians, there are several groups of villages, more or less isolated, whereof the population is not only other than Russian, but where it is Fin; and where it is not only Fin, but where it is of the particular division called Karelian.

South of Lake Onega lies one of these settlements, separated from the ordinary Karelians of Olonets, and in immediate contact with a mass of Tshuds. It has also a few patches of Tshuds to the north.

South of these and south of *all* the Tshud localities, lie the Karelians of the Government of Novogorod; and south of these those of Tver and Yaroslav. There are others in the Government of St. Petersburg.

The number of the Russian Karelians is as follows:—

| | | |
|---|---|---|
| In Government of Archangel | . | 11,228 |
| ———— Novogorod | . | 27,076 (*sporadic*) |
| ———— St. Petersburg | . | 3,660 (*sporadic*) |
| ———— Tver | . | 84,638 (*sporadic*) |
| ———— Yaroslav | . | 1,283 (*sporadic*) |
| ———— Tambov | . | ? |
| ———— Olonets | . | 43,810 (*some sporadic, others not*). |

Word for word, Karelian is Coralli, the name of a population of the middle ages credited with cannibalism —"*Coralli*, gens paganorum ferocissima, carnibus crudis utens pro cibo." I also think that, word for word, it is the *Kur-* or *Cour-*, in *Kur*land (*Cour*land).

*The Tshuds.*—What is meant by the word *Tshud?* It has just been used; the populations which bore it being contrasted with the Karelians of their neighbourhood. Word for word, I, along with many others (many others holding a decidedly contrary opinion), believe it to be *Scytha*. It is a word which the Slavonians of Novogorod applied to the Non-slavonic populations with which they came in contact. We shall see its import more clearly after a notice of the Vod, and the Vesp.

(1.) *The Vod.*—A few villages within the circles of Oranienbaum and Yamburg, in the Government of St. Petersburg, and in the district called Ingria, Ingermannia, or Ingermannland, are the occupancies of a small population whose dialect, dress, and manners have presented sufficient peculiarity to draw the attention of more than one investigator. At first they were pronounced to be a separate people; but this was by an inquirer who knew nothing of either the Estonian or the Fin; but who judged of their isolation from a specimen of their language in the shape of a song which he was unable to construe. The men and women who spoke this called themselves Vadjalaiset, the plural of Vadjalaine, both of which names are so thoroughly Fin in their form that they tell their own story. Other forms were Vadi, and Vaihsi, the latter being the adverb. *Loquerisne Voticé* is *tunnet pajattaa Vaihsi*, a fact which is by no means without its importance as an instrument of criticism, as will be seen hereafter. The Fins call them Vatjalaiset, the Swedes Voter, or Vatlanders; their country being Vatland. The Russian designates them as Tshud.

In 1848 the whole number of Vod amounted to 5148 souls; a small number to represent the original population of Ingria—for this the Vod are. They are the Fins whose area most closely touches the present capital of Russia; intermediate in their ethnological characters, as well as their geographical position to the Finlanders on one side, and the Estonians on the other.

The name appears in the early annals of Russia. They resisted for a time the Slavonians of Novogorod; though before the end of the thirteenth century they were reduced. Their area, then, formed one of the five divisions of the Novogorod domain, and was called the Vodskaya pyatina or the Vod fifth.

It is in parishes of Kattila and Soikena where the existing remains of the Vod are to be found. Of their language there is a grammar and glossary by Ahlqvist, published within the last two years at Helsingfors, and, on their relations to the other members of the Fin stock, a valuable paper by Sjögren in the Memoirs of the Academy of St. Petersburg.

*Vod Wedding Song.*

| | |
|---|---|
| Neitsüeni ainagoni ! | Single, dear daughter-in-law ! |
| Menet kaiwolle, kanani ! | Thou goest to the spring, chicken ! |
| Wesitielle, wierakkoni ! | The water-way, dear stranger ! |
| Alä waad warjoa wetee ! | Give way to the reflection on the water |
| Wesi wetab kaiuiu. | For the water takes away thy charms. |
| Meill on naised nagrajad ; | We have fair wives ; |
| Meill on cinainaad eliäd. | We have fair meadows ; |
| Alä mene kurjossa kujalle ! | Keep aloof from the house of the flatterer. |
| Pääpaikas parapi muita, | Bright is the cap of thy head, |
| Körja muita körkääpi. | Higher than that of all the rest. |
| Neitsüseni ainagoni ! | Single, dear daughter-in-law ! |
| Neitsüt aianagoanoni ! | Dear daughter-in-law, single only ! |
| Alä tuskaa tuloa, | Never may thy coming rue thee, |
| Kao katsche lähtego ! | Never may thy journey trouble ! |
| Emmä pannu pakasialle, | I did not betrothe you to a deserter, |
| Emmä wienüd wöhkasuolle, | Took you not over the mossy moor, |
| Panimma poisile üwälle. | But I gave you to the good youth. |

(2.) *The Vesp.*—At some distance to the east of the Vod lie the Vesp, in the Governments of Novogorod and Olonets; some on the banks of Lake Onega, some on the White Lake, or Bielozero. When Sjögren, in 1830 or 1832, described them, he carried their numbers as high as 21,000. In 1848 they were reckoned at about 15,600.

The ancestors of the Russians who, in the eleventh and twelfth centuries, had to make their way, and keep their footing in their country, sword in hand, called them Yam, or Yem. In 1042, Vladimer, the son of Yaroslav, marched an army against them, fought a battle, and won it. His success, however, was incomplete, for he lost his horses by a murrain. The Yam, however, though vigorous in their resistance, were eventually reduced; their present representatives being the fifteen thousand and odd Vesp in the aforesaid localities.

The Russians call them Tshud, just as they do the Vod.

The Vod, like the Vesp, are connected with the Yam; for we have seen that one of their localities is in the circle of Yamburg.

The language of the Vesp and Vod are, according to the decision of the most competent Fin scholars, connected by special affinities.

The names, however, of the two forms of speech are different. The term by which Tshuds of Novogorod and Olonets designate their speech is Luudin kiele, the Luudin language, or Lingua Ludina. Upon the similarity of this to the word Latina I say nothing. Latium is a long way from Lake Onega. Its likeness, however, to the name of what was once the contiguous language of the Lets and Lithuan-ians deserves notice. So does the word Vais. The Ves are mentioned by Nestor: the Vesi, by Sidonius Apollinaris, as members of the armies of Attila.

*Numbers.*

| | | |
|---|---|---|
| *Vod*— | Of the Government of St. Petersburg | 5,148 |
| *Vesp* | — . . | 8,550 |
| | — . . | 7,067 |
| | | 15,617 |

Now comes the practical application of the difference between the Tavastrians and the Karelians. The former are supposed to represent the older inhabitants of the parts nearest to Novogorod and St. Petersburg, to be the *Yam*, or *Ham*ailaiset, and to form a class to which the so-called Tshuds, the Vod and Vesp, belong. The Kirialaiset, on the other hand, are colonists from a more distant part of the Fin area, and of comparatively recent origin.

## CHAPTER XX.

### The Ugrians of Estonia or Rahwas.—The Liefs.

ESTONIA differs from Finland in its frontier; inasmuch as the Ugrians which occupy Estonia are in contact with the Germans and Lets, rather than with the Swedes and Laps. For this reason the foreign influences have been German rather than Swedish. The difference, however, is of no great importance. The alphabet is Roman, the religion Protestant; just as it was in Finland.

At one time, when all Ingria was Ugrian, the Estonian and Fin populations must have been in contact. The Vod, at the present time, is believed to represent one of the intermediate forms of speech.

The Estonians call themselves Rahwa, and their country Marahwa, or Rahwa-land; the parts north of the river Salis being their chief area.

| | |
|---|---|
| In Liefland the Rahwa number . . | 355,216 |
| — Estonia ———————— . . | 252,608 |
| — Vitepsk ———————— . . | 9,936 |
| — Pskov ———————— . . | 8,000 |
| — St. Petersburg ———— . . | 7,736 |
| | 633,496 |

Some of the purest blood in Europe must be to be

found amongst the southern, the eastern, and the central Rahwas; the admixture of foreign elements being greatest on the northern and western frontiers. In the south, too, and the east, the greatest number of national characteristics present themselves. This they do in the way of language, in the way of physiognomy, and in the way of manners and customs. In the ordinary works on comparative philology, the Estonian language is divided into two main dialects; one with Reval, the other with Dorpat as its centre; so that we hear of the Dorpatian and the Revalian forms of speech as paramount. I believe, however, that almost every parish presents some peculiarities, and I am no means sure that the distribution of the numerous dialects and sub-dialects thus developed corresponds with the usual classification. Nevertheless, it represents the written language; for there is the Reval New Testament and the Dorpat New Testament exhibiting notable differences of idiom.

A love for song and music is exhibited throughout the Rahwa country; and of this we may judge by more than one collection of songs, legends, charms, nursery rhymes, and the like. The harp was the instrument—with wires, not strings; the harp or *kandel.* With this the bards, the exact analogues of the Gaelic bards of almost our own days, musical and locomotive, used to wander from place to place, as the harvest-home, or the wedding-feast, might tempt them. There are none such now alive, the last having died in 1813. He had no fixed residence; but was known, and welcomed, whithersoever he chose to roam, as the *wanna laulumees,* or the old singer.

Neuss, whose account I am following, maintains that the true Estonian popular minstrelsy died out with him; perhaps a little before his time. At the beginning of the last century it flourished. Towards the end of it it declined. At the beginning of the last century religious and other compositions after German models were afloat in Estonia; but only as oil on water. They touched the native style; but without affecting it. Now, however, they are imitated; and just in proportion as these prevail, the older poetry dies off.

This is the first time we have had an opportunity of enlarging upon the character of the Ugrian poetry. The notice, indeed, has yet to take its full dimensions and prominence. We shall, ere long, talk of epics, and the like. In Estonia, we can only find tales, wedding songs, harvest songs, songs for the sowing-time, riddles, and the like; a little in the way of narrative; a little redolent of heathenism—much what we expect. Elements, too, we find of what might be developed into the Satyric drama; if we had Greeks instead of Ugrians to develope it.

Those who apply classical names to modern phenomena describe the Ugrian metres in general as trochaic; sometimes being dactylic, but never iambic. This means that the accent is on the first, third, and fifth syllables, rather than the second, fourth, and sixth; a fact which arises out of the structure of the language.

The common formula is – ⏑, – ⏑, – ⏑, – ⏑; sometimes with – ⏑⏑ instead of – ⏑, more rarely with – –, or the so-called spondee; *e. g.*

Töulis rebbust Körge-sare,
Muña walgest Tüttar-sare,
Muña tumest teised sared.

or,

Kotkad lensid Some-male,
Some-maalta Saksa-male.

Add to this that, within a certain interval, a certain number of words must begin either with a vowel, or, if with a consonant, with the same; as

> Minna *s*ulg ei annud *s*uda
> Egga *p*ärg ei *p*öörnud *p*eada.

This is the alliteration of the old German metres; almost to its minutest details. It is held, however, to be no more German in origin than the German is Ugrian.

Archaic words are, in Estonia, as elsewhere, poetical; a fact which creates trouble and perplexity to modern commentators; indeed, many expressions which have wholly dropped out of the current language are to be found in the songs. Like the ballad-mongers of our own country, who, when they wanted a double rhyme and could not get it out of a monosyllabic ending, would tack on an *-a*, and write

> With cloves and nutmegs from the line-*a*,
> And even oranges from China,—

the Estonian changes *isfal*, *mind*, &c., into *isfal-a*, *mind-a*, &c.

Notwithstanding the little communication between the different sections and sub-sections of the Estonian population, the same details appear in different parts of the country with slight modification. The story, of which the venue lies, in one district, on such or such a hill or bank, lies in another in such a one. *Mutatis mutandis*, the same tale is told. This is evidence in favour of the antiquity of the poetry altogether; and as such it has been received. Some of it points to the times of Estonian heathendom—some, but not much; the little that does so being obscure.

Perhaps the face of the country itself shows the most remains of paganism. Finland has its numerous *pyhävesi*, *pyhäjärvi*, and *pyhäjoki*, or the *holy waters*, *holy lakes*, and *holy rivers*. So has Estonia. In Estonia there is a particular stream which has long been the object of reverence, the Wohhanda. It joins the Meddä, which falls into the Peipus Lake. It is, of course, a *pöha jögge*, the Estonian for *pyhäjoki*. In the olden time, no Estonian would fell any tree that grew on its banks, or break one of the reeds that fringed its watercourse. If he did he would die within the year. The brook, along with the spring, that gave it birth, was purified periodically, and it was believed, that if dirt were thrown into either, bad weather would be the result. Gutslaf tells a tale of a bold, bad German, whose hardihood and avarice induced him to build a mill across its stream, and to stop its waters with his mill-dam. Soon after the grinding had begun, a bad season set in, and lasted as long as the mill stood, which was only until the peasants of the parish and parts around became incendiaries, and burnt the whole establishment down to the very ground. Earlier still, tradition speaks of offerings—sometimes of little children—having been made to Wohhanda; the river-god being a little man in blue and yellow stockings, sometimes visible to mortal eye, resident in the stream, and in the habit of occasionally rising out of it.

| English. | Fin. | Karelian. | Olonets. | Ingrian.* | Estonian. |
|---|---|---|---|---|---|
| *Man* (*vir*) | miös | mijazh | mes | mês | mees |
| —— (*homo*) | ingémin | inegmine | mes | mês | innimęne |
| *Head* | pöja | pijä | pä | pä | peja |
| *Hair* | iwusa | tukka | tukka | —— | karw |
| *Eye* | silme | silmä | silmä | silmä | silm |
| *Ear* | kyrwa | korwa | korwu | körwa | körw |
| *Nose* | njena | nena | nena | nenä | ninna |
| *Mouth* | suu | shun | su | sû | sun |
| *Tongue* | kieli | kijali | keli | ćèli | keel |

* Or Vod.

| English. | Fin. | Karelian. | Olonets. | Ingrian. | Estonian. |
|---|---|---|---|---|---|
| *Hand* | kesi | käsi | käsi | čäsi | kässi |
| *Foot* | jalka | jalja | jalgu | jalka | jalk |
| *Blood* | weri | weri | weri | weri | werri |
| *Sun* | pöiwa | päiwäne | pewen | päiwa | paw |
| *Moon* | kou | kuudoma | ku | kû | kuu |
| *Star* | tögyt | tägti | techte | —— | tjecht |
| *Fire* | tuli | tuli | tuli | tuli | tulli |
| *Water* | wesi | wesi | wesi | wesi | wesi |
| *Tree* | pún | puu | pu | pû | pu |
| *Stone* | kiwi | kiwi | kiwi | čiwi | kiwwi |
| *One* | yks | juksy | juksi | ühsi | yks |
| *Two* | kaks | kaksi | kaksi | kahsi | kaks |
| *Three* | kolmi | kolmje | kolshe | kölme | kolm |
| *Four* | nelja | nellä | nelli | nell'a | nelje |
| *Five* | wisi | wiisi | wizhi | wisi | wis |
| *Six* | kusi | kuuzhi | kusi | kûsi | kuus |
| *Seven* | seitseman | zhitshemän | setshemi | seitsê' | seitse |
| *Eight* | kadeksän | kagekshan | kacsak | kahetsê' | kattesa |
| *Nine* | ydeksän | iujekshan | igokse | ühetsê' | uttesa |
| *Ten* | kymmemen | kymmen | kümmene | čümmê' | kuemme |

*The Lief.*—The Lief are the remains of the population that gave its name to Liefland or Livonia.

They amount to

| | |
|---|---|
| In Livonia . . . . . | 22 |
| — Courland . . . . . | 2052 |
| | 2074 |

Word for word, I believe Lief to be Lap. I also believe it to be the element Lem of the word Lemovii in Tacitus. The Estonians, however, are not the Æstyii of that writer.

That Æstyii, Estonia, Esten, and Estland, are the same words I believe; also believing that they all mean the eastern country. I only doubt about the eastern end of the Baltic having been the same in the time of Tacitus as now. In the time of Tacitus it must have begun at Memel, where the coast-line turns suddenly to the north. *Now* it means the Gulf of Finland. If so,

The Æstyii of Tacitus were Old Prussians.
— Lemovii —————————— Lief.
— Rugii —————————— Rahwas.
— Fenni —————————— Laps.
— Sitones —————————— Kwains.

How far the names were native is another question. One of them, Æstyii, is German; the oldest German gloss we have. It is the 'Ωστιαῖοι of Strabo speaking of the voyage of Pytheas.

# CHAPTER XXI.

The Laplanders—of Russia, Sweden, Norway.

*Laps of Russia.*—A Lap calls himself Sabme, a Russian calls him Lopar. The Laps of Russia, entirely confined to the Government of Archangel, amount to about 289. They are all Christians (more or less imperfect), of the Greek Church. This is the point in which they most especially differ from

*The Laps of Sweden,* who are Lutheran Christians, and occupants of Lapmark. They differ from the Laps of Norway in being called Laps, and in their dialect.

*The Laps of Norway* differ from those of Sweden in their dialect, and in being called Fins. It is the Norwegians, however, who call them so; though the name is occasionally adopted by the Laps themselves. They apply it with satisfaction, perhaps with pride. The Kwain repudiates it. A Lap of Norway lives in Finmark, Lapmark being the occupancy of the Swedish Sabme. For Sabme is the true name. Word for word, it is the first part of Suome-laine.

For the most northern population of Europe the Laps are favoured in respect to climate; no part of the world equally arctic being so warm—or, rather, so little cold. It is only when we approach the North Cape that we get beyond the region of trees—the birch being found as high as N. L. 70-71°; the Scotch fir up to 69-70°; and the spruce fir to 67°. The elm, lime, oak, hazel, and alder have, however, long been passed; so has the latitude at which fruit ripens. On the other hand, as far north as 67°, barley ripens at the level of 800 feet. Potatoes, too, pay for cultivation even farther north. So do cabbages, turnips, spinach, and carrots.

The Lap, except so far as he has adopted the industry of his neighbours, is a nomad, essentially so. His country is that of the reindeer-moss, and the reindeer that feeds on it. Its streams are prolific with salmon; but the main aliment is the flesh of the reindeer, itself migratory.

The Sabme may fairly be looked upon as the least industrial, and the least civilized tribes of Christian Europe. They are herdsmen rather than agriculturists. The Norwegian of their neighbourhood plants potatoes, the Finlander keeps cows, but the Lap attaches himself to the reindeer and adapts himself to its habits.

Essentially nomad as they are, the habits of the Sabme have been considerably modified by the influences of the populations with which they come in contact; and it cannot be denied that, upon the whole, the attention bestowed upon them by the different Governments under which they live, has been, as things go with the weaker populations of the world in general, praiseworthy, even if insufficient. I state this with more confidence respecting the Norwegian than the Swedish, and with more confidence respecting the Swedish than the Russian, Laps. The language has been reduced to writing, and that well. As the adapters of the Lap alphabet had no preconceived views in the way of etymology, they have spelt the speech as they found it, created new letters when they were necessary, expelled old ones when superfluous, and limited the power of each sign to the expression of a single sound, each sound having also its appropriate sign. The effect of this is, that, other things being equal, a Lap child learns to read easier than another.

The Christianity of the Laps is of the same imperfect character with their industry and culture. The original heathenism of the country still tinges the better creed. The old creed shows itself through the new, and the superstitions of the Sabme of the time anterior to Christianity are seen almost as clearly and transparently now as they were seen in the days of their unmodified paganism. There was not much to get rid of, and of that little more than a fair portion has been retained. There was not much to get rid of, for the Sabme superstitions were simple, and the mythology far from elaborate. Neither does it seem to have been wholly native. At least *one* of their objects of veneration has a Norwegian name.

The being who has the Norwegian name is the Storjunker, pronounced Stor-yunker; a name which means *great noble*. A full-grown reindeer, with full-sized antlers, used to be the proper sacrifice to the Storjunker. A thread was put through his ear, and this thread had to be a red one. No other colour would suit the Storjunker's reindeer. When the feast was over, and the flesh had been eaten by the feasters, the antlers were fixed in the ground so as to mark a certain space—a space which was thus made holy; women, most especially, being forbidden to approach it.

Next amongst the Lap gods to the Storjunker, was Tiermes. The third was Baiwe. The rites of Tiermes are much the same as those of the Storjunker, but those of Baiwe exhibit a difference in some of their details. The string which is put through the ear of the victim is a *white* one. A red one would be out of place. The reindeer is a *young* one. An old one would be inappropriate. Then, as the young reindeer has no antlers, the sacred enclosures of deers' horns are wanting to the sacrificial grounds of Baiwe, or the Sun; for that is the object symbolized.

But there was a deity higher than any of these, who seem to have been mere subordinates. This was Jubmel—but more will be said of Jubmel hereafter.

In one sense the old Lap religion was a religion without a priesthood. There were no roofed temples, no officiating ministers. The head of the family performed his rites himself. His proceedings were as follows. About a bow-shot from his tent he chose a convenient piece of ground and marked it out by rows of boughs; of the birch-tree in summer, of the fir in winter. The area within was holy ground; pre-eminently holy, and, like most of the Lap enclosures, forbidden to females. The path from this to the tent was also marked out by branches. In the centre stood the representative of the deity—of wood or stone as the case might be; of *wood* for Tiermes, who was thence called the *wooden*, of stone for the Storjunker, who was similarly known as the *stone*, god. Wood and stone were the materials; to which the workmanship was scarcely equal. Indeed, there was none, or next to none. Instead of fashioning an image with his own hands, the Lap thought himself lucky if he found one ready-made, the workmanship of Chance or Nature. Hence, if a birch-tree grew crooked and contorted about the roots, if it were knobby and knotty on the stem, if its branches grew in abnormal clusters, it was looked upon as a deity already represented. The same with stones. Those that were water-worn, rubbed, or drilled into strange shapes, became divinities; or rather, the divinity grew out of the shape of the symbol. If it suggested a bird, the idea of the Storjunker became birdlike; quadrupedal if the likeness were that of a beast. He would, too, be a fish, as often birch-roots grew fish-shaped. The same with Tiermes. He might fly one year, swim the next, and go upon four legs the third; or, as the sacrifices took place twice a year, he might be a pike at Midsummer, and an otter at Christmas. A piece of reindeer flesh was the offering to him; the heart or liver by preference.

When the worship took a more public character, and approached the form of a festival, the drum came in request; the drum being the most important of all the articles in a Laplander's pontifical *apparatus*. This was a skin drawn across a frame of birch-wood; rudely painted with figures of the chief deities. In the middle was fixed a ring with bobbins (much like those used in lace-making) attached to it. The drum is beaten and the bobbin dances about. The beating leaves off and the bobbin lies quiet. The drummer then sees on whose figure it lies. If on that of Baiwe, Baiwe has to be honoured; if on that of Tiermes or the Storjunker, it is Tiermes or the Storjunker accordingly.

These are the most specific of the Lap superstitions. That certain wizards have the power of selling favourable winds to sailors is believed not only amongst the Laps themselves, but by the Norwegians, the Swedes, and the Russians of their neighbourhood.

The most characteristic, perhaps, of their habits or accomplishments, is what we may call by a name coined for the occasion—*she-running*. The *skide* (pronounced *she*) is a snow-skate upwards of six feet long. Up-hill the Lap toils with a stick: down-hill he drives with the rapidity of an arrow. The Tshapodzhir does the same.

I have said that the civilization of the countries to which they belong has told upon the Laps. I believe this to be the case in both Russia and Scandinavia. In Norway, however, we can measure the extent to which it has done so; this meaning the extent to which, within the last ten years, a nomad population has become stationary.

| Parishes and Towns. | In 1845. Laps. In fixed habitations | In 1845. Laps. Nomadic. | In 1845. Laps. Total. | In the year Laps. In fixed habitations | In the year Laps. Nomadic. | In the year Laps. Total. |
|---|---|---|---|---|---|---|
| Röros | — | 31 | 31 | — | 45 | 45 |
| Trondhyem Town | — | — | — | — | — | 31 |
| Sælbo | — | 44 | 44 | — | — | — |
| Stördal | — | 10 | 10 | 16 | — | 16 |
| Skogn | — | — | — | 10 | — | 10 |
| Værdal | — | 7 | 7 | — | — | — |
| Ytterö | — | — | — | 12 | — | 12 |
| Inderö | 2 | — | 2 | — | — | — |
| Sparbo | 8 | — | 8 | 14 | — | 14 |
| Stod | 12 | — | 12 | 17 | — | 17 |
| Snasen | — | 41 | 41 | — | — | — |
| Beitstaden | 9 | — | 9 | 5 | — | 5 |
| Overhalden | — | — | — | — | — | 2 |
| Grong | 8 | 89 | 97 | — | 97 | 97 |
| Fosnæs | — | — | — | — | 14 | 14 |
| Brönö | 6 | — | 6 | 1 | — | 1 |
| Bindalen | — | — | — | — | 39 | 39 |
| Alstadhoug | 28 | — | 28 | — | — | 36 |
| Vefsen | 253 | — | 253 | — | — | — |
| Nesne | — | — | — | 2 | — | 2 |
| Kemnes | 47 | 36 | 83 | 38 | 27 | 65 |
| Rödö | 25 | — | 25 | 29 | — | 29 |
| Mo | 59 | — | 59 | 26 | 77 | 103 |
| Gildeskaal | 4 | — | 4 | — | — | 21 |
| Skydrstad | 240 | — | 240 | 230 | — | 230 |
| Saltdalen | 119 | — | 119 | 94 | — | 94 |
| Bodö | 53 | — | 53 | 49 | — | 49 |
| Folden | 60 | — | 60 | 69 | — | 69 |
| Stegen | 9 | — | 9 | 1 | — | 1 |
| Hamerö | 54 | — | 54 | 52 | — | 52 |
| Lödingen | 140 | 9 | 149 | — | — | 163 |
| Lofoten | 522 | — | 522 | 570 | 7 | 577 |
| Hadsel | 80 | — | 80 | 84 | — | 84 |
| Bö | 28 | — | 28 | 34 | — | 34 |
| Oxnes | — | — | — | — | — | 98 |
| Dverberg | — | 5 | 5 | — | 8 | 8 |
| Vaagen | — | 14 | 14 | — | 14 | 14 |
| Borge | — | — | — | — | — | 8 |
| Trondenes | 202 | — | 202 | 231 | — | 231 |
| Kraedfyord | 112 | — | 112 | 118 | — | 118 |
| Ibestad | 653 | — | 653 | 734 | — | 734 |
| Tranö | 207 | — | 207 | 235 | — | 235 |
| Lenvik } | 329 | — | 329 | 380 | — | 380 |
| Maalselven } | | | | 109 | — | 109 |

of the Census 1855.

| Social Condition. Heads of Families. | | | | | | | Besides of mixed origin, and included in the Norwegian population. |
|---|---|---|---|---|---|---|---|
| Landed proprietors. | Farmers. | Cotters with land. | Cotters without land. | New Settlers in waste lands. | Mechanics. | Captains of vessels. | Norwego-Lapps. |
| — | — | — | — | — | — | — | — |
| — | — | — | — | — | — | — | — |
| — | — | — | 2 | — | — | — | — |
| — | — | — | — | — | — | — | — |
| — | 1 | — | — | — | — | — | — |
| — | — | — | — | — | — | — | — |
| — | — | — | — | — | — | — | — |
| — | — | — | 4 | — | — | — | — |
| — | — | — | 2 | — | — | — | — |
| — | — | — | — | — | — | — | — |
| — | — | — | 1 | — | — | — | — |
| — | 20 | — | 1 | — | — | — | — |
| — | — | — | — | — | — | — | — |
| — | — | — | — | — | — | — | — |
| — | — | — | — | — | — | — | — |
| — | — | — | — | — | — | — | — |
| — | — | — | 1 | — | 2 | — | 10 |
| — | — | — | — | — | — | — | — |
| — | — | — | — | — | — | — | — |
| — | — | 8 | 4 | — | — | — | — |
| — | — | — | — | — | — | — | 27 |
| — | 19 | — | 1 | — | — | — | 7 |
| 1 | — | 1 | 1 | — | — | — | 13 |
| — | — | — | — | — | — | — | 43 |
| 2 | 4 | 3 | 13 | — | — | — | 31 |
| — | — | — | — | — | — | — | 10 |
| 1 | 6 | 1 | 2 | — | — | — | 87 |
| — | — | — | — | — | — | — | 8 |
| — | — | — | — | — | — | — | 3 |
| 7 | 6 | 8 | 8 | — | — | — | — |
| — | — | — | — | — | — | — | — |
| — | 8 | 13 | — | — | — | — | 19 |
| — | 3 | 2 | — | — | — | — | — |
| — | 16 | 1 | 4 | — | — | — | — |
| — | — | — | 4 | — | — | — | — |
| — | — | — | — | — | — | — | — |
| 1 | — | 29 | 4 | 9 | — | — | 62 |
| 14 | 4 | 1 | 7 | 3 | — | — | 32 |
| L.* 41 | 27 | 28 | 32 | 12 | — | — | — |
| F. 1 | 1 | 1 | 1 | — | — | — | — |
| — | — | — | — | — | — | — | 19 |
| L. 16 | 25 | 6 | 26 | 5 | — | — | 78 |
| F. 1 | — | — | — | — | — | — | |
| L. 11 | 4 | — | 6 | 2 | — | — | 14 |
| F. 6 | 1 | 2 | 8 | 1 | — | — | |

* L. means Lap; F., Fin, or Kwain.

| Parishes and Towns. | In 1845. Laps. | | | In the year Laps. | | |
|---|---|---|---|---|---|---|
| | In fixed habitations. | Nomadic. | Total. | In fixed habitations. | Nomadic. | Total. |
| Tromsö Parish | 600 | 10 | 610 | — | — | 720 |
| Tromsö Town | 3 | — | 3 | — | — | — |
| Karlsö | 844 | — | 844 | 708 | — | 908 |
| Lyngen | 1460 | — | 1460 | 1601 | — | 1601 |
| Skyservö | 1447 | — | 1447 | 1620 | — | 1620 |
| Alten | 1069 | — | 1069 | 1019 | — | 1019 |
| Loppen | 550 | — | 550 | 569 | — | 569 |
| Hammerfest Parish | 1011 | — | 1011 | 1166 | — | 1166 |
| Hammerfest Town | — | — | — | — | — | — |
| Kistrand } | 664 | 1026 | 1690 | 763 | 405 | 1168 |
| Koutokeino } | | | | 122 | 705 | 827 |
| Lebesby } | 919 | 116 | 1035 | 233 | 20 | 253 |
| Næsseby } | | | | 1303 | 85 | 1388 |
| Vardö Parish | — | — | — | — | — | 65 |
| Vardö Town | 4 | — | 4 | 5 | — | 5 |
| Vadsö Parish | 1093 | 93 | 1186 | 564 | 110 | 674 |
| Vadsö Town | — | — | — | 3 | — | 3 |

That the Swedes and Norwegians have encroached upon the Sabme is certain; indeed, the belief that the whole of the Scandinavian peninsula was once Lap is as general as it is well-founded. How far, however, the eastern members of the family may, by extending southwards, have occupied portions of the present Duchy of Finland is a question upon which less evidence has been brought to bear. It has been thought that the conflict between the men of Kalevala and Pohjola, the subject of a poem which will be specially considered in the sequel, expresses the struggles between the Laps and Finlanders. Be it so. That the evidence of their language suggests a more southern locality than the present for the northmost Finlanders is certain. The differences of dialect of the Census 1855.

| Social Condition. Heads of Families. | | | | | | | Besides of mixed origin, and included in the Norwegian population. |
|---|---|---|---|---|---|---|---|
| Landed proprietors. | Farmers. | Cotters with land. | Cotters without land. | New Settlers in waste lands. | Mechanics. | Captains of vessels. | Norwego-Laps. |
| — | — | — | — | — | — | — | — |
| — | — | — | — | — | — | — | — |
| — | — | — | — | — | — | — | 8 |
| L.* 23 | 127 | 43 | 129 | 8 | — | — | |
| F. 19 | 42 | 22 | 66 | 2 | — | — | |
| — | — | — | — | — | — | — | 116 |
| L. 162 | 16 | — | 7 | 7 | — | — | |
| F. 84 | 2 | 2 | 2 | 16 | — | — | 28 |
| L. 60 | — | 2 | 30 | 6 | — | — | 19 |
| F. 1 | — | — | 3 | 8 | — | — | |
| — | — | — | — | — | — | — | 50 |
| — | — | — | — | — | 3 | 6 | 2 |
| L. 154 | — | — | 2 | 1 | — | — | 12 |
| F. 51 | — | — | 2 | 1 | — | — | |
| — | — | — | — | — | — | — | — |
| L. 8 | — | 26 | 11 | — | — | — | 8 |
| F. — | — | 1 | — | 4 | — | — | |
| L. 236 | — | — | 4 | — | — | — | — |
| F. 14 | — | — | 2 | 19 | — | — | — |
| — | — | — | — | — | — | — | 11 |
| — | — | — | — | — | — | — | — |
| L. — | — | — | — | 113 | — | — | 12 |
| F. 10 | — | — | — | 31 | | | |
| — | — | — | — | — | — | — | — |

increase as we go south. The affinities with the Estonians indicate a southern origin; as do those with the Votiak.

This northward movement of the Finlanders implies the obliteration of more than one population, which may fairly be supposed to have been transitional or intermediate; a fact to be remembered whenever we speculate upon the difference, in physical form, between the Laps and the Finlanders.

Of this difference, full enough has been made. The Laps are a short people. The Finlanders are, by no means, tall. Nevertheless, they are the taller of the two; being better housed, better fed. Between the skulls of a

* L. means Lap; F., Fin, or Kwain.

Lap, a Finlander, and an Estonian, there is but little difference. All are broad rather than long. In all the occipital protuberance is slight, the orbits large, the nasal bones more depressed than elevated.

Of the external form of the Finlanders there are many individuals who have had means of judging for themselves, and that without visiting Finland. The prisoners, who, during the late war with Russia, lay at Lewes, were numerous enough to serve as fair specimens of their countrymen in general. They were undersized and small-boned. Strong beards were rare; and there was, with many of the men, a peculiarly glabrous skin. The complexion varied. Of red-haired heads I saw fewer than the current accounts had led me to expect. Of truly Mongol faces there were a few. There were an equal number that might be found amongst the agricultural labourers of England. The hair was brown, the eyes generally dark. Upon the whole, however, few would be mistaken for anything but what they were. Less European than the Swedes and Norwegians, less Asiatic than the true Mongols, they were more like Slavonians than aught else except Fins. They were almost all Tavastrians.

| English. | Lap. | Fin. | Norwegian. |
|---|---|---|---|
| *Man (vir)* | olma | mios | mana |
| —— *(homo)* | almaz | ingemin | menneske |
| *Head* | oike | pöja | hoved |
| *Eye* | tjülme | silmo | öje |
| *Ear* | pelje | kyrwa | ohn |
| *Nose* | njuone | njena | näse |
| *Mouth* | nälme | suu | mund |
| *Tongue* | njuoktem | kieli | tunge |
| *Hand* | ket | kesi | hand |
| *Foot* | juolke | jalka | föd |
| *Sun* | peiwe | poiwa | sol |
| *Moon* | mano | kou | maane |
| *Star* | tüste | tögit | sterne |

| English. | Lap. | Fin. | Norwegian. |
|---|---|---|---|
| *Fire* | tollo | tuli | ild |
| *Water* | tätse | wesi | vand |
| *Stone* | kedke | kiwi | sten |
| *One* | akt | yks | en |
| *Two* | kwekt | kaks | to |
| *Three* | kolm | kolmi | tre |
| *Four* | nelje | nelja | fire |
| *Five* | wit | wisi | fern |
| *Six* | kot | kusi | seks |
| *Seven* | kjeta | seitseman | syv |
| *Eight* | kaktsat | kadeksan | otte |
| *Nine* | aktfe | ydeksan | ny |
| *Ten* | tokke | kymmemen | ti |

Until the publication of Rask's grammar, the Fin and Lap languages were supposed to be less alike in their structure than in their vocabulary. Especially was it thought, that out of the fifteen cases in Fin, the Laps had only eight or nine. Traces, however, of the others were found by those who knew how to look for them; and, at the present time, both languages being well known, the evidence of the grammarian, as to their close affinity, is admitted to agree with that of the lexicographer.

In a sort of preface to one of the earliest vernacular translations of the Psalms of David, a copy of Fin verses, by Bishop Agricola, enumerates the heathen gods and goddesses, who, notwithstanding the nominal Christianity of the Finlanders, were still more or less believed in. It is a list which contains more than twenty names. In a poem published within the last thirty years a great number of these names re-appears. In other words, there was a pagan element in Finland in the sixteenth century, and there is a pagan element in the nineteenth. There is more of this in Lapland, and much of it in Estonia.

Towards the end of the last century these remains of

the original heathenhood commanded the especial attention of Ganander and Porthan; the latter the founder of the present school of mythological investigators. Then followed Topelius, who gave the germs of a system by arranging the legends round their several subjects. He collected, for instance, those that appertained to a fabulous individual named Wainamoinen. Lönröt went further, both in the collection of legendary poems and in their arrangement. The result is the Kalevala; a Fin Ossian with fair claims to authenticity. It grew into form gradually and was the work of more investigators than one. It is a pagan poem in respect to its machinery, though not without allusions to Christianity. Towards the end the names of even Herod and the Virgin Mary (Marietta) appear; but this is in a kind of appendix to the poem, rather than the poem itself.

The Kalevala is a series of rhapsodies; the word being used in that technical sense in which it appears in the numerous writings on the Homeric poems. It is in the language of the present time, and the metre of Longfellow's Hiawatha; or rather, Hiawatha is in the metre of the Kalevala. The heroes are Wainamoinen, Illmarinen, and Lemminkainen, whose actions, like those of Diomed or Ulysses in the Iliad, though separate, are still capable of being connected in such a manner as to give unity to the poem in which they are exhibited. The scenes are, for the most part, in Kalevala and Pohjola. All three of the above-named agents agree in acting more or less in concert. They represent Kalevala as opposed to Pohjola. Those who love to find the symbolic in the material may make out of this dualism an antagonism, and out of that antagonism a moral, a meteorological, or a historical struggle, according as they see in it the contrast between good and evil, summer and winter, light and darkness, the Laplanders and the Finlanders. For our present purpose it is enough to consider it simply as a vehicle for so much fantastic narrative.

There is a contest, and a long one—not the less remarkable for the negative fact of its being, comparatively, bloodless. There are fights in it more than one; but not fights with the sword or spear. It is the skill of the enchanter that is most particularly tried; the skill of the man of powerful spells and sweet sounds, the skill of the man of a crafty head and a cunning hand, the skill of the musician and the metallurgist. Wainamoinen is much of a smith, and more of a harper. Illmarinen is most of a smith. Lemminkainen is much of a harper and little of a smith. The hand of the daughter of the mistress of Pohjola is what, each and all, the three sons of Kalevala strive to win; a hand which the mother of the owner will give to any one who can make for her, and for Pohjola, Sampo. Wainamoinen will not: but he knows of one who will—Illmarinen. Illmarinen makes it, and gains the mother's consent thereby. But the daughter requires another service. He must hunt down the elk of Tuonela. We now see the way in which the actions of the heroes are, at one and the same time, separate and connected. Wainamoinen tries; Illmarinen tries (and eventually wins); Lemminkainen tries. There are alternations of friendship and enmity. Sampo is made and presented. It is then wanted back again.

"Give us," says Wainamoinen, "if not the whole, half."

"Sampo," says Louhi, the mistress of Pohjola, "cannot be divided."

"Then let us steal it," says one of the three. "Agreed," say the other two.

So the rape of Sampo takes place. It is taken from

Pohjola, whilst the owners are sung to sleep by the harp of Lemminkainen; sung to sleep, but not for so long a time as to allow the robbers to escape. They are sailing Kalevalaward, when Louhi comes after them on the wings of the wind, and raises a storm. Sampo is broken and thrown into the sea. Bad days now come. There is no sun, no moon. Illmarinen makes them of silver and gold. He had previously made his second wife (for he lost his first) out of the same metals. However, Sampo is washed up, and made whole. Good days come. The sun and moon shine as before, and the sons of Kalevala possess Sampo.

But what is Sampo? "A temple," say some. Others say a "talisman." Others, a "mill." Wainamoinen found it hard to make. Speculators on Wainamoinen find it hard to understand. Let us take the order for it simply as so much fantastic narrative. It was to be made out of a swan's feather, a lock of wool, and a grain of corn, and it was to bring prosperity to the possessor.

Wainamoinen, &c., are heroes rather than gods. First amongst the gods is Jumala.

All the importance we attach to such words as Zeus, Jupiter, Baal, Odin, &c., in the Greek, Latin, Syrian, Scandinavian and other mythologies, we must give to the word *Jumala* in the Ugrian, or if not to the exact word, to its several modifications, some of which, though real, are obscure. The *cultus* of *Jumala* is one of the great Ugrian characteristics. It is widely spread. It originated early. Languages, wherein the names of the minor and newer divinities are different, all agree in containing the root *Jum*—for the syllable *-la* is a derivational affix. Thus, in the Samoyed, the word is *Num*, from probably *Nyum*, the change from *y* to *ny* being common. The Tsherimis form is *Juma*, the Ziriańian *Jen* (from *yenm*, or *yeml*). The Estonian and Lap names are *Jummal* and *Jubmal* respectively.

We may talk, then, of the Jumala-cultus as being the chief cultus of the Ugrians. Its meaning, like its form, varies—being threefold. Jumala means, (1) the Sky or Heavens ; (2) the God of the Sky or Heavens ; (3) God in general ; the present Finlanders, who have been Christianized, using it in this third sense at the present moment, notwithstanding its relation to their old heathen mythology ; just as we use the word *Hell* from the Goddess *Hela*.

Ukko bears a name with, apparently, a very definite signification. In the Magyar, *agg* means *old*. In Ostiak *yig* does the same. In a secondary sense this latter word is *father*. Word for word, it is the *aga*, or *aka*, of the Turk dialects, wherein it has almost as many meanings as forms. All, however, imply seniority, and the respect which seniority demands. In Yakut it is *father*, in other languages elder brother, uncle, grandfather. In the Osmanli it is a title expressive of rank. The Mantshú *aga* = Sir, or Master ; whereas in Mongol it re-appears as elder brother—*c'est une expression respectueuse comme, en français, Monsieur*. In pursuance with this, Ukko is, as Lencvist writes, *totius aulæ celestis senior et præses ;* his designation being a title, or form of address, rather than a true and proper personal name. It is only this, however, in its primary etymology. It is a true and proper personal name as well. If so, Ukko is not only Pater and Princeps, but Diespeter, Jupiter, or Zeus. Like Zeus he is the God of Heaven.

Ukko, who art in the heavens ;
Ukko, father of the heavens ;
Ukko, in the clouds that rulest,
And the clouds and breezes drivest ;
Rule the clouds, and rule the heavens,—
Rule the sky, and rule it kindly ;

Send a cloud from east to westward,
Send a cloud from north to southward,
Send a cloud from west to eastward,
From the south send clouds and showers—
Clouds whose showers drop like honey, &c.

Tapio, of Tapiola, or Tapio-land, heads the list of the genii of the forest, presiding over the beasts, both of the chase and the homestead, more especially, however, those of the chase. Yet his apparel and harness are scarcely those of the hunter. His cap is made of the needles of the fir, his jacket of the lichens. His jacket fits tight, and his cap is like the mitre of a bishop; at least it bears the same name, *hippa*. His beard is brown, and his neck is long, so that he is sometimes called *knippana* (long-necked) on that account. But he has many names besides this; or, at any rate, many circumlocutions under which he is invoked. He is the Lord of Tapiola; the Old Man of the Woods; the Elder of the Hills; the King of the Forest; the Master of the Waste; and the like.

His more especial epithet is *tarkha*, that is, the *exact* or *careful*, for where need a man be careful and exact if not in hunting?

He has a wife, a maid, and a son. The son is noticed first; because when he has been noticed the whole of the male part of Tapio's family is disposed of. Yet the family is a large one. It is large; but it is a family of daughters. The gods of the Fin forest are chiefly goddesses. The Fauni and Silvani are Dryads and Oreads. Nyyrikki, however, or Pinneys, is the son; son of Tapio; son and heir-male; well-shaped and comely, with a high cap on his head, like his father; but no jacket of lichens on his body. He has a blue vest instead of this, and bears himself nobly in it. When the ways are foul, and the bogs deep,

Nyyrikki, or Pinneys, makes bridges, or lays stepping-stones; or, this being done already, directs the feet o the wandering huntsman to where they are. He marks too, the trees, and, so doing, shows which way i: to be taken, which avoided. Tapio, the father, give: the game. Nyyrikki, the son, gets it pursued ir safety.

The mother of Nyyrikki, and his numerous sisters, i: Miellikki. She has many names besides; but Miellikk is, probably, the commonest. She is the hostess of th woods; the mistress of the court of Tapio; the quee of the woodland; the mother of the honeycomb—o which she is the consumer as well. One of her name is Simanten; *sima* meaning *honey*. A damsel of her trai is named Honeymouth.

How is she dressed? That depends upon the season—not the season in respect to its heat or cold, but th season in respect to its goodness or badness in the eyes c the hunter who invokes her. If things go but badly, sh is an ugly old woman dressed in rags, and those rag dirty. But if game be abundant, she is loaded wit golden ornaments; rings on her fingers, rings on her toe rings on her wrists, rings on her ankles, and ear-rings all of gold. Golden, too, is the band round her fore head; and of gold the wires and pins of her hai But her eyebrows are adorned with pearls. Her stock ings are blue, and her garters red.

"Take off thy old and mean garments, and dre thyself in thy noble attire. Put on the 'giving smock.' So prays the hunter to Miellikki; much as he does Tapio as well. Though not so regularly; for the contra between Tapio's best and worst, his Sunday-clothes a his work-a-day dress, is less. He is a quiet dresser general; as has been already remarked.

As are the garments, so is the dwelling; so, at least, according to Castrén's interpretation, runs an obscure passage in the Kalevala. Lemminkainen sings that one day, when he was a-hunting, he saw three houses, one of wood, one of bone, one of stone. The mansion of stone was the residence of Tapio when he was free and liberal in sending game. When he was chary, he lived in the lodge of wood; and when an actual niggard, in the bone-house. He owned treasures; of which honey in abundance was the chief. The key of the storehouse was of gold, and his wife, or housekeeper, kept it on a ring by her side.

For Tapio had a housekeeper as well as his Miellikki. This was Tellervo, or Hillervo. She had a round and full figure and golden hair. She dressed herself in a fine linen smock, with ornamented edges. I call her housekeeper, because I am uncertain about her actual relation to Tapio; who may have been a polygamist. She is called Tapio's maid, and the maiden of the woods. She is once, however, if not oftener, called Tapio's wife, and occasionally she is confused with Miellikki.

She has a name to herself. So has the good-natured Tuulikki. The rest of the children, or maids, of Tapio, are known only by their function; which is to look after the wild and tame. Collectively, however, the female portion of them (which, with the exception of Nyyrikki, means the whole) is called *Luonnottaret*, or *Luonnon tyttärat*. One of these is more especially *Metsän püka*, or the wood-maiden, short in stature, fond of music, fond of honey. Indeed, this is the young woman who has already been named as Honeymouth (*Sima-sun*). Her flute is *Sima-pilli*, or honey-flute. She wakes the milkers with this, by blowing it in their ears if they be too late of a morning.

The name of Kekri presented itself in the translation of Agricola's poem.

> At curat pecudem Kekri, atque propagine læta,
> Respondet votis pastor avare tuis.

He is not to be found in the Kalevala, though found in the practices of the country people. All-Saints' day is called, in some parts of Finland, Kekri. It is the time when much corn is thrashed, so that, probably, Kekri is the genius of harvest, or the threshing-floor.

Ahti is the god of the sea; Wellamo being his wife. The land of the dead is either Tuonela, or Manala. Ukko, however, and Tapio, are by far the most prominent gods of the Pantheon.

I conclude this sketch with the three following extracts. They give us the mundane egg of the Ægyptians. They give us a cosmogony common to the Scandinavians and the Fins. They give us (as in the Estonian narrative) a specimen of the transformation or, as some would say, the degradation, of a myth.

### Fin of Finland.

Old true Wainamoinen
Floats here and there,
On the great bosom of the sea;
Under him floats the water,
Over him waves the sky.
Then comes an eagle from Turialand;
Seeks a place for itself;
A place where it can rest.
Now the old Wainamoinen
Heaved up his knees out of the sea,
So that out of the sea there was a sod,
Over-grown with straw, withered.
The eagle from Turialand
Finds a place for it to build,
Marks the sod on the sea,
Drops on Wainamoinen's knees,

Builds for himself a nest of hay,
Lays in it six eggs :
Golden were the six eggs,
But the seventh was an iron egg.
Then she sits on the eggs,
The eagle warms the end of the knees,
Thereupon old Wainamoinen
Felt the heat in his knees,
Moved when his limbs were warm ;
Suddenly he moved his knees,
Shook his limbs.
The egg rolled in the water;
The egg split in pieces ;
The eagle flew off in the air.
Then said old Wainamoinen,
" The lower part of the egg
Shall become the earth ;
The upper part of the egg
Shall be changed into the sky;
All the white of the egg
Shall be the sun in the sky;
The yolk of the egg
Shall be the moon in the dark;
And all the little bits of the egg
Shall be the stars of the sky."—*From the Kalevala.*

### Norse.

Out of Ymer's flesh
The earth was made;
Out of his sweat the sea;
The hills out of his bones ;
The trees out of his hair;
Out of his brow the sky;
And, from his hair,
The gods made
Midearth for the sons of men :
And out of his scalp
Was there made
All the sky.—*From the Older Edda.*

### Estonian.

The eagle of the north, the cunning bird,
Built a nest in the fir-trees of the island,
In the middle of the rocks of Kalleva.
There were in the nest three eggs :
Two were of the hen of the eagle.

The third was of the hen of Kalleva.
This was the nest-egg of Kalleva.
The eagle flew forth to Finland,
Thence from Finland through Saxony;
Secretly did I slip to the nest,
Took the egg of Kalleva,
Carried it to the town,
Raised it with a crane into a boat,
Hastened homewards in the skiff.
The egg sunk to the bottom of the sea;
Smashed in two on the rocks.
Out of one shell came a man of war;
Out of the other was a merchantman;
Out of the shard barges.
Out of the yolk came Kargesare,
Out of the white came Tutlarsare,
Out of the embryo the other islands.*

*From Neuss Estnische Volkslieder.*

Word for word, the Norse Ymer is the Fin Jumala. Sare is the Estonian for an island. Dagö and Osel, &c., seem to be alluded to.

* The original of the last six lines of the Estonian poem are remarkably regular in their metre, for which reason I subjoin them.

Sääl korest sõa-laiwa,
Teisest korest kauba-laiwa,
Kore kildest killa-padid.
Tõusis rebbust Kõrge-sare,
Muña walgest Tüthar-sare
Muña tumest teised sared.

## CHAPTER XXII.

The Ugrians of Vologda, Permia, &c.—The Komimurt, or Permians and Zirianians.—The Udmurt, or Votiak.—The Biserman.

*The Komimurt.*—The Komimurt in the eyes of a Russian fall into two divisions, one occupant of the Government of Vologda and called Zirianian, the other called Permian, occupant of the Government of Perm. It is only, however, in the eyes of a Russian that this distinction exists. A Permian calls himself Komimurt, and he calls the Zirianian so as well. The Zirianian does the same. In short a Zirianian is a Permian of Vologda, and a Permian a Zirianian of Perm. So it is now. So it was in the times of the old Scandinavians and Anglo-Saxons, who call the whole country Biarmaland, and Beormaland, *i. e.* the land of the Beormas, a population of no small commercial importance, a population whose early history, whether read in the old Norse sagas, or deduced from the examination of their antiquities, is well worth investigating. Indeed, the commercial history of the Beormaland would be the commercial history of the White Sea, a history of bold explorers, active traders, and, doubtless, unscrupulous pirates. It would be important, too, in its relations to the populations of Central Asia.

Notwithstanding the historical prominence of the ancient Beormas, their descendants, the present Komimurt, have no recollections of their ancient nationality, no traditions, no explanation of the several monuments of antiquity in which their country abounds. Of their ancient renown they know as little as they do of the distinction which the Russian draws between their Zirianian and Permian elements; a difference which is political and geographical rather than ethnological. Both populations occupy a region of streams and woods, both being fishers and foresters. The Permian, however, is in a mining district, and is, in his present occupations, a miner. Both have asufficient aptitude for trade and labour; both are active and hard-working.

The Komimurt are, to a man, Christians, Christians of the Greek Church, and of long standing, the history of their conversion being that of St. Stephanus, in the fourteenth century. An inscription from the Church of Vozhemsk, in Vologda, though not yet deciphered, is believed to be Zirianian.

The Zirianians and Permians call themselves *Komimurt*.
——————————— Wotiaks *Wotiak*.
——————————— Woguls *Wagol*.
——————————— Samoyeds *Yerang*.
——————————— Russians *Kotsh*.
——————————————— *Rodsh*.

*The Udmurt, Udi,* or *Votiak.*—The Udi, or Udmurt, were first visited by the Russians of Novogorod in 1174, who settled a few colonists in their country, and established a trade, the settlement being, more or less, independent. It was not until the reign of Ivan Vasilievitsh, who subjected the great town of Novogorod itself to tribute, that the whole area of what is now the Government of Viatka was thoroughly reduced. Nor was this reduction absolutely final. In 1553, a rebellion of the Udmurt, Tsherimis, and Tartars of the conterminous districts, though quashed, took formidable dimensions.

At present it is in the circles of Glasov, Malmysh, Yelabuga, and Sarapul, all in the Government of Viatka, that the bulk of the Udmurt is to be found. Sometimes it bears all the characters of a separate substantive population, retaining the Udmurt language, the Udmurt customs, and the Udmurt creed. At others, one or more characteristics is lost, and the language is Turk or Russian, the creed Christian or Mahometan.

Word for word, Udmurt is a compound of *murt* = *man*, like *Komimurt*, the name of the Permians and Ziri-nians. It is native. The Russian term is Votiak; the Votiaks of the river and Government of Viatka being Udmurt under a Russian name. The Tartar name for them is Ari. From this we may learn that, at one time, the Udmurt, or Votiak, area extended further south than it does now; since there is a locality on the river Kasanka called the Fortress of the Ari, or Arskoi Prigorod. It was one of the last strongholds that yielded to the Tartars, and exhibits, at the present time, remains of its ancient defences.

In person the Votiak resembles the Finlander, as he does in temper. His hair is often, very often, red; indeed the Votiaks have the credit of forming the most red-haired nation in the world.

The men dress like the Russians, the women only adhering to the ancient costume. Of this the most important part is the *aishon*, or cap, made of the white bark of the birch, with a band of blue linen round it, and silver ornaments, often coins, in front. To these decorations add streamers behind and embroidery on the borders, and you have the aishon of the Votiak, or Udmurt, woman. She resides with her family, in small villages erected on clearances in the forest. Her business is to weave, to spin, to felt, and to tend bees; for the Votiak area is in the heart of the bee country, a country of limes and birches. In the vast woods of these trees the Udmurt lives, like the German of old, in tribes, with wastes or woodlands as marks between the villages. These take their name from the tribe to which they belong; for the tribual organization belongs to the Votiak country, and, though many of their nobler families have become extinct, some few still remain. When the ground of a settlement has been exhausted, the tribe, or village, removes itself to a fresh spot. Like so many other rude nations the Udmurt is, at one and the same time, migratory and agricultural. To Russia they pay a capitation-tax, either in money or peltry, but beyond this are left to themselves, *i. e.* to the government of their own elders.

The Votiak Christianity (to say nothing about the truly pagan portion of the country) is of an imperfect kind. It just overlies, or surmounts, a basis of original superstitions. The chief deity is Juman, resident in the Sun; then Tasa Buss the Bad, and Urom Bus the Good, deity; then a lot of little household gods called Modor. Not seldomer than three times a year solemn sacrifices, in the deepest and gloomiest parts of the forest, are made to Urom and Tasa Bus, the chief offerings being milk, honey, sheep, and poultry. The priest is called Tona, the festival Nunal, the locality in which it takes place Keremets. At the great feast of the Keremets Nunal, a horse, a chestnut horse if possible (but never a black one), is sacrificed. His fat is burnt, his hide taken home, his skull left to bleach in mid-air. In praying, the priests look to the sun at noon.

The Votiaks are generally considered to be a very pure-blooded population, intermarrying but little with the Tsherimis, and less with the Turks and Russians.

| English. | Permian. | Ziriauian. | Votiak. |
|---|---|---|---|
| *Man (vir)* | aika | weres | kart |
| —— *(homo)* | mort | mort | mura |
| *Head* | jor | jor | jor |
| *Hair* | jors | jorsi | jirsi |
| *Eye* | sin | sin | sin |
| *Ear* | pel | pel | pel |
| *Nose* | nyr | nyr | nyr |
| *Mouth* | im | wom | im |
| *Tongue* | kyl | kyv | kyl |
| *Tooth* | pin | pin | pin |
| *Hand* | ki | ki | ki |
| *Foot* | kok | kok | pud |
| *Sun* | shondc | shonde | shunde |
| *Moon* | tyles | tyles | toles |
| *Star* | kod | kadzil | kesele |
| *Fire* | by | bi | tul |
| *Water* | wa | wa | wu |
| *Tree* | pu | pu | pu |
| *Stone* | is | is | is |
| *One* | otyk | ytyp | odyk |
| *Two* | kyk | kyk | kik |
| *Three* | kwiu | kuim | kwin |
| *Four* | njula | njul | nil |
| *Five* | wit | wit | wit |
| *Six* | kwet | kwait | kuat |
| *Seven* | sysim | sisim | sisim |
| *Eight* | kykamys | kekames | kiyamis |
| *Nine* | okmys | ykmis | ukmys |
| *Ten* | das | das | das. |

*The Beserman.*—In my work on the Native Races of Russia, I stated that in the Government of Viatka, there were 4545 *Besermanians;* this being all I could say. What was meant by the term I knew not; neither did I know who these Besermanians were.

I have since learned that, word for word *Beserman,* is *Mussulman;* the *B* being changed to *M;* just as, on the banks of the Lena, the huge fossil mastodon that the Arabs (for Arab trade forced itself thus far north) called behemoth, took the name by which it is now known in Europe, *i. e.* that of mammoth.

Beserman, then, is Mussulman, and the Besermanians are the Ugrians whom the neighbourhood of the Turks of Viatka converted to Mahometanism.

The Komimurt and Udmurt languages are sufficiently like the Fin Proper to suggest the likelihood of all four having originally belonged to the same area, *i. e.* to the Governments of Viatka, Perm, Vologda, Kostroma (a Fin name), Yaroslav, and Novogorod. This fixes them in the centre of Russia rather than in the extreme north. Northwards, however, they have extended themselves; for the Zirianians of the Government of Archangel, in contact with the Samoyeds, Voguls, and northern Ostiaks, and on or within the Arctic Circle, appear to be intrusive.

The distribution of the Komimurt, Udmurt, and Beserman, is as follows:—

Komimurt—

*Zirianians :*

| | |
|---|---|
| In Archangel . . . . | 6,958 |
| — Vologda . . . . | 64,007 |
| | 70,965 |

*Permians :*

| | |
|---|---|
| In Perm . . . . | 47,605 |
| — Viatka . . . . | 4,599 |
| | 52,204 |

Udmurt—

| | |
|---|---|
| In Viatka . . . . . | 181,270 |
| — Kazan . . . . . | 5,500 |
| — Orenburg . . . | ? |
| — Samar . . . . . | ? |
| | 186,770 |

Beserman—

| | |
|---|---|
| In Viatka . . . . . | 4,515 |

The Turks of Viatka (those who, being in the closest contact with the Beserman, are the most likely to have effected their conversion) amount to 57,944. Besides which there are 3617 Bashkirs, also Mahometan.

There is, probably, some Komimurt blood in Siberia. A village on the Obi is named Zirianovskoe. The Yeniseians call the Russians Zirianians. Castrén states that there has been, within the last three centuries, a direct Zirianian settlement in some part of the Government of Tobolsk.

# CHAPTER XXIII.

The Ugrians of Viatka, Kazan, &c.—The Mari, or Tsherimis.—The Mordvin.

*The Tsheremis.*—Word for word, I believe *Tsheremis* to be *Arimaspi*. It is no native name. The native name is Mari = man.

The Tsheremis census is as follows:—

| | |
|---|---|
| In Viatka . . . . | 75,450 |
| — Kazan . . . . | 71,375 |
| — Perm . . . . | 7,938 |
| — Nizhni Novogorod . | 4,330 |
| — Kostroma . . . | 3,357 |
| — Orenburg . . . | 2,626 |
| | 165,076 |

The face of the Tsheremis is flat, the beard scanty, the stature moderate.

Haxthausen saw none but dark-skinned, dark-eyed, and dark-haired individuals. Other observers report differently, and speak of light complexions, with hair to match.

Though he is said to delight in the flesh of the horse, the Tsheremis abominates that of the hog; and this even where his habits are unwarped by any influence from his Tartar neighbours.

The price that a Tsheremis pays for his bride, and, as

polygamy is allowed, he may pay it for several, is called *Olon*. The Votiak word was *Yerdon*.

The following hymn shows that Christianity has yet to displace the original heathendom of the Tsheremises; indeed, to say nothing about the imperfect and inchoate religion of the converts, the number of unmodified pagans is far greater than with the Mordvins.

1. May God give health and happiness to him who offers a sacrifice.

2. To the children who come into the world, give, O Yuma, plenty of good things, gold, bread, cattle, and bees.

3. During the new year make our bees to swarm and give much honey.

4. Bless our chase after birds and after beasts.

5. Give us our fill of gold and silver.

6. Make us, O Yuma, masters of all the treasures buried in the earth, all over the world.

7. Grant that in our bargains we may make three times the value of our goods.

8. Enable us to pay our tribute.

9. Grant that, at the beginning of the spring, our three sorts of cattle may find their ways back by three different paths, and that we may keep them from bears, from wolves, and from robbers.

10. Make our cows with calf.

11. Make our thin kine fatten for the good of our children.

12. Enable us with one hand to sell our barren cows, and with the other to take the money.

13. Send us, O Yuma, a true and trusty friend.

14. When we travel far, preserve us, O Yuma, from bad men, from sickness, from fools, from bad judges, and from lying tongues.

15. As the hop grows and throws out its scent, so, O Yuma, grant that we wax strong through goodness, and smell sweet from reason.

16. As the wax sparkles in burning, so let us, O Yuma, live in joy and health.

17. Let our existence be as calm and regular as the cells of a honeycomb.

18. Grant, O Yuma, that he who asks may obtain the object of his prayer.

When this prayer is finished, the head, heart, lungs, and liver are offered up to the deity to whom it is addressed. A feast follows. The remains are burnt.

*The Mordvin.*—The Mordvin men dress like the Russians, live like the Russians, and are, with few or no exceptions, Christians. They speak, however, a Ugrian language.

They amount to—

| | |
|---|---|
| In Penza . . . . | 106,025 |
| — Simbirsk . . . | 98,968 |
| — Saratov . . . | 78,010 |
| — Samar . . . . | 74,910 |
| — Nizhni Novogorod . | 53,383 |
| — Tambov . . . | 48,491 |
| — Kazan . . . . | 14,867 |
| — Orenburg . . . | 5,200 |
| — Taurida . . . | 340 |
| — Astrakan . . . | 48 |
| | 480,242 |

They fall into three divisions:—

1. The Ersad on the Oka;
2. — Mokshad — Sura;
3. — Karatai about Kazan.

The name is native.

Among the Ersad red hair is not uncommon; elsewhere it is brown, rather than black.

In Taurida and Astrakan they are recent settlers.

| English. | Tscheremis. | Mordvin. |
|---|---|---|
| *Man (vir)* | mara | mirda |
| *— (homo)* | edem | loman |
| *Head* | bui | prä |
| *Hair* | ip | tsher |
| *Eye* | shinsha | syälme |
| *Ear* | piliksh | pilye |
| *Nose* | ner | sudo |
| *Mouth* | ushma | kurgo |
| *Tongue* | yolma | kel |
| *Tooth* | pü | päi |
| *Hand* | kit | ked |

| English. | Tsheremis. | Mordvin. |
|---|---|---|
| *Foot* | yal | pilge |
| *Sun* | ketshe | tshi |
| *Moon* | tilsye | kov |
| *Star* | shuder | teshtye |
| *Fire* | tul | tol |
| *Water* | wüt | wät |
| *Tree* | pu | tshufto |
| *Stone* | ku | käv |
| *One* | iktet | wait |
| *Two* | koktet | kafto |
| *Three* | kumut | kolmo |
| *Four* | nilit | nilye |
| *Five* | wisit | wäze |
| *Six* | kudut | kota |
| *Seven* | shimit | sisem |
| *Eight* | kandashe | kauksa |
| *Nine* | indeshe | wäiksye |
| *Ten* | lu | kämen |

Word for word, Mordvin is the root *mard* = *man*, in so many Asiatic languages. It is also, in all probability, the same name as Amardi, a name belonging to the ancient geography of Persia.

Word for word, Ud seems to be Vod.

## CHAPTER XXIV.

**The Ugrians of the Ural.—The Mansi, or Ostiaks and Voguls.**

*The Mansi, or Ostiaks and Voguls.—The Ostiak Mansi.*— Under the name of Mansi I include two populations, akin to each other in all the chief ethnological characters, and in immediate geographical contact. The first of these is known by the Turk and Russian designation of Ostiak, and, as its occupancy is the river Obi, the Ostiak of the Obi appears somewhat conspicuously in the ethnology and geography of Siberia. The other is called, by the Russians, Vogul.

The Ostiaks have no general or collective name at all. So at least I infer from the description of them. The nearest approach to one is Kondiko; but, as this merely means the occupants of the river Konda it has only a partial application. In like manner, the terms, Asyakh = river-men, and Tyukum = morass-men, are anything but general.

Undersized and deficient in muscle, the Ostiak is nevertheless hardy. In youth he is healthy; but, as age comes on, scorbutic and cutaneous diseases, evidently connected with his filthy habits of life, set in. The winter hut is close and fetid with the reek of damp fuel and putrid fish. The winter provender is dried or frozen; for salt is scarce. The product of the summer's fishing is stored in abundance and over-abundance, some part of it for human use and some for the dogs; some having been previously bartered away. The cold weather drives them from the river-side to the forest, where, on long snow-skates, like those of the Lap, or on dog-drawn sledges, they search for bears, foxes, sables, and squirrels. Their clothing is the skin of the reindeer doubled—hair in and hair out.

The women are partially tattooed.

It is only the winter cabin of the Ostiak that aspires to the name and dignity of a house. It is half sunk in the soil and sodded over with turf by way of a roof. The summer habitation consists of a few slanted poles, with wattles, or birch-bark, for a wall. Where the winter house takes its full dimensions it becomes the joint occupancy of some three, four, or six families, in which case as many as thirty individuals of all ages and either sex may be cabined and confined together, cooking, smoking, and sleeping.

The tribual system of the Ostiak Mansi, though exhibited on a smaller scale than that of the Turks and Mongols, is eminently instructive not only to the ethnologist, but to the civil historian, who, in many cases, would do well if he trusted less to testimony and more to induction. The Mansi Ostiaks are both tribesmen and pagans; a fact which gives us a double division. It is the parts about Obdorsk of which our informant, Castrén, most especially speaks. There are several tribes in its neighbourhood. Each has a head, with elders under him. This head, chief, or prince has large powers; being judge in all cases for which, in Russian law, the penalty is less than death. But the subordinate elders are appealed to in the first instance. They also take cognizance of minor quarrels, offences, and suits.

Members of the same tribe, whether large or small, consider themselves as relations, even where the common ancestor is unknown, and where the evidence of consanguinity is wholly wanting. Nevertheless, the feeling of consanguinity, sometimes real, sometimes conventional, is the fundamental principle of the union. The rich, of which there are few, help the poor, who are many. There is not much that can change hands. The little, however, that is wanted by the needy is taken as a right rather than a favour. This makes the hunting-grounds, and (in a less degree) the product of the hunt common property.

The names of the following tribes, or *Megh*, are from Klaproth :—

1. Luhung Megh.
2. Waghu Megh.
3. Tormiogon Megh.
4. Pyhm Megh.
5. Agon Megh.
6. Endl' Agon Megh.
7. Ay Agon Megh.
8. Lokatsh Megh.
9. Palakh Megh.
10. Salâhm Megh.
11. Tahsen Megh.

Such are the names of the Asyakh divisions; occupant of the Obi. The principle on which they are given seems to be other than uniform. The second, third, and fourth are geographical, the Waghu Megh, the Tormiogon Megh, and the Pyhm Megh being the tribes of the rivers Wakh, Tohrm-yogan, and Pyhm. It is probable, too, that this is the case with the sixth and seventh, where *yogan* (*river*) takes the form *agon*. The Luhung Megh has a different derivation. So at least writes Klaproth, who objects to deriving it from *Lung*, an *idol*, as some of his predecessors had done. He prefers the root *Lun*, the name of a bird. If so, the principle that gives us the Hare, Tortoise, Wolf, and other tribes in America gives us the Owl, or Hawk tribe in Siberia. The other names may or may not be local. I should have been glad to have found that some of them were personal: for this is what is expected *à priori*. The principle of eponymy (*i. e.* the principle of naming the tribe after a real or supposed progenitor) is so common that the absence of a body of Ostiaks bearing the name of some chief or hero is remarkable. When the eponymus is real (as he rarely is) the tribe takes its name from him in reality as well as in appearance. When the eponymus is fictitious or conventional, and the name of a hypothetical ancestor is an after-thought to account for the name of a tribe, the denomination is fictitious, and the hero takes his name (and existence as well) from the tribe.

The Ostiak tribes, however, have local rather than personal denominations; and the Ostiaks are Wak-men or Pym-men, rather than the sons of A, or the children of B.

The Megh is a political division. But besides the political division, there is a religious one. The use of the same consecrated spot, or the same priest, is also a bond of union; and I infer, from the notice of Castrén, that the two divisions thus formed by no means necessarily coincide.

The priest is a Shaman, *i. e.* priest, sacrificant, sorcerer, prophet, and medicine-man at once; capable of working himself into real or mock frenzies; fond of the sound of the drum.

Some of the idols are called ***Lung***, others ***Yilyan***. ***Mean*** and ***Kuly*** are the names of two of the minor divinities; each malevolent rather than kind. The highest deity is ***Torom***. Of oaths, the greatest, like that of the Yeniseians, is that which is taken on the head of a bear, and concludes with the imprecation "if I swear untruly, may a bear eat me." Other Siberians, besides the Ostiaks and the Yeniseians, reverence the bear. The old Zirianians did so, and, probably, the Pèrmians as well. Indeed, if an ordinary huntsman meets his death in the forest, and a bear have killed him, he is generally accused of having forsworn himself during life.

The practice of interring the weapons and accoutrements of the deceased along with the corpse, common in so many rude countries, is common amongst the Ostiak.

Polygamy is allowed. But it is not common. For a plurality of wives the country is too poor. Brothers marry the widows of brothers. Two brothers, however, may not marry two sisters.

Of the two branches of the Ostiaks, the hunters and the fishers, the latter are the poorest.

The Ostiaks call the river Obi As. The As-yakh, Men of the As, Asicolæ, or Obicolæ, call

| | |
|---|---|
| The Ostiaks of the Demianka | *Tshonto-yakh.* |
| ——————— Irtysh | *Long-gol-yakh.* |
| ——————— other rivers | *Nang-wanda-yakh.* |

Narym, and the banks of the river Ket, are the most eastern points of the Ostiak occupancy, and there they come in contact with the Samoyeds. Now the term for *man* changes here, and is—

In the singular number, *kup* = *homo.*
—— plural ——— *kula* = *homines.*

Hence the compound Gentile names all end different, and a Narym Ostiak calls himself *Dshumul-kula.*

| | |
|---|---|
| The Surgut Ostiaks . | *Tangyl-kula.* |
| — Russians . . | *Ruzhil-kula.* |
| — Turks in general . | *Tül-kula.* |
| ———— of the Tshulim | *Tshulim-ku-kula.* |
| ———— Tungusians | *Guellon-kula.* |
| ———— the river Obi | *Koldy.* |
| ——————— Tym | *Kasükh-kü.* |

Koldy is also the Samoyed name of the Obi.

The Asjaikh of Surgut call themselves *Kaxta-yakh.*
——————————— the Ostiaks *Narym Nyorom-*
——————————— Samoyeds *Yeryan-yakh.* [*yakh.*
——————————— Turks *Katan-yakh.*
——————————— Russians *Rutsh-yakh.*
——————————— Germans *Nimet-yakh.*

Word for word, *Njorum* is *Narym,* meaning fen, and, as a Ugrian gloss, it is an instrument of criticism. Where the root *Nar* and a swampy locality go together, we have a presumption in favour of either a Ugrian occupancy or a Ugrian neighbourhood.

| English. | Ostiak. | Samoyed. |
|---|---|---|
| *Man* (*vir*) | kuim | khayodu |
| —— (*homo*) | koiet | meñatshe |
| *Head* | ugol | ngaiva |
| *Hair* | upat | ngeepta |
| *Eye* | sem | sou |
| *Ear* | pel | khau |
| *Nose* | näl | ngpuie |
| *Mouth* | lul | nyan |
| *Hand* | ket | uda |
| *Foot* | kur | ngai |
| *Sun* | syunk | khaer |
| *Moon* | tylesh | yirri |
| *Star* | koz | numge |
| *Fire* | tyod | tu |
| *Water* | ying | yi |
| *Tree* | yog | pya |
| *Stone* | kiw | pai |
| *One* | ogy | ngob |
| *Two* | ketto | zidde |
| *Three* | kholym | nyahar |
| *Four* | nül | tyet |
| *Five* | uet | sambalyank |
| *Six* | kut | mat |
| *Seven* | labut | ziu |
| *Eight* | nuul | zidden-tyet |
| *Nine* | yirteng | khasoai-yu |
| *Ten* | iyani | lusto-yu |

*The Vogul Mansi.*—The Voguls hold a cheerless and inhospitable tract of land along the ridge of the Ural in its northern parts, and on its eastern aspect, being bounded by the Zirianians, Samoyeds, and the Kondicho, whom they call by the name they give themselves, viz. Mansi. The Mansi, or Voguls, ruder than the populations to the west of them, are, there or thereabouts, on a level with Kondicho and Samoyeds, their villages being small and far apart, their clearances in the forest imperfectly cultivated, their habits those of the hunter.

As Beresov was the great mart for the Ostiak, Obdorsk is the emporium for the Vogul. Thither he takes the produce of his long and wearisome hunts, the skins of the reindeer and elk, shot by the bow or gun, and caught by the trap or pitfall. Of hunting on horseback the Vogul has none; neither are dogs common in his country, a country of bog and wood, where the wealthy proprietor keeps but a few cows, and where agricultural industry is only inchoate.

In the south part of the Vogul country Christianity has advanced a little; feebly and imperfectly, but still a little. In the north, paganism prevails. The head of the family is the priest. The chief object of the prayer is success in hunting. To ensure this, images in the shape of the beast more especially sought for, rudely shaped out of wood or stone, are set up; so that a Vogul divinity is elk-shaped, fox-shaped, or sable-shaped, as the case may be.

The Voguls call themselves *Mansi.*
———————— the Ostiaks *Mansi.*
———————— Samoyeds *Torran-kum.*
———————— Turks *Nyurma-kum.*
———————— Russians *Rus.*
———————— river Obi *As.*

| | | |
|---|---|---|
| The Voguls call the Irtish | | *Shap.* |
| ———————— | Tawda | *Tagget.* |
| ———————— | Konda | *Khonda.* |

The Vogul language is the least known of all the Ugrian tongues; there being no grammar of it, and only short vocabularies.

| English. | Vogul. | Ostiak. | Samoyed.* |
|---|---|---|---|
| *Man* (*vir*) | kom | kuim | khayoau |
| —— (*homo*) | klas | khoiet | menatshe |
| *Head* | pank | ngol | ngaiva |
| *Hair* | ata | upat | ngeepta |
| *Eye* | sham | sem | seu |
| *Ear* | bal | pel | khau |
| *Nose* | nöl | näl | ngpuie |
| *Mouth* | tozh | lul | nyan |
| *Tongue* | nelma | nälim | nyami |
| *Tooth* | ping | penk | —— |
| *Hand* | kat | ket | uda |
| *Foot* | lal | kur | ngai |
| *Sun* | kotal | syunk | khaer |
| *Moon* | yankop | tylesh | yirri |
| *Star* | kenza | koz | numge |
| *Fire* | taut | tyod | tu |
| *Water* | wit | ying | yi |
| *Tree* | yo | yog | pya |
| *Stone* | ku | kiw | pai |

*The Magyars.*—The vernacular name for the natives of what we are in the habit of considering the pure and proper Hungarian districts of Hungary, as opposed to the Germans, Slavonians, and Rumanyos, is Magyar—Magyar, and not Hun. This latter, the commoner and more current denomination, is foreign to the real Hungarians. It is Slavonic in origin; being Uhri in Bohemian, Wegry in Polish, and Vengri in Russian. It was adopted, however, by the Germans,

* Of Obdorsk.

and that at an early period, inasmuch as the first notices of the western annalists speak of the Hungarii. They give them a bad name, and depict them as the wildest of the wild. They come from Scythia. They fight (as the Tsheremises are described to have done) with the bow; the bow made of horn. Where the sword kills its tens, the arrow destroys its hundreds. They are very savage; indeed, they are like the Britons in their fierceness. However, the Britons use darts rather than arrows. In doing this they exhibit their chief difference between themselves and Hungarians. These Britons are the Britons of Brittany. The Hungarians are the Magyars. Nomads and warriors, they occasionally got called Hagarens, as if they were Arabs. From Agar to Ishmael the transition is short, and, in one of the notices, we hear of Billa and Bocsu, who found a place called Pest, at the head of a great multitude of Hishmaelites, who came from the land of Bular, *i. e.* Bulgaria.

They are more excusably confounded with the Turks; for they both came from a Turk district, and settled in one. They came from the kingdom of Bulgaria and the frontier of the Khazars and Petshineks, and they settled in what had, a few centuries back, been the land of the Huns, and, nearer to their own time, that of the Avars. Add to this that the Magyars effected during one of their marches an alliance with the Comanians or Polovczi. There was much, then, to connect them with Turkestan. No writer does this more than the imperial historian Constantine Porphyrogeneta, writing about two centuries after their first appearance. With the Huns they were confused in the tenth century by learned writers in Constantinople. With the Huns they are confused at the present moment by learned writers in Berlin and Vienna—by some, though not by all. Now, whatever the Magyars may have been, they were not the strength of the armies of Attila.

Another name, found in Porphyrogeneta, is Savartoyasfal (Σαβαρτοιάσφαλοι); and a mysterious name it is. It is said to be an older name than Turk; Turk being no true name at all. We must, however, take the word as the author who supplies it, took it. Can it be German? One of the Slavonic denominations for the Magyars was Czernij Ugri, or black Ugrians; and Zeus suggests that the first part of the name Savartoyasfal is Swarthy. Who, however, applied it? The Russians (he further suggests), before they had become Slavonic, and when they were the Scandinavians of Rurik. In the topography of eastern Hungary the termination *-val* (*fal*) is common. We must be satisfied, however, for the present, with leaving the name Savartoyasfal unexplained.

With such a choice of denominations it is not surprising that the native name Magyar has been limited to the Magyars themselves; who use it now, when they speak of themselves, and who used it at the beginning of their historical period. Its Latin form is Mogerii, its Greek, Μαζαροι.

The original Magyar-land fell into three kingdoms, Bostardia, Dentia, and Magaria; the first of which is the land of the Bashkirs, a name variously transformed, and which appears, in different writers, as Bashkart, Bastarque, and Pascatir, and (to pass from a verbal to real designation) Great Hungary. *Baschkart, ou Pascatir, qui est la grande Hongrie.* So writes Rubriquis, A. D. 1255.

To return, however, to the use of the word amongst

the Magyars themselves. It appears in two compounds; Dentu-moger, and Hetú-moger, or the seven Magyar. To the Hetumoger were seven chiefs.

1. Almus, the father of Arpad.
2. Eleut, the son of Zobolsu, from whom are descended the Saac.
3. Cundu, the father of Curzan.
4. Ound, the father of Ete, from whom are descended the Calan and Colsoy.
5. Tosu, the father of Lelu.
6. Huba, from whom are descended the Zemera.
7. Tuhut, the father of Horca.

The sons of Horca were Gyyla and Zombor, from whom are descended the Moglout.

This list, though it gives us no true genealogy, gives us an historic fact, that of there being, at the time of its concocter, certain tribes, clans, septs, or families (*genera*) named Moglout, Zemera, Calan, Colsoy, and Saac. Let these fall into divisions and subdivisions, and the number increases. They did do so; and, according to other so-called traditions, the tribes of the Magar amounted to 108.

Word for word, I suspect that Magar is the Ostiak Mekh. At any rate, the seven tribes of Hungary would be—

| | |
|---|---|
| In Ostiak . . | *labut mekh* |
| — Vogul . . | *satu mekh* |

the Vogul form being nearest to the Magyar.

That the Government of Orenburg is the original Magyar country is shown by the remark of the writer (Rubriquis) who speaks of the Bashkir country as being the Great Hungary, adding that its language is that of Hungary in Europe.

The best-ascertained facts in the way of chronology respecting the movement westwards turn upon the names of Leo the philosopher and the German emperor Arnulf. The former employed the Magyars against the Bulgarians, the latter against the Slavonians of Moravia.

That a branch settled in Persia is also fairly attested. Porphyrogeneta writes of his Savartoyasfal that some are in Persia "even until now." The minuter details of the invasion are obscure.

All the blood in Hungary must be mixed. Before the Magyars settled in it, it had been occupied by Dacians, Jazyges, Romans, Huns, and Avars, to which add Cumanians, and other less important elements.

That many females accompanied the Magyar invaders is unlikely. The first generation was one of half-bloods.

The Magyar is not only Ugrian, but Ugrian of the Mansi branch. The Ostiak and Voguls, however, are amongst the most northern members of the stock. The Magyar affinity suggests that, in their present localities, they are intrusive; for the Magyar affinity brings them southwards. So, it is said, do some of the traditions of the Ostiaks themselves, according to which they came from the upper Irtish.

I think, with others, that, word for word, Bashkir is Magyar, the M being changed into B, upon the principle which converts *M*ussulman into *B*iserman, and *b*ehemoth into *m*ammoth. I think that Meshtsheryak is the same; also that in the Ostiak and the Magyar languages we get the names for the Montes Rhipæi and the Volga or river of Bulgaria. In the former, *rip* = *hill;* in the latter, *volgy* = *valley*. In Arabic *wadi* means not only the valley through which a river flows, but the river itself. The *Guad*alquivir is, not the valley of the Iberis, but the Iberis itself.

| English. | Magyar. | Other Ugrian Languages. |
|---|---|---|
| *Eye* | szem | sem—*Ostiak, &c.* |
| *Belly* | has | waz—*Fin* |
| *Tree* | fa | pu—*Fin and Permian* |
| *Hill* | hegy | kuruk—*Tsheremis* |
| *Leaf* | lewel | lybet, &c.—*Ostiak, &c.* |
| *Blood* | wer | wyr—*Ditto* |
| *Bad* | kar | kurya—*Fin* |
| *Bread* | kenyer | kinda—*Tsheremis* |
| *Thou* | te | ty, &c.—*Permian, &c.* |
| *Ice* | jeg | yenk, &c.—*Ostiak, &c.* |
| *Egg* | mony | muno—*Tsheremis, &c.* |
| *Feather* | toll' | tuul—*Vogul, &c.* |
| *Fire* | tüz | tut—*Ostiak, &c.* |
| *Finger* | uij | lui, yoi—*Ditto* |
| *Fish* | hal | kul—*Ditto, &c.* |
| *Spring* | tawasz | kawed—*Karelian* |
| *Foot* | lab | lal—*Vogul* |
| *Goose* | lud | lont—*Ostiak, &c.* |
| *Grass* | pasit | pady, *Ost.*—pizhe, *Mordvin* |
| *Throat* | torok | tur—*Ostiak, &c.* |
| *Good* | jo | jowo—*Fin* |
| *Cock* | kakas | kikkas, &c.—*Estonian* |
| *Neck* | nyak | naugol—*Ostiak* |
| *Hand* | kez | ket—*Ostiak, &c.* |
| *House* | haz | kat—*Ditto, &c.* |
| *Heart* | sziv | sem—*Ditto* |
| *Sky* | meny | manen—*Mordvin* |
| *Horn* | szarv | sarv, &c.—*Estonian, &c.* |
| *Cold* | hideg | itek—*Ostiak* |
| *Bone* | czont | koint—*Fin* |
| *Head* | fo | pa—*Ditto* |
| *Herb* | fu | pum—*Ostiak* |
| *Slow* | lassan | lasy—*Vogul* |
| *Live* | elet | let, &c.—*Ostiak, &c.* |
| *Easy* | könmu | kunna—*Vogul* |
| *Man (vir)* | fery | veres—*Zirianian* |
| *Mouth* | szaj | su—*Fin* |
| *Night* | es | at—*Ostiak* |
| *Take* | elvenni | wain—*Vogul* |
| *Ear* | ful | pel—*Ostiak* |
| *Horse* | lo | lo—*Vogul* |
| *Rye* | ros | oros—*Ditto* |
| *Red* | veres | vyr—*Ditto* |
| *Sow* | vetek | vidik—*Mordvin* |

| English. | Magyar. | Other Ugrian Languages. |
|---|---|---|
| *Sand* | humok | yema—*Vogul* |
| *Sleep* | alom | olm—*Ditto* |
| *Swift* | gyors | tshuros—*Fin* |
| —— | sereny | sarag—*Ostiak* |
| *Black* | fekete | puqqete—*Ditto* |
| *Sister* | hugom | iggem—*Ditto* |
| *Silver* | ezyst | esys—*Permian* |
| *Son* | fui | pu—*Vogul* |
| *Sun* | nap | nai—*Ostiak* |
| *Stone* | ko | ku—*Vogul* |
| *Star* | tsillag | tisil—*Permian* |
| *Deep* | mely | mil—*Ostiak, &c.* |
| *Dead* | hallal | kul—*Ditto* |
| *Drink* | iszom | asokh—*Vogul* |
| *Over* | felette | pällä—*Fin* |
| *Under* | allat | alla—*Ditto* |
| *Water* | viz | wisi—*Ditto* |
| *Wind* | szel | tyl—*Permian* |
| *Winter* | tel | telli—*Ostiak* |
| *We* | mink | mung—*Ditto* |
| *Worm* | fereg | perk—*Vogul* |
| —— | nyii | nynk—*Ditto* |
| *Tooth* | fog | penk—*Ostiak* |
| *Tongue* | nyelu | nalem—*Ditto* |
| *One* | egy | ogy—*Ostiak* |
| *Two* | ketto | ketto—*Ditto* |
| *Three* | harom | korom—*Vogul* |
| *Four* | negy | nül—*Ostiak* |
| *Five* | ot | uet—*Ditto* |
| *Six* | hat | kut—*Ditto* |
| *Seven* | het | sat—*Vogul* |
| *Eight* | nyoltz | nuul—*Ostiak* |
| *Ten* | tiz | das—*Permian.* |

Word for word, Eleut and Saac seem to be Olöt and Sak, suggesting Mongol elements.

The Magyar language, in respect to its phonesis, uses the secondary sounds like *f* and *h*, rather than the primary sounds *p* and *k*.

The Mansi forms of speech have special affinities with the Tsherimis.'

# CHAPTER XXV.

The Samoyeds.—Northern Branch.—Yurak.—Tawgi.—Ostiak.—Southern Branch. — Soiot or Uriankhai. — Mati. — Koibal. — Karakas. — Soiot Proper.—Kamash.—The Andon Domni, or Yukahiri.

THE Samoyeds are a small population widely spread. That some of them lie within the Arctic Circle is shown rather ostentatiously in the ordinary maps. Look to the parts between the White Sea and the Lena, and the word Samoyed is one of the few that meets your eye. It will probably appear twice; once on the borders of Europe, once in Asia. It fills up the vast vacancy between the Petshora and the Chatunga; and suggests the idea of intense cold and discomfort suffered by a population of savage nomads. As a set-off to this, the Samoyed tribes seem to have the country all to themselves; and a very cheerless country it is. It is a tundra; *i. e.* a tract of moss, a swamp, beyond the tree-line, bleak, damp, foggy, boggy; for the Northern Samoyeds are pre-eminently the tundra population of the Old World. The Laplanders are the same, but in a far less degree, and only partially. The Northern Samoyeds are wholly so.

The word Northern is by no means unnecessary. Far as the Samoyed area extends in the direction of east and west, it extends equally as far from south to north. There are Samoyeds within the Chinese frontier, on the Upper Yenisey, and on the drainage of the Lake Baikal;

—of course, under very different conditions from those of the Arctic Circle and Icy Sea.

*The Northern Branch.*—Of the Northern Samoyeds the chief divisions, according to Castrén, who founds them upon the differences of dialect, are three; (1), the Yurak; (2), the Tawgi, and (3), the Ostiak.

(1.) The Yurak Samoyeds are those that lie in the closest contact with the Russians; those, also, that are the best known. They are those, too, who are not only Asiatic but European as well—common to the two continents. To them the name Samoyed was first applied. It is a name which is, by no means, native. The native name is Kasovo (Hasawayo), or Nyenek = Men.

The Yurak Samoyeds, or the Samoyeds of Yugoria, appear on the eastern coast of the White Sea, to the north of the river Mezene. On the lower course of the Petshora they are more abundant still. They are separated from the Russian Laplanders by the sea and by the valley of the Dwina; for the parts about Archangel have long been wrested from them, and Russianized. Neither is it certain that the Russians were the first who pressed upon them in this direction. The Karelian Fins may have done so before; so may the Zirianians of Vologda.

Between the Petshora and the Ural, the Samoyed is bounded on the south by the Zirianian area. On the Obi he comes in contact with the Ostiak; and that at the very mouth of the river. In the parts, however, about Obdorsk, Samoyed is spoken. From the Obi to the Tas, all is Yurak Samoyed. On the Tas, however, there is a break; beyond which the details are obscure. The Yurak division is generally carried as far east as the Yenisey. We will here, however, carry it to the Tas.

The Yurak proper is only one dialect out of five; the

other four being represented by the (1), Kanin and Timan; (2), the Ishim; (3), the Bolshizemla and Obdorsk; (4), and the Kondin or Kazym forms of speech.

(2.) The Tawgi division reaches from the Lower Yenisey to the Chatunga; the tribes which belong to it being sometimes called the Avam Samoyeds.

(3.) The Ostiak Samoyeds have the disadvantage of being described by an inconvenient name. The true Ostiaks are something else, as has been seen. That they form a natural class in the way of dialect I hold on the authority of Castrén; or rather his editor Schiefner. That their habits are, more or less, peculiar, is an inference from the difference of the physical conditions under which they live. We have left the cheerless regions of the Arctic Circle. We have left those of the swampy boggy tundras. We are in the region of the woods and forests, on a river prodigal of fish. We are in contact, too, with the northern members of the great Turk stock. We are not far from the Chinese and Tartar frontiers. We are in a region of an improved civilization; a barbarous region, nevertheless. We are beyond the latitudes where wheat can be grown; though we are south of that of St. Petersburg, Stockholm, Christiania, and the Shetland Isles. We are, in short, in the very middle of Siberia, and, on an elevated portion of it. We are high-up on the streams of the Obi and the Yenisey, and we are, more or less, on the elevation which forms the watershed between them.

The Ostiak Samoyeds are to be found not only in the districts to which they are indigenous, but in more than one locality beyond them; the evidence of their language, and (to a certain extent) that of their history, pointing to one or more movements northwards and eastwards.

Of the dialects, however, *in situ*, the most northern is that of the parts about the Tym and Narym; next comes that of the river Ket; thirdly, that of the Tshulim. The Ket forms of speech extend as far as the rivers Parabel and Tshaya, on the frontier of the Barabinski Steppe, feeders of the Obi. The dialect of the Circle of Pumpokolsk is also akin to the Ket.

The migrations are represented by the Karasin and Tas forms of speech; the former being spoken in the parts to the north of Turukansk, on the Yenisey, and the latter by the Tym and Karakon tribes of the Tas; tribes that use the reindeer and call themselves Mokase.

Such are the three principal divisions of northern Samoyeds, called also Kasovo or Nyenek. We are scarcely prepared to hear them called "powerful." That epithet, however, has been applied. As compared to some of the Ostiaks, they may be so. Indeed, it is specially stated by Castrén, that where the Ostiak and Samoyed frontiers touch, the Samoyed nationality prevails. The dress of the Ostiak then becomes Samoyed; his habit Samoyed; his creed Samoyed; his language Samoyed. There are, certainly, many Ostiaks disguised as Samoyeds.

*The Southern Branch.*—The Southern Samoyeds may be called Soiot, or Uriankhai, according to the political position of their occupancy. When it lies in Russia or Siberia they are the former. When it lies within the Chinese frontier it is the latter. A Soiot is an Uriankhai of Russia. An Uriankhai is a Soiot of China. The names, perhaps, are more convenient than strictly accurate. One population, indeed, is common to the two areas. Hence, it is partly Soiot, partly Uriankhai. I will notice it first, and then follow out the details of the less equivocal names.

The population in question is that of

*The Mati, Motorians, Matlar,* or *Modorzi.*—The last of these names is Russian, the last but one Turk, in form. The root is Mat. The Russian Mati are, probably, either extinct, or amalgamated with the Turks of their neighbourhood. They are, probably, in the same category with the Tubalar, of which they may be (or may have been) a part. I think this because the banks of the Tuba were their occupancy. They came, however, from the main stream of the Yenisey. They are, probably, extinct or amalgamated, because, in 1722, they numbered only ten families.

*The Samoyeds of the Koibal division.*—Before the Russian conquest of Siberia a powerful people, divided into tribes and sub-tribes, bore the name Koibal, a name which has since changed its signification. The natives of the parts about Krasnoyark and Abakansk are, at the present moment, divided into four divisions; the Katshinzi, the Sagai, the Kisilzi, and the Koibal.

The Koibals fall into eight families, or clans, whereof three are believed to be Yeniseian, and five Samoyed. They call themselves Tufa. In 1830, they amounted to 635 males, and 493 females. In 1847, a few aged individuals alone spoke the original Koibal language; by which, I presume is meant, the language of the Samoyed, rather than the Yeniseian, portion of the group. I presume, too, that it is the language represented by the following specimens from the Asia Polyglotta.

| English. | Koibal.* | Motorian.* | Kamash. |
|---|---|---|---|
| *Head* | ulu | nambam | ulu |
| *Hair* | abde | ipti | apty |
| *Tongue* | zeka | kashte | shika |
| *Tooth* | tyme | tyme | —— |
| *Eye* | zima | zime | saimo |

* Collected by Klaproth not later than A.D. 1823.

| English. | Koibal. | Motorian. | Kamash. |
|---|---|---|---|
| *Mouth* | an | agma | ang |
| *Blood* | kam | kem | —— |
| *Hand* | oda | udam | udam |
| *Foot* | musta | hoi | uyu |
| *Nose* | piya | eyem | peya |
| *Ear* | ku | kuma | ku |
| *Sky* | num | num | num |
| *Sun* | kuya | kaye | kuya |
| *Moon* | kuii | kishtit | kü |
| *Star* | kynsygei | kindzhikei | kinsygai |
| *Fire* | ziu | tuck | shu |
| *Water* | bu | bu | bu |
| *Stone* | pi | dagia | phi |
| *Tree* | pa | kha | unet-pfa. |

The language which has replaced the original Samoyed is the Turk; the present Koibals (whether Samoyed or Yeniseian in blood) being Turks in speech, imperfect Christians in creed, and, more or less, agricultural in habit. They possess horses, oxen, and camels.

The Koibal districts lie on the Yenisey, between Abakansk and the Chinese frontier; the right bank of the Abakan, from its junction with the Yenisey, upwards as far as the Tabat, being one of their districts; as is, also, the right bank of the Yenisey itself as far as the Sogda, a feeder of the Tuba. That the Tuba is a Samoyed river has already been stated.

The name Kyzdym, or Kishtim, is sometimes applied to the Koibal. It is Turk in origin, and means servants. It implies that certain Turks pressed upon certain Samoyeds, and reduced them. It also suggests the likelihood of a certain amount of intermixture. That this has taken place is a historical fact. Koibal blood is to be found amongst the Kirgis; inasmuch as, when the latter nation moved westwards and southwards, some of the Koibal accompanied them.

*The Karakas.*—Word for word, *Karakas* may be a compound of the Turkish *kara* (= *black*), or the term Kirgis. The population to which it applies, has its occupancy on the rivers Oka, Uda, Biryusa, and Kan. It is nomad in habits, and amounted, in 1851, to 284 males, and 259 females. Small as is the Karakas group, it falls into no less than five sections, tribes, or families.

| | |
|---|---|
| The Kash, | The Tyogde, |
| — Sareg Kash, | — Kara Tyogde, |

The Tyeptei.

The last is on the Buriat frontier, and, more or less, Buriat in habits, and dialect.

Samoyed in blood, the Karakas are Turk in language. They are poor, like

*The Soiot Proper,* who live about Tunkinsk.—It is especially stated, by both Müller and Pallas, that they speak Samoyed. The only vocabulary, however, which Klaproth succeeded in procuring, was Turk. This, however, is not conclusive. A part of them might still use the language of their ancestors. A part, too, (indeed a large part) is Buriat, rather than Turk. Samoyed in blood, it is Mongol in speech, and Buddhist in creed.

*The Kamash, Kangmash,* or *Kamashinzi.*—Nomads, and Shamanist pagans, on the head-waters of the Kan and Mana, the Kamash are the weak representatives of a once powerful tribe. Most of them speak Turkish. From one division, however, which still speaks Samoyed, Klaproth has procured specimens of their vocabulary, and Castrén of their grammar.

*The Uriankhai.*—There are four tribes of the Uriankhai :—

1. The Matlar, already noticed.
2. — Bagar, on the Russian frontier.
3. — Tozhin.
4. — Ulek.

Lake Ubsa (a Turk name) lies in about the centre of the Uriankhai area. The name seems Chinese; being applied to other populations. The Uriankhai, along with the Teleut, were subjects to Dzungaria, until reduced, by the Chinese, in 1744–1755. Two of their chiefs, at that time, mustered 10,000 men between them. I mention this to show that one member of the Samoyed group, at least, has borne an appearance of something like power and organization.

I have given the divisions and subdivisions of the Samoyed family only so far as I feel satisfied with the arrangement. The two main sources of our information are the Asia Polyglotta of Klaproth and the grammars and lexicons of Castrén. Castrén's works, however, are posthumous; so that it is, by no means, in all cases, an easy matter to ascertain what rests on the original investigations of the author, and what has been added by the editor from works already published, especially Klaproth's. It is only certain that the details of the two chief authorities are not exactly the same. Klaproth lays the Tawgi in the same class with the Yurak, along with which he places the Pustosersk, the Obdorsk, the Mangaseia, and the Turukansk dialects. His second class contains the Tas, Tomsk, Narym, Ket, Tym, and Karass forms of speech along with a short specimen of what he calls the Lak. Finally, a list headed *Taigi* (the import of which is not explained), finds place in the third division; a natural and accurate class, containing the Motorian, the Koibal, and the Kamash.

Even in Castrén the details and value of a fourth section called (most inconveniently) the Yeniseian are obscure. The class itself is small. Its name gives the locality of its members. They lie between the Yurak and Tawgi divisions, on the Lower Yenisey. They lie, too, in the parts about Mangaseia, or Turukansk, using two sub-dialects; the Khantai-Karassin, and the Baikha. But, as has already been stated, certain members of the so-called Ostiak division, have intruded themselves into these parts, have been described by the same names as the older occupants, and have engendered an amount of confusion, which future researches may advantageously rectify.

Again, for the Yurak Samoyeds, from the Lower Obi to the White Sea, Klaproth gives us, besides the specimens of their language, the tribual divisions. Evidence that these coincide with the divisions suggested by the philologue is still wanting. The divisions themselves are as follows:—

(1.) *The Vanoita.*—The Vanoita, the most western members of the Yurak, or Kasovo, group, occupy the rivers Mezen and Petshora, as well as the coast of the White Sea, and Arctic Ocean, as far as the parts about Obdorsk.

(2.) The Tyzya Ilogei belong to the interior of the Government of Archangel.

(3.) The Khyryutshi, or Karatsheya, are Siberian rather than European. The Circles of Obdorsk, and Beresov contain their chief districts.

The text continues:—"This divisi[illegible] of the kinsmanships" (*Geschlechter*) "is so rigidly ob[illegible]ved that no Samoyed takes a wife from the kinsmanship to which he himself belongs. On the contrary, he seeks her in one of the other two." That this practice of going out of the family, clan, or tribe of the bridegroom in search of a bride, is common amongst the ruder populations is well known. I doubt, however, whether the fact be exactly as Klaproth gives it. From Archangel to Beresov, or from Obdorsk to the Petshora, is a long way to go for a wife. The observation, more probably, applies to some of the divisions, or subdivisions of the larger groups.

Nevertheless, it may be as it is said to be; so that I draw attention to the statement in order to improve the evidence on which it rests.

The terms Katshinzi, Sagai, Kisilzi, and Koibal, are political rather than ethnological, artificial rather than natural. As a general rule, however, they apply to populations which are Turk in speech, other than Turk in origin. The Katshinzi are the Katsha tribes already noticed as Turks, though, perhaps, Samoyed or Yeniseian in blood. They fall into two divisions.

A few hundred (the males amount to 240) are still to be found on the banks of the Katsha, their original area, near, or in, the town of Krasnoyarsk. Wholly Russianized, they represent that portion of the group which stayed at home, when the remainder emigrated to the valley of the Abakan. The descendants of this division amounted, in 1830, to 3460 males, and 3119 females; in 1847, to 9436 individuals. They reach as far as Askyz; where they are succeeded by

The Sagai, amounting in 1830 to 3897 males, and 4011 females, and extending to the head-waters of the Abakan.

The Kisilzi (2283 males, 2080 females), like the Katshinzi of the Katsha, are all but Russians.*

| English. | Yurak. | Tawgi. | Ostiak. |
|---|---|---|---|
| *Man (homo)* | nyenyeato | anasang | kum |
| —— *(vir)* | hasawa | kuayumu | teb |
| *Head* | aewa | aewua | ol |
| *Hair* | nobta | abta | opt |
| *Eye* | saeu | saime | hai |
| *Ear* | ha | kou | ko |
| *Nose* | puiyea | unka | potsh |
| *Mouth* | nya | ang | ak |
| *Tongue* | nyami | sieya | se |

* These details are taken from the preface to Castrén's Koibal and Karagass Grammar; a work which was not published until the notice on the Siberian Turks had been printed.

| English. | Yurak. | Tawgi. | Ostiak. |
|---|---|---|---|
| *Tooth* | tyibea | tyim | tsheu |
| *Hand* | uda | yutu | ud |
| *Foot* | ae | oai | tob |
| *Sun* | hayen | kou | tyel |
| *Moon* | yiry | kityada | äre |
| *Star* | numgy | fatayea | keska |
| *Fire* | tu | tui | tü |
| *Water* | yi | bê | öt |
| *Stone* | pae | fala | pö |
| *Tree* | pea | fa | po |
| *One* | ngob | ngoai | oker |
| *Two* | side | siti | sede |
| *Three* | nyar | nagur | nagur |
| *Four* | tiet | tyata | tet |
| *Five* | samblang | sangfalanka | somblang |
| *Six* | mat | matu | muktet |
| *Seven* | seu | syaibua | seldye |
| *Eight* | sidendyet | sitidata | sedetshan |
| *Nine* | hasawayu | ameaityuma | okertshan |
| *Ten* | lusayu | bì | kot |

The numerals of the so-called Yeniseian division are as follows:—

| English. | 1st Yeniseian.* | 2nd.† | 3rd.‡ |
|---|---|---|---|
| *One* | ngo | ngo | ngo |
| *Two* | sire | zide | zire |
| *Three* | nehu' | nehu | negu |
| *Four* | teto | tetto | tetto |
| *Five* | soborleggo | sabbareggo | zoborriggo |
| *Six* | notu' | motu | motu |
| *Seven* | seo' | zeo | zeo |
| *Eight* | sirioto | ziditte | ziriotto |
| *Nine* | êsâ | neesa | aza |
| *Ten* | biu' | bü | bün |

It is more likely that the northern part of the Samoyed area should have been conquered from the south than *vice versâ*. Such being the case, the Northern Samoyeds are, probably, intrusive. Castrén believes that they were, and also that the previous occupants of the northern parts

* From Castrén. † The Mangaseia of Klaproth. ‡ The Turukansk of Klaproth.

of Siberia were Fins proper. He infers this from the names of the rivers Ishma, Tsylma, Pyosha, Oya and Kuloi, all of which are significant in the language of Finland. Then there is the story of the Sirtye. The Samoyeds called the Fins by this name. Now the Sirtye fled before the Samoyeds, and hid themselves underground, where they live at the present moment, with abundance of beavers, foxes, and mammoths. I can scarcely think that the aborigines of the North Samoyed area were actual Fins, though they were, probably, an allied population; perhaps more Lap than aught else.

Of the Samoyed mythology we know little, which is a pity; for, as the Samoyeds are amongst the rudest of the Ugrians, a knowledge of their superstitions would be of great value, for the light it would shed over the otherwise obscure creeds of the Laplanders, Finlanders, Estonians, and the like. However, of the Samoyed mythology we know but little. Perhaps, there is not much to know. We know, however, that the word Num is the name of the chief object of their cultus; and this is an important word. It is applied to the thunder, and this in what appears to Castrén, its original sense. It applies also to the sky in general, and to the sun, as the chief luminary. A Samoyed woman, stricken in years, and the observer of old customs, which she spoke of with regret as dying away, used morning and evening to leave her tent and prostrate, or bend, herself before the rising or setting luminary, saying, "When thou, O Yilibeambaertye, risest, so, also, out of my bed rise I," and "When thou, O Yilibeambaertye, settest, so, also, do I go to rest." This is so little of a prayer, that it may only be a receipt for early rising. I give it, however, as I find it.

Yilibeambaertye is a sort of synonym, or epithet for Num. It means, Guard over the hearths. The tribes who use it most are those that have taken a tincture of civilization and Christianity; indeed, it is used, occasionally, to denote Christ. The ruder the Samoyed the more exclusively he speaks of Num, the sky, or the God of the Sky; the God of the Sky in the second instance, though, probably, the God of Thunder in the first. The tribe which most restricts its meaning to the original sense is that of the Kangmash.

Occasionally the name is given to physical phenomena other than atmospheric; other, at least, than those that belong palpably and visibly to the sky. Castrén once heard it applied to the earth; and once, when on the coast of the Icy Sea, he asked "Where is Num?" his attendant said "There," pointing to the waves.

The Tawgi tribes give to a deity named 'A or 'Nga the same importance that the others give to Num. To judge, however, from the Yurak creed, 'Nga is a subterranean, rather than a super-celestial, being. He dwells underground, dark and in darkness; sending to men and beasts death and disease. Do the souls or bodies of deceased men go to him? Castrén doubts this. He finds the idea of any place whatever for the reception of the spirits of the dead all but non-existent. Nevertheless, there is an approach to it in the residence of 'Nga.

There is also an approach to it in the Tadebcyo of the Tadibeas. A Tadibea is the Samoyed Shaman, or Medicine Man—a mere priest of ordinary flesh and blood, alive amongst living men. But the spirit, with whom he has the power of putting himself in contact, and who is called his Tadebcyo, is immaterial, and invisible; at least to ordinary eyes. The Tadibea, however, can see him, speak to him, propitiate him, learn the future events from him. In short, the Tadibea is the mediator between the uninitiated believer, and the Tadebcyo.

Where Christianity has taken root, the Tadebcyo is an evil, rather than a good, demon. Where paganism, however, remains intact, he is more good than bad. A Tadibea would repudiate the idea of dealing with anything diabolical. He will admit, however, that his friend is capricious, hard to please, accessible only through a proper mediator. If he were not so, what would be the use of a Tadibea?

In explaining this Castrén takes an opportunity of stating that the antagonism between absolute good and absolute evil finds no place amongst the Samoyeds. There are no extreme divinities; no Ahriman, no Auramazdes; nothing, in short, divine at all. The human temper is the divine temper also, good and bad mixed; more of the former than the latter. He adds, too, that the Samoyed, in worshipping a material object, such as a rock, tree, or the like, has no secondary ideas in respect to any divinity enshrined therein. He simply worships the object, stock or stone as the case may be. The negative character of this assertion must be borne in mind. It must also be borne in mind that negative statements are, pre-eminently, subject to correction.

The Itarma are the souls of departed Tadibeas.

In some tribes the Tadebcyo are called Los, Loh, and Koika.

The Samoyed analogies of the Roman Penates now claim our attention. They are of two kinds; those made by nature, and those made by human skill. Those of nature's making are odd-shaped stones, especially such as can be compared to the human form. Of course, these are essentially local. They are usually called Hahe.

The Yilyan,* on the other hand, are artificial. One

* Word for word, this is the first element in *Yili*beambeartye, as well as the Ostiak Yilyan.

kind is called Syadaci, from Sya = face. They are sometimes naked, sometimes clothed. They are naked when they stand out of doors, on the moor, in the bog, or on the tundra. They are clothed when they are placed under cover; thoroughly domesticated, and made inmates of the Samoyed dwelling-house.

A certain variety of these requires great care in its fabrication. It must be made partly by a Tadibea, partly by a spotless virgin. The Tadibea takes the skin of a squirrel, an ermine, or a sable, and twists it into something like the shape of a human being; when it has to be dressed, and when the work of the vestal begins. A virgin has to stitch the clothes; a virgin to make the basket in which it lies.

One of the most famous of the Samoyed objects of adoration seems to have been of neither native nor natural workmanship. Castrén thinks it was a Mongol piece of art. It stood near the village of Karbin on the Ket, and had a hut built over it for its special preservation. In vain. It was destroyed a few years ago by a band of Tungús marauders.

But the great repository for the Hahe was the island Waygatz, before its purification by some recent missionries, who (in 1827) burnt, on one spot, 420 Hahes; Waygatz being to the Samoyed what Heligoland was to the Angle, and Rugen to the Pomeranian heathens. It contained three most especial Hahe localities. The first was the Hahe-salye, or the Promontory of the Hahe, the most south-western projection in the island. It was here where the 420 were burnt. The chief of them, named Wesako, or the Old One, had three heads.

The second locality is in the centre of the island; ennobled by the stone Ya Yieru Hahe = the Hahe the Lord of the Land. It lies in a hole. It did not lie there always. It came there by a miracle. It looks like a man with a peaked head, a head like that of Thersites; a head which both the Samoyeds and the Ostiaks are fond of giving to their artificial Hahè. Nyebe-hahe = The Mother Hahe is either a second stone in the same district, or the Ya Yieru Hahe under another name.

The third locality is in the north-west. Castrén heard it called Ya Mâl Hahe, or the Land's End Hahe; Islavin names it Nyu Hahe = Son Hahe. Concerning which he adds, that it was the son of Wesako Hahe and Nyebe Hahe, the parents of three other stones besides, (1) Minisei, a peak of the Urals; (2) Yabmal, a peninsula to the west of the Gulf of Obi; and (3) a stone about twenty versts from Mezene, surrounded by Hahe of wood; which the missionaries treated as they did the 420, and burned.

*The word Samoyed.*—Samo-yed is one of those words that an etymologist can play tricks with; and that in more languages than one. Wherever the root *sam* = *self* and *ed* = *eat*, we may translate it *self-eater*. It does this in Russian. It nearly does so in English, where the word *same* and *self* are closely allied in meaning. It does so to some extent in Latin, where *edo* means *I eat*. But as men are not in the habit of devouring themselves, we must allow a little latitude, and consider *self-eater* to mean merely an *eater of beings like himself*, an *eater of his own kind*, a *cannibal* in short. And for cannibals the Samoyeds have passed. Herberstein tells us that "beyond the river Petshora, near the mountain Camenipoyas, and the sea and island in its neighbourhood, lie various and innumerable nations, called by the common name of Samoged, which being interpreted is *eaters-of-themselves*"—"uno ac communi nomine Samoged (quasi diceres *se ipsos comedentes*) nuncupantur." Doubtless, there have been other blunderers in things appertaining to the Samoyeds, besides the etymologists. I find in the preface to Castrén's grammar that some one committed himself to the doctrine that they shrieked and chattered like apes instead of speaking, and that some one else, once, took the credit of a discoverer when he notified the fact of their using the languages of articulately-speaking men. Physiologists, too, have related strange things concerning them.

Having stated what the word Samoyed is not, I will now say what I think it is. Word for word, I believe it to contain the root of the Fin Suomelaiset, a word which means the *men of a fen, marsh, morass,* or *swamp.* It was applied by the Karelians or Zirianians to the country occupied by their Samoyed neighbours, and taken up from the Karelians or Zirianians by the Russians, from whom it spread over the learned world of Europe at large. If this be true, it is the same word as Samogitia, distant as the latter locality is from the Samoyeds; since a case may be made out for believing that word to be Lithuanic, only in the way that such a name as Britain is English, *i. e.* not at all. As Britain belonged to the language of a population, occupant of a given locality, anterior to the Angle conquest, so did Samogitia apply to a district which was either Ugrian or on the Ugrian frontier before it became Lithuanic.

At present

The Zirianians call the Samoyeds *Yarang.*
— Ostiaks ———————— *Yeryan-yak.*
— Voguls ———————— *Yorran-kum.*
— Tungusians ———————— *Dyandal.*

The Russians, as aforesaid (and, after the Russians, the French, English, and Germans), say Samoyed. But it is only the Kasovo, or northern branch, that they so denominate. The southern Samoyeds have been called Ostiaks; which they are not.

The ordinary interpretation of such a fact as two populations so distant from each other as Herberstein's Samogedi and the Samogitæ of Lithuania, bearing names so similar, is that they both belonged to the same class. The true inference is, that they are in a certain relation to some third population which lies between them, which touches their two frontiers, and which supplies the name common to the two.

This is the principle upon which the natives of Wales, of Italy, of the Valais in Switzerland, of the Walloon country in the Ardennes, are all *Wel*-sh (*Weahl-as*). They all lie in contact with populations sufficiently allied to each other to denote their neighbours by the same term.

*The Andon Domni*, or *Yukahiri*.—A fragmentary population on the lower part of the Kolyma and Indidzhirka calls itself Andon Domni, and is called by its neighbours Yukahiri and Atal. Before the Samoyed was shown to be Ugrian, I placed it in the same class as the Yukahiri. A vocabulary of the language of these last, along with the names of some of their now extinct tribes, is nearly all we have in the way of *data* for their ethnology. They are said to be fine-looking men, though not strong enough to hold their own against the Yakut on one side, and Tshuktsi on the other. The Tungús, too, seem to have pressed on them. Of all the primary tribes of Siberia this seems to be the nearest its dissolution.

| English. | Yukahiri. | Koriak. | Yakut. | Tungús. |
|---|---|---|---|---|
| *Head* | monoli | lawut | baz | dyll |
| *Eye* | angdzha | lalat | kharakh | eha |
| *Ear* | golendzhi | vyilut | kulgakh | zen |
| *Nose* | yongyul | enigytam | murun | ongokto |
| *Mouth* | angya | zekiangin | ayak | hamun |

| English. | Yukahiri. | Koriak. | Yakut. | Tungús. |
|---|---|---|---|---|
| *Hair* | manallae | katshugui | az | nyuritta |
| *Tongue* | andzhub | gügel | tyl | ingni |
| *Tooth* | tody | wannalgyn | tiz | ikta (!) |
| *Hand* | tolondzha | myngakatsh | ili | ngala |
| *Day* | bondzhirka | hallo | kun | inangi |
| *Sun* | bugonshe | tyketi | kun | ziguni |
| *Moon* | kininshe | geilygen | ui | bega |
| *Star* | lerungundzhia | lelapitshan | zulus | haulen |
| *Fire* | yenyilo | milugan | wot | togo |
| *Water* | ondzhi | mimal | u | mu |
| *Tree* | tshal | uttepel | maz | mo |
| *Stone* | kall | guggon | taz | dzholo |
| *One* | irken | onnon | bir | omukon |
| *Two* | antaklon | nioktsh | ike | dzhur |
| *Three* | yalon | niyokh | uz | ilyan |
| *Four* | yekalon | niyakh | tirt | dygyn |
| *Five* | onganlon | myllangin | ves | tongo |
| *Six* | malhiyalon | onnanmyllangin | alta | nyungun |
| *Seven* | purkion | langin | seta | nadan |
| *Eight* | malhielekhlon | niyokh-myllangin | agys | dzhapkun |
| *Nine* | khuni-izkeel-lendzhin | khonnaitshinkin | dogys | yagin |
| *Ten* | kuniella | mynegytkin | on | dzhur |

The root *malhi*, in the Yukahiri numerals for *six* and *eight*, is the *malhuk* (*malguk*) = *two* of several of the dialects of North-west America. *Yakut* and *Aino* are also (along with several others) American glosses. East of the Lena decidedly American characteristics present themselves; and that prominently.

# CHAPTER XXVI.

Doubtful Ugrians.—The Yeniseians.—The Tshuvash.

The present chapter is possibly the place for three populations already noticed—the Bashkirs, the Meshtseryak, and the Teptyar, all of which, though Turk in speech, are probably Fin in blood. It is probable, too, that others besides are in this predicament.

(1.) *The Yeniseians.*—In all the works anterior to the publication of the Asia Polyglotta, in 1823, a number of tribes occupying the valley of the Yenisey were known under the name of Ostiak. As, however, they were a different population from the true Ostiak, Klaproth called them Yeniseians.

Their area lies along the Yenisey from Abakansk, in 53° N. L., to Turukansk, in 66°. A few are found on the Ket, a feeder of the Obi. The Yenisey, however, is their river; on the left bank of which they are more numerous than on the right.

The Yeniseians proper, or Könniyüng, between Yeniseyisk and Turukansk, amount to about 1000 men, who pay tribute, split up into different tribes. They live in movable huts, consisting of a few poles, encircled by the rind of the birch, and, with a few reindeers, but more dogs, subsist chiefly by fishing and hunting; skilful in both pursuits; skilful, too, as smiths and smelters of iron; still retentive of their original paganism, paying particular respect to the bear.

Small as is this branch of the family, that to which the Kot belong is smaller still; Kot being the name by which its members are noticed by the writers of the last century. At present they consist of a few families on the river Agul, a feeder of the Kan, which constitute a single village. They hold fast to their language and nationality, as it is wise in them to do; being lighter taxed than if they were counted as Russian. Nevertheless a few Russianized families have attached themselves to the settlement; of which the pure Kot make a trouble. This little Agul village is in the country of the Kamass Samoyeds. Castrén saw five individuals of the stock, and took down of their language enough to form the last of his numerous and valuable works. It is now in the course of publication.

There are, possibly, a few other members of this group which still retain their original language. The greater part, however, of the tribes has lost it. The forms of speech which they are most likely to have adopted are, of course, those of the tribes with which they come in contact, viz. the northern and southern Samoyeds, the Obi Ostiaks, the Tshapodzhir, the other Tungús tribes to the east of the Yenisey, and, finally, the Sayanian Turk.

It is an historical fact that this last-named language is that which has been adopted by the Arini, or Arintsi, south of Krasnoyarsk. As long ago as 1721 the Arini amounted to no more than forty or fifty individuals, and in 1735 to no more than ten; of which only two spoke their native tongue. The rest had either died off, or become assimilated to the Turks of the river Katsha. Their power was broken at the time of the Russian conquest of the parts about Tobolsk and Tomsk; and it was broken by a blunder. When the Russians were fighting against the other Siberians, the Arini sent to Tobolsk an arrow, some red earth, and a black fox, *as a symbol of friendship*. It was mistaken for the contrary, and the nation was attacked accordingly.

The *Deng*, or *Denka*, as they call themselves, are called also the *Sable Ostiaks;* though less correctly. In 1723, Messerschmidt took a vocabulary of their language, and remarked, that it carried its numerals no further than *five*. Their locality was on the Tunguska.

Of the *Yesirti* and (? or) *Dzesirti* I can only say, that, along with the Arini, they bury their dead as follows: —The bow and arrows are placed in the grave of the deceased, over which his best horse is slaughtered and flayed. The skin is then stretched over a pole, set up on the grave, and the flesh is feasted on.

The women, after their confinements, wash themselves three times within the first seven days, and then fumigate themselves with a herb named Irben. The first friend that visits them names the child.

Their oaths are taken over a bear's head, of which the swearer fixes his teeth in the nose.

When a sentence equivalent to banishment is pronounced against a culprit, he is placed between a dog and a reindeer. These are then set free. Whichever way they run must be taken by the man also, who is no longer allowed to remain where he was. Even a draught of water from his old locality is forbidden. So is all further intercourse with any of his original neighbours.

For no population throughout Siberia are our notices more scanty than they are for these Yeniseians.

The name *Arini* is probably Turk rather than native.

It is said to mean *wasps;* the population to which it applies being so denominated from their warlike activity. But it most likely means nothing of the kind. Word for word, it is *Yarang,* &c.

| English. | Inbazk. | Pampokolsk. | Assan. | Kot. | Arini. |
|---|---|---|---|---|---|
| *Man* (*homo*) | ket | kit | hit | ilit | khitt |
| —— (*vir*) | tshet | ilset | hadkip | hatkit | Lirkhanyat |
| *Head* | tsig | kolka | takai | tagai | kolkya |
| *Hair* | tonge | khynga | khingayang | hingayang | khagang |
| *Foot* | toigen | aning | pulang | pulang | pil |
| *Eye* | des | dat | tesh | tetshagan | tieng |
| *Ear* | hokten | —— | klokan | kalogan | utkhonong |
| *Nose* | olen | hang | an | ang | arkhui |
| *Mouth* | ko | kan | hohui | hohu | bukhom |
| *Tongue* | ei | ilygyl | alup | alup | alyap |
| *Sun* | i | hikhem | oga | ega | ega |
| *Moon* | khip | khep | shui | shui | eshui |
| *Star* | koogo | kaken | alak | 'alagan | ilkhoi |
| *Fire* | bok | butsh | hat | khott | khott |
| *Water* | ul | ul | ul | ul | kul |
| *River* | ses | tom | ul | kem | sat |
| *Hill* | kai | khai | yii | dzhii | kar |
| *Tree* | oksa | oksy | atsh | atshshi | kush-oshtshe |
| *Stone* | tshugs | tshys | shish | shish | khez |
| *Egg* | ong | eg | shulei | shulei | ang |
| *Fish* | isse | gite | tyg | tig | ilti |
| *God* | eis | es | etsh | esh | es |
| *Sky* | eis | es | etsh | esh | es |
| *House* | khush | hukut | hush | hush | hu |
| *Milk* | mamel | den | —— | —— | tengul |
| *Snow* | begges | tyg | tik | tik | the |
| *One* | khus-em | khuta | hutsha | hutsha | khusei |
| *Two* | un-em | hinneang | üna | inya | kina |
| *Three* | dong-em | donga | tongya | tongya | tyonga |
| *Four* | zi-em | ziang | sheggiang | tshegs | shaya |
| *Five* | gag-em | kheilang | geigyan | kega | khala |
| *Six* | ag-am | aggiang | gedudzhiang | kelutsha | ögga |
| *Seven* | enh-am | onyang | gdiliniang | kelina | unnya |
| *Eight* | unem-boisan-khogen | hing-basi-khaiyang | geiltaniang | kheltonga | kina-mant-shau |
| *Nine* | khusem-boi-san-khogen | khuta-yamos-khaiyang | godzhi-buna-giang | hutshabunaga | kusa-mant-shau |
| *Ten* | khogen | khaiyang | hagiang | haga | khoa |

(2.) *The Tshuvash.*—In the Government of Kazan reside as many as 300,000 Tshuvashes, differing from the other Ugrian populations in their somewhat superior civilization, and from the so-called Tartars in the fact of their being Christians rather than Mahometans. Respecting their language much has been written; some inquirers maintaining that it is essentially Ugrian upon which a great deal of Turk has been engrafted; others that it is Turk at bottom, but Ugrian in respect to its superadded elements.

| English. | Tshuvash. | Osmanli. | Tsheremis. |
|---|---|---|---|
| *Head* | puz | bash | bui |
| *Eye* | kos | gos | shinsya |
| *Ear* | khulga | khulak | piliksh |
| *Nose* | sumsah | burun | ner |
| *Mouth* | zuvar | aghis | ushmu |
| *Hair* | zuz | satsh | ip |
| *Tongue* | tshilge | dil | elmye |
| *Tooth* | shil | dish | puntshal |
| *Hand* | alla | el | kit |
| *Sun* | khwel | gyun | ketshe |
| *Moon* | oikh | ai | tilsye |
| *Star* | zuldur | yildis | shuder |
| *Fire* | wot | od | tul |
| *Water* | shiva | su | wut |
| *Tree* | evyz | agatsh | pu |
| *Stone* | tshol | tash | kü |
| *One* | pra | bir | iktet |
| *Two* | ikke | iki | koktot |
| *Three* | vise | utsh | kumut |
| *Four* | dwatta | dort | nilit |
| *Five* | pilik | besh | visit |
| *Six* | alta | alty | kudut |
| *Seven* | sitshe | yedi | shimit |
| *Eight* | sakar | sekis | kandashe |
| *Nine* | tukhon | dokus | indeshe |
| *Ten* | wonka | on | lu |

Schubert reckoned the Tshuvash at 370,000; a high number for a Ugrian, or even a Turk, population. At the present moment they are more numerous still, being an increasing population.

Their distribution of the Tshuvash is as follows :—

| | |
|---|---|
| In Kazan . . . . . | 300,091 |
| — Simbirsk . . . . | 84,714 |
| — Samar . . . . . | 29,926 |
| — Orenburg . . . . | 8,353 |
| — Saratov . . . . | 6,853 |
| — Viatka . . . . . | 17 |
| | 429,954 |

The Tshuvash (for the name is not native) call themselves Vyres, Vereyal, and Khirdyal.

NOTE.

I originally placed the Yeniseians in the same category with the Samoyeds. (See "Varieties of Man.") Castrén, however, so decidedly denies that the Yeniseian language is Ugrian that, in deference to his opinion, I suspend my judgment until the publication of his forthcoming grammar of the Kot. I may also add that, when I connected the Yeniseian with the Samoyed and Yukahiri I overlooked some notable Turk affinities, some of which may be seen in page 273 of the present volume. Whatever the Yeniseian may be, the Yukahiri is Samoyed.

# CHAPTER XXVII.

The Koreans.—The Koriak and Kamtskadales.—The Kurilians or Aino.—The Japanese and Lúchú Islanders.

(1.) *The Koreans.*—The natives of the peninsula of Korea resemble both the Chinese and the Japanese in their physical appearance, having flat faces, oblique eyes, broad cheek-bones, strong black hair, scanty beard. They are strongly made, and they vary in respect to the colour of the skin. Sometimes it is tawny or yellow rather than brown, sometimes brown. Siebold calls it "wheat-coloured" and "straw-coloured." He also calls it "reddish yellow." This means that it has a maroon tint; as has that of some of the Chinese.

The chief foreign influences that have acted on Korea are those of China and Japan; the religion being Buddhist. The alphabet, however, is other than Chinese. So is the language. The former is phonetic rather than rhematographic; the latter agglutinate rather than monosyllabic.

How far the Koreans are a pure or a mixed race is uncertain. The Chinese, according to Klaproth, make some of them descendants of the Sam Han, and others descendants of the Sienpi. But everything about the Sienpi is obscure.

Again—Siebold writes that many individuals depart, in

their physical appearance, from the Mongol type and approach the European; having sharp profiles and beards.

That the Korean area extended beyond its present limits is an inference from the word Solgo. This is what a Mantshú calls a Korean. Word for word, it is Solon, the name of a Mantshú tribe in contact with the northern Mongols.

| English. | Korean. | Japanese. | Mantshú. |
|---|---|---|---|
| *Eye* | nuon | mi | yasa |
| *Head* | mati | kaobe | udzhi |
| *Ear* | kui | mimi | shan |
| *Nose* | ko | khana | okoro |
| *Mouth* | yip | kuti | anga |
| *Tongue* | hie | sita | veikhe |
| *Tooth* | ni | kha | ilengu |
| *Hand* | sun | te | gala |
| *Foot* | pal | asi | betkhe |
| *Sun* | heng | fi | shun |
| *Moon* | oru | zuki | bia |
| *Star* | peru | fosi | uzhikha |
| *Fire* | pol | fi | tua |
| *Water* | mu | midz | make |
| *Tree* | nan | ki | moo |
| *Stone* | tu, tol | isi | vekhe |
| *Fish* | koki | ivo | nimakha |
| *One* | hodzhun | fito | emu |
| *Two* | tupu | fitak | dzhuo |
| *Three* | sai | miz | ilan |
| *Four* | nai | yots | duin |
| *Five* | tashu | izuts | sundzha |
| *Six* | ishu | muts | ninggun |
| *Seven* | iki | nanats | nadan |
| *Eight* | ita | yats | dzhakun |
| *Nine* | yahao | kokonots | uyun |
| *Ten* | ye | tovo | dzhuan |

(2.) *The Koriak.*—To the north of the peninsula of Kamtskatka lie the Koræki, or Koriak, Shamanist, or imperfect Christians of the Greek Church, those of the Circle of Okhotsk being more Russianized than the rest.

*The Tshuktshi.*—The Tshuktshi are a branch of the

same stock, more exclusively Shamanist than the Koræki; and more independent of Russia. They lie on the edge of the Arctic Sea between the Yukahiri and the Namollo Eskimo.

*The Kamtskatkans*, or *Kamtskadales*, whose native name is Itülmen, occupy the parts to the south of the river Tigil, in the peninsula that bears their name; the extreme point of which, however, is not Kamtskatkan but Kurilian. They are few in numbers.

| English. | *Koriak. | †Kamtskatkan. | Namollo. |
|---|---|---|---|
| *Head* | lawut | kobbel | naskok |
| *Eye* | lalat | elled | ik |
| *Ear* | vyilut | ilyud | tshintak |
| *Nose* | enigytam | kayako | tatuk |
| *Mouth* | zekiangin | tskhylda | —— |
| *Hair* | katshugui | tsheron | nuyak |
| *Tooth* | wannalgyn | —— | gutuk |
| *Tongue* | gügel | dydzil | ullyu |
| *Hand* | myngakatsh | tono | —— |
| *Day* | hallo | taazh | gannak |
| *Sun* | tyketi | koatsh | shekinak |
| *Moon* | geilygen | quingan-kuletsh | tankuk |
| *Star* | lelapitshan | ezhingin | igalgetak |
| *Fire* | milugan | pangitsh | annak |
| *Water* | mimal | i | mok |
| *Tree* | uttepel | oo | unakhtshjk |
| *Stone* | guggon | kual | uigakh |
| *Egg* | lygly | nygagada | —— |
| *Fish* | kokayalgatyng | etshuda | zalyuk |
| *River* | waim | küg | kiuk |
| *God* | anggang | kutkhai | istla |
| —— | —— | —— | aghak |
| *Sky* | khain | kokhal | kiulah |
| —— | —— | kollaa | keilak |
| *Snow* | kalatyg | kolaal | annu |
| *One* | onnon | dysyk | atashek |
| *Two* | nioktsh | kaas | malgok |
| *Three* | niyokh | tsúk | pigayut |
| *Four* | niyakh | tshaak | ishtamat |
| *Five* | myllangin | kúmnak | tatlimat |

* Of the Kolyma. † Middle of the Peninsula.

| English. | Koriak. | Kamtskatkan. | Namollo. |
|---|---|---|---|
| *Six* | onnan-myllangin | kylkoak | sevinlak |
| *Seven* | langin | etakhtana | malguk |
| *Eight* | niyokh-myllangin | tshonutono | pigayuk |
| *Nine* | khonnai-tshinkin | tshanatana | aginlik |
| *Ten* | mynegytkin | tshemyktagona | kulla |

The Kamtskatkans of A.D. 1701 are contrasted with their northern neighbours the Koræki (Koriaks), and Lutorzi, or occupants of the coast of the Gulf of Pendzinsk. The Koræki were beardless, and spoke a language unintelligible to the Kamtskatkans. The Kamtskatkans spoke a language unintelligible to the Koræki, and were bearded. The Koræki made their huts of reeds and reindeer skins. The Lutorzi dwelt underground. So did the Kamtskatkans in the winter. In the summer, however, they dwelt in the air, in huts erected on a wooden frame, into which they ascended by ladders. Three or four hundred of these built close together, made a village. This implies that the population was, comparatively speaking, dense. Along the river Yelovka alone, a Kosak sent for information as to the occupancy of the parts near the sea, reported as many as 160 forts. These seem to have consisted of one large and several smaller buildings; the large ones holding from 150 to 200 men. Near each of these every man had a smaller one for himself, built on posts, the covering being of hides. The reporter added that since the Russians had been in the country, the number of these forts had been increased. The Russians, however, soon destroyed them. They burnt the buildings, and killed the inhabitants as they came out. Against a warfare of this kind, and men armed with fire-arms, the ordinary weapons of the Kamtskatkans, slings, pointed poles, and clubs, were of little avail. The diminution of the population proceeded at a sad and rapid rate. Besides the wooden forts there were some earthworks; but these were carried as easily as the forts. The fire-arms frightened away the defenders. Amongst themselves they went to war, during the winter, on snow-skates. The Koræki used, as war-chariots, their sledges. The Koræki drove reindeer; the Kamtskatkans dogs.

They were foul feeders; their meat being eaten either raw or frozen, and the cookery being of an incredibly prerude character. To boil their messes of putrid fish (previously put in a hole in the ground and covered up to keep), they used a wooden trough, into which they flung hot pebbles till the water boiled.

They are stated to have gone naked during the summer. Sometimes they were brave, sometimes panic-stricken cowards. Much, indeed, has been written concerning the moral qualities of the Kamtskatkans, the basis of which is the account of the naturalist Steller, who lived long amongst them, and became almost as much of a Kamtskatkan as the Kamtskatkans themselves.

They were excitable, not to say (for men) hysterical. A light matter sent them mad; or made them commit suicide. Their stimulants were strange and nauseous. Their sexual appetites morbid. In all this they seem to differ from the ruder nations of the north. The difference, however, may be more apparent than real. It may arise out of the fact of the description of its elements being fuller. The dances of the Tungús seem to resemble those of the Kamtskadales. The tendency to male hysteria is Lap. So is much of the Kamtskatkan excitability.

The Kamtskatkan sledge is drawn by dogs. So is that of the Dog Tungús, and the Eskimo. Indeed the dog as a domestic beast of draught now replaces the reindeer.

The maker of the earth and heavens is Katshu, whose

sister is Katligith, whose daughter is Sidanka, and whose son is Tigil. Tigil, however, is, also, the name of a river.

(3.) *The Kurilians*, or *Aino*.—The Kurilians, or Aino, occupy two localities on the main land, and all the islands between Kamtskatka and Japan. The localities on the main land have been already mentioned. One was at the mouth of the Sagalin, one at the southern extremity of Kamtskatka. Of the latter we know but little; not knowing much more about the former. We know the people, however, under the name of Gilak. We know that the peninsula of Tarakai is Kurilian.

Some of the Aino are subject to China, some to Japan, some to Russia. They are said to be dark-skinned, but as the iris is light, their depth of colour may be apparent rather than real. Mongol features are common; yet prominent noses, and comparatively thick beards, are by no means wanting. Indeed, the phenomena that appear in Korea, suggestive of the notion of a double population, re-appear in Kurilia.

In the island of Karafto, at least, Kamoi is the chief deity; Kami being the name of a god in Japanese, and of a Shamanist priest in Mongolia.

In their marriages the Aino avoid near relationships. The northern occupants of Karafto take their wives from the south.

That the Kurilian area, like the Korean, once extended inland beyond its present frontier, is likely. The numerals of the Mantshú of the frontier, seem to have taken the Aino ending in *f*.

| English. | Aino of Kamtskatka. | Tarakai. | Yeso. |
|---|---|---|---|
| *Man* (*vir*) | okkaiyu* | okkai | oikyo |
| —— (*homo*) | ainuh | ainu | ainu |
| —— | guru | guru | —— |
| *Eye* | sik | shigi | —— |
| *Head* | gpa | shaba | —— |

* Oyakotsh, *Koriak*.

| English. | Aino of Kamtskatka. | Tarakai. | Yeso. |
|---|---|---|---|
| *Hair* | ruh | numa | karnu |
| *Ear* | gsahr | kisara | —— |
| *Nose* | ahdum | idu | —— |
| *Mouth* | tshar | paru | —— |
| *Tongue* | aukh | ai | —— |
| *Tooth* | imak | nimaki | mimak |
| *Hand* | dek' | tegi | —— |
| *Foot* | kehmma | kima | —— |
| *Blood* | kehm | kim | —— |
| *Sun* | tshupu | tshukf-kamoi | touki |
| *Moon* | tshupu | tshukf | zuki |
| *Star* | kytta | nodzi | noro |
| *Fire* | apeh | undzhi | abe |
| *Water* | peh | raka | vakha |
| *Tree* | nyh | nü | —— |
| *Stone* | poinah | shioma | —— |
| *Egg* | nokh | nuku | —— |
| *Fish* | tshep | zepf | zizf |
| *One* | syhnap | shnepf | senezb |
| *Two* | dupk | tup | zuzb |
| *Three* | raph | repf | rezb |
| *Four* | yhnap | inipf | inezb |
| *Five* | ahsik | ashiki | asaranfof |
| *Six* | ihguahn | yuvambi | yuiwambe |
| *Seven* | aruahn | aruvambi | aruambe |
| *Eight* | duppyhs | tubisambi | zuyemambe |
| *Nine* | syhnapyhs | shnebishambi | sinesambe |
| *Ten* | upyhs | wambi | fambe. |

| English. | Aino of Kamtskatka. | Kamtskatkan proper (South). |
|---|---|---|
| *Eye* | sik | nannin |
| *Head* | gpa | tshysha |
| *Hair* | ruh | kubün |
| *Ear* | gsahr | igiad |
| *Nose* | ahdum | kaiki |
| *Mouth* | tshar | telun |
| *Tongue* | aukh | nitshil |
| *Hand* | dek | sittu |
| *Sun* | tshupu | galen-kutelsh |
| *Moon* | tshupu | koatsh |
| *Star* | kytta | ashangit |
| *Water* | peh | asamkh |
| *Tree* | nyh | nuda |
| *Stone* | poina | uvatshi |
| *Egg* | nokh | lylida |
| *Fish* | tshep | entshudu. |

I cannot think that it is by mere accident that the root *kor* appears in the names *Kor*-ea, *Kur*-ile, and *Kor*-iak; nor yet that it is by accident that, when we reach the Baltic, the same syllable appears in *Kar*-elia, and *Kur*-land; also appearing in the name of the Government of *Kur*-sk. In Siberia, similitudes between the geographical names occur where the languages (in the present state of our classification at least) belong to either widely-different groups or to different sections of the same group. Thus, Tagil is the name of a river as far westward as the Government of Perm, Tigil the name of a river as far eastward as Kamtskatka. Tagil is on the boundaries of Europe. Tigil flows into the Pacific. Neviask, one of the oldest mining establishments in Siberia, is on the eastern side of the Ural, on the river Neva. St. Petersburg, in the Ingrian portion of the proper Fin country, is on a Neva as well. The Kolyma is, apparently, word for word, the Tshulim. There is also a river Kialim. The Tshuvash of Kazan have already been spoken of. The Tshuvants were a tribe of the Yukahiri.

(4.) *The Japanese and Lúchú Islanders.*—In its essentials the civilization of Japan is that of China. The Japanese, like the Chinese, have towns, arts, commerce, agriculture, a central Government, a Buddhist creed, and a lettered language. The language, however, is agglutinate rather than monosyllabic, and the alphabet, like the Korean, is phonetic rather than rhematographic.

There are differences in the details of the Buddhism. In Japan the traces of the primitive creed are numerous. There is the cultus of the deity of the sun, the son of Izanagi and Izanami, husband and wife, the last king and the last queen of the seventh dynasty of gods, each of whom reigned thousands, or even millions of years. The Amat-sukami, whose name is a compound of kami =

deity, ruled before the world began. I cannot say that this is not Buddhism. It is certainly something more than mere Shamanism.

Thunberg's description of a Japanese is that of an ordinary Mongol, with a flat face, black hair, broad cheek-bones, and oblique eyes. Siebold's is somewhat different. He notices two types. The field-labourers have broad faces, brown hair with an occasional tinge of red, flat noses, large mouths, and a comparatively light complexion. The fishers of the sea-coast have prominent features, with their noses inclining to the aquiline. Their hair is black, and crisp; wavy and with a tendency to curl.

The nobles, writes Kæmpfer, are somewhat more majestic in their deportment than the generality, and are more like the Europeans.

We have now had the details of the double type. It has appeared in Mantshuria, in Korea, amongst the Koriaks, amongst the Aino, and in Japan.

*The Lúchú Islanders.*—In language and physical form the Lúchú islanders resemble the Japanese; their Buddhism being more imperfect and their manners more simple.

| English. | Japanese. | Lúchú. | Aino of Tarakai. |
|---|---|---|---|
| *Eye* | mi | mi | shigi |
| *Head* | kaobe | busi | shaba |
| *Ear* | mimi | mimmi | kisara |
| *Nose* | khana | honna | idu |
| *Mouth* | kuti | —— | para |
| *Tongue* | sita | stsha | ai |
| *Tooth* | kha | kha | nimaki |
| *Hand* | te | ki | tegi |
| *Foot* | asi | shanna | kima |
| *Sun* | fi | tida | tshukf-kamoi |
| *Moon* | zuki | gwazi | tshukf |
| *Star* | fosi | fushi | nodzi |
| *Fire* | fi | fi | undzhi |

| English. | Japanese. | Lúchú. | Aino of Tarakai. |
|---|---|---|---|
| *Water* | midz | mizi | raka |
| *Tree* | ki | ki | nü |
| *Stone* | isi | ishi | shioma |
| *Fish* | ivo | io | zepf |
| *One* | fito | tizi | shnepf |
| *Two* | fitak | tazi | tup |
| *Three* | miz | mizi | repf |
| *Four* | yots | yuzu | inipf |
| *Five* | izuts | —— | ashiki |
| *Six* | muts | mutsi | yuvambi |
| *Seven* | nanats | nanatsi | aruvambi |
| *Eight* | yats | yatsi | tubisambi |
| *Nine* | kokonots | kannizi | shnebishambi |
| *Ten* | tovo | tu | wambi. |

The small islands between the Lúchú group and Formosa are in the same category with the Lúchús themselves, *i. e.* they are Japanese rather than Malay. The names of them end in *-sima* (Madzhiko*sima*, &c.), meaning *island*.

## CHAPTER XXVIII.

Relative importance of the preceding Groups in the History of the World. —Burmese.—Siamese.—Chinese.—Tibetans.—Mantshú.—Mongols.—Ugrians.—Turks.—Paramount importance of the latter.—Turks proper.—White Huns.—Alans.—Avars, &c.—Khazars.—Ghuznevids.—Seljukians, &c.—Mameluks.—Ottomans.—Petshinegs.—Uz.—Kumanians.—Huns.—Scythians.[1]

We may now look back upon the divisions and subdivisions of the numerous groups that have been under notice, with a view of deciding upon their relative importance as material or moral forces in the history of the world. How far has a given influence been extended? How far and in what direction? When did it begin, when did it cease to act? Was it moral rather than material, or material rather than moral?

As a general rule the forces in question have been material. None of the great religions, nor yet any of the important literatures, have originated with any of the foregoing populations. Or, if they have so originated, their development and diffusion have been effected by others.

In that great class of which the Tibetan, the Nepaulese, the Burmese, the Siamese, and the other allied groups, were sections, the civilization is, for the most part, of Indian origin. So, at least, it appears to those who put the same low value as myself upon the pretensions of the Chinese to an indigenous and independent culture.

*The Burmese* are the dominant members of the class to which they belong; the direction in which they have intruded and conquered being from north to south. The annexed table illustrates the extent to which the nume-

| | Khamtí. | Siamese. | A'ká. | A'bor. | Mishimí. | Burmese. | Karen. | Singpho. | Jilí. | Gáro. | Manipurí. | Songpú. | Kapwí. | Koreng. | Marám. | Champhung. | Luhuppa. | N. Tángkhul. | C. Tángkhul. | S. Tángkhul. | Khoibú. | Maring. | Anamese. |
|---|---|---|---|---|---|---|---|---|---|---|---|---|---|---|---|---|---|---|---|---|---|---|---|
| Khamtí . . . . | | 92 | 1 | 1 | 5 | 8 | 8 | 3 | 10 | 3 | 3 | 1 | 0 | 1 | 0 | 0 | 0 | 0 | 0 | 0 | 0 | 0 | 5 |
| Siamese . . . | 92 | | 0 | 0 | 3 | 6 | 8 | 8 | 10 | 1 | 3 | 1 | 0 | 1 | 0 | 0 | 0 | 0 | 0 | 0 | 0 | 0 | 5 |
| A'bor . . . . . | 1 | 0 | | 47 | 20 | 17 | 12 | 15 | 15 | 5 | 11 | 3 | 10 | 3 | 8 | 8 | 8 | 5 | 6 | 10 | 8 | 10 | 0 |
| A'ká . . . . . | 1 | 0 | 47 | | 20 | 11 | 10 | 18 | 11 | 6 | 15 | 6 | 11 | 5 | 8 | 6 | 8 | 8 | 8 | 10 | 10 | 18 | 0 |
| Mishimí . . . | 5 | 3 | 20 | 20 | | 10 | 10 | 10 | 13 | 10 | 11 | 0 | 11 | 0 | 3 | 5 | 6 | 8 | 6 | 13 | 10 | 8 | 1 |
| Burmese . . . | 8 | 6 | 17 | 11 | 10 | | 23 | 23 | 26 | 12 | 16 | 8 | 20 | 6 | 11 | 11 | 11 | 10 | 13 | 13 | 16 | 16 | 1 |
| Karen . . . . | 8 | 8 | 12 | 10 | 10 | 23 | | 17 | 21 | 8 | 15 | 10 | 15 | 8 | 12 | 4 | 12 | 8 | 12 | 12 | 10 | 15 | 2 |
| Singpho . . . | 3 | 3 | 15 | 18 | 10 | 23 | 17 | | 70 | [illegible] | 25 | [illegible] | [illegible] | [illegible] | [illegible] | [illegible] | [illegible] | [illegible] | [illegible] | [illegible] | [illegible] | 18 | 5 |
| Jilí . . . . . . | 10 | 10 | 15 | 11 | 13 | 26 | 21 | 70 | | [illegible] | [illegible] | [illegible] | [illegible] | [illegible] | [illegible] | [illegible] | [illegible] | [illegible] | [illegible] | [illegible] | [illegible] | 20 | 3 |
| Gáro . . . . . | 3 | 1 | 5 | 6 | 10 | 12 | 8 | 16 | 22 | | 10 | 5 | 6 | 5 | 8 | 5 | 8 | 13 | 11 | 5 | 5 | 5 | 3 |
| Manipurí . . | 3 | 3 | 11 | 15 | 11 | 16 | 15 | 25 | 16 | 10 | | 21 | 41 | 18 | 25 | 28 | 31 | 28 | 35 | 33 | 40 | 50 | 6 |
| Songpú . . . . | 1 | 1 | 3 | 6 | 0 | 8 | 10 | 10 | 10 | 5 | 21 | | 35 | 50 | 53 | 20 | 23 | 15 | 15 | 13 | 8 | 15 | 6 |
| Kapwí . . . . | 0 | 0 | 10 | 11 | 11 | 20 | 15 | 18 | 21 | 6 | 41 | 35 | | 30 | 33 | 20 | 35 | 30 | 40 | 45 | 38 | 40 | 5 |
| Koreng . . . . | 1 | 1 | 3 | 5 | 0 | 6 | 8 | 11 | 13 | 5 | 18 | 50 | 30 | | 41 | 18 | 21 | 20 | 20 | — | 10 | 15 | 3 |
| Marám . . . . | 0 | 0 | 8 | 8 | 3 | 11 | 12 | 11 | 11 | 8 | 25 | 53 | 33 | 41 | | 21 | 28 | 25 | 20 | 16 | 23 | 26 | 3 |
| Champhung . | 0 | 0 | 8 | 6 | 5 | 11 | 4 | 13 | 11 | 5 | 28 | 20 | 20 | 18 | 21 | | 40 | 20 | 20 | 16 | 15 | 25 | 3 |
| Luhuppa . . . | 0 | 0 | 8 | 8 | 6 | 11 | 12 | 15 | 18 | 8 | 31 | 23 | 35 | 21 | 28 | 40 | | 63 | 55 | 36 | 33 | 40 | 5 |
| N. Tángkhul. | 0 | 0 | 5 | 8 | 8 | 10 | 8 | 13 | 20 | 13 | 28 | 15 | 30 | 20 | 25 | 20 | 63 | | 85 | 30 | 31 | 31 | 3 |
| C. Tángkhul . | 0 | 0 | 6 | 8 | 6 | 13 | 12 | 25 | 20 | 11 | 35 | 15 | 40 | 20 | 20 | 20 | 55 | 85 | | 41 | 45 | 41 | 1 |
| S. Tángkhul . | 0 | 0 | 10 | 10 | 13 | 13 | 12 | 13 | 13 | 5 | 33 | 13 | 45 | 11 | 16 | 16 | 36 | 30 | 41 | | 43 | 43 | 5 |
| Khoibú . . . . | 0 | 0 | 8 | 10 | 10 | 16 | 10 | 20 | 20 | 5 | 40 | 8 | 38 | 10 | 23 | 15 | 33 | 31 | 45 | 43 | | 78 | 3 |
| Maring . . . | 0 | 0 | 10 | 18 | 8 | 16 | 15 | 18 | 20 | 5 | 50 | 15 | 40 | 15 | 26 | 25 | 40 | 31 | 41 | 43 | 78 | | 3 |
| Anamese . . . | 5 | 5 | 0 | 0 | 1 | 1 | 2 | 5 | 3 | 3 | 6 | 6 | 5 | 3 | 3 | 3 | 5 | 3 | 1 | 5 | 3 | 3 | |

rous vocabularies, collected by the Rev. Mr. Brown, and published in the Transactions of the Asiatic Society of Bengal, represent like or unlike languages. The numbers give the percentage of words that agree. And it is clear that they tell a long tale briefly. They give, indeed, not only the nucleus of the Burmese group, but most of its details. They show, too, that the Anamese, on the one side, and the Siamese and Khamti on the other are strangers to it. A language that is spoken so far south as Pegu, yet has its nearest congeners on the frontier of Asam, is evidently a language that has spread itself at the expense of others, and that to a great extent. Such a language is the Burmese proper. Such a language is the Karien. That

*The T'hay* tongues have done the same, and that their

direction has been vertical, is shown by the resemblance of the Khamti to the Siamese proper; the distance from the extreme points of the two areas being upwards of twenty degrees.

*The Bhot* of the Tibetans has also diffused itself within a comparatively recent period. Such, at least, is the inference from the great extent of ground over which it is spoken with a *minimum* amount of difference of dialect. Its original *situs* is on the east. This is an inference from its affinities with the Burmese and T'hay.

So much for the leading members of what may be called the northern or north-eastern division. The Tibetan has stretched itself westward; the Burmese and T'hay southward.

Of the southern group

*The Môn and Kho* are more allied to each other than they are to the interjacent Burmese and Siamese.

*The Chinese* has its nearest congener in the Anamitic; its differences of dialect decreasing as we go northward. This suggests that its diffusion has been from south to north.

We now pass from the domain of the nations whose language is monosyllabic to that of the Turanian populations.

*The Tungús.*—The Tungús have spread themselves at the expense of the southern Koriaks and the Yukahiri. The Mantshús have conquered China; and, again, the Chinese are pressing upon the Mantshús.

*The Mongols.*—The influence of the Mongols is measured by their occupancy of China and by the Temuginian conquests.

*The Ugrians.*—The Ugrians have, as a general rule, been encroached upon by others. It will be seen, however, in the notice of Persia, that there are fair reasons for believing that one Ugrian nation, at least, has effected conquests to the south of the Caspian. The most definite event, however, in the history of Ugrian influence is the Magyar conquest of Hungary.

*The Turk stock.*—The place of the Turks in the world's history is, in every way, conspicuous. They show themselves in most parts of the field. They are seen amongst its earliest objects.

It is only, however, in the latter half of the sixth century of our æra that the Turk proper—the Turk *eo nomine*—appears. The name *Turc*ilingus has been found earlier, but, though this is a form which the simpler term Turk may reasonably be supposed to have taken in the mouth of a Goth, it is not the actual term. The actual term appears, for the first time, A.D. 558; and it is the Alans and Avars who utter, and the Romans of Constantinople, under the reign of Justinian, who hear, it. I take the name as a landmark, and use it as a text for a commentary upon those divisions of the great Turk stock, of which we have clear and undeniable notices. And first I mention

*The Turks proper,* occupants of the parts around the Ektag, whose king was Dizabulus, and whose ambassador was Maniach. They are, to all appearance, the ancestors of the Tshagatai; at any rate, Transoxiana, or Kokan and Fergana, is their country. They have pressed, and they continue to press, upon Persia. They hold as subordinates

*The Epthalites, Nepthalites, Cidarites, Chionites,* or *White Huns,* who have but recently been conquered, and who, not long before, had conquered Sogdiana. It was the Sogdian subjects of the Epthalites who more especially traded in silk, and who were most particularly displeased, (their displeasure being mixed with amazement,) when they were shown that the silkworm had found its way into Europe. The Epthalite occupancies are now Uzbek and Turkoman.

In Caucasus, where at present we find the Basiani, Karatshai, and other Turk tribes (not to mention the names Avar and Kumuk), the leading nation is that of

*The Alans*, under their king Sarosius. The Romans are engaged in the war against the Colchians of Lazistan, and Justin is commanding. To Justin the Alans make known the request of

*The Avars.*—The Avars have been either the enemies or the dependents of the Turks, from whom they are flying westwards. From this I infer that their occupancy was the present tract called Independent Tartary. How far it extended northwards is another question. I have elsewhere suggested that *Bara* in *Barama*, the *land of the Bara*, may be, word for word, *Avar*. Be this, however, as it may, the Avars fly before the Turks, and appeal to the Alans for a recommendation to the court of Constantinople. It is granted. The embassy of A.D. 558 results. It ends in a portion of Pannonia being granted to the Avars; who, from henceforth, are a European population; a European population of what is now Magyar Hungary, but which was then what its name denotes, *i. e.* the land of the Huns of Attila; of the Huns of Attila, shorn of their strength, and encroached upon by both Gepidæ and Lombards.

I think that Avar was the name by which the Avars designated themselves.

The Turks called them *Varkhonitæ*.<br>
—— Slavonians —— *Obri*.<br>
—— Germans —— *Hun*.

They are said to have belonged to the Ogor nation. Word for word, this is Uigur.

The Avars conquer

*The Zali*, especially called a *tribe* (φῦλον not ἔθνος is the word) of the Huns;

*The Savir* (Σάβειροι), of whom little is said, and

*The Utigur* (*Ut-igur*), who, along with

*The Kotrigur* (*Kotr-igur*), are a portion of the Huns of the Thracian frontier under Sandilkh and Zabergan, *i. e.* Zaber-khan. A chief of the Avars is as regularly called Khakhan (Χάχανος) as Darius or Xerxes was called the Great King. This is to be noted; inasmuch as the word is an instrument in ethnological criticism. Again, when Sandilkh, the Utigur, is requested to declare war against the Kotrigurs, he half excuses himself by saying that "it would ill become him to act as enemy against his tribesmen (ὁμόφυλοι), who use the same language (ὁμόγλωσσοι), the same arms (ὁμόσκευοι), and who, though under different chiefs, are our kinsmen (συγγενεῖς)."

Whether any of these populations may have been the same as certain Turks of the Don, who have been called descendants of the Massagetæ, and whom the Persians called

*Kermikhion*, is uncertain. It is only possible that the Kermikhion, though specially named Turks, were neither exactly Turks proper, nor yet Avars. They *begged* the Romans not to receive those fugitives. They begged and sent presents. The Turks commanded and threatened. The difference, however, in the tone of the legations thus suggested is not conclusive.

*The Khazars.*—The Khazars appear somewhat later, *i. e.* in the seventh, rather than in the sixth century. In A.D. 626 Heraclius forms an alliance with them. They are said to come from Berzilia, *i. e.* the parts between the Volga and the Jaik.

And now the two known extremities of the Turk area

are Fergana on the Amur, and Hungary on the Danube, the former being the land of the Turks proper, the latter that of the Avars.

The history of the Avars is but brief. They conquer quickly. They are quickly conquered. When Nestor writes his history, his countrymen talk of nations who have been wholly obliterated, as nations who have "passed away like the Avars."

The Slavonians more especially cut them off. Between, however, their settlement and their fall they had been more formidable to their neighbours than even the Huns were. They had overrun Thrace, Mœsia, and Macedon. They had touched the Adriatic on the south, and the upper Elbe on the north. The Frank kings had fought with Avars (Huns as they called them) in Thuringia.

*The Turks* play a far greater game. For a time, however, their movements are obscure. As a general rule they are in alliance with Rome, and in hostility to Persia. They are always on the frontier of this latter kingdom; often on that of Armenia; for it is in an Armenian war that we find the Zali and Saviri taking part; as do the Alans and the Dilmain (Διλμαινον ἔθνος). Word for word, I imagine that Dilmain is Dhilem. I also think that the Dhilemites were Turks. The history, however, of the Turk name, during the reigns of the latest Sassanidæ is obscure. So it is under those of the earlier Kaliphs. As the power, however, of the Abassides breaks up, the name re-appears, and we hear of the Turk guards—the Prætorians of Bagdad.

There were the Prætorian Turks in the heart of the Kalifat. There were the Turkomans of the Persian frontier; and there were (to the back of them) the Turks of Bokhara, Kokan, Kashgar, and Yarkend, frontagers to the Mongols, and probably ancestors to the Tshagatai, Uigurs, and Uzbeks.

To the Turks who, rendering military service to the later Abassides, must be looked upon as settlers in Persia rather than as actual immigrants, I refer, after Gibbon,

A.D. 868–905. (1.) *The Tulinides* and

A.D. 905–968. (2.) *The Ikshidites of Ægypt.*

(3.) *The Ghuznevids* of Caubul.—Sebek-tegin (mark the name and mark the title) was the father of Mahmud, whose capital was Ghuzni, whose conquest was India, and whose title was Sultan. Gibbon writes that he was the first who bore it. His editor, however, remarks that the authority of Ibn Chaldun is in favour of its having been first assumed by the Bowids. If so, the Bowids were Turk; as were their predecessors: who will appear when we treat of the dynasties of Persia. In like manner the Indian branch of the line of Mahmud will appear when we notice Hindostan. In the west the star of the Ghuznevids waxed pale before that of

*The Seljukians* (*so called*)—the Seljukians of the house of Togrul. It seems that Mahmud of Ghuzni encouraged the immigration into Persia of the tribes from beyond the Oxus, tribes that he introduced into his dominions to the ruin of the power of the Ghuznevids. He asks a chief named Ismael "how many men he can supply"; Ismael being a Turk of Bokhara. "If you send," is the answer, "one of these arrows into our camp, 50,000 of your servants will mount on horseback."

*Mahmud.*—"And if that is not enough?"

*Ismael.*—"Send this second arrow to the horde of Balik, and you will find 50,000 more."

*Mahmud.*—"But what if I need the whole force of your tribe?"

*Ismael.*—"Dispatch my bow, and 200,000 horse will appear."

I give the dialogue (from Gibbon) because it fixes the locality. Bokhara is the land of the present Uzbeks. Balik (Balig) is a name either Mongol or belonging to the Mongolian frontier.

If the conqueror of India was able to control these bold and numerous tribesmen, his son Masúd was too weak for them. He is defeated on the
A.D. 1038.
field of Zendecan. The conquerors then elect their king, and "if the probable tale of a Latin historian deserves any credit, they determined by lot the choice of their new master. A number of arrows were successively inscribed with the name of a tribe, a family, and a candidate; they were drawn from the bundle by the hand of a child, and the important prize was obtained by Togrul Beg, the son of Michael, the son of Seljuk, whose surname was immortalized in the greatness of his posterity. The Sultan Mahmud, who valued himself on his skill in national genealogy, professed his ignorance of the family of Seljuk; yet the father of that race appears to have been a chief of power and renown. For a daring intrusion into the harem of his prince, Seljuk was banished from Turkestan. With a numerous tribe of his friends and vassals he passed the Jaxartes, encamped in the neighbourhood of Samarcand, embraced the religion of Mahomet, and acquired the crown of martyrdom in a war against the infidels. His age, of an hundred and seven years, surpassed the life of his son, and Seljuk adopted the care of his two grandsons, Togrul and Jaafar, the eldest of whom, at the age of forty-five, was invested with the title of Sultan in the royal city of Nishabur."

Word for word, I believe Seljuk to be Seleucus; so that the Seljukian Turks are neither more nor less than the Turks who, along with the empire, assumed the title of the Seleucidæ. Seljuk the Turk, *eo nomine*, has no historical existence. If so, the ignorance of the Sultan Mahmud is better than the learning of the historians. Alp Arslan is the nephew of Togrul, and Malek Shah the son of Alp Arslan.

The empire of Malek Shah includes (1) Georgia, Armenia, and Asia Minor on the west; (2) Kashgar on the east.

A.D. 1092. It breaks up, however, after his death, into the minor kingdoms of Persia, Kerman, Syria, and Roum.

(1.) *Persia.*—The little that is known concerning the kingdom of Persia suggests the idea that it was broken up by fresh invasions from Turkestan. At any rate its

A.D. 1151. Sultan Sangiar is defeated and taken prisoner by the Uz.

(2.) *Kerman.*—The history of Kerman is darker than that of Persia. Not so that of

(3.) *Syria*, which is, to a great extent, the history of the first and second crusades. It is against not merely the Mahometan but the Turk Mahometan, that the Christian puts on his armour.

In Syria,

A.D. 1127–1174. *The Atabegs* (Turks with a Turkish title) make themselves masters of Aleppo, Damascus, Edessa, and Mosul, encroaching on the Kurd frontier, as preliminaries to their conquest of Ægypt. Ægypt, however, they soon abandoned to the great Kurd, Sultan Saladin; only, however, as rulers. There are still Turks in the valley of the Nile, and of these come

A.D. 1250. *The Baherite Mameluks.*—Baherite as opposed to Borgite; the Borgite Mameluks being of Circassian origin. When Selim I. invaded Ægypt, the "military force of the Mamelukes consisted of three classes of warriors; all cavalry superbly mounted and armed, but differing materially in rank. First, there were the Mameluks themselves—properly so called—all of whom were of pure Circassian blood, and who had all been originally slaves. The second corps was called the Djebbans, and was formed principally of slaves brought from Abyssinia. The third, and lowest in rank, was called the Korsans, and was an assemblage of mercenaries of all nations. There were twenty-four beys or heads of the Mameluks, and they elected from among themselves a Sultan, who was called also Emirol Kebir, or Chief of Princes. He reigned over Egypt and Syria, and was also recognised as supreme sovereign over that part of Arabia in which the holy cities of Mecca and Medina are situated."*

(4.) *Roum, Anatolia, or Asia Minor.*—The Seljukians of Roum are defeated by the Mongols. A fragment, however, of their power is preserved in the little kingdom of Konieh (Iconium); connected with which is the history of

*The Chorasmian Turks.*—We find formidable bodies of Turks, called Chorasmians or Karismians, in Persia, in Syria, and in Asia Minor, between the death of Malek Shah and the death of Kazan Khan, the last descendant of Tshingiz who governed Persia. They must have come from western rather than eastern Turkestan, from Khiva rather than Kokan or Kashgar. I believe that they were Uz. It was they who dethroned Sanjiar. It was they who, under Mohammed, were attacked and defeated by the Mongols under Tshingiz-khan. It was they who, under Gelaleddin, attempted the recovery of their lost empire after the decline of the power of the Mongols, and who, after the

A.D. 1304.

A.D. 1218–1284.

* Creasy's Ottoman Turks, vol. 1.

death of their chief, broke up and separated; some for Syria, some for Palestine, some for the service of the Sultan of Iconium. Amongst these last was Soliman Shah, the father of Ortogrul, the father of Othman, the founder of the dynasty of

*The Ottoman Turks*, or the Turks of the present Turkish empire—occupants of Rumelia, masters of Bulgaria, Bosnia, Macedonia, Anatolia, Syria, suzerains to Moldavia, Wallachia, Ægypt, Tripoli, Tunis.

*The Tokhar.*—This is the name of one of the tribes of the north-east. They are expected by the Romans as allies against some of their enemies on the west. A district of Persia took from them the name Tokharistan.

*The Tshagatai.*—It is the Tshagatai Turks whose history is so pre-eminently mixed up with that of the Mongols, whose history is that of Timur, and of Baber, conqueror of India, and founder of the Great Mogul dynasty. Yet he was a Turk, notwithstanding. So was Timur. The notice, however, of the Turks of India will appear hereafter.

I now return to

*The Khazars.*—It is in the seventh, eighth, ninth, and tenth centuries that they are conspicuous. The Khanat of Astrakhan is Khazar. The Arab name for the Caspian is the Sea of the Khazars. Meanwhile the Khanat of Kazan is Bulgarian, *i. e.* Turk and Ugrian.

As the Khazars recede from the field of history,

*The Petshinegs* grow prominent. Wallachia and Moldavia are their area; and they are known to the Hungarians as Bisseni and Bessi, the etymon of Bessarabia. Out of the rougher form of the word has grown the name Budziak.

*The Uz.*—Whether this be a name of a new group, or

a name of general application, is uncertain. The Arab form is Ghoz. There were, as has been seen, Uz in Karismia. There were Uz in Moldavia.

*The Cumanians.*—These have been already noticed. They overrun Volhynia, parts of Galicia, and parts of Hungary. Their language was spoken A.D. 1770—so that they are all but an actually-existing tribe.

The Khazars, the Petshinegs, the Cumanians, and the Osmanli are pre-eminently the Turks of Europe; of which the Danubian Principalities, Bulgaria, Rumelia, and parts of Hungary are (in blood at least) the most Turkish portions.

All the tribes of the preceding list agree in being not only Turks, but Turks of the historical period. Sometimes they are Turks *eo nomine.* Oftener, however, the place in the Turk family is expressly stated by some competent authority. In the instance of the Cumanians we have a specimen of the language. In all cases, however, the evidence is direct, satisfactory, and generally recognized. With

*The Huns*, and with

*The Scythians* there are differences of opinion. That both were of Asiatic origin is universally admitted. That, Mongolia, however, rather than Turkistan was their original area has been not only suggested but insisted on; and that by able writers and influential authorities. Nor can it be denied that the accounts of the physical appearance of both the subjects of Attila and the Herodotæan Skoloti suggest Mongolian affinities to those who only know the Turks as they are represented by the Osmanlis of Constantinople. The Osmanlis, however, to say nothing of the effects of their long residence in Europe, are Georgian, Circassian, and much else beside in blood. As for the identification of the

Huns with the ancestors of the present Magyars, it is a careless inference from the word *Hun*gary. The evidence that they were in the same category with the Avars is as conclusive as the evidence that the Avars themselves were Turks.

Satisfied as I am that the Scythians of Herodotus were members of the Turk family, I am not prepared to say that *all* to whom the name Scythia applied were the same. I think that some particular divisions of the name may have been Mongol. The further we go east the likelier this is to have been the case. The Persian equivalent to the word Scythæ was Sacæ. Hence what was Scythia in Europe became Sacasthan in Asia. Now, Sok is the name by which, at the present moment, a Tibetan designates a Mongolian. An ancient Persian, I think, most probably applied it to both; oftenest to the Turk. Some few of both the Scythæ and Sacæ may have been Ugrian. As a rule, however, the names applied to Turks.

For the purposes, however, of the present inquiry the details of the difference are unimportant. The minute ethnology of the Turks is one thing. The extent to which tribes akin to the Turk, if not actually Turk, whose original occupancies were the distant steppes of Central Asia, extended themselves southwards and westwards, is another.

Now, I wish to show not only that the Turks have been remarkable amongst migrants and conquerors for their conquests and migrations, but that at the beginning of the historical period the general character of their distribution over the face of the earth was much as it was in the fifth, sixth, and seventh centuries. The degree to which India, Persia, and Syria, and even parts of Africa, were just as Turkish in the reign of Cyrus as they were under the Seljukians will be considered when the proper ethnology of those countries comes under notice.

I conclude this chapter with drawing attention to very remarkable details in the history of the Alan name. The Alans were what the Huns were. They were, too, what the Avars were. Their name shows itself early, and lasts long. The Huns of Dacia and Pannonia are closely connected with the Alans of Caucasus; and when Attila fights the great battle of Chalons, the king of the Alans is his ally. So, the Alans find their way into Gaul. They also find it into Spain, as joint invaders with the Vandali Silingi and the Suevi. They occupy a portion of the kingdom of Genseric. But Genseric effects settlements in Africa. Suppose any portion of his Alan subjects to have accompanied him, and you have Turks in Tunis in the fifth century; Turks in Tunis who reached their African locality, after traversing the whole breadth of Europe, and sailing past the *western* half of Africa.

They have fought their way through France and Spain, to settle in the neighbourhood of Carthage, and to be engaged in the sack of Rome. Their fathers lived under the shade of Caucasus and their present king is a Vandal from Silesia.

